Kearsley
An Illustrated History

Simon Colley

First published 2019
© Simon Colley

The rights of Simon Colley to be identified as the author of this work have been asserted by him in accordance with the Copyright, Designs and Patents Act of 1988. All rights reserved; no part of this publication may be reproduced, stored in a retrieval system, or transmitted in any form or by any means, electronic, mechanical, photocopying, recording or otherwise without the prior written consent of the publisher or a licence permitting copying in the UK issued by the Copyright Licensing Agency Ltd. www.cla.co.uk

ISBN 978-1-78222-654-3

Book design, layout and production management by Into Print
www.intoprint.net
+44 (0)1604 832149

Special Thanks

Liz McLellan for her patience and advice in proofreading whilst also correcting my grammatical inaccuracies.
Arron Raw at Raw Tattoo, Bolton Road, Kearsley, for the wonderful cover design.
Stephen Tonge and all the great people at The Churches On The Mount. Lily Alker, Springfield Road, Kearsley. Betty Bostock, Springfield Road, Kearsley. Maude Haydock, Ringley Road, Stoneclough. Dave Lomax, Bent Spur Farm, Kearsley. Marion Keyte, Ramsbottom. Susan Oliver, The Visitor Centre, Clifton Country Park. Adam Bietrich and all the staff at Farnworth Library. Bolton History Centre, Bolton Central Library. The Lancashire Archives, Preston. The British Library, Euston Road, London.

In January 2005 our world was turned upside down by the sudden death of my father, Ken Colley. Aside from being an exemplary Dad, he had served on Kearsley Urban District Council during the 1960's, and as a teacher at Kearsley West County Primary School for nearly thirty years. His love of football and local history were no secret to all that knew him, and it had been his intention to chronicle the history of the town he had lived in all his life. Around twelve months after his unexpected passing my mother gave me all of his old maps and a suitcase containing some documents and pictures. After looking through it, it became clear he had not got started, so I decided to have a go myself, and informed everyone it would probably take a couple of years. That was twelve years ago, and now I can say it is finished.

The original idea was to produce something straightforward from the contents of the suitcase and maps, but once you look into a subject, the more interesting it can become, and more information and pictures can be found if you dig hard enough.

This book is not as complete as it could be, as there is still much to uncover, and hopefully someone will have another go in the future and find the information that has evaded me. It has been a joy, and a strain at times, but I must thank all those who have helped even in the smallest way. Many of those have been kind enough to invite me into their homes to share stories, memories, documents and pictures, and this has been by far the most enjoyable part of the whole process. I have endeavoured to provide the most accurate information possible from the best sources available, but this is certainly not above criticism or question, and any imprecision will be amended in future editions.

Simon Colley, December 2018.

For Dad

The Long 'S'

You may notice whilst looking at some of the documents and articles in this book the odd looking symbol ' ʃ ' which is often thought to be a letter 'f.' It is in fact a Latin lower case form of the letter 's.' It is called the 'long s' and was used frequently in English until the end of the 18th century, after this its decline in use was rapid and became almost obsolete within a couple of decades.

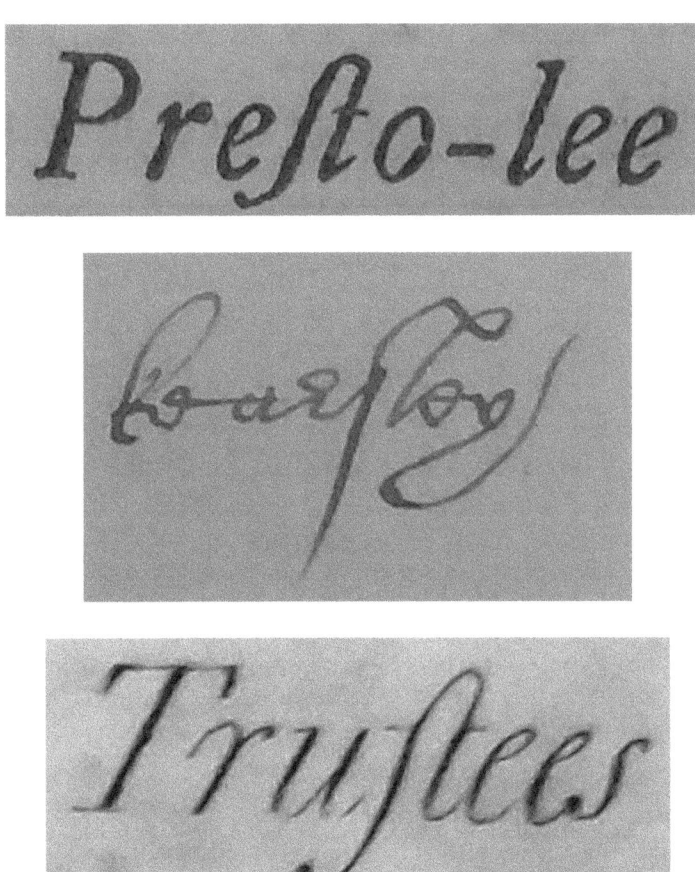

It is beyond the scope of this book to explain exactly when and how the long s was utilized, but its written use among these pages is, as best as possible, how it would have been in the articles and documents that are referred to.

Introduction & Early Records
Kearsley

It may seem like an average suburban township sitting quietly in-between Bolton and Manchester, and that's because it is. There are hundreds of towns all over Britain that are similar in size and stature, and Kearsley, like all the others, can at first glance look to be as unremarkable as the next one. But each place has its own history and story to tell, and this is what makes each place remarkably unique and fascinating.

Kearsley has a captivating and endearing narrative, particularly from the years onwards of the industrial revolution, a time when the town grew and adapted to changes of enormous proportions in lifestyle and culture. Great strides were made in living standards, education, leisure and health matters, as fresh running water, schools, sports facilities and General Practitioners became more available and accessible. Roads were improved, canals were constructed without any mechanical machinery, and the railways emerged to carry the ever-increasing amount of goods and passengers.

But not all of these changes were welcomed, or were for the betterment of its inhabitants, because even though great feats of engineering were made and the infrastructure of an emerging society were beginning to be established, the people had to work long hours in the often dreadful conditions of the treacherous mines and mills. Some would have no doubt fell foul of the enclosure acts that displaced them and removed self sufficiency, and those that fell into unimaginable poverty, often by no fault of their own, would end up in the dreaded workhouse.

A great deal of Kearsley's noted early history can be ascribed to Prestolee, Stoneclough, Ringley and the once picturesque Irwell Valley. Chemical works, paper manufacturers, extensive cotton mills and a vast electricity generating station all sprang up along the banks of the formerly clean waters of the powerful River Irwell. Effluent from all of these industries devastated the resident wildlife to such an extent that to this day it has never fully recovered. Today all of the industries that utilised the Irwell for power, or as a means to deposit waste, have faded away, and considerable efforts are still being made to clean the river.

Very little is known about ancient Kearsley, but like much of Britain prior to the industrial revolution there would have been only a few scattered farms and cottages connected by roads that were little more than dirt tracks. The whole district remained fairly sparse until the middle part of the 19th Century, and it is hard to imagine the area without the rows of houses, and vehicles, that now line the main roads, or the crowded housing estates that presently dominate the landscape.

Today we see great changes during our own lifetimes that are continuously altering the way we live, but prior to the 17th century medieval Britain would have remained comparatively indistinct from one decade to the next, or even from one century to the next.

The first known written mention of Kearsley appears in the charters of Cockersand Abbey, which was located in the city of Lancaster. The document is a deed dated around 1222 in which the landowner, Lady Edith Barton, donates the whole of her lands in Kearsley to God and the Canons of Cockersand. It also seems that at this time Kearsley was merely regarded as a portion of Farnworth. The deed (in Latin) reads as follows:

> "SCIANT, etc., quod ego domina Edit de Barton, assensu et 1. consensu domini mei Gilbert! de Notton, dedi, etc. Deo, Ferne- etc., quandam porcionem terrae meae infra diuisam de Feme- w [] rtne ' worthe, scilicet, totum Kersleie, cum omnibus pertinenciis suis Edit, infra has diuisas, sicut profundum lac exit de Urwil, ascendendo uersus Stokebruge, et ita sequendo illud lac descendendo uersus Flethithaleth usque in praedictum Urwil ; in liberam, puram, etc., libere et quiete ab omni seculari seruicio et exactione, cum omnibus libertatibus et eisiamentis quae infra has diuisas et eius pertinenciis sunt uel fieri potuerunt, sicut aliqua elemosina liberius et quiecius, etc. ; pro salute animae Johannis filii mei, etc.
> Cum warantia et testibus"

Translation in English below:

> "Grant in frankalmoign from Lady Edith de Barton for the health of the soul of her son John, and with the consent of her husband Gilbert de Notton, to God [and the canons of Cocker-sand], of a portion of her land in Farnworth, 1 to wit, the whole of Kersley, within these bounds, where the deep leach issues forth of Irwell, going up the same towards Stock-bridge, following that leach and going down towards Flethithaleth unto Irwell aforesaid;
> with liberties and easements existing and prospective."

Donating land to religious institutions was not uncommon in the early thirteenth century, and the "Grant in Frankalmoign" clause at the beginning of the deed was a tenure in English law by which a religious corporation holds lands given to them and their successors forever, usually on the condition of praying for the soul of the donor and their heirs.

It seems Lady Edith and her husband handed the land over to the Monks at Cockersand Abbey in the hope that their prayers would keep them, and their son John, safe and well. It is worth noting here the early spelling of both Kearsley (*Kersleie*) and Farnworth (*Femeworthe*), as well as the River Irwell (*Urwil*).

Exactly how much land Lord Gilbert and Lady Edith Barton donated to the Monks is unclear, as there were other families that seem to have had rights to certain land in Farnworth and Kearsley around the same period. The Salford Hundred records of 1278 show that Richard De Redford and another man named Richard the Chief of Farnworth were Lords of the manor, and in 1295, William, son of Richard the Chief sold all of his lands in Kearsley to Adam De Lever and further parts of his estate to Henry De Hulton.

The Manchester Barony Survey of 1320 shows that Farnworth, of which Kearsley was merely a portion at this time, was held by three principal land owners, Adam De Lever of Great Lever, Henry De Hulton and Richard De Redford, of which the largest share was held by Hultons. It is believed the Kearsley area was predominantly owned by the Hultons and Redfords, and by 1473 records show the Redford portion had been divided into the hands of Adam Prestall and George Seddon (1).

The Hulton family remained as predominant landowners into the following centuries as records show in 1598 that George Hulton made a complaint to the authorities that 'certain persons were intruding on his land and digging coal pits there.' He died on 19th March 1609 holding the manor of Farnworth, with the capital messuage and various lands (2). The Prestall share of the land stayed in the family until late into the 16th Century, but eventually descended to heirs who sold it on to a Ralph Assheton of Great Lever and the Trafford family of Manchester (3).

Around the same time the Seddon share descended to Giles, Ralph and Thomas Seddon, of which the Thomas Seddon share descended to his two daughters, Elizabeth and Cecily. The younger daughter, Cecily, married a Peter Seddon and they had a son, Ralph, described 'as of Pilkington.' Elizabeth married Thomas Marcroft and had a son Robert who sold his lands to a Richard Ashton who in turn sold them to the Starkie family of Huntroyde in 1651.

At the implementation of the Farnworth and Kearsley enclosure act in 1798 the Hultons and Starkies, amongst others, were still prominent landowners, with William Hulton Esq residing at Kearsley Hall and being regarded as lord of the manor.

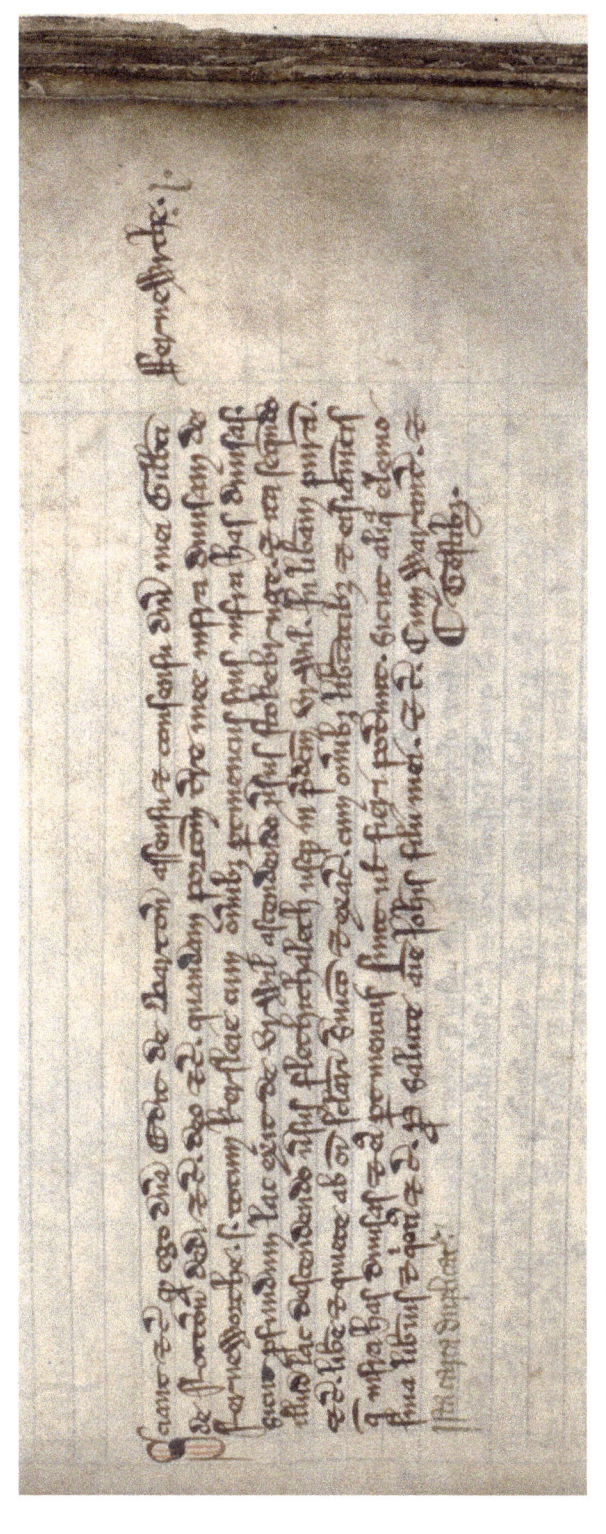

This is the actual entry from the Charters of Cockersand Abbey dating from around 1222 and is the earliest known written record of Kearsley (3rd line 3rd word). It is held at the British Library in London and is so delicate that only a small number of their curators are allowed to handle it. Special permission was granted to have it photographed for the purpose of using it in this book. You will notice the spelling of Kearsley as *'Kersleie'* and the use of the latin 'long s'.

The examples of Kearsley land ownership, and how it was sold on or descended to heirs, that have been described are only a small sample of the many documents that survive from the medieval period, but it is almost impossible to piece together a conclusive account of who owned what and when, especially as there is an abundance of conflicting and inconsistent information and details.

Today it is difficult to ascertain who all of the current landowners are around Kearsley without applying for (and paying for) information on each property on each street and road from the UK Land Registry service.

(1). An indenture of 1394 has been preserved, made between Ellen and Alice, daughters and co-heirs of Richard de Redford, concerning land called Herefield in Kearsley; from this agreement for partition it appears that Ellen was then the widow of (Adam) de Prestall and Alice the widow of Jordan de Tetlow; Lever Chartul. no. 260.

(2). The capital messuage would have most likely been a large house including all of its outbuildings and surrounding lands.

(3). On the North Western boundary of Kearsley an area of land most likely partly in both Kearsley and Farnworth was known as Prestall. It took its name from its former landowner in the 15th Century, Adam Prestall. Presto Street takes its name from this family.

KERSLEY

Commons and Waste Lands contain in Statute Measure exclusive of the Turbary Grounds

			A.R.P
Stone contains			0.0.0
Sand			0.2.20
William Hulton Esq. both as Lord of the Manor and in right of his Lands	20A.2?B.20C.20?.20?.E.20?F		18.0.28
Duke of Bridgewater	21A.21B.21C		9.0.19
Earl of Derby	22A.22B.22C.22D.22E.22F.22G.22H.22J.22K		44.0.17
S.Jn Parker Mosley	23A.23B.23C.23D		17.3.4
L.C.P. Starkie Esq.	24A.24B.24C.24D.24E.24F.24G.24H.24J		35.2.4
Rev.d Walter Bagot	25A.25B.25C.25D.25E.25F		9.1.16
Matthew Fletcher Esq.	26A.26B.26C		0.2.24
M.r John Seddon	27A.27B.27C		8.1.28
Peter Seddon	28A.28B.28C.28D		7.3.35
Jonathan Dorning	29		10.3.25
M.rs Kirkhams	30A.30B		4.0.20
M.r Samuel Holt	31		1.1.35
Trustees of M.r Hathorn Charity School	32A.32B.32C		0.1.9
M.rs Hardman	33		1.2.38
Robert Whittaker	34A.34B		0.3.27
James Macantifs	35		0.1.21
Thomas Smith	36A.36B		1.1.17
Trustees of Roskow	37A.37B		1.1.31
			220.0.34½
Roads			2?.1.2?½

List of landowners on the 1798 Enclosure Act document. Note the second from bottom entry and the spelling of 'Roskow,' this land was at the bottom of what is now Roscow Road and is how it took its name. It is unknown why the spelling altered.

The Development Of The Valley

In the 17th and 18th Century the Irwell valley, including Prestolee, Ringley and the surrounding area must have seemed idyllic with lush green meadows, extended woodland and the odd scattered farm or cottage. The original Ringley Chapel, standing solitary on the site of the present church, would be a notable landmark, not least with it being the only place of worship for miles around. Close-by is the sturdy stone pack-horse bridge that still holds firm today was one of only three bridges between Ringley and Manchester crossing the sparkling clear River Irwell that was used for boating, bathing and fly-fishing.

The River Irwell has been the catalyst for the development of much of the industry along or near the river terraces, and its 39 mile length has, as stated by Newbigging, "performed more work than a hundred rivers of greater pretensions". The first known mention of the river is found in the charter of Brandwood, by Roger De Lacy about the year 1200. Its name is most probably derived from the old English words 'irre' and 'welle' meaning the 'angry' or 'wandering winding river'.

The source of the Irwell is in Cliviger at Irwell Springs on Deerplay Moor north of Bacup. The moor was once a part of the Forest of Rossendale. The river flows through Bacup, Rawtenstall, Ramsbottom, Radcliffe, Little Lever, Prestolee, Ringley, Clifton, Salford and into the Manchester Ship Canal behind Chester Road, Manchester. Its main tributaries are the Roch at Bury, the Croal at Farnworth, the Irk near the Cathedral at Hunt's Bank, Manchester, and the Medlock just before it empties into the ship canal.

The lower valley of the Irwell is heavily faulted by the Irwell and Pendleton Fault which runs from the Mersey to the gritstone hills north of Bolton. At Little Lever there is a prominent outcrop of sandstone well over 100 feet thick known as Nob End Rock, this was also known locally as 'red rock.'

Prior to mass industrialisation there would have been a few scattered farms, the odd corn mill and a couple of small paper mills using the River Irwell for power and other purposes. Handloom weaving would be carried out in the farms and weavers' cottages, and a small amount of coal would be dug from the shallow pits in the valley slopes, the river terraces and on the flat plateau above the valley. Ample peat and turf was available for burning from turbary land, so there was little demand at first for coal, until greater supplies were needed in the burgeoning cities. This stimulated the growth of the mining industry, and coal from pits at Kearsley and the surrounding area would be trundled into Manchester along the rocky, uneven tracks by horse and cart or pack horses.

The Irwell was the magnet that attracted industry along its terraces, it being ideal for power processes and the disposal of effluent. As early as 1786 the Irwell and its tributaries provided power for over 50 waterwheels, 40 of these being on the swifter flowing tributaries and only 10 on the main river. Weirs were built on sandstone outcrops on the riverbed to create heads of water to help drive the waterwheels.

During the latter eighteenth and early nineteenth century the industrial revolution stretched out across Britain, and the Irwell Valley played its part, with substantial bleachworks, chemical works, paper mills, dyeworks, coal mines, fulling mills and spinning mills springing up across the landscape.

Circa 1910. View showing the giant Irwell Bank Mills (now the Riverside Drive housing estate) in the background, with the River Irwell meandering past Fletchers Paper Mill (now the Ringley Lock Housing Estate). Wells House (currently used as a children's nursery) can be seen to the left.

The Industrial Revolution

It is generally considered that what we now refer to as the Industrial Revolution began around 1750, and lasted more or less a hundred years. Some will argue that it began as much as 200 years previous to this time, but it is certainly from 1750 onwards that the growth rate of industry increases at a phenomenal rate. This in turn dramatically changed the landscape of Britain, and indeed, its effects rippled out across the globe.

For the 500 years or so before this, very little in the way of everyday life in Britain had changed, and three quarters of the population still lived in the countryside. Most worked together as a family within small communities to provide the things everyone needed, and farming would have been the most predominant line of work.

Kearsley and its surrounding area would have been no different, with families working in the fields by day and perhaps spinning wool into yarn by candlelight in the evening, or some would have worked full-time on their handlooms. Local merchants, known as 'putter's out' or 'chapmen' would drop off raw materials such as wool or cotton, and would return to pick up the finished goods, which had then been woven into material. This was known as the 'Putting Out' system, in fact many households came to rely upon the income from spinning and weaving as much as that from agriculture. The phrase 'cottage industries' comes from the handloom weavers and spinners of this time, working in their homes and cottages.

Mechanisation and the advent of industrialisation changed all this, and in turn resulted in the biggest social transformation these islands had ever experienced. Possibly the main catalyst in this sea change was the textile industry, which gathered pace with the invention of new machinery that could greatly increase spinning and weaving productivity from the home workers in their cottages.

It is worth considering why Lancashire became the number one location in the world for producing textiles, with mill towns such as Manchester, Bolton, Blackburn, Oldham, Rochdale, Ashton, Bury, Preston – and many others working at full capacity to meet the enormous demand for their products. A valid reason is that the climate is, for a large part of the year, damp and wet, and this favours the spinning of cotton considerably. This is a sensible assumption, but not the whole answer. Lancashire also has many streams and rivers near at hand in the dales and valleys, which not only drove the water wheels but also provided abundant water for scouring, bleaching and dyeing cloth, as well as, unfortunately, being a convenient place to discard the unwanted effluents. Add to this a rapidly expanding population which provided a ready made workforce, as well as newly built canals, together with much improved roads as a result of the Turnpike acts, and everything was in place. You can now see why Kearsley and its surrounding area became such a sound location for the numerous mills and factories that sprang up during the nineteenth century.

Britain was experiencing a population explosion in the late eighteenth and early nineteenth century, for example the population in Bolton went from 37,414 in 1801 to 105,957 in 1851, this meant wool and cotton thread were in constant demand. The invention of the 'Flying Shuttle' by John Kay allowed cloth to be woven much faster and in wider lengths, and the 'Spinning Jenny' invented by James Hargreaves meant that eight threads of yarn could be spun at once. These machines were small enough to be installed at home, but the industrialists had other ideas, as they began to build small factories and then huge mills with further advances in mechanical technology, such as Samuel Crompton's Spinning Mule that allowed one operator to work over a thousand spindles.

Another factor that affected much of the population was the 'enclosure acts' which were passed by Parliament during this period. These removed local people's previously existing rights to carry out activities on common land, such as growing food, grazing animals or digging turf for fuel. In 1798 an enclosure act was passed entitled "an Act for dividing, allotting and enclosing certain commons and waste lands, within the Manors or Lordship of Farnworth and Kersley, which parcels of common and waste land are called Halshaw Moor, Dixon Green and Blackhurst Green." This meant the principal landowners were allowed to evict the occupants of the small farms and cottages from their lands, and basically fence them off or 'enclose' them.

Picture Taken from above Kearsley Train Station showing Kearsley Mill, Prestolee, Circa 1907.

The main reason cited for the enclosure acts was that the land could be used to its optimal agricultural potential to supply the rapidly expanding population, and it is true that measures were necessary to achieve this, but more often than not it would be the principal landowner who would press for an enclosure act, because it was they who would have most to gain.

The principal landowners, or persons deemed to have rights to the land, concerned with the Farnworth and Kearsley Enclosure Act, were, amongst others, William Hulton Esq, of Hulton Park; The most Noble Francis, Duke of Bridgewater; The Right Honorable Edward Smith Stanley, Earl of Derby; The Right Honorable Henry, Lord Bradford; Sir John Parker Mosley, Baronet; Le Gendre Starkie, Esquire; the Reverand Walter Bagot and Peter Rasbotham, Esquire. See picture on page 13.

It is unclear how much hardship the introduction of this Enclosure Act brought to Kearsley and Farnworth, but around Britain the effects of enclosure on the people in the small farms and dwellings who were forced from their homes was devastating. Gone was the self sufficiency, and in most cases the only option was to work for someone else, and the mills and coal mines provided the answer.

It has often been stated that this was how the British people became landless, with a small amount of people being allocated large areas of land. Evidence that this rings true may be seen in a 2010 land survey which showed that a mere 0.6% of the population owns 50% of the rural land of Great Britain.

Left. The original enclosure document of 1798, which is held in the Lancashire Archives at Preston. It is over two feet square with around twenty pages, and well worth a visit to study for yourself.

Above. Two postcards from around 1900 that perfectly illustrate the sentiments of the working classes, as they toiled for long hours in the harsh, and often dangerous, industries of the era. Coal powered the factories and heated the homes, but the smoke that belched from the chimneys polluted the air and badly impacted on their health.

It is no coincidence that factories, mills and coalmines began to spring up all over Kearsley and Farnworth, with Cromptons Paper Mills alongside the River Croal, plus Prestolee old cotton mill and Seddons Paper Mill a little further down at the confluence with the Irwell, being some of the first of these large scale manufacturing facilities in Lancashire.

In the late 19th century Britain had become the largest manufacturer of cotton cloth in the world, and there were an estimated 2650 mills in Lancashire alone, employing around 440,000 persons, and by 1906 the River Irwell and its tributaries the Roch, Irk and Medlock were being used by 327 mills and factories. The Health of Towns Commissioners report in 1844 found that the sewage waste from the growing populations in the towns of the Irwell basin was also mostly finding its way into local streams, and that the Irwell was receiving so much effluent that it never had the opportunity of purifying itself, and in times of drought the impurities in the water became so concentrated that deposition occurred on the stream bed. Large amounts of cinders and ash were also continually being tipped into the river, and from Wilson's chemical works at the confluence of the Croal and Irwell the persistent disposal of solid waste not only devastated the wildlife, it also reduced the width of the river by a third, forcing water to erode the opposite bank.

By the mid 1800's there were numerous factories and mills that sprang up alongside the rivers in the Irwell valley. For example, from Farnworth and Little Lever through to Ringley the following industrial works are all using the Croal and Irwell for various purposes at this time;- Farnworth Old Paper Mill, Prestolee Old Cotton Mill, Seddons paper mill, Prestolee print works, Creams paper mill, Lever Bank Bleach works, Ladyshore Colliery, Mount Sion Print works, Wilson's Chemical works, Clammerclough Cotton Mill, Clammerclough Pottery works, Prestolee New Cotton Mills and Fletchers Paper Mill.

Below is an extract from an account of working class life given by Bolton born writer Charles Allen Clarke in his book 'The Effects of the Factory System' written in 1899, when the Lancashire cotton industry reigned supreme. Charles Allen Clarke was born in 1863 at the height of the Lancashire cotton famine. He began to work at the tender age of eleven as a 'little piecer' helping to piece together the broken threads on a gigantic spinning mule. He was far from satisfied with the working-class lifestyle:

"Everywhere you will find steam hissing and smoke scowling; factories, chimneys, coal pit heads, streams fouled by chemical works. In 1770 the population of

Bolton was about 5000; it is now twenty times that......change from a happy hamlet to mighty centre of filth and fume, hundreds of high chimneys belching forth. People growing up stunted, dying prematurely... have been used to nothing better. The death rate is much higher in the factory town compared with rural districts. Often families of a dozen sleep in two rooms. If a mill girl is lucky she may get a warm cup of tea before starting out of a morning. Breakfast at work is cup of tea and slice of bread and butter, sitting in a corner in the dust and dirt. The dinner hour only allows time to gulp food..a repetition of the breakfast menu with perhaps a little meat or jam."

The dreadful anachronism of half-time employment of boys and girls in the cotton mills and other industries continued well into the twentieth century, and undoubtedly did untold harm to both physical and educational development. Typical hours could be from six in the morning until noon one week, and from mid-day to half-past five in the alternate week with meagre wages being paid. Around the turn of the century this could be as little as half-a crown per week, which equates to approximately 12 ½ pence in today's money. Children from working-class families began working 'half-time' in the factories when they were very young. Half-time working was intended to be a preparation for a lifetime in the mill. They left school at 13 to begin full-time work of 55.5 hours per week.

Prestolee Old Cotton Spinning Mill and Paper Mill

Located at the convergence of the Rivers Croal and Irwell, Prestolee old spinning mill was built in the late 18th century and originally managed by a Mr John Todd who lived at Leigh House in Farnworth. Leigh House was a large residence which sat between King Street, Cross Street and Bank Street, there are industrial units named King Street Retail Park on the site at present. Nearby Leigh Street is so named as it once led up to the house and its impressive grounds. The cotton mill was later purchased by three Scottish gentlemen named Scott, Dalziel and McNairn. The Local trade directories of 1836 show that James Dalziel is listed as *'Cotton Spinner, Prestolee Old Mills.'* The mill is still shown on the Ordnance Survey map of 1848, but is believed to have burnt down around 1871.

Next Page. Shown is an Indenture dated 1798 between Benjamin Rawson and Robert and Thomas Seddon.
At the convergence of the River Croal and the River Irwell the drawing shows the original Prestolee Cotton Spinning Mill, it is not known exactly when it was built, but it is shown on a map from 1786. The mill was powered by a waterwheel that was fed from goits which took their water from the Rivers Croal and Irwell. The Seddon brother's paperworks are shown along with Rawson's Vitriol works, which produced acid for local print and bleach works. Note that the artist has named the River Croal as the River Lever, and the gap between the letters 'L' and 'E' across the river is what we know today as Wilsons Bridge. This bridge was known at the time as Rawson's bridge. It was a stone structure without any sidewalls and people were known to have fallen to their doom in the pitch dark or fog.

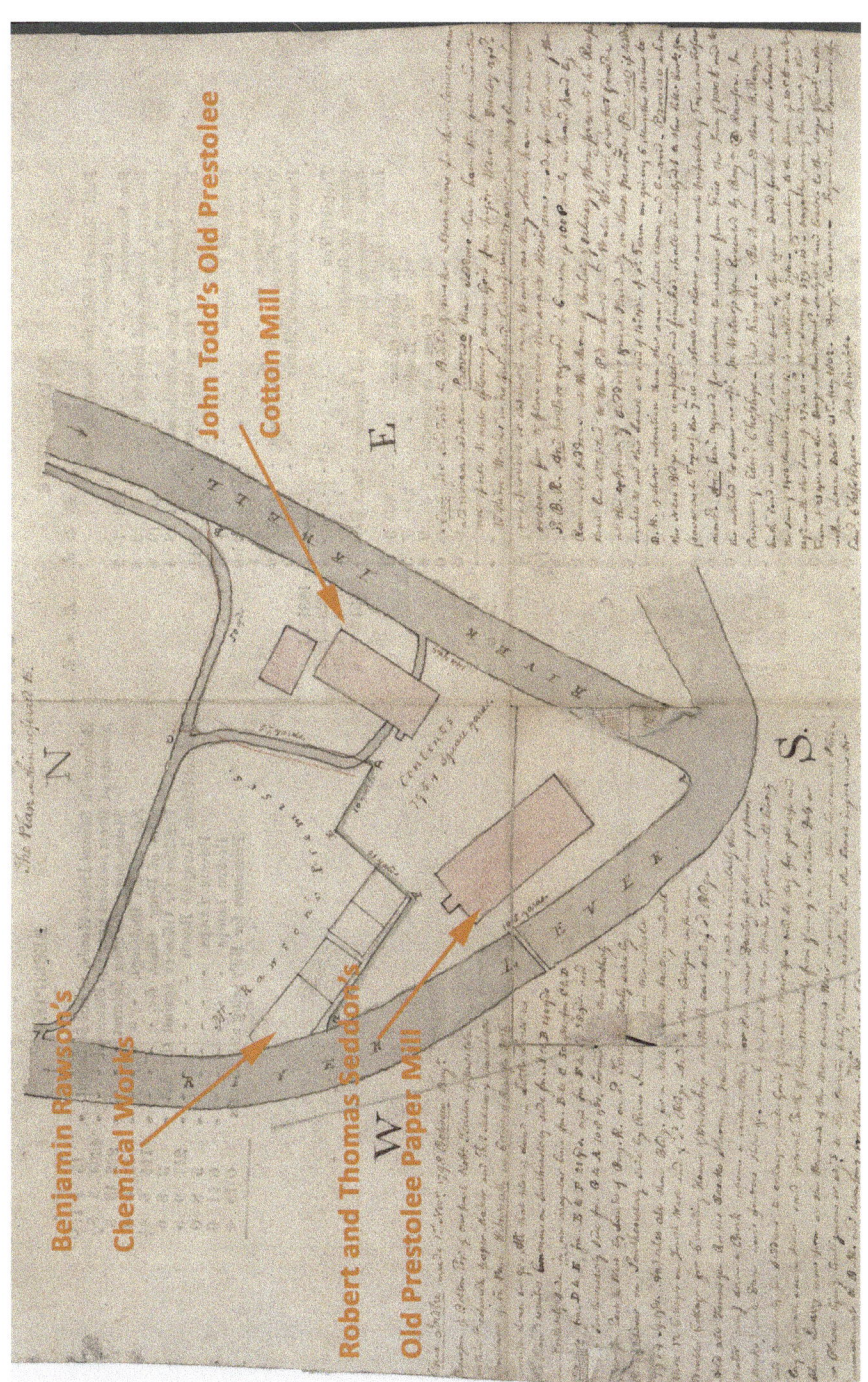

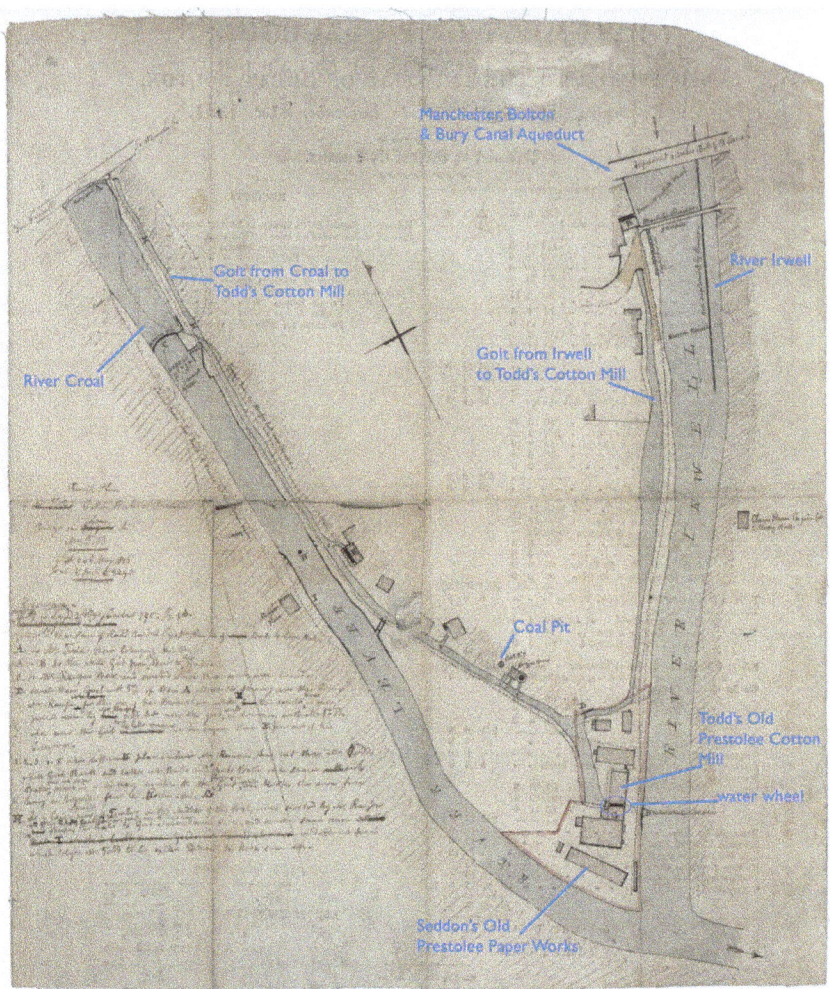

Above. Sketch drawn in 1816 of John Todd's Old Prestolee Cotton Mill and the goits (or leats) that drove its waterwheel, a coal pit is also visible which provided a most convenient supply for the factories. It is notable that the mill has been enlarged somewhat from the drawing of 1798 shown on the previous page. The river was used to dispose of most of the waste for all of the industries, resulting in a disastrous effect on the wildlife in and around this area of the Irwell valley. Rawsons chemical works ceased manufacture around 1834 when the price of vitriol began to decline. The works were then sold on to a Mr. Wilson, but eventually closed for good around 1875. The site is now completely cleared with no evidence of the factories, buildings, coal pit, waterwheels, goits and millraces that once occupied the area. In fact, only the recently rebuilt Wilsons Bridge over the River Croal remains as a clue to the industrious past of this now innocuous, but historically important, patch of land.

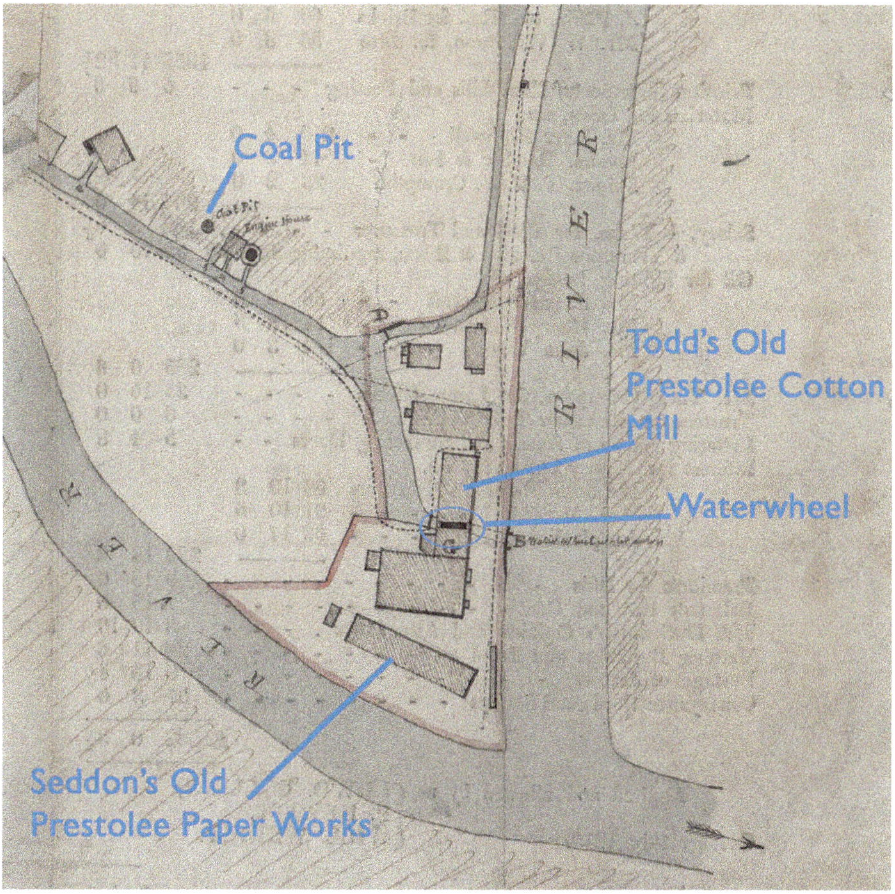

Above. Close up view showing the confluence of the Croal and Irwell in 1816. The waterwheel of Prestolee Old Cotton Mill is clearly shown with its tailrace flowing into the Irwell. **Below.** Some details concerning the weirs, goits and buildings.

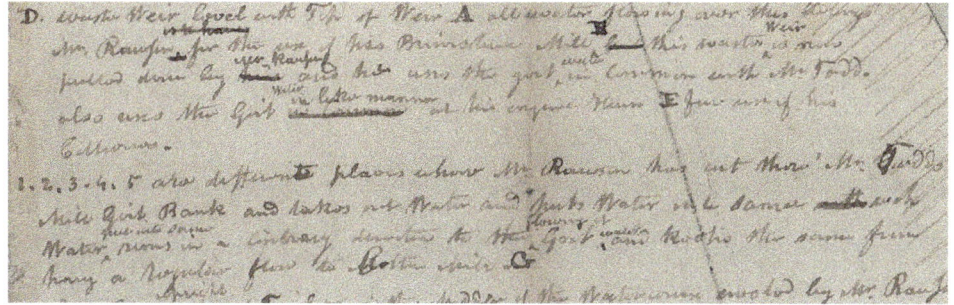

MACHINERY.

To be SOLD by AUCTION,

On Wednesday the 22d September, 1819, and following days.

THE MACHINERY belonging to *John Todd*, of the Prestolee Factories, near Bolton, consisting of 17 carding engines, 18 inches, nineteen ditto 36, 12 double heads of drawing and 14 single do. three 8 inch bobbin and fly frames, 24 spindles each, two do. 12 spindles, three 6 inch bobbin and fly frames, 72 each, two do. 60 each, four billies 120 each, fifteen mules, 240, nineteen 252, six 288, nineteen 300, and thirteen 312 spindles each, forty reels, of 30 hanks, two making up presses, and other requisites belonging to the spinning business.

A good Water wheel, Oak shaft 2 feet diameter, and about 16 feet long, also 70 bags of Waste.

May be viewed at the premises, any day previous to the Sale, and further particulars known, by applying to Mr. *W. Lomax*, Auctioneer, Bolton.

Above. The sale of machinery from Prestolee Old Cotton Mill as advertised in the Manchester Mercury, September 14th 1819.

Above. April 1921. The original stone bridge across the Croal which was built when Benjamin Rawson was proprietor of the vitriol works. As you can see it is falling apart with a large section already in the river. Note also it has no sidewalls, just a wooden fence which would have been added at a later date. The bridge became more commonly known as Wilson's Bridge after Rawson sold the works.

Rawson's dangerous stone bridge remained until the 1920's when it became unsafe and began to collapse. It was replaced in 1927 with a steel trestle girder bridge at a cost of £816 with the cost split between the County Council, Farnworth Council, Bury Rural District Council, Little Lever Council and Kearsley Council. This bridge lasted until 1968 when it too became unsafe and had to be replaced. Then in 2008 that bridge became unsafe and was replaced with the current bridge, which was opened in May 2014 at a cost of around £1.8 million.

Above. April 1927, the opening of Wilson's New Bridge by Messrs, N. Wardle, J.P., and J. Robertson, J.P, Chairmen of Little Lever and Kearsley Councils, with Messrs. H. Martin and J. Seddon, clerks watching on.

Thomas Bonsor Crompton, Prestolee New Cotton Mill and Irwell Bank Mill

Thomas Bonsor Crompton was born in Farnworth on May 20th 1792, and by the time of his passing on the 5th September 1858 he had become one of the most industrious and influential men in the area, as well as the main benefactor for the construction of Prestolee Holy Trinity Church (see page 292).

His Grandfather owned a paper mill and bleachworks at Great Lever, and in 1828 he also built a bleachworks and the famous Farnworth Paper Mills on the banks of the Croal, which were powered by water wheel and serviced by mill ponds that are now known as Crompton Lodges. Thomas Bonsor had two brothers, John and Robert, and it was their father, also named John, who had decided to build Rock Hall as a family residence, but he passed away as work on the house neared completion around 1807. Thomas Bonsor and brother John became partners in the Mills at Farnworth, and Robert took control of paper mills at Worthington near Wigan.

Thomas Bonsor Crompton became a skilled paper maker, and first came to prominence in 1820 when he obtained a patent for new machinery that allowed for continuous drying of paper after pressing, and for the cutting of the paper in suitable lengths. The three former millponds from the old paper works are today known as Crompton Lodges, and along with the Crompton family former residence Rock Hall, now form part of the 750 acre Moses Gate Country Park. The site is regarded as a local nature reserve.

In 1833 he built Prestolee New Cotton Mills which were situated between the Manchester Bolton Bury canal, which it used for coal and cotton transport, and the River Irwell which was used for power and water for the boiler. The mill had three water wheels, two steam engines, a condensing beam engine and a pair of horizontal engines. Water power was apparently used for around 9 months in the year and steam power for the rest. Thomas Bonsor Crompton passed away on the 5th September 1858, after which his nephew, William Jackson Rideout, took over running of the mill.

To celebrate the coronation of Queen Victoria a dinner was held at Prestolee New Cotton Mill. The following account was given in the Bolton Chronicle, Saturday June 30th 1838.

PRESTOLEE NEW MILLS.- The proprietor of this large establishment. **Thomas Bonsor Crompton, Esq***, being desirous that all his workpeople should rejoice and be merry on the occasion of the coronation, had a large room fitted up for the purpose of dining all the hands, about 600 in number. The room was most splendidly decorated on the occasion with flags, emblems, &c. The room was 85 yards long, and 22 yards wide; there were three tables, each 40 yards long, with two cross tables, for the chair and vice, laid out and well furnished with good roast beef, mutton. All the hands assembled in the mill yard at eight o'clock in the morning, and at half-past eight formed themselves in procession in the following order :- Band. Manager on his beautiful grey horse, highly decorated. Standard bearer, bearing a splendid blue silk banner, with the following inscription, in large gilt letters; on one side, "Prestolee New Mills;" on the other side, "Thomas Bonsor Crompton, Esq., proprietor;" "Success to the cotton trade." Watchman, with his lantern and blunderbuss. Engineer, bearing a model of the two large and splendid engines lately erected at the works. Mechanics, bearing a large flag, with emblems of their trade. Scutching-room hands, carrying a large and beautiful cotton tree, under which were four black boys. Card-room hands, bearing a flag, and a many beautiful emblems of their trade. Throstle-room hands, bearing a flag, with the bobbin doffers carrying blue and white wands, highly ornamented. Mule spinners, bearing a flag and emblems. Reelers, bearing a handsome flag, with a reel, highly ornamented - splendid crown. Makers-up, carrying highly ornamented emblems of their trade. Sunday scholars belonging to the Prestolee New Mills Sunday school, with flags, bearing the inscription, "Prestolee New Mills Sunday School; T.B. Crompton, Esq. proprietor." Labourers, &c. carrying a flag, with their pick-axes, spades, &c. - All the hands were very respectably dressed, having rosettes and medals; all the females wearing very neat caps and rosettes. The procession moved off in beautiful order, the band playing "Rule Britannia," and proceeded on to Farnworth paper mills, another very large establishment belonging to the same gentlemen, where both establishments joined together, and gave three cheers for the Queen, three for Mrs. Crompton, and three for T.B. Crompton, Esq. The procession then moved on, headed by the Farnworth establishment, who were beautifully decorated with emblems of* *their trade, to Halshaw Moor, where the two establishments separated, the one to join the Farnworth procession, and the other to join the Kearsley procession. Before joining the Kearsley procession, all the hands assembled in the dining room to partake of lunch, and a most splendid sight it was to see all the females in the centre, neatly and well dressed, with the males outside. After lunch all the hands sang "God save the Queen," after which the procession was again formed and proceeded to Blacus Green, to join the Kearsley procession. After the procession, the hands again assembled in the dining room, to partake of the dinner provided, to which they did ample justice. The manager, Mr. Heywood, officiating at one end, and Mr. Chapman, cashier, at the other. After dining, the chair was taken by Mr. Heywood, and the vice chair by Mr. J.P. Fletcher. The Queen's health was drunk with 3 times 3. Mrs. Crompton's, with 3 times 3. T.B. Crompton, Esq, with 3 times 3. "Success to the cotton trade," 3 times 3. The chairman, vice-chairman, &c. made some beautiful and appropriate speeches, which much increased the harmony of the meeting, and were well received and applauded. After that, the hands joined together in country dances, and separated soon after eight o'clock, all well pleased with the day's enjoyment. All the hands are deserving of praise for their good and orderly conduct. The house of Mr. Heywood, the manager, was splendidly illuminated in the evening, with a brilliant transparency, representing the Queen on horseback with the initials "V.R. Britain's Glory."*

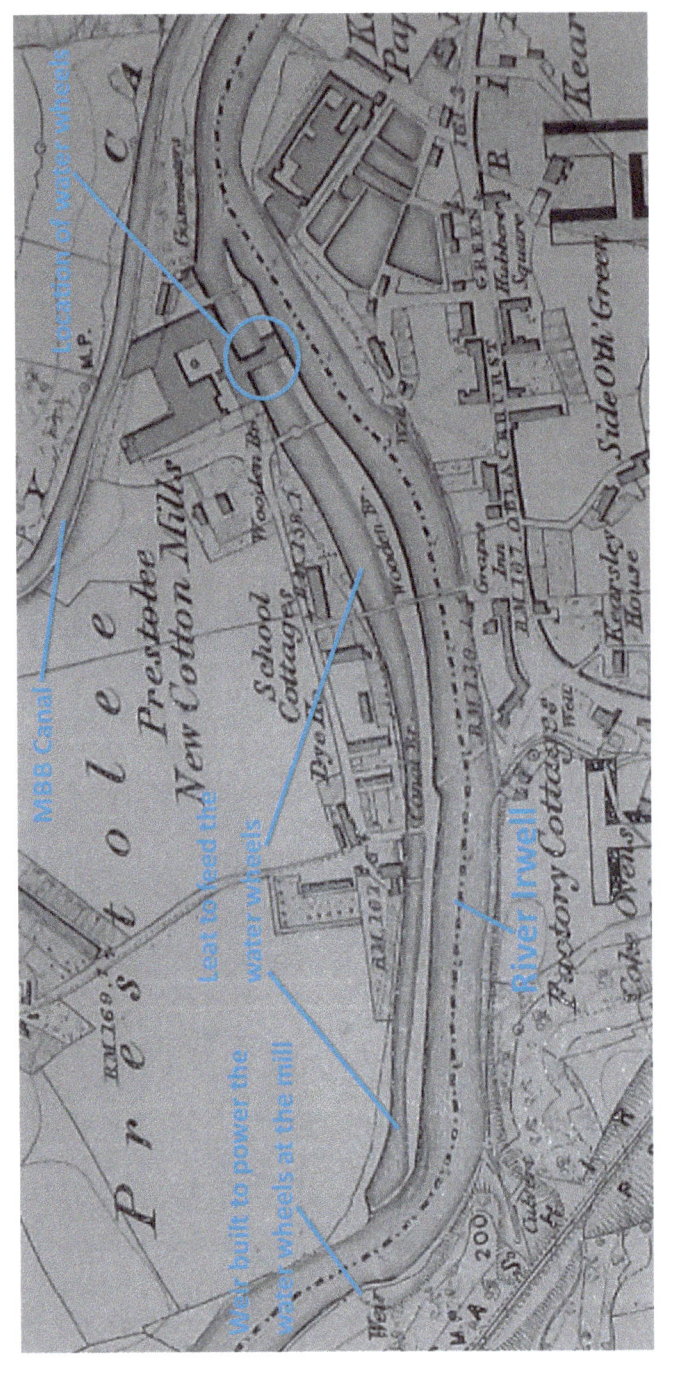

Above. Map of 1848 showing Thomas Bonsor Crompton's Prestolee New Cotton Mill, and how it was powered by water from a leat cut all the way along the riverbank to the Weir that was constructed for this purpose. The leat is quite substantial as it had to drive 3 water wheels, and a number of bridges can be seen crossing it. The location of the Grapes Inn is shown and the bridge next to it at this time is noted as being of wooden construction.

The original mill shown on the 1848 map was extended somewhat over the following decades, but was rebuilt completely in 1894 whilst under the ownership of the Irwell Bank Spinning Company. The new mill was approximately 259 feet long by 133 feet wide inside, and six storeys high in addition to the basement, which extended the whole length of the building. To achieve sound foundations for such a heavy building, a depth of 30 feet below the cellar floor line was needed. The mill employed around 800 persons and contained approximately 133,000 mule spindles which ran from 116 spinning mule machines. The towers adjacent to the River Irwell incorporated water tanks which connected to a sprinkler system on all floors.

Irwell Bank Mill was again extended over the next decade to make it one of the largest in the country, with work finishing in September 1904.

Left. Farnworth Journal Newspaper Report 15th September 1894 on the opening of the newly built Irwell Bank Spinning Mill.

IRWELL BANK SPINNING COMPANY.

LORD DERBY STARTS THE NEW ENGINES.

The splendid new spinning mill at Prestolee, Stoneclough, upon the site of old mills belonging to Messrs. T. B. Crompton and Co., and erected for the Irwell Bank Spinning Co., are almost completed, and yesterday the magnificent engines were started and christened by Lord Derby in the presence of a large and influential gathering of shareholders and friends. Amongst those who joined in the proceedings were Messrs. A. Wood, of Pendleton, chairman of directors, who acted as controller of the gatherings, and John Baxter, of Southport, G. Chatton, of Southport and Little Lever, L. Reddaway, of Pendleton, C. Howarth, of Manchester, W. Pass (manager), and C. B. Grover (secretary), directors of the concern, Jesse Stott, of Stott and Sons, architects, of 5, Cross-st., Manchester, J. Wood, of John and Edward Wood, ironfounders, of Bolton, the Rev. J. W. Brooker, Colonel Mellor, J.P., and Messrs. R. Marsh, I. K Whittaker, T. Boardman, T. H. Chatton, Joseph Rivett (Liverpool, manager of the old Prestolee Mills), J. Prestwich, J. Fletcher, J. Entwistle, Job Openshaw, T. Statter, E. Gittins, Dr. J C. Eames, and Mr. T. Heywood, who had superintended the erection of the engines. The party assembled in the engine-house at four o'clock, when Mr. A. Wood, in introducing Lord and Lady Derby, said the directors and shareholders felt very keenly the high honour done them by that visit. (Hear, hear.) The undertaking from its inception was purely and simply a business one, and for the money invested they expected a good return. To ensure success they had laid themselves out to erect and equip a mill second to none for spinning Egyptian cotton which would command a ready sale with profit to the company. They had in every department brought into operation all approved modern appliances for economy and proficiency in the art of cotton spinning. The site of the mill presented many advantages, as from the river they enjoyed free water, and the Manchester, Bury, and Bolton canal, which was at their door, would give them communication with the Manchester Ship Canal docks, one loading hoist serving for the conveyance of goods by road or canal. There was a large number of collieries surrounding them, which would mean cheap coal, and they were sheltered from north and east, a consideration of great value in spinning fine counts. Apart from being a good investment the undertaking would be of benefit

Irwell Bank Mills at Prestolee circa 1913.

Slightly damaged photo of the maintenance crew at Irwell Bank Mill during the 1920's. They were dubbed 'the black gang' as they were frequently covered in oil and grime from the machinery.

Jack Howard of Prestolee with his son Simeon in the engine room at Irwell Bank Mill in the 1920's.

THE JOURNAL, FRIDAY, SEPTEMBER 27, 1946

RIVER IRWELL IN FLOOD

CAUSES STOPPAGE AT TWO MILLS

HEAVIEST RAIN FOR NEARLY 60 YEARS

The floods in the Farnworth district last week-end, the worst for nearly 60 years, left behind them a story of damage and loss, though their effect was not so severe as in other parts of the country. The worst damage was at Prestolee and Stoneclough, where the River Irwell, overflowing its banks below the Prestolee Bridge, flooded the Irwell Bank Spinning Company's mill, causing a stoppage of work there, and also caused a similar stoppage at Messrs. R. Fletcher and Sons, Paper Mill. An official of the Irwell Bank Spinning Company said, although they had had floods before in his 40 years' association with the company, he had never known the mill to have to close down.

A "Journal" reporter visited the mill during the time the floods were at their height. The card room, which is one of the largest in the trade, was flooded to a depth of nearly a foot, and water was still bubbling up through the floor and rushing in through the main and emergency exits. Entrance to the cardroom could only be gained by a window opening on to the mill yard on the side furthest away from the river, there being from three to four feet of water in the main entrance to the room. Card cans, brooms, shoes, oilcans, cotton were floating about in the muddy water, and the only occupants of the room were a few workmen who, wearing gumboots or barefoot, with trousers rolled up to their knees, worked to secure what movable objects they could. The machinery beneath the looms was under water, and before work can begin again this will have to be taken down, cleaned and oiled.

The flooding began shortly before eight o'clock, and at first only six frames were affected. The water continued to rise and unable to do anything to stem the flood, the management were forced to close down the mill and send the employees home just before noon. Although the engine room was well above the water level, the exhausts from the engines were under water and the engines had to be stopped.

Serious Setback to Production

Normally the mill is some yards from the river but in the early afternoon the water was lapping along the window-sills and when one of the windows was opened, at eye level one looked across the swollen waters of the river. Across from the mill on the further bank of the river a red white and black marker had been placed to measure the level of the water, and this was watched anxiously by officers. As the rain slackened off, prospects became more hopeful as the river falls quickly and an hour later it was evident that the level was dropping.

The mill was only reopened in February after having been closed during the war period under the concentration scheme. In the cardroom nearly 100 per cent running had been achieved, and the flooding is a serious setback to the company.

At Messrs. Fletcher's Paper Mills, only the boiler room was affected by the floods, and at 9-30 the mill was closed down and the employees sent home. The boiler room was flooded to a depth varying from a foot to two or three feet, but here the position was not so serious, so immediately the water receded the work of pumping out the water could be begun. The mill was back on normal working on Monday.

The river overflowed again at the Ringley new bridge, where five wooden hen coies, normally well above the water level on the river bank were partially submerged.

Flooding also occurred in the fields on either side the mineral railway across Buckley-lane, Farnworth, and at Smith's croft below Moses Gate.

There was further flooding at the Alder Forest Housing Estate, Winton, property on the west side of Worsleyrd. opposite the estate and at Monton, where the Bridgewater Canal, for the first time within living memory, overflowed its banks and poured thousands of gallons of water on to the Westwood Park Estate and flooded the lower rooms of a block of low-lying cottage property in Parrin-lane. Early on Friday morning the Worsley Brook (on which work is already in progress to prevent such flooding) overflowed its banks. Residents of the Alder Forest Cottages arose to find the lower rooms flooded and they could do nothing to abate the flow. Only by wading through water two or three feet deep could they be reached and they were marooned in the upper storey. Worsley-rd. itself became submerged beneath the flood and motor traffic had to carefully negotiate a passage. As each vehicle ploughed its way through, waves washed against the adjacent property.

Considerable damage was done to gardens which were flooded to a depth of several feet and many private garages were flooded out. N.F.S. men who visited the scene could do nothing but wait for the flood to subside. Had they started pumping there was no place to get the water away, gulleys and sewers being taxed to their full capacity by the onrush.

Picture shows workers retrieving equipment from the flooded cardroom of the Irwell Bank Spinning Co's. Mill, Stoneclough, where the Irwell, swollen by the heavy rains, flooded the cardroom of the mill on Friday.

Above. Article from the Farnworth Journal of 27th September 1946 showing the flooded cardroom of Irwell Bank Mill.

Irwell Bank Mill finally ceased working as a cotton spinning mill in 1959 and the building was taken over by domestic appliance manufacturer A.J Flatley Ltd, but unfortunately they went out of business in 1962.

Reputed to be two of the largest Mills in the world, they are now the main centre for the famous FLATLEY domestic appliances. Fitted out with fully automated production lines capable of fantastic quality and quantity production. The latest in office equipment and administrative methods, plus a delivery fleet of over 200 modern vehicles - the Mills now provide the need of every housewife in the world - low cost, efficient and safe domestic appliances.

A. J. FLATLEY LTD., IRWELL BANK MILLS
STONECLOUGH Nr. MANCHESTER

. . . . . . She deserves a Flatley!

Left. Advert from 1960 for Flatley Domestic Appliances at Irwell Bank Mills.
Note the tagline "She deserves a Flatley!" which would be considered offensive today.

Oddly they had decided to remove the tops of the towers from the buildings in the picture, even though they were still in place up until its demolition.

Irwell Bank Mill was demolished in 1977 and the Riverside Drive housing estate built on the site.

On Boxing Day 2015 exceptionally high rainfall caused the River Irwell to once more flood the area causing extensive damage to the houses that now cover the site, with some families trapped in their homes and having to be rescued by boat.

Irwell Bank Mills being demolished in 1977

Above. View from Prestolee Bridge on Boxing Day 2015 showing the extraordinarily high level of the River Irwell. The houses to the left are on the site formerly occupied by Irwell Bank Mills.

Kearsley Mill, Prestolee

Work began on the construction of Kearsley Spinning Mill at Prestolee in June 1904 by Messrs W Brown of Manchester, the same contractor who had built the nearby Irwell Bank Mills as well as the Midland Hotel in Manchester. By March 1906 it was reported that the building work was complete and that the mill was being fitted out with machinery from textile engineers, Messrs Hetherington's of Manchester, and that it hoped to be in full production by September the same year. It was to be one of the first in the country to be electrically driven.

The construction is a rectangular block of five storeys on top of a basement. The top storey is of cream brick with the lower storeys all red brick. The South East corner incorporates a stair tower, which has a domed roof with an integral water tank, this connected to each level of the factory to supply water in case of any major outbreak of fire. This was an important feature, as at this time the nearest fire brigade resided at Darley Street, Farnworth, and their 'fire engine' consisted of a horse drawn cart with a steam powered boiler which drove water through the hoses. A large fire at a mill of this size would have proved almost impossible to control by this means. See the picture of Farnworth Fire Brigade on page 44.

The West side of the building has a single storey block that was formerly the engine house, and a full size chimney with the wording V/ER Kearsley, signifying its Edwardian era construction. Also on the West side is a protruding tower, which contained the electrical motors for each floor that would have driven the machinery via a line shafting. The electricity would have been generated onsite by steam turbine generators in the engine house, but at a later date the mill was connected to the national grid.

There is no definite information as to who the original shareholders of Kearsley Mill were, but it is interesting to note that as the nearby Irwell Bank Mills had the same building contractor, textile machinery supplier and both mills were inviting investment from the same agent, so it is not inconceivable that they were both possibly being run by the same consortium. It is known that in the late 1920's Kearsley Mill was owned by a joint-stock company called Combined Egyptian Mills Ltd, which had been setup to buy, and make profitable again over 30 other mills, and this made it the world's second largest cotton spinning company with 3.2 million spindles under its control. In 1953 the company changed its name to Combined English Mills, but following a further decline in the textile industry it was declared in June 1965 that Kearsley Mill was to close as a cotton spinning mill, with the loss of 240 jobs.

Kearsley Mill during the latter stages of construction around 1906. Horse drawn carts can be seen delivering materials, and in the background are the former cottages that stood at the bottom of Seddon Lane with the Prestolee Farmhouse buildings just to the right on Crompton Road. Further back is the spire of Holy Trinity Church with Irwell Bank Mills barely visible to the right.

Left. The impending closure of Kearsley Mill makes the front page of the Journal on June 3rd 1965.

In May 1966 the mill was taken over by Outlook Supplies Ltd, which was a subsidiary of Robert Sinclair Ltd of Newcastle-Upon-Tyne, wholesalers of tobacco, cigarettes and confectionary goods, who in turn were a subsidiary of the Imperial Tobacco Company. Outlook Supplies had won the contract for supplying gifts for the Players No. 6 cigarettes gift token scheme and the mill was now to be used for warehousing purposes. The mill re-opened in August 1966, utilising just the bottom two floors and employing only around 30 people. At the time of writing the Mill is owned by The Ruia Group, and the business supplies household textiles and hosiery to retailers and hospitality organisations.

Above. Kearsley Mill, January 1979. The chimney bears the Royal Cypher V ER, which is perplexing, as it should read EVII R to signify it was built during the reign of Edward VII (E for Edward and R is for 'Rex' which is king in Latin). The word 'Kearsley' also curls upward in an unusual fashion so it can be read fully without the letters being lost to view.

Circa 1905. Farnworth Fire Brigade outside their original premises in Darley Street. They moved to larger premises on Albert Road, beside Frederick Street, in 1914 until 1979 when the current station further along the road opened. The old Albert Road station became Brando's nightclub in the 1980's. There is a Lidl supermarket on the site at present.

The Lancashire Cotton Famine

The cotton industry of the mid 1800's dominated the British economy, but it took a crippling blow, caused by a far-away political conflict completely beyond its control. The American Civil War 1861-1865 was fought largely over the issue of slavery, and most of the cotton that arrived for production in Lancashire was Southern American slave grown cotton.

In March 1861 the newly appointed Republican President Abraham Lincoln immediately set about abolishing slave labour from all of the then 34 states, but seven of the southern states declared their independency from this and formed the Confederate States of America, or as it became better known, The Confederacy or simply The South. This then grew to eleven, and as their economies were principally cotton based they strongly opposed Lincoln's measures to put an end to slavery, in fact six of the Confederate states had a population made up of up to 48% slaves.

In April 1861, shortly after the first shots were fired, Lincoln ordered the blockade of all the Sothern sea ports, cutting off supplies of all goods, in and out, for the duration of the war. This immediately cut the supply of raw cotton to the Lancashire mills, causing many to close or go on to 'short time'. Some mill owners and cotton traders had actually stockpiled cotton, and while some of these used the reserves to keep the mills going as long as possible, some kept hold of it hoping for a higher price as it became less available, and others even exported it for greater profit to other European countries and sometimes even back to the United States.

The knock-on effect in Lancashire was calamitous with over half the cotton operatives out of work by November 1862. Up until this time most of the workers, traders and mill owners had paid no thought to how and where the cotton was harvested and by whom. But this now came into sharp focus, and it is interesting to note that most people sympathized with Abraham Lincoln and his just cause to abolish slavery, even though it was his army that continued to blockade the Southern ports.

Northern British towns suffered terribly as the mills closed and families were forced into unimaginable poverty. The Government set up relief funds and soup kitchens, and as people became more desperate they took to singing on the streets or begging. Some sold or pawned off personal possessions including furniture, clothes and bed linen. As one observer wrote "the pawnbrokers stores were glutted with the heirlooms of many an honest family."

The unemployed workers became widely acknowledged for their diligence and acquiescence during these harsh times. On the rare occasions where protests turned to violence it was due to the unfair dispensation of relief in which unemployed cotton operatives were treated the same as the work-shy and drunkards or 'stondin paupers.' Their anger was justified, as through no fault of their own these previously hard working folk were now denied a means to make a living, but were shown no preference over those who chose not to work even when they could. This unrest prompted the Government to provide relief projects to provide work.

In April 1865 Abraham Lincoln's Northern Union army accepted the surrender of General Robert E. Lee and his Southern Confederate Army. The ports were re-opened and the flow of raw cotton quickly started to make its way across the Atlantic Ocean to Lancashire and the world. The thirteenth Amendment was ratified on January 31st 1865 and slavery was made illegal in the United States. It is again interesting to note that many of those who had been forced to work as slaves in the cotton fields continued to do so, only this time as free men and women.

The next serious decline began with the outbreak of the First World War, as a ban was imposed on exporting to foreign markets, and this had the knock on effect of other countries starting their own cotton weaving industries. When exporting started again British manufacturers found it difficult to compete financially, and the British cotton industry began a downturn from which it has never recovered. Locally the effects of this downturn were not fully felt until the great depression of the 1930's, in fact the proportion of the employed population engaged in cotton in Farnworth, Kearsley and Little Lever was over 41% in 1931. This figure dropped by half over the next two decades as many mills closed down.

Right. From the Bolton Chronicle of 14th October 1865. Details of the Farnworth and Kersley Relief Committee that was officially setup on 22nd October 1862 to provide assistance to those affected by the cotton famine. Even after the paralyzing effects of the cotton famine years the industry recovered and thrived once more, but 50 years later it would again be circumstances out of its control that would deal it another devastating blow.

MEETING OF THE FARNWORTH AND KERSLEY RELIEF COMMITTEE.

A meeting of the general committee connected with the Relief Fund was held in the Board-room, Darley-street, on Monday afternoon. Amongst those present were Alfred Barnes, Esq., in the chair; the Rev. W. Woodman, Mr. D. Crossley, secretary, Mr. Samuel Gee, Mr. Greenhalgh, and Mr. Thornley. The Secretary read the following report from the Executive Committee:—

"The Executive Committee have now the pleasing duty of presenting what they hope may be their last report to the General Committee and the subscribers to the fund, and, in doing so, would briefly epitomise the labours of the committee from its commencement. The first meeting having reference to this question was convened, by circular, and held in the Mechanics' Institution on the 25th of August, 1862, when, after a long conversation, it was resolved:—That an Interim Committee be appointed to watch the state of trade in this district, and to call together a more general meeting so soon as circumstances seem to require the formation of a Public Relief Committee.' Unfortunately, the necessity was soon felt; as on the 17th of October a public meeting of the inhabitants was called in the same place, Thomas Barnes, Esq., M.P., in the chair, when it was resolved:—'That it is the opinion of this meeting that there exists in Farnworth and Kersley a degree and kind of distress which calls for special efforts from all who are able to give assistance.' A subscription list was then opened, with what success the balance sheet will testify. On the 21st of the same month the Executive Committee was appointed, and held its first meeting on the day following, October 22nd, 1862, A. Barnes, Esq., in the chair. The first relief was given on the 6th of November. For a short time the committee met twice a week, and once regularly afterwards, until April 30th, 1864, when they adjourned till the 24th of September, at which time it was found needful to request all the subscribers to pay up say seven months' subscription. The committee have held 192 meetings, and with the exception of £20 13s. (given in money as a Christmas gift,) all the relief has been given in kind. The committee have signed and issued about 5500 food tickets, and 900 tickets for clothing, clogs, &c. In addition to the amount stated in the balance sheet, there has been distributed by the committee about 550 tons of coal, all of which have been weighed and distributed by ticket received from the visitor of each district. In like manner the committee have distributed 99 barrels of flour, 70 of which were a part of the cargo of the George Griswold; about 1000lb. of bacon, and two boxes of bread. The money value of these articles would be about £240. This sum added to the sum stated in the balance sheet would raise the amount of actual relief granted to £2052 10s. 2d., and the total expenditure of the committee to £2321 1s. 10d. The sum expended by the committee in distributing is under £160, from which £27 7s. must be deducted for furniture sold, and the proceeds paid into the Bank. The labours of the committee have sometimes been of a difficult character, but in the main it is believed that the object contemplated by its formation has been fully realised, and that many of the hard-working and honest poor have been kept from a condition of poverty, that would have been to them the greatest humiliation. Your committee would record their devout thankfulness to Almighty God, for the very favourable circumstances this district has shared, both as regards the employments for many, and the liberality of those to whom He has entrusted the means of aiding the needy. Your committee have now, in brighter days, to tender you, the trust they received, with the hope that the same All-wise Providence may so order our affairs, that we may not again have the necessity laid upon us of providing for those who are willing to work for bread, but have to mourn that work cannot be found. In conclusion, your committee believe that the inhabitants of few places will be abler to look back with more satisfaction to these trying times than the men of Farnworth, as from the cotton famine of 1863 will date the commencement of its sanitary and other arrangements, all tending to a healthier and better requisited population."

—The report was adopted.—Mr. GEE spoke in complimentary terms of the services rendered in the committee's operations by the secretary, Mr. Crossley.—In the course of the meeting it was stated that the balance in hand would be about £167. It also transpired that some of the subscribers to the relief fund had paid ten months' subscriptions, whereas the majority had only paid seven. It was therefore agreed to return all subscriptions given for more than seven months: about £25. It was said would here to be returned in this way. With respect to the final balance, it was decided to leave the money in the bank for the present.—A committee was appointed for the purpose of arranging for the presentation of a testimonial to Mr. Crossley for his services as honorary secretary.—A vote of thanks was awarded to A. Barnes, Esq., for his services as chairman of the Executive Committee, in acknowledging which that gentleman expressed his gratification that the end of their labours as a committee had come, and that there now appeared no further need of relief in the district.

Bankfield Mill, Ringley

This mill started as a cotton weaving shed in mid 1800's but ceased cloth production during the 1930's. In 1891 it was owned by Baker and Whittaker and boasted 150 looms manufacturing checks, ginghams, cotton lynseys & stripes.

During the Second World War it was used as a storage depot, but in December 1945 it was purchased by Norman Evans & Rais Ltd, Chemical Manufacturers, of Manchester, who produced paint driers and metallic soaps. The mill is currently occupied by ITAC Ltd, manufacturers of industrial coatings and adhesives.

Above. Bankfield Mill, Ringley, during the 1950's whilst under the ownership of Norman Evans & Rais Ltd.

Moss Rose Mill

This mill is believed to have been originally opened by a Mr Giles Gee, with the company name being G. Gee and Sons by 1871, when both Isaac and Samuel Gee had joined their fathers business. On the map of 1848 the mill is named 'Rose Cotton Mill' but by 1871 it is listed in local trade directories as Moss Rose Mill.

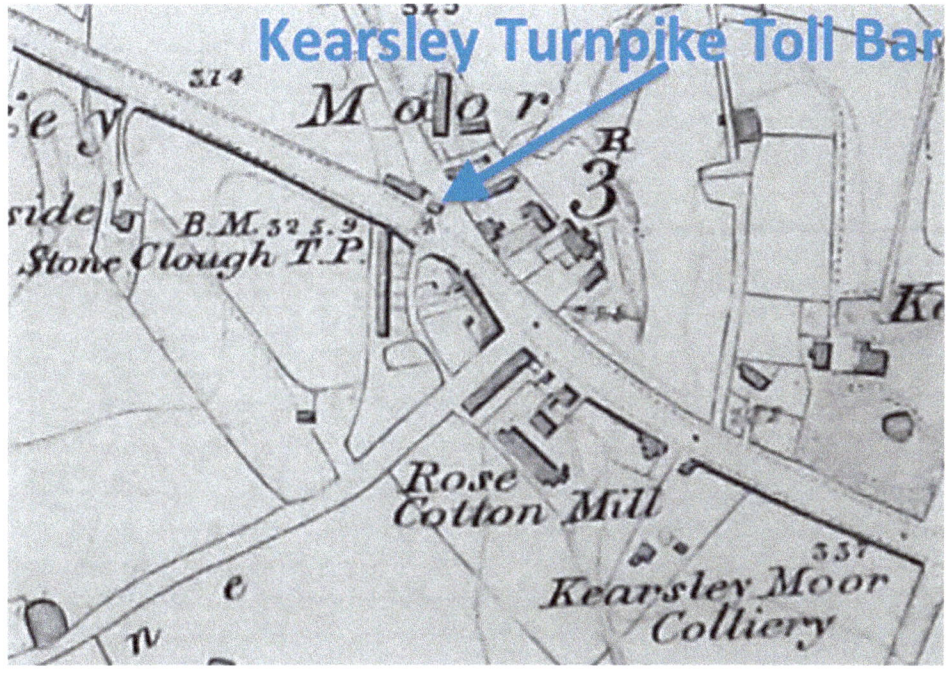

Above. Rose Cotton Mill in 1848. The map also shows the location of the Kearsley Toll Bar, at the junction of Roscow Road, Bolton Road and Manchester Road, which was part of the Stoneclough Turnpike Trust. Kearsley Moor Colliery can also be seen at a location to the rear of where the Kearsley Social Club now stands.

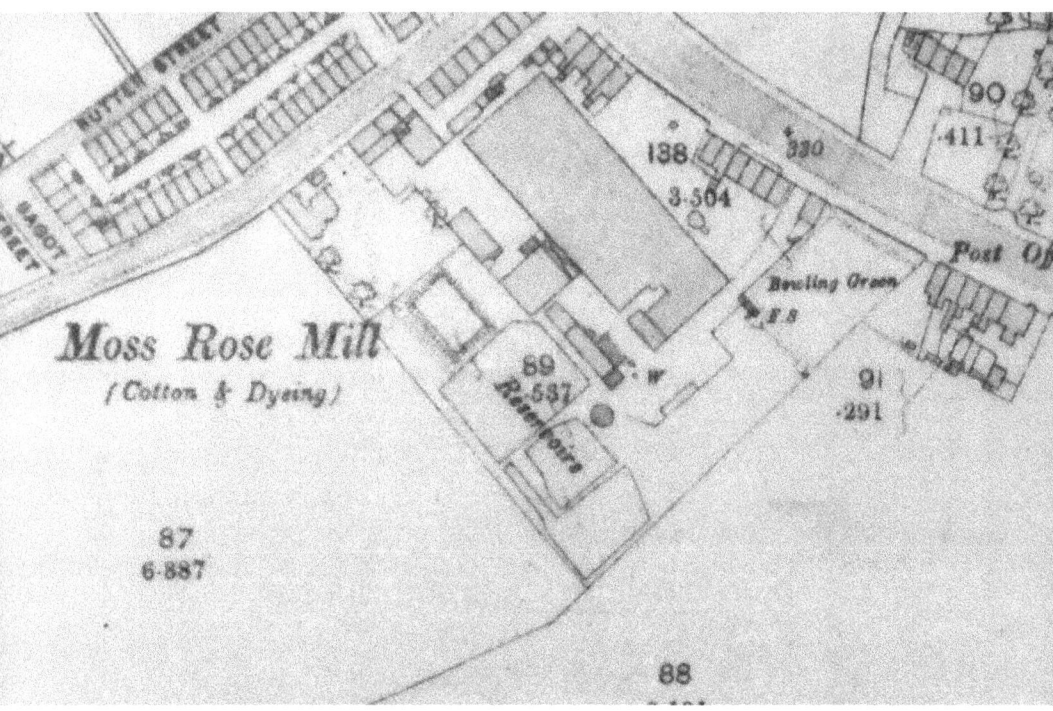

Above. Map of 1890 shows the mill is larger and reservoirs have also been added. Moss Dene House can also be seen on Taskers Lane (Springfield Road) to the left.

Moss Rose Mill was purchased from a Mr. G. F. Cooke by John Holden in 1903, but he passed away in August 1904 at Moss Dene house and control of the business passed on to his son. At present the John Holden group of companies still occupy the mill at the end of Springfield Road, which also retains the name Moss Rose Mill. They use the latest technologies in fabric laminating and textile coating for a wide variety of industries worldwide.

Kearsley Manufacturer's Death. The death occurred on Saturday morning, at his residence, Moss Dene, Tasker's-lane, Kearsley, of Mr. John Holden, who recently purchased Moss Rose Mill from Mr. G. F. Cooke. Previous to commencing business in Kearsley Mr. Holden resided at Blackburn. He was a staunch Churchman and held the offices of Sunday school superintendent and churchwarden in connection with the parish church of that town. The end was unexpected, acute peritonitis being the cause of death. The deceased gentleman was attended by Drs. Robinson (locum tenens to Dr. Affleck) and Grannar (Blackburn.) The funeral took place on Tuesday, when the remains were placed in the family vault in St. James' Churchyard, Lower Darwen, the officiating clergymen being the Revs. J. Morgan, vicar of St. Stephen's, Kearsley, and G. Sumner, vicar of St. James's, Lower Darwen. Deceased leaves one son and two daughters.

Above. Report on the passing of Moss Rose Mill owner John Holden, from the Farnworth Journal 26th August 1904.

Below. The former site of the Kearsley Royal British Legion premises on Springfield Road in June 2003. Holden's mill is seen in the background.

Kearsley Mill to Reopen

There is some good news for Kearsley people this week. Moss Rose Weaving Mill, owned by Messrs. John Holden and Son, Ltd., and closed since 1941 under the concentration scheme, is to be reopened in a few months by the new proprietors, Messrs. W. H. Sciama and Co., rayon manufacturers, of 82, Princess-st., Manchester.

Moss Rose Mill was acquired by Mr. John Holden in 1903. It was then an old mill, but additions were made to the premises in 1912, and when the closure came 473 looms were in operation. The mill was established under a limited company in 1929, with a merchandising office in Manchester, under Mr. A. M. Holden as managing director. Mr. Holden died in 1943. Since 1936 Counc. J. Crankshaw, of Kearsley, has had charge of the Manchester establishment as general manager.

The new proprietors, who have acquired both the Kearsley and Manchester premises, are intending to manufacture rayon products here. Before they open, however, they are planning several improvements which include the installation of electricity for power and lighting, and respacing the looms. It will be a modern mill when completed, and should provide employment for between 150 and 170 people.

Left. Article from the Farnworth Journal, December 1946. The British Government had introduced a concentration scheme in 1941 which aimed to minimize the resources used by less essential industries, without destroying their markets. Rather than working all mills at reduced capacity, which would have been wasteful of fuel and factory space, production was restricted to selected mills, with the result that about a third of the industry's spinning and weaving capacity was closed during the wartime years. Moss Rose Mill had been closed since the establishment of this scheme in 1941 and Moss Dene house was utilized as the headquarters for the Kearsley air raid wardens.

The cotton mills of Baker Street

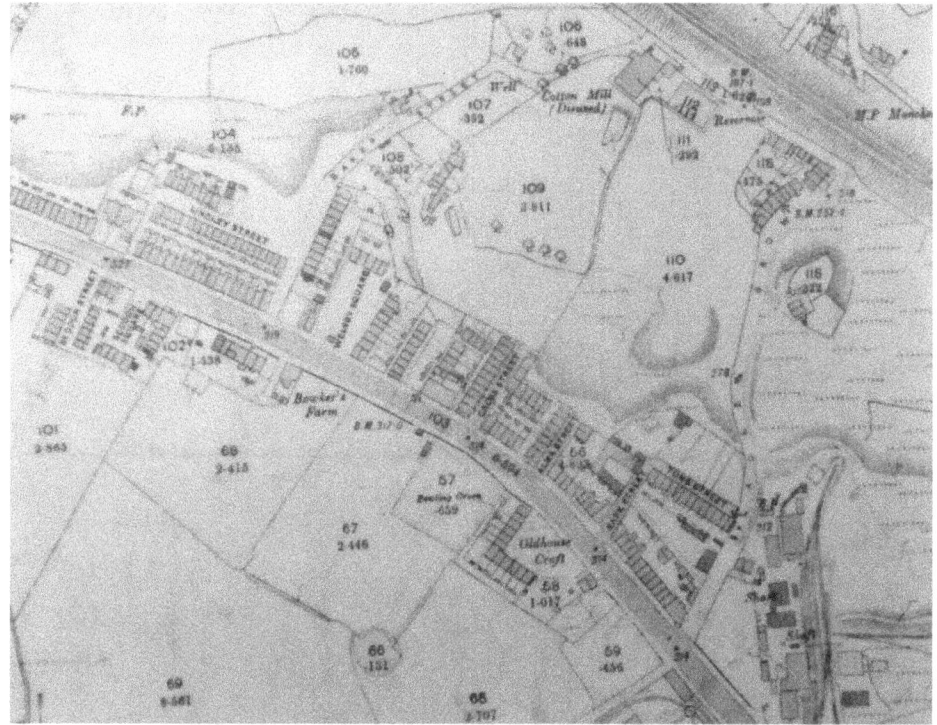

Above. Baker Street takes its name from the Baker family who were the proprietors of Mount Vale Mill, which was located between the bottom of Baker Street and the tunnel under the railway at the bottom of Slackey Brow. The mill does not show on the map of 1848, but is shown, albeit disused, on this map of 1890. In 1871 Noah Baker is listed in local trade directories as 'Cotton Spinner and Manufacturer' residing at nearby Mount Vale house, which was also on Baker Street overlooking the mill and the former site of a smaller mill owned by the family. Today there is no trace of the mills or reservoir shown.

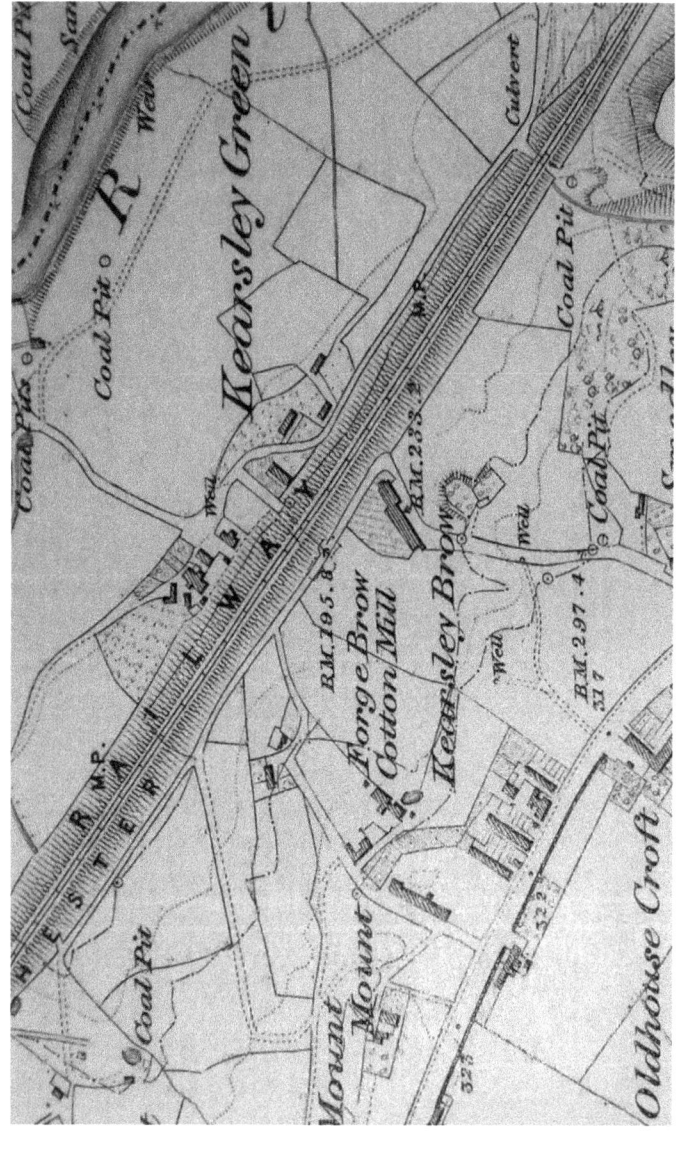

Above. On this map of 1848 the original mill is named Forge Brow Cotton Mill and located further up the hillside. It is interesting to note the two wells close to Slackey Brow and one at Kearsley Green, all of which could have been used by the locals as a source of fresh water.

The paper mill of Robert Fletcher & Sons Ltd, Stoneclough.

In 1823, the Earl of Derby granted a lease to a bleacher in Prestolee named Ralph Crompton, for a plot of land on the right bank of the river Irwell, on which to build a bleachworks, and Stoneclough Mill, then known as Kersley Bleachworks was born. Ralph Crompton had previously been in business with his brother, James, as bleachers at Prestolee, as far back as 1805, but this partnership was ended in 1813 by the death of James.

When James's two sons, Roger and James, came of age, they were taken into partnership by their uncle, trading as Ralph Crompton and Nephews, Bleachers of Prestolee, The Old Boar's Head, Hyde's Cross, Manchester.

Ralph Crompton would only enjoy the prosperity of Kersley Bleachworks for three years, as he drowned in the Irwell during 1826, at which point the business passed into the hands of his nephews, Roger and James the younger. Later, Roger undertook to act as guardian to uncle Ralph's two younger children, Rachel and James Roger, of whom the latter was born in 1827 after his father's death.

The original business at Stoneclough Mill was textile bleaching, but in 1829 the Mill began papermaking and a year later acquired the services of Robert Fletcher, who it is believed was a relative of the Crompton's. Fletcher was a skilled bleacher, and he impressed his employers so much that he was made general manager within seven years, on both the textile bleaching and papermaking processes. At first he turned down the offer because of his own lack of experience of papermaking, other than what he had picked up during the seven years at the mill, so one of the conditions for him taking up the post was that if he failed as a papermaker, which he did not claim to be, he was not to be dismissed from the Crompton's service, but was to be allowed to resume his former work as head of the cloth bleaching department.

The Crompton brothers' decision to promote Robert Fletcher soon turned out to be a wise one, as he rapidly acquired the same mastery of papermaking as he had already acquired in the art of textile bleaching. From this time onwards, fortified by his strong, religious convictions, he became a dedicated man. He had been brought up by his parents in an atmosphere of strict puritanical nonconformity, and he himself attributed his later success to what he termed 'a good Sunday school education', and this may well have been the only education he had ever received.

Specific details of the inner workings of the mill are unavailable, but within the first 20 years of producing the first sheet of paper it had gained the

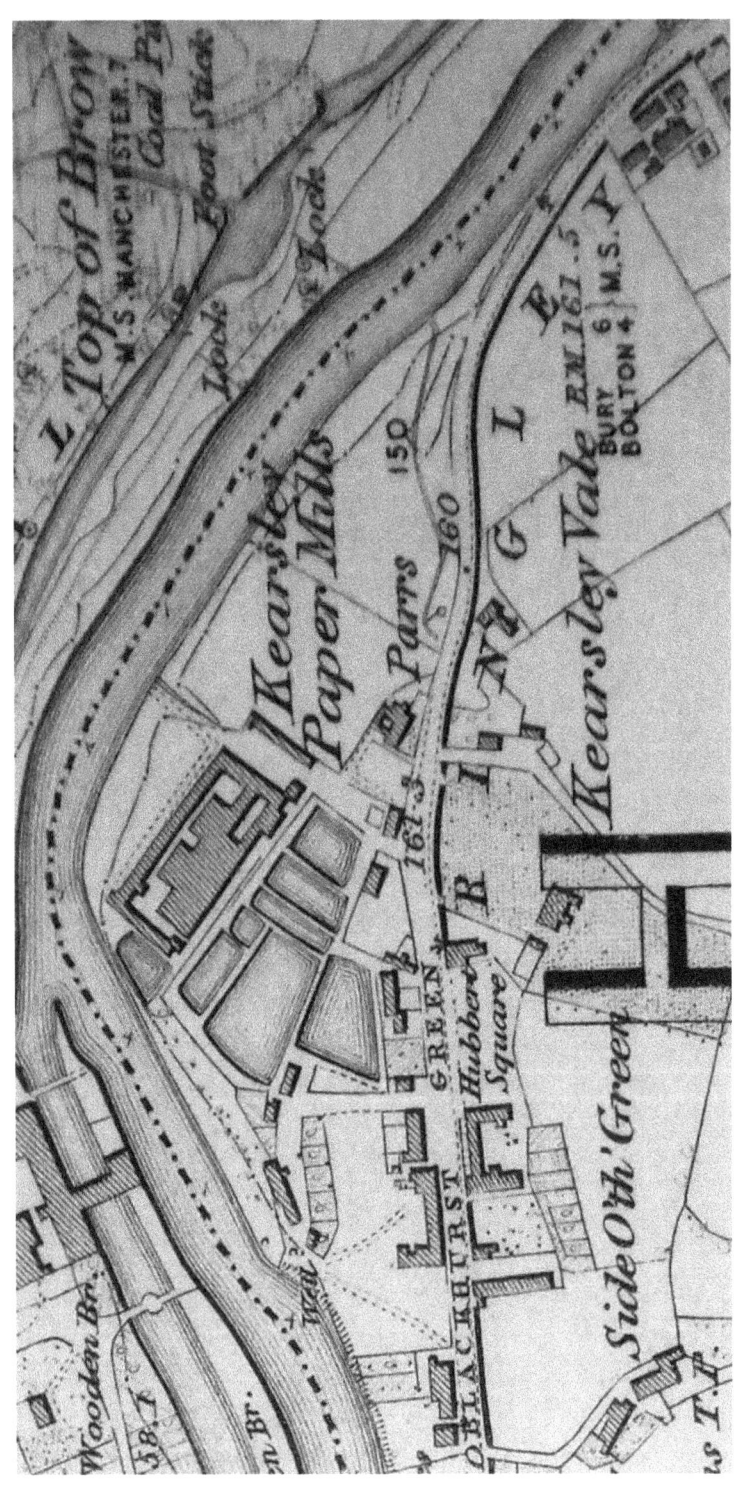

Kearsley Paper Mill in 1848 which, at this time, was owned by Roger Crompton, nephew of Ralph Crompton whom had acquired the original lease for the land to build the works in 1823. Robert Fletcher was general manager until he purchased the factory in 1859. It is worth noting the area from Stoneclough to Ringley was also known as Blackhurst Green, a name that is no longer in use.

Above, Circa 1910, Ringley Locks and Lock House on the Manchester Bolton & Bury Canal with Fletchers Paper Mill across the Irwell to the left. The imposing Irwell Bank Mills stand in the background with Holy Trinity Church spire seen between the towers. Numerous factory chimneys fill the skyline giving some attestation of the industrial nature of the Kearsley area during this period.

reputation of being one of the world's leading manufacturers of fine tissues. In the meantime the bleaching of textiles had been discontinued and all the efforts of the mill were thereafter concentrated solely on the manufacture of paper. Thus in 1844, Roger Crompton was still officially described as both a textile bleacher and a papermaker. By 1851 on the other hand, his firm is recorded in local directories solely under the heading of papermaking: the mill now being referred to as Kearsley Paper Works. The discontinuance of textile bleaching must therefore have taken place sometime during the late 1840's.

In April 1844, the death of James Crompton brought the partnership between himself and his younger brother, Roger, to an end. He was 52 when he died, was unmarried, and left his entire estate, including his share in the business, to his brother, Roger. This must have been considerable - another indication of the firm's success – for Roger was now able to acquire a house in Regents Park, London, where he entertained frequently, and had many servants and staff. From then on he divided his time between his London and Stoneclough homes. During his time away from Stoneclough the affairs of the paper works were left in the capable hands of Robert Fletcher, and in 1859 when Roger passed away in his London home at the age of 62, his will, in recognition of their fruitful business association and personal friendship, not only named Robert Fletcher as one of his three executors, but also gave him the option to purchase the business under most favourable terms. This offer was immediately taken up, and control and ownership of the mill was passed to Robert Fletcher, who then made his elder son, James, then aged 26, a partner and gave the firm the new title of Robert Fletcher And Son: a title that was not changed when his younger son, John, was also later taken into the partnership.

The Fletcher family also moved into the Crompton's old home at Kearsley Vale House, and it was about this time the trademark 'Archer' was adopted because of the coincidence that the word fletcher means a maker of arrows. The fortunes of the company continued to prosper under the ownership of Robert Fletcher, but he was beginning to suffer ill-health, and after a long illness he died in Vale House on 17th May 1865, aged 61. He was buried in the churchyard of the Parish Church of his native Radcliffe in what was to become the family vault. He was followed only a few months later by his wife, Tabatha.

On the death of Robert Fletcher the business passed into the hands of his two sons, James aged 32 and John, aged 26. James then took over the management of the mill at Stoneclough, and John, who had lived at

Southport since his marriage, continued to look after the Manchester office. James was married to his cousin, Charlotte Leak of Manchester, and they had been living in a house in Blackhurst Green, later known as 78 Market Street, Stoneclough, but on the death of his parents they moved into Kearsley Vale House. The company continued to prosper and was now exporting papers all over the world, an important market for the Stoneclough papers at this time was the United States, the range included white and coloured tissue papers as well as fine bible papers.

The company did however face competition at times from cheaper foreign imports, but managed to defeat this threat by upgrading their own machinery and the superior organization and technical skill of his works. James Fletcher died in Kearsley Vale House on November 9th 1887, just over twenty years after himself and his brother took over the business on the death of their father. He had taken part in the public life of the district and from 1861 until 1865 he was chairman of the local highway board, one of the many *ad hoc* bodies that were formed in this country until the implementation of the Local Government Act of 1888.

In 1865 James Fletcher was among those who strongly and successfully opposed the swallowing up of Kearsley by the neighbouring township of Farnworth at a meeting of owners and ratepayers at the Grapes Inn, Stoneclough, on August 30. It was, in fact, as a result of this meeting, and in particular of a resolution seconded by James Fletcher that Kearsley was able to continue its separate existence and that a new board, the Kearsley Urban Sanitary Authority was set up under the Local Government Act of 1858, this was the forerunner to the Kearsley Urban District Council that was established in 1899. He was also very interested in local ecclesiastical affairs, and although brought up as a strict Wesleyan he came under the influence at a very early age of the Swedenborgians of the New Jerusalem Church in Kearsley (see New Jerusalem Church, Page 238).

The Fletcher partnership now consisted of John and his two nephews, John Robert, born in 1855, and James, born in 1859 who were the two eldest sons of James Fletcher. This new partnership would only last two years though, as John Fletcher, the senior partner, was murdered by poisoning on the evening of February 26th 1889 after attending an afternoon sale at the Mitre Hotel near Manchester Cathedral. He had decided to visit some of the stalls in the neighbouring Old Market and was unfortunate enough to succumb to the sharp tongue of a man named Parton, who quickly summed him up as easy prey. The pair hailed a cab and went for a drink in the Three Arrows Hotel on Deansgate, where the cabby was told to wait, about twenty minutes later the pair came out with the older man looking worse for drink, Parton ordered the cabby to drive to a house on Stretford Road. On the way there a passer-by alerted to the cabby that one of his doors was open, the cabby went to close the door and noticed that the younger man had disappeared and only his companion remained on the back seat, but with his head forward on the front seat. The cabby fetched a policeman and they drove to the infirmary, where John Fletcher was found to be dead.

It was first thought that he had died of excessive alcoholism, but subsequent police enquiries revealed that while the two men were in the Three Arrows Hotel young Parton had poured some chloral hydrate from a small phial into his companions drink and then bundled him into the cab while he was still capable of walking. His victim will have soon become completely bemused, and it will have been a simple matter for the young man to rob him of all his money, plus his gold watch and chain – said to be worth £120 – and as soon as he thought the coast was clear to jump out of the moving cab and escape with his haul as fast as his legs could carry him. John Fletcher was a widower, his wife had died nearly five years earlier, and as they had no children his interest in the business passed into the hands of his two nephews and junior partners, John Robert and James.

When the two brothers took over the business from their unfortunate uncle in 1889 the threat of foreign competition was sufficiently serious enough for them to realize the need to significantly reduce running costs as a matter of urgency. The mill machinery was operating at its maximum rate, and the brothers did not seem to want to purchase new and faster machinery, and thankfully nor did they wish to take the easy option of simply reducing the wages of the workers, which were already desperately low. For example, an adult worker in the beater-room or machine-house was already working 15 hours a day from 06:00 to 21:00 hours Monday to Friday inclusive and 10 hours a day from 06:00 to 16:00 hours on a Saturday when the mill shutdown for the week-end. In other departments the hours worked were slightly less. Even boys of no more than 10 years of age, when not in school as half-timers, worked up to 12 hours a day. And there were only a few days' holiday in the year.

In return for these appalling conditions a beaterman or a machineman, at the maximum rate of 6½d (3p) an hour, or a worker in any of the other departments, at a maximum rate of 5¾d (2½p) an hour, could not earn more than 44/3d (£2.21) and 36/- (£1.80) respectively. For boys on full time the weekly rate was 4/11d (24½p), and for half-timers only 2/5½d

(12½p). These rates must of course be considered in relation to the cost of living of the time. Rents, for example, were no more than a few shillings a week, coal was about 6d (2½p) a hundredweight, eggs could be had for 9d (4p) a dozen, and an ounce of tobacco cost only 3d (1p).

The wages provided no more than a bare existence for a working man and his family, and it must be borne in mind that the Welfare State was still more than half a century away. If a worker lost his job through sickness, the sack or scarcity of work, nothing stood between him and abject poverty but the humiliation of charity, however well intentioned that may have been, or separation from his wife and family in the hated workhouse.

Fortunately John Robert and James Fletcher decided on a new, and at the time innovative, method of workers on shift systems that would keep the factory running 24 hours a day, and enhance the welfare of their employees. Introduced at Stoneclough in 1890, the experiment started in the preparation department as a two-shift system, each shift working 12 hours a day. By running the machines continuously their production increased by some 75 per cent for the same overhead charges, and with only small additions to the labour costs with the workers hourly rates being increased to compensate for their reduction in hours worked per day from 15 down to 12. Even though by today's standards these are extremely long hours, for dreadfully low wages, a sound principal on which to build had been established.

On October 4th 1897 the partnership between the two brothers was terminated, and the firm became a private limited company with John Robert as its first chairman and his brother James as his co-director. The first secretary was James Sutcliffe who became known for keeping a tight hold on the company's purse strings. The company continued to thrive and produce an even wider array of fine papers, but in 1907 the Fletcher family connection to the business began to disband with the death of John Robert on September the 20th. James Fletcher was also beginning to suffer ill health, and as none of the brothers had sons to follow them in the business James sold a portion of his interest in the company to Henry Whitehead, a bleacher, of Walshaw, Bury, and a new board of directors was formed.

This consisted of Henry Whitehead, his son, Sydney Dean Whitehead, Joseph Dixon, W S Horton and James Fletcher, the latter retaining his position as chairman. Joseph Dixon and W S Horton soon left the firm, however and on January 22, 1915, James Fletcher died suddenly in Vale House, where he had been born nearly 57 years before, he was succeeded as chairman by S D Whitehead. The Fletchers' association with the company had lasted three generations over a period of 85 years, and they had sole control for 52 of those years. James Fletcher like his father before him had not only been a businessman, but had served the community in which he had lived and worked. He had been a member of the Kearsley Sanitary Board and was its chairman from 1895 until it was dissolved in 1899 and the Kearsley Urban District Council was formed.

Sydney Dean Whitehead,
1886 - 1961

Sydney Dean Whitehead was now in full control of the company, and as the First World War began to rage across Europe a new opportunity arose from these lamentable circumstances. France was, at the time, the major producer of cigarette papers, but the German invasion compromised this sufficiently enough that British papermakers were required to fill the void. The Stoneclough mill had never produced fine cigarette papers before, but S D Whitehead made a decisive decision, and within a year they were rolling off the reels.

Such was the efficiency of the mill and quality of the cigarette papers that in 1918 the Imperial Tobacco Company acquired a financial stake in the business, and subsequently, in 1936 they took complete control.

The rapidly increasing demand for cigarette papers meant the Stoneclough mill could not maintain the required output, so in 1920 the company bought Greenfield Mill, at Chew Valley near Oldham, which would be solely devoted to the manufacture of cigarette papers. The mill was originally a textile mill and later a bleachworks, but had been standing idle since the end of the war where it had been used for the manufacture of gun cotton under the control of the War Ministry. The whole site including already installed machinery was bought for £39,000. It is believed that the stripped out machinery was later sold for more than what the mill had been bought for.

The Stoneclough mill also continued to be developed, and in 1922 a new 80 inch wide machine was installed and became the first in the company to be electrically driven, and in 1931 an electricity generating plant was installed which would provide 50% of the power demands of the mill.

It is worth noting that the firm's development between the wars was by no means solely technical. Sydney Dean Whitehead was especially conscious of the needs of the disillusioned men returning from the terrors and dreadful conditions endured whilst fighting for their country. He referred to the *"steadfast patience and faith in themselves that had enabled them to triumph over apparently insurmountable difficulties,"* he added that *"the same spirit is needed now by everyone if we are to emerge triumphantly out of the present difficulties in which the world is plunged."*

His first concern was over hours of work. The factory was still running the two 12 hour shifts that had been introduced in 1890, but he thought this was still too excessive, so a new three shift system of 8 hours each was introduced in 1919, with no reduction in the employees basic earning power. In the same year he set up a works committee, which consisted of four members representing the workforce, and four members representing the management. The purpose of this committee was to settle any differences or potential grievances as they became apparent, and this system was such a success that it remained in place until the mill closed in 2001. An example of its constructive influence was shown in 1922 when the workers' representatives put forward a claim for three days' holiday pay, this was unusual because at that time paid holidays were out of the ordinary in industrial working life, and they were not confident that their request would be positively received.

Above. The Archer logo used by the works Journal.

To their astonishment however, the management did not offer three, but 10 days paid holiday pay for every works employee that had been in service for over a year. This made Fletcher's the first papermaking firm in Lancashire, and one of the first in the country to grant this concession.

In January 1920 the works first journal, *The Archer*, was produced. It was initiated and edited by George Tatlock, who had been in charge of costing since his return from the war, it was printed by the local firm of McCardell & Son and published quarterly as a 30-page octavo pamphlet. Unfortunately the publication ceased in 1922 when George Tatlock was transferred along with a number of other experienced and skilled engineers and craftsmen, to the Greenfield Mill at Oldham to take over key posts and train the newly recruited workforce. It was revived in 1938 but ceased again during the second world war before resuming again in 1946 with George Tatlock joined by C G Hampson as joint editor.

In 1921 the two remaining daughters of the late James Fletcher departed Vale House, with Miss E M Fletcher marrying W H J Winstanley of Stockport and her sister Miss D E Fletcher leaving to live in Cheshire. It was Sydney D Whitehead who had the idea of putting the house to better use, and work began immediately with a bowling green being laid, two hard tennis courts constructed and interior alterations to the house which provided a big room for dances, concerts, and social events plus a billiards-room and bar.

The outbreak Second World War on September 3rd 1939, caused an enforced interruption to all major schemes of development at the factory, but Sydney D Whitehead continued to take bold steps in ensuring greater financial security for the workforce. On May 1st 1943 the first contributory pension scheme was introduced by the company for all employees regardless of their status. Clauses were also introduced to provide pensions for the widows of members who died either during their service with the firm or after retirement. Other initiatives brought in were the setting up of canteens with food at reasonable costs, factory doctors visiting the mills and day release without loss of earnings for employees to attend courses at technical colleges.

After the Second World War things slowly began to return to normal and with war-time restrictions being lifted the company updated and upgraded its machinery as it now began to export around the globe. The need for increased accommodation for raw materials was provided by the erection of a large new building on the other side of the road (Roughly where Tanfield Drive is now situated) at Tickle Farm, a few years later a further extension doubled its capacity.

Another notable project at Stoneclough at this time was the construction of a new water purification plant at a cost of some £50,000. The Plant had relied on the Irwell for its water supply, but it had become too polluted and was a serious threat to the manufacturing process. The new water plant came into operation in 1948 and was designed to deal with around two million gallons of water per day.

Above. Situated to the rear of the Market Street Tavern the former Fletchers Paper Mill Water Treatment Plant in 1971.

In June 1950, having reached the age of 65, S D Whitehead went into a well earned retirement after almost 40 years of service. He had not only shown tremendous vision while in charge of the company, but displayed genuine compassion, empathy and respect for the dedicated workforce of the firm.

Look At Work No. 2 —

Paper making has, for 138 years, been associated with Stoneclough and in the second article of our series on local industries, personalities and projects Terry Walker writes on:—

PAPER BY THE M-I-L-E . . . .

World-wide sales of products from Stoneclough mill

THE MILL IN THE VALLEY is the home of a pioneering paper manufacturing firm, Robert Fletcher and Son, the 138-years-old Stoneclough firm, whose go-ahead activities have kept them abreast of all the latest developments and methods in the paper-making industry, and have provided employment for generations of people in Kearsley and the surrounding districts.

THE AVERAGE HOUSEHOLD must surely contain several products from Fletcher's. That cigarette paper, the inner tissue of the wrapping on a tablet of soap, the sweet wrapping, piece of carbon paper, that Bible . . . the list is almost endless.

Other fine quality papers made at the mill in the valley are used for air mail paper, writing paper, packaging, and a host of other things.

And every day, in most countries of the world, someone picks up a piece of Fletcher's paper in the shape of an overseas edition of our national newspapers and magazines.

The Stoneclough firm makes the paper required for these overseas editions which, as they are flown out by air-mail, must be of a very light weight.

AND THAT'S WHERE FLETCHER'S COME IN. Whatever the use tissue is required for, they can produce the necessary paper of the right colour, weight, width and strength.

Later we'll see how paper is made, the ins and outs, how demo and the solutions, but now what about the people who work there, the bosses, the production staff. You get the idea?

First I met the man who has been a director of the firm for 17 years and has been associated with the mill in the valley for 21.

The quiet man

He's a quiet man, with a deep interest in paper making. His problems — these are a few at Fletcher's — and is in fact the ideal man to be company secretary.

Mr. Lingard is a traveller too, his journeys taking him at home and abroad — including Russia — from where the raw materials for production come — have given him an insight into the International paper markets.

Fletcher's have succeeded, in spite of the growth of rival firms of the world's market for high quality specialist papers, and sales product is increasing all the time.

The chairman and managing director of the firm is Mr. E. J. Pitt. The general manager at the mill is Mr. W. E. [...]

Prep' department

reminiscent of a cha-cha, shaking out all the surplus water and fills all the water along the edges of the wire ensure that the paper will come out with straight edges.

But there is nothing out of this world about this process. What it is probably the most important to date. It takes out lumps and impurities from the pulp, white pulp matter, by simmers and shivers its way through the drying cylinders after leaving the gauze mill damp.

Cha-cha

By now the porridge has been reduced to a milk-like substance by adding water, and this now is fed on to a phosphor-bronze wire, pours at one end of the 25 yards or so long paper making process which reaches upwards for two storeys.

The wire, with a movement [...]

Made, the instruments on which the paper slides are broken, balanced and boiled in readiness for the actual process of making the paper.

He said: "I enjoy the work here. I started off with the firm at their other mill at Greenfield, near Oldham, 33 years ago. In 1942 I came to Stoneclough as foreman of the preparation department.

"My work involves seeing that everything runs smoothly in the first part of the process of manufacture. It usually does, but you never know."

Weird machine

Nearby were several spherical iron coilers, rotating on shafts, which is the process of being "cooked" for from six to 12 hours.

Some of the wood pulp comes to the mill already "cooked" and ready to be popped into the popping machine. This title is a "popper" but you must be misled by the name — it only washes the residue of the boiling liquids used in the processing of flax, hemp and jute.

It is neither from chlorine

pending on the type of paper speed, it is pushed away in the speedy manner.

But there is nothing out of this world about this process. What it is probably the most important to date. It takes out lumps and impurities from the pulp, white pulp matter, by simmers and shivers its way through the drying cylinders after leaving the gauze mill damp.

Science-fiction?

Next the mixture is carried by pipes into a beating machine which, with the thickness and time allowed for this process depends on the type of paper required. Coloured papers, at their rainbow over a steam blanket are produced on the wire, giving at one end of the 25 yards or so long paper making appeal to all science-fiction fans greet the eyes . . . rows of semi-transparent tubes containing white or coloured liquid [...]

CADET DIVISION WAS FOUNDED 21 YEARS AGO

FORMED during the early days of the war in [...]

● This "GIANT" produces paper from TINY pulp particles. As the paper travels further along it can be seen going lighter in colour due to the drying process.

leave Tom's care they may receive other processes.

When the giant rolls of paper leave Tom's care they may receive other processes.

But when Mrs. Margaret Howcroft, of 27 Vale-ave., Stoneclough, takes the picture the paper comes out in a great roll.

Mrs. Howcroft, who works in the finishing department, must deal with sheets of paper at great interest.

First Mrs. Fletcher, the pile of blanks get four fingers, then the "felt" with over four of the "felts" which means the has counted from her firm finger, second finger and so on to Mrs. Howcroft, counting room of 140 sheets using her first finger again. So six fingers, combine for a sheet 30 times over makes 200. Howcroft counts five sheets in six.

Three giants

Thomas Fairbrother, of 22 Mollyfield, Kearsley, has been with Fletcher's for 45 years. He was a maintenance [...]

There are 50 women working at Fletcher's, mainly in the finishing department.

At Fletcher's their products are used for packaging, greet wrappers etc. Some supply of paper coming for possibly being used at Fletcher's.

Water cleansing

A water softener used by first were made from water, softeners considerable, different times from installed it's a cost of £700 plant can soften 6,000 gallons of water an hour and the water passes through filters to be softened to soap particles.

After going through the pulp pulp mills the water then is purified so that it is pure enough to be pumped into the river.

Car Mr. Lingard: "We were recommended to instal [...]

Pioneers

It was in 1835 that Roger Crompton, the last of the family who founded the mill in 1829, and Mr. Robert Fletcher became partners. After that it was Fletcher for the mill. In 1911 Mr. Fletcher's grandson James had control of the mill with his son assuming the role, who in due course to Mr. E. J. Williamson who was in the firm from 1910 until his retirement in 1960.

There has been a steady change in the production of the mill from wrapping papers to specialist papers for writing and packing, and the writers [?] at Stoneclough, and the many types of quality papers [...]

Finishing off

"It is easy to work, but my fingers are very sore and warm-ing from handling all that paper [...]

Above. Fletchers Number 4 machine, a Black Clawson 144 inch Fourdrinier designed specifically for the manufacture of fine tissues.

When S D Whitehead retired, he was succeeded as chairman of the company by H C I Rogers, at that time chief engineer of the Imperial Tobacco Company and a member of its board of directors. Further investments were made to the mill site with the installation of a new effluent plant to meet the growing problem of preventing further pollution of the River Irwell. New machinery was brought in and existing machinery was upgraded, with much of this work being carried out by their own staff under the supervision of chief engineer Mr W Lord. The largest of these projects was the installation of what became known as No.4 machine, this was a Black Clawson 144 inch Fourdrinier designed specifically for the manufacture of fine tissues, running at 1000ft per minute. The machine was housed in a building 403ft long and 59ft wide, which included a new laboratory, instrument workshop and various testing and control offices. The original order was placed in 1962 but it would take over two years of preparation and construction before it could be started up in June 1965.

Above. Fletchers Paper Mill in the early 1970's.

Financial Pressure and Final Closure

The increased cost of raw materials such as wood pulp, along with rising energy prices, plus the strength of sterling, had begun to place a strain on the company finances towards the end of the 1990's, and in the year 2000 the Stoneclough site posted losses of £1.8 million. By the end of January 2001 the workforce of around 170 were told that the mill would be closing by June of the same year, but there would be 50 jobs available at the Greenfield mill.

The company was in such a dire financial state though that just a few weeks later several creditors applied to have the company wound up, and the Greenfield site went into receivership and closed overnight in July 2001.

In 2004 Warrington based property developers Countryside Homes applied to Bolton Council to build 86 apartments and 132 houses on the 14 acre site. Part of the original planning application conditions were that land would be made available for a community centre, this never materialized, but the homes were built, and they are now known as the Ringley Lock estate, which takes its name from the canal locks that were once situated on the old Manchester Bolton & Bury Canal on the opposite side of the River Irwell. See Page 57

Above. The gates of Fletchers Paper Mill shortly after it closed for good in 2001. This is now the entrance to the Ringley Lock housing estate. **Below.** March 2005. The Ringley Lock estate under construction on the former Fletchers Paper Mill site. The former offices can be seen on the left, these have been converted into residences named Fletcher Court. Interestingly to the right we can see that a bat roost is an early addition to the site.

Above. March 2005. As the Fletchers Paper Mill buildings were being demolished the new houses for the Ringley Lock estate were simultaneously going up on the site. **Below.** March 2005. The former water treatment plant of the paper mill that sat to the rear of The Market Street Tavern awaits destruction.

Children of the Prestolee Council School who gave a colourful pageant at the Garden Party at Vale House, Stoneclough, on Saturday in aid of the Kearsley Comforts and Prisoners of War Fund.

Above. Kearsley Vale House, August 1944.
Below. August 1946. A welcome home party was held at Vale House for employees and staff of Fletchers Paper Mill who had returned from service with the armed forces.

Above. Mr. and Mrs. S.D. Whitehead at the front of Vale House with some of the employees, staff and their families during the welcome home party in August 1946.
Below. Some of the regulars enjoying a drink at Vale House in May 1968.

Vale House finally closed on October 31st 1987, sadly, whilst left derelict it was vandalized then partly destroyed by fire. Eventually it was developed into housing during the late 1990's with the frontage of the original building being restored. It is now known as The Parklands.

Creams Paper Mill

Formerly located on the banks of the River Irwell, a short distance from the locks at Nob End, Creams Paper Mill was built around 1677 and is thought to be one of Bolton's oldest manufacturing concerns. It was founded by the Crompton family and stayed in their hands until around 1812 when the death of Adam Crompton saw it pass to his nephew Joseph Bealey. Bealey became bankrupt in 1816 and the mill passed to the Hughes family. Thomas Hughes became sole proprietor, but he too was declared bankrupt in 1834, and the mill was taken over by his creditors. William Broadbent bought the mill around 1840 and ran it until his death in 1862.

A Mr Joseph Lyddon bought the mill in 1945, and upon his death in 1960 it was acquired by Trinity International, but Joseph's nephew Mr Dennis Lyddon remained as managing director until his retirement in 1987, at this time the mill still employed over 120 full time staff.

It eventually closed in December 2004 under the ownership of Mondi Paper UK, with the company blaming 'drastically deteriorating' market conditions, caused by escalating energy costs,' resulting in the losses of more than £1 million in 12 months. Mergon Properties, which owns Bolton-based Westgate Estates, bought the mill for more than £1 million in October 2007 and built houses on the site in 2012.

Above. Creams Paper Mill circa 1904.

Creams Paper Mill on the bank of the River Irwell, circa 1920

Coal

Deep beneath our feet, still even today, are millions of tons of coal. Interestingly though it is not all at the same depth. At various depths there are different seams of coal. These seams were known as mines, and each mine of coal had its own particular attributes, but as a very general rule though, the deeper the mine the better grade of coal.

These seams, or layers of coal were formed around 280 to 320 million years ago when Britain had a much different climate than today. Much of the country was covered in vast tropical swamps filled with vegetation, as well as insects, molluscs, crustaceans and all manner of prehistoric aquatic life. The dead vegetation and inhabitants of these tropical swamps would sink to the bottom, and over millions of years the contents became repeatedly buried and compressed.

At different times the earth changed, and layers of earth and sand formed on top, before further swamps appeared and the cycle continued. These prehistoric swamps at different depths dried and hardened with the weight pressing down on them, forcing out the oxygen and leaving them rich in carbon and energy. After millions of years it is these swamps that became coal.

Until the mid 1700's the demand for coal was still fairly minimal. The usual source of energy used for domestic or small scale industrial purposes was wood or peat, otherwise known as turf. In fact peat, if compressed for tens of million years will turn into coal.

We know the inhabitants of Kearsley burned peat, and one of the main sources for this was on Kearsley Moor, down what is now Bent Spur Road. At this time the road was not called Bent Spur Road, it was known as the Turbary Road. Turbary meaning 'the road to the turf.'

In the latter half of the 18th century the industrial revolution took hold in Britain. Vast cotton mills, as well as paper mills, chemical works, iron works and other large manufacturing concerns began to spring up across the landscape, and they all required power to drive their pumps, engines and machinery. A rapidly increasing population provided a ready-made workforce, which too required an energy source for domestic heating and cooking. The answer to all these increased energy needs was coal.

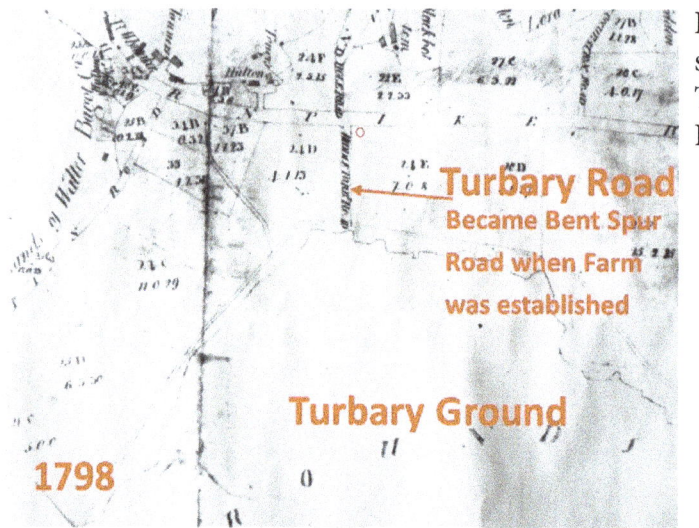

Left. 1798 map showing the Turbary Ground on Kearsley Moor.

Not only did we seem to have an endless supply of it, but coalmining itself would also provide work for more people. But there were several big problems with retrieving coal, especially in the 1800's. It was deep underground and only basic mechanical machines and tools were available, electricity was not an option as its power had still not been harnessed. The dust from digging out coal caused lung disease and other respiratory problems. Digging out coal meant the roof above could fall down and possibly crush you, or dangerous and explosive gases that lay hidden could seep out without warning. To say coal mining in Victorian times was dangerous is an understatement.

A Government report in 1914 showed that between 1850 and 1908 there were nearly 71,000 mine workers killed in Britain, which works out on average at around 24 killed per week, every week, for nearly 60 years. The number of injuries also runs into the millions. Coal mining wasn't just dangerous, it was deadly.

The men, women, boys and girls who went deep underground under these circumstances, on a daily basis, literally took their life in their hands, just to earn a pittance of pay to put food on the table and keep a roof over their heads. It was only in 1842 that a law was passed to prevent women, and children under the age of 10, from working underground, this was raised to the age of 12 for boys in 1862.

THE CHRONICLE.

BOLTON, SATURDAY, MARCH 16, 1878.

THE KERSLEY COLLIERY EXPLOSION.

A considerable portion of our space to-day is occupied with the harrowing details of the most fatal colliery explosion which has ever been experienced in the mining districts immediately around Bolton. The scene of this terrible catastrophe was the Unity Brook Colliery, owned by Messrs. J. Stott & Co., and no less than 43 men and boys who were apparently well and hearty at noon on Tuesday are now lifeless corpses, many of them almost beyond identification. In January of last year, as may be remembered, 18 colliers lost their lives by an explosion at Messrs. Roscow & Lord's Stonehill Colliery, Farnworth, and soon after the opening

Here in Kearsley, and the surrounding area there were many coal mines, dozens of them in fact, and accidents and fatalities happened just like everywhere else. But Tuesday 12th March 1878 became Kearsley's darkest day. The single worst disaster our town has ever known struck in an instant, and took the lives of 43 men and boys at the Unity Brook Colliery.

The Unity Brook Colliery Disaster – Kearsley's Darkest Day

Tuesday March 12th 1878 remains the most disastrous day in our town's history, as a ruthless and powerful explosion at Unity Brook Colliery cut down 43 men and boys as they toiled in the grim subterranean tunnels. In an instant this one detonation brought an unimaginable horror that left 26 widows and 76 fatherless children.

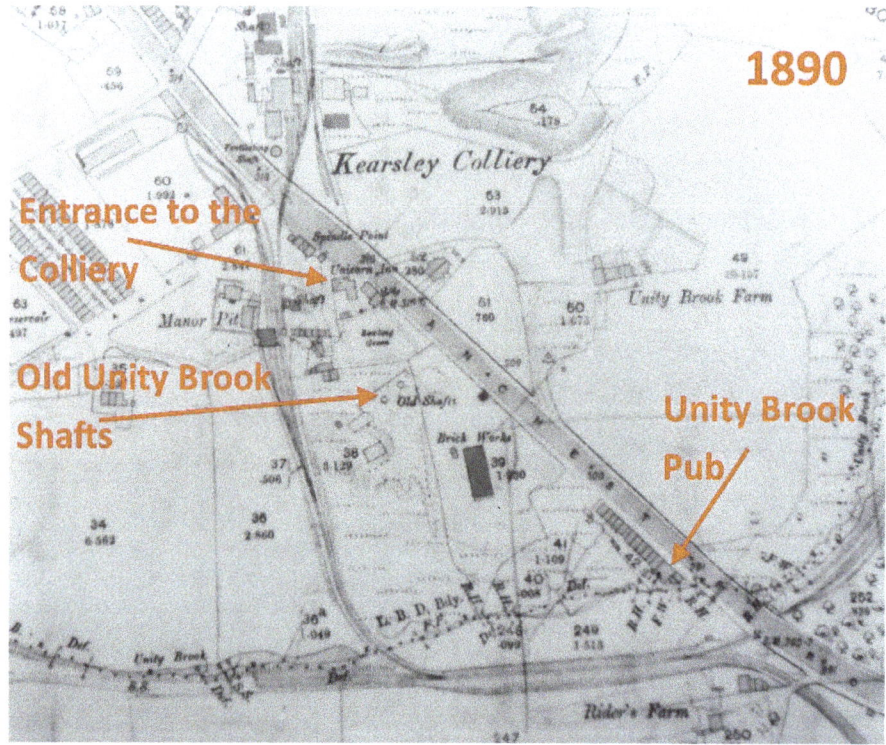

Above. Map c1890. The location of the two shafts of Unity Brook Colliery just off Manchester Road are clearly shown, as is the entrance to the colliery at the side of the Unicorn Inn. Note the close-by Manor Pit which was accessed from Moss Lane. Also seen is the mineral railway that served the Spindle Point, Manor and Unity Brook collieries going under the road near to Rider's Farm before it connects to the main Manchester to Bolton line at the Unity Brook Sidings.

The Unity Brook Colliery, owned by Messrs, James Stott & Co was located at a place approximately two thirds of the way up the hill towards Moss Lane from the Unity Brook public house, and around 60 yards south of the main road. The colliery had opened in 1868, and up until the time of the disaster it was considered a safe mine to work in, as there had been no fatal accidents and few reports of gas, or firedamp*, as it was known. Indeed The Mines Regulation Act of the time actually made special provision for these so-called 'safe mines' and allowed the relaxation of the more stringent levels of precaution where it could be shown no dangerous escape of inflammable gas had taken place for some time. One of these precautions would have been the use of safety lamps, in which the naked flame was enclosed inside a fine metal gauze that made it almost impossible for the lethal gasses to ignite. Another benefit of the safety lamps was that the flame would also change colour slightly in the presence of any gas, or it would extinguish completely where the oxygen levels were too low.

Unfortunately though, there were two big drawbacks regarding the safety lamp. The first was that because the flame is enclosed inside an arrangement of metal gauzes the light levels given off were poor, and often the miners thought that this made the working environment even more dangerous. The second downside was the miners had to provide their own lighting, and, rather than pay for an expensive lamp the more cost effective option was to simply buy candles. Because this colliery had been deemed as 'safe' the miners at Unity Brook had been allowed to use the naked flame of their candles to illuminate their work area.

This false sense of security of working in a supposed 'safe' pit with its relaxed safety precautions was a tragedy waiting to happen, and it is also incredible to think that this was just one of many similar such catastrophes that occurred all over Britain.

The Unity Brook Colliery had two working coal seams, the Trencherbone mine, which had been worked since the pit had opened in 1868, and the Cannel mine, which had only been worked for around 3 months, (in this part of Lancashire the coal seams were called mines) the former mine being around 300 yards down and the latter around 64 yards below this. The two mines at Unity Brook were inspected twice a day by the colliery Underlooker and his deputy, the colliery fireman. It was their jobs to inspect the workings for any potential problems, such as possible roof collapses or the presence of firedamp. They could then take a decision not to let the miners begin work if it was considered too dangerous.

The colliery Underlooker at Unity Brook was a Mr James Holt, who lived a short distance away at Cross Place off Manchester Road, and the colliery fireman was a Mr William Mayoh who lived near the old Toll Bar location, near to what is now the Moss Rose public house.

On the day of the disaster James Holt found there had been a partial roof collapse in the West workings of the Cannel mine. This roof collapse had been reported by James Partington earlier that morning, and he also described how he had heard the noise of the roof 'weighting' above him. Partington was considered to be an experienced and careful miner and had, according to his duty and normal practice, reported this to the colliery fireman, William Mayoh, who reported it to his superior, Holt.

Together Holt, Mayoh, and some other men, propped up the roof and saw no reason to take any further action or precautions, as they also found no evidence of gas. It is this incident that came under intense scrutiny at the inquests which followed.

Holt then went to the Trencherbone mine above to continue his inspection of those workings. It is interesting to note that the daily inspections by the Underlooker and Fireman would normally have been carried out using safety lamps, and once they were satisfied that the mine was safe to work in it would often be the fireman who would then light the miners candles.

Note* *The hazardous, and often, lethal gasses found in coal mines acquired the names firedamp and afterdamp. Firedamp was a gas that was potentially flammable and, usually, methane. Afterdamp was a noxious mixture of chemicals produced after an explosion, which often caused further fatalities for those unable to escape it. The terms are thought to derive from the German word 'dampf' which means vapour. Firedamp was therefore the 'firevapour.'*

At just before 1pm Holt was satisfied that everything was in order and signalled for the cage to pick him up from the mouth of the Trencherbone mine. The cage had been lowered to the Cannel mine to collect a miner named Ralph Welsby who had arranged to finish early that day to attend his sick child, both men reached the surface at just after 1pm. The men and boys below were now resuming work in both mines after their lunch.

James Holt lived less than a quarter of a mile away at Number 1 Cross Place, which is where Cross Street is now located, and had decided to go home for his dinner. Just as he approached his front door the enormous explosion resonated out, he knew where it had come from, and he immediately ran back to the colliery.

A devastating blast had occurred in the Cannel mine, most likely to have been sparked by one of the miner's candles. Later inspections of the Cannel mine confirmed the location of the blast was near to where the earlier roof collapse had occurred. It is thought that either more of the roof must have given way, or that a shot was fired (this is a controlled explosion to remove or break down obstructions such as rock) and this released the lethal incendiary gas.

The force of the explosion must have been tremendous, as all of the 42 persons in the Cannel mine perished, plus another man, Thomas Hilton, who had been near to the mouth of the Trencherbone mine 60 yards above, and had been sucked down by the blast. The cage, which only minutes before had carried Holt and Welsby to the surface, was propelled upward and had smashed into the head gearing, the wreckage plummeting back down the pit. Ominous plumes of black smoke made their way up into the air, whilst around the mouth of the shaft a man named Thomas Worrall, the colliery Banksman, and a boy named William Haslam had both been thrown by the blast. The former badly injuring his hip, and the latter having several of his teeth knocked out.

Preparations were made to go down the shaft and discover the fate of the 60 or so persons in both mines, speedily some ropes and a hoppet were rigged up and James Holt, plus two brothers named John and Joseph Teesdale, descended first to the Trencherbone Mine where they found a number of men and boys suffering from asphyxia, or afterdamp, from the explosion in the Cannel mine below. These men and boys were taken up in groups of three or four, and at around half past four 21 had been rescued alive. At the surface they were treated by Drs. A Kershaw, B. Eames, C. Clark, W.Y. Ruthin and J. Eames who administered restoratives, after this the men and boys who were still unable to walk were taken home in spring carts.

A boy of 13 named Henry Johnson, who was the son of the colliery manager Isaiah Johnson, was considered to have had perhaps the most miraculous escape from death. His statement was that he worked with Thomas Hilton, the hooker-on in the Trencherbone mine, and that at the time of the explosion he was standing about a yard from him, asking about making up another train of wagons. All that he remembers afterwards was finding himself at home, being attended to by his mother, he had suffered injuries to his face. An elderly miner named Jones stated that the scene in the Trencherbone Mine immediately after the explosion was painful to witness, for as he was making his way out of the mine from his working place he came across several of his fellow workmen, in health and strength only a few minutes before, lying prostrate on the ground and praying most fervently. He added, "the sight was one that would have softened the hardest heart", after this he set himself to the task of assisting all needing help to the surface, he being the last to ascend.

With all the persons rescued from the Trencherbone mine Holt then went back down the shaft with Mr. Joseph Dickinson, her Majesty's Inspector of Mines who had been summoned to the scene by telegram that afternoon. Dickinson had visited the mine only 9 days earlier and had declared it satisfactory in every way.

At the bottom of the shaft they found it impossible to get down into the Cannel mine due to the amount of wreckage and large pieces of timber blocking the way. They called down to the mine, but received no answer.

A number of carpenters were dispatched down the shaft to clear the debris, which they accomplished at shortly after six o'clock. Immediately after this James Holt and several men descended in the hoppet to at last reach the mouth of the Cannel mine, here they found the body of Thomas Hilton, his face blackened and blood still trickling from his nostrils. The exploring party then only managed to proceed a short distance before they were forced back by the noxious air, so they returned to the surface along with the body of Hilton. Ventilation of the mine was restored shortly after this by lighting the furnace at the bottom of the upcast shaft, this allowed Joseph Dickinson, Herbert Alfred Woodward, who was the manager of nearby Spindle point colliery and two other men to return and explore virtually the whole mine.

The first bodies were discovered around 100 yards from the pit eye, and those nearest to the scene of the blast were found to be much mutilated, with one being decapitated and another his skull so smashed his brains were protruding. During the night all of the bodies were taken to the pit eye and placed in order ready to be sent up to the pit bank, they had been wrapped from head to toe in tarred sheeting and secured round the extremities with string. At approximately one o'clock on Wednesday afternoon, more or less 24 hours after the explosion, the commencement of bringing the dead to the surface began.

Two at a time the bodies were placed feet first into the hoppet, and a collier known as 'Yorkshire Bill' and a companion also got in, the former supporting the dead in an upright position with his arms around them, and the latter steadying the hoppet. On arrival at the pit bank the deceased were placed onto stretchers and carried to the wheelwrights shop by men who had been waiting in the nearby Tally Cabin. Here they were each dressed in a clean shirt and stockings, which had been brought by their relatives. They were then replaced onto the stretcher and taken to the colliery stables and another small stables belonging to the Unicorn Inn, both of which had been prepared with clean straw in readiness for them.

The first to arrive was Robert Enion aged 39, along with one of his two sons who had worked with him, these were Jonathan aged 12 and David aged 13. They had all worked at the pit for less than 6 weeks. A patent lever pocket watch was found on Robert Enion which had stopped at seven minutes past one o'clock, this is perhaps the best indication to the time of the explosion. The grim task continued until 20 past six when all but two men, John Peak and William Mayoh, were still unrecoverable under a mass of debris in the dib-hole or sump, these two were not recovered until Thursday morning. This macabre and distressing work was observed by hundreds of onlookers who had gathered on a piece of ground adjacent to the colliery yard.

Above. The Unicorn Inn Public House which stood on Manchester Road across from the uppermost entrance to Unity Brook Farm. The entrance to the colliery was to the right. The pub dated from the early 1800's and survived into the late 1930's before it was demolished.

The colliery yard was accessed via a passage at the side of the Unicorn Inn, but on Wednesday 13th March, the day after the explosion, this had to be blocked to prevent the flood people attempting to get in. Entry to the colliery was now only possible through the lobby of the Unicorn Inn, and this was strictly supervised to allow access to only persons on important business at the pit and relatives of the deceased. The scene was attended by an artist, named Mr. S.H. Ashley Oakes, of Silverwell Street, Bolton, who drew the two very special pictures on the following pages.

As the deceased are brought from the pit they can be seen being carried by stretcher to the colliery wheelwright shop to be cleaned and dressed in fresh clothing brought by relatives. After this they were taken to the stables of either the colliery or the Unicorn Inn for identification.

A distraught woman identifies the body of a relative as the constable pulls back the sheet. It is not known if this is the stables of the colliery or the Unicorn Inn.

The following account is from the Bolton Chronicle, Saturday 16th March 1878:

"Sorrowing trembling women clustered around the entrance to the stables and eagerly peered at the faces of the deceased as their bodies were uncovered and placed side by side on the straw. The scene was heartrending. The wife of Christopher Moore was ushered into the stable to identify the body of her husband, which lay third in rotation from where she was standing. The faces were uncovered, and the poor woman immediately recognized that of her husband, moaning in chants so piteous that the hearts of those present were touched: "Aye, that's my lad, that's my poor lad . I hope I shall soon be wi' thee.' On being shown the clogs which were laid on the clothes at the head, she exclaimed, "Aye, them's his, I know 'em, he only nailed them on Monday."

List of the deceased

Robert Clarke, aged 18, Jackson's Buildings, Kearsley,
Peter Fogg, aged 26, of 32 Bolton Rd, Clifton,
John Harrison, aged 40, Old House Croft, Kearsley
Thomas Hilton, aged 20, Fletcher's Houses, Kearsley,
Alfred Isherwood, aged 31, Stoneclough,
William Leach, aged 24, Lower Kearsley,
William Mayoh, aged 38, of 53 Manchester Rd, Kearsley,
James Partington, aged 44, 54 Primrose St, Kearsley Moor,
Thomas Peak, aged 17, of 109 Manchester Rd, Kearsley Mount,
Joseph Welsby, aged 18, Kearsley Moor,
Thomas Wolstenholme, aged 41 Old House Croft, Kearsley,
James Beattie, aged 19, Manor Houses, Kearsley
Thomas Byron, aged 28, Warm Hole, Kearsley,
Robert Enion, aged 39, Kearsley Moor,
Jonathan Enion aged 12,
David Enion, aged 13,
Richard Featherstone, aged 18, Albert St, Kearsley,
John Hamblet, aged 31, Seddon St, Kearsley
John Haynes, aged 21, Manor Cottages, Kearsley,
James Hobson, aged 30, Old House Croft, Kearsley,
George Jackson, aged 28, 110 Manchester Rd,
Thomas Lever aged, 18, Mount Pleasant, Kearsley,
George Lindley, aged 47, Kearsley Moor
Ellis Lord (or Lindley) aged 14, Kearsley Moor,
John Tickle Lomax, aged 31, Eckersley Buildings,

Thos. Ed Mace, aged 19 Taskers Lane, Kearsley,
Christopher Moore, aged 26, Lindley's Houses,
Andrew Walker, aged 23 (22), of Green Lane, Stoneclough,
Samuel Wolstenholme, aged 47, Lindley's Houses,
William Wolstenholme, aged 21, Kearsley Moor,
James Chadwick, aged 38, Primrose St, Kearsley
Joseph Hobson, aged 26, Kearsley Moor,
William Morris, aged 15 Taskers lane, Kearsley
Charles Tonge, aged 16, of 55 Taskers Lane, Kearsley
William Barnes, aged 38, Stoneclough
Absolam Barnes, aged 14, Stoneclough
George Booth, aged 21, from Denton
James Byron, aged 32, from Slater-field, Bolton
John Greenhalgh, aged 34 (26), Jane-Lane, Swinton.
Amos Lomax, aged 17, Irwell Bank, Kearsley
Thomas Lomax, aged 28, Irwell Bank
Wright Lomax, aged 26, Irwell Bank, Kearsley
Richard Wallwork, aged 25, Swinton

Thirty-six of the deceased were kept in the stables of the colliery and seven at the Unicorn Inn stables. It was not until Thursday evening that the 43 coffins, made by Messrs Coop Brothers, were delivered and the corpses placed carefully inside. One burial took place at St. Stephen's on Friday 15th March, but the majority were on Saturday the 16th and Sunday the 17th.

The first inquest into the disaster was held only three days afterwards, on Friday 15th March in an upper room of the Unicorn Inn before district coroner J. Broughton Edge, Esq. The following gentlemen of the Township were also present and sworn in as the Jury.

    Benjamin Bowker, grocer (Jury Foreman)
    Thomas Coope, beerseller
    William Davies, Landlord, Lord Nelson
    Thomas Gee, provisions dealer, Mount Terrace
    John Grundy, beerseller
    George Lomax, beerseller
    John Longworth, grocer
    Solomon Jackson, beerseller, Unity Brook
    Thomas Thompson, grocer
    James Warburton, butcher

Joseph Seddon, grocer
John Prest, boot and shoemaker
Isaac Wardle, beerseller
Ralph Wood, beerseller
William Kelsall, beerseller

Messrs J.L. Topp and J. Taylor were excused from serving on the Jury on the grounds of deafness and age!

Also present were a Mr Edwards (deputy coroner), The Rev C. Lowe M.A, (vicar of St, Stephens, Kearsley), Mr. A Holden (Holden and Holden), representing the colliery firm, Mr. James Atherton, Surveyor to the colliery firm; and Mr. S Stansfield, who represented the Lancashire and Cheshire Miners' Association.

A considerable amount of evidence was taken from relatives and witnesses during the several inquest hearings that followed, and small samples of these statements are as follows:

Eliza Hobson said James Hobson was her husband, and lived at Kearsley Moor. He was turned 30 years of age and was a collier. He had worked in the mine eight years and had always spoken of it as safe.

Ann Lomax said John Tickle Lomax was her husband. He was 31 years of age and they resided at Eckersley Buildings, Kearsley. He had worked a fortnight in the cannel mine. He had said to me that the coal was hard but has not said that the place was dangerous.

Sarah Isherwood said Alfred Isherwood was her husband. He was 31 years of age and lived at Stoneclough. They have seven children and Tuesday was the first morning he had been employed at the pit.

Margaret Leach said William Leach was her son, and resided with the deceased Alfred Isherwood at lower Kearsley. He was 24 years of age, and was a collier. He had been working at Clough-Side colliery and had only commenced to work at Unity Brook on the morning of the accident.

John Lomax identified Amos Lomax as his grandson. He was seventeen years of age. He was a ganger. He lived with him at Irwell Bank, Kearsley. He had only worked in the mine a fortnight. He had never said anything to him about the mine. He also identified Wright Lomax as being his son. He lived at Lower Kearsley, was a collier, and was 26 years of age. He said there was very good air, but his place was giving way at the roof. He had worked at the mine only a few weeks.

Alice Lomax, said "the deceased Thomas Lomax was my husband. He lived at Stoneclough and was 28 years old. He has only worked at the place two or three months. He has told me it was very dangerous working at this pit because the places fell. His place had fallen.
Note* Thomas Lomax was also the brother of Wright Lomax.

Mary Hamblet said John Hamblet was her husband, and lived at Seddon Street, Kearsley. He was 31 years old, and was a collier. He had worked at the mine about 3 months and had made no complaint about the mine.

Ann Harrison said John Harrison was her husband and lived at Old House Croft, Kearsley. He was 40 years old, and had only worked at the colliery 3 weeks. He had told her he liked the mine very well.

George Woodward, Kearsley Moor, collier, declared that Joseph Welsby was his cousin and was a waggoner, he was 18 years of age. He had been working there about two years, ever since the Cannel Mine started. He had passed no opinion upon the state of the mine.

"Martha Moore said Christopher Moore was my husband and lived at Lindley's houses Kearsley, we have three children. He was a getter in the coal-pit and was 26 years old. He told me that working in the pit was as safe as being at home."

Alice Tyldesley, widow, Moss Road, Farnworth, said that William Mayoh was her nephew. He lived near Kearsley Bar (the old toll bar location close to the Moss Rose), and was a fireman. He was 33 years of age. He said the working-place was quite safe and there was plenty of air. He left a wife and one child.

Ralph Welsby, "I live at Kearsley Mount and am a collier. On the 12th of this month I was working at Unity Brook Colliery. I went down that morning at about ten minutes to six o'clock. I worked in No. 3 east level of the cannel mine. John Welsby and Thomas Edward Mace worked along with me. I came out of the mine at one o'clock on Wednesday, and Holt came out of the Trencherbone mine at the same time. That was not my usual time to leave, but I had asked

Mayoh to let me off early that day for I had a child ill at Farnworth, and I wanted to get home.

Nancy Enion; the deceased Jonathan Enion is my son, and he lived with me at Mount Terrace, Kearsley. He was a hooker-on at the pit, and was 12 years old. He has worked in the pit for about five weeks. He has never said anything to me about the place except that he liked it. We have only lived here about seven weeks and came from Wharton, near Liverpool. The deceased Robert Enion, was my husband and was a metalman at the mine. He was 32 years old, and had worked here about seven weeks. He told me that he liked his work very well, for it was as safe as being in a house. David Enion, another deceased, was also my son. He assisted his father, and was 13 years of age, and went to work first at the pit at the same time as his father.

Further inquests were held at the Bowling Green Inn, Farnworth and the Antelope Public House, Kearsley, with the final hearing at the Bowling Green Inn on Monday the 25th March.

At this final inquest hearing Joseph Dickinson gave the following account of his first inspection of the stricken mine at around 6:15pm on the day of the disaster: *"My first object was to run through the mine, as it were, to see if any of the men could be got out alive. All the bodies we found were dead and cold, and more or less burned. The pressure of the blast must have been so strong that that alone would have killed the men. All the deaths must have been instantaneous, and I don't think the men went a yard after they were struck."* He then continued, *"On the next day I inspected the mine to ascertain the cause of the explosion, and also on the 19th. From my inspection I have no doubt the cause of the explosion was the fall in the West workings, at James Partington's workplace, between levels 1 and 2. The evidence given entirely confirms that. The fall had been from the crack which has been referred to. There is no fall at the higher side. The blast all radiated from that fall."* As to whether he felt any blame should be apportioned to the colliery underlooker, James Holt, he said *"When there is a fall of roof it is not at all safe to work with naked lights; they ought to be taken away when there are indications of falls. Had poor Holt, when he found that morning the roof weighting and ground was shifting, ordered all the men out it is probable the jury would not be sitting in that room. I would be sorry to do Holt an injustice, for he acted most nobly after the explosion."*

On the subject of safety lamps Joseph Dickinson also stated *"I believe it probable if you were to put the same questions which I did to some witnesses about the use of lamps they would give the same answer. Are we to force lamps upon the* men? They know the danger of them, had there been self-extinguishing lamps such as Stephenson's or Muster's, the gas would have got away without the explosion, but had it been the Davy lamp, the rush of gas from the fall and the strong rush of air through the mine would have fired through the gauze. The current of air was a little over 600 feet per minute. I think the proprietors will be bound to take extra precautions. Indeed , I think they will be bound to put on safety lamps. The Davy lamp has many advantages, and some disadvantages over the other. It will be for them to select the best. There are a large number of collieries working in the same way as this, well ventilated, and working with naked lights, where explosion may occur at any time. I know no part of the kingdom where mines are better and systematically worked than they are here, but they are behind other districts in the use of lamps."

Mr James Stott, one of the principal proprietors of the mine also gave evidence at the inquest, stating; *"All was done that could be done to make the work safe, for we have been very particular to get a competent staff of men and secure good discipline. We shall not continue the use of candles and shall take into our serious consideration what kind of lamps we shall use. It is only one possible precaution more that we can take and we shall certainly adopt it."* Somewhat surprisingly though, the district coroner, Mr J.B. Edge, Esq, later presented the following opinion; *"So far as I am concerned I should prefer to use candles, because I consider that a good man down a pit with a candle is better than a bad man with a lamp. Candles give more light, more work can be done, they are more portable, and greater precaution is used by all when the men know that all are using naked lights. I would rather carry a candle myself than a lamp in a strong current. You may make an examination with greater facility with a candle than a lamp."*

It is not known whether James Stott followed through on his pledge to abolish the use of candles in his mines, or if any mines at all in the locality decided to adopt a policy of only using safety lamps. But what is known is that the majority did not, and, most notably, just 3 miles away at the Clifton Hall Colliery in 1885, a lighted candle ignited a blast which caused the deaths of 178 miners.

Further evidence showed that a roof fall had occurred in the same area on the 7th March, and after inspection no traces of gas were found, just as on the day of the explosion. James Holt was exonerated from any blame as his decision not to withdraw the men from the mine was regarded as an error of judgment of which could have befallen many other others in a similar position.

At five minutes past one in the afternoon, the Jury of the Unity Brook Colliery disaster inquest retired to consider their verdict. Just ten minutes later they returned to the large room in the Bowling Green Hotel, where the Foreman, Mr. Benjamin Bowker said; *"We are all unanimous in our opinion that the explosion occurred from a pure accident, and we all believe that everything that could be possibly be done was done. We don't find the underlooker or anyone else to blame. We think that to the manager of the colliery, to Mr. Dickinson, and to everybody concerned great praise is due for their prompt action in this matter."*

A Mr. John Prest, a juror, then spoke; *"We are thoroughly satisfied at the same time with the general working of the pit, both as to the men, their officials, and everything being carried out that could tend to their safety previous to the accident."* Another juror said; *"they, as a jury, could not force upon them to use lamps; indeed, the evidence upon that score was so conflicting that they could not say that candles should not be used."*

The Coroner said; *"it appeared the jury would rather leave the question of naked lights to the consideration of the legislators and to more practical men."*

A juror said; *"Yes."*

The Coroner; *"Your verdict then is accidental death."*

The Foreman; *"Yes it is."*

The selection of local men chosen for the jury caused discontent amongst some in the locality, with them questioning the suitability of so many persons who held licenses to sell beer. Some even wrote to the local papers to vent their displeasure at the situation, prompting the jury foreman, Benajamin Bowker, to defend those whose character had been brought into question. His letter printed in the Farnworth Journal 30th March 1878 states;

"As the foreman of the jury empannelled to inquire into the cause of the deaths of the 43 men and boys who lost their lives at Unity Brook Colliery on the 12th instant, I was much pained when my attention was drawn to the offensive criticism upon the selection of the gentlemen who acted upon that jury. I am informed not by the police, but on good authority that the order for the police to summon a jury was not received until about six o'clock in the evening preceding the morning of the inquiry, and an effort was at once made to summon a jury out of the township of Kearsley. It is somewhat strange that no less than seven out of the eight licensed victuallers and beersellers summoned upon the jury had had practical experience of the working of coal mines, seven of them as coal getters and one as a pit carpenter. All of these with the exception of one or two, has had over 20 years' practical experience in pits. And yet in spite of all this their respectability and their intelligence are called into question. If they are not the men who are likely to be able to understand evidence given by colliers, their officials, and mining inspectors, who are? The verdict they returned is, I find, thoroughly

coincided with by all whom I have conversed with on this matter; it was entirely compatible with the practical and scientific evidence adduced, and could not have been unanimously agreed to by fifteen jurymen if eight of them had been so wanting in intelligence as the writer of the letter would have the public believe."

Now we have to remember that these were not the days of uninhibited compensation claims. Nor was there any state run benefits system to fall back on. There were now 25 widows with somewhere in the region of 71 to 76 fatherless children (**see note below), and their main breadwinners of the family had been taken from them. These families would now have to rely on the goodwill of others among the community to help them through this difficult time.

A relief fund was opened for the widows, orphans and relatives of the deceased, with the Rev. C. Lowe immediately donating £15, the Bishop of Manchester £20 and the owners of the colliery Messrs. James Stott & Co contributing £200. For around five years afterwards widows would attend the Local Board offices at 41 Bolton Road for their relief money. The allowance was 5 shillings for the widow (as long as she did not re-marry) and a half-crown for each child.

Unity Brook Colliery reopened for business shortly after the disaster, but by May 1881 work had ceased in all its mines and it was finally abandoned for good.

**The number of reported dependents actually varied over the following weeks of the disaster from between 71 and 76, as some women found they were expecting another child, and some others came forward claiming to be mistresses of the deceased with whom they either already shared a child or were expecting one. I have been unable to find the definitive number.

Above. Meeting at the Kearsley Local Board Office on 15th March 1878 chaired by Mr James Fletcher, with the purpose of considering the most advisable steps to take in order to raise a public subscription for the relief of the widows and orphans and relatives of those who lost their lives in the disaster.

Left and Below: One of the subscription books that were left at the factories, mills, public houses and churches to raise money for the relief fund of the Unity Brook disaster.

The following extract is from the St. Stephens Bazaar Booklet of March 1914.

On the afternoon of 12th March 1878, at about a quarter past one, there occurred a terrible calamity. A violent explosion in the Cannel Mine of the Unity Brook Colliery resulted in the sudden death of no less than 43 men and boys, leaving one hundred relatives, fatherless children, and widows to mourn their loss.

The remains of 19 men and boys were laid to rest in our Churchyard. A relief fund on behalf of the dependents of those who lost their lives was opened.

A sum of £4,000 was required. Thanks to the indefatigable efforts of the Rev. Charles Lowe, and the widespread liberality of many sympathisers, the amount subscribed soon exceeded £4280. This allowed a provision of 10/- for each widow and 2/6 for each child to be made. These amounts were paid for upwards of ten years.

In a colliery village like ours it is hardly necessary to refer to the many deeds of heroism displayed on this occasion; how fellow colliers begged to go down, at the risk of their own lives, to explore the wrecked mine, in the hope of helping some unfortunate comrade. There was no shortage of such heroes, and many who were first to descend the mine after the explosion refused to ascend until every unfortunate man and boy had been accounted for.

Such deeds of heroism are so common amongst our colliers that they press unnoticed; yet on a similar occasion, at the Clifton Hall Colliery, 18th June 1885, when 176 lives were lost, they received a fitting tribute of praise.

Shortly after the explosion the Bishop of Manchester, Dr Fraser, appeared on the scene. He saw men descend the mine, hoping to carry succor to some unfortunate brother below; some of Kearsley's best sons had gone down to the rescue in the first cage. It was rumoured several times that another explosion had taken place. Volunteers to descend the mine had been called for.

Scores were pressing forward; all ready, if need be, to give their lives for their fellow-men. The good Bishop stood speechless, with tears in his eyes, to see these oft-slighted men, men considered low in social scale, with their patched trousers, scrubby beards, ready and willing, if necessary, to be a willing sacrifice. The saintliest of Bishops returned to Manchester and, addressing the city merchants, said of these colliers, "I have looked into the faces of angels."

Did ever a man earn greater praise? Did ever a man deserve greater praise than these rough diamonds? Unpolished they may be, yet their hearts are as clear as crystal, and they will always respond to humanity's call.

A memorial service, organized by Stephen Tonge and Kearsley Churches on the Mount, was held at St. Stephen's Church on 18th March 2018 to commemorate the disaster and remember those who died that fateful day. The Miners' Hymn to the tune Gresford was sung as well as Jerusalem, and I was also lucky enough to be asked to give an address. Children from St. Stephen's, St. Gregory's, St. John's, St. Saviours and Spindle Point read excerpts from the inquest and sang whilst the Kearsley Youth Brass Band played. On Sunday 17th June the same year a permanent memorial was placed at Manchester Road on the site of the long gone Unicorn Inn public house.

Above and below, June 2018. The Unity Brook disaster memorial on the former site of the Unicorn Inn public house on Manchester Road. I was fortunate enough to be asked to unveil the memorial plate, upon which I had written a brief description of its significance and the names of those lost in the tragedy. The circular graphic shows the Colliery wheelwright building and pithead with ghostly images of the men and boys. This was created by local artist Paul Cooper, who also produces various designs for St. John Fisher Roman Catholic Church. The coal tub was unveiled by local lady Bernie Lomax, whose great grandfather John Tickle Lomax had perished in the disaster. The tub features an image of a patent lever pocket watch with the hands stopped at seven minutes past one, just like the one found upon Robert Enion.

Above. The Bowling Green Hotel, Farnworth circa 1895.

The Clifton Hall Colliery explosion

An explosion, resulting in the loss of 178 men and boys, took place in the Trencherbone Mine of the Clifton Hall Colliery at around 9:20 a.m. on Thursday the 18th of June 1885. The colliery was located in Pendlebury, at the bottom of Rake Lane where it meets Lumns Lane, just on the northern side of the Manchester-Bolton railway line, and was owned by Messrs. Andrew Knowles and Sons Limited, who also owned several other collieries in the district. The first shafts were sunk at Clifton Hall Colliery in 1838, and eventually it came to comprise of eight seams at the following depths:-

Bin Mine	----	129 ½ yards
Shuttle Mine	----	159 ¼ yards
Crumbouke Mine	----	161 ½ yards
Rams Mine	----	212 yards
Dow Mine	----	422 yards
Five Quarters Mine	----	436 ¼ yards
Trencherbone Mine	----	534 yards
Cannel Mine	----	595 ½ yards

The Trencherbone Seam was first worked in 1865 and comprised an area of around 727,000 square yards of coal at a thickness of six feet, and as a rule it was worked with naked lights. The use of safety lamps at Clifton Hall appears to have been looked upon as an almost unnecessary precaution, and at most they were only convenient for the preliminary checks of the working places before candles were then employed by the workers. The manager of the colliery at the time of the disaster, Mr. Jonathan Hall, admitted that he had always been in favour of the adoption of lamps throughout the mine, and that when he first came, he determined to bring about the change, on the ground that greater security would be obtained. He found however, that the feeling of the men was so strong on the subject that had he attempted to enforce it there would have been a strike.

The procedure at the colliery was that the firemen would inspect the workplaces with a safety lamp and leave a mark showing the day of the month, written on a prop or other prominent place to show it was free from gas and in a safe condition. The firemen would then meet the next shift and sanction their proceeding to work. The men however were not allowed to light their candles until the firemen paid a second visit to their working places and made another examination. In fact it was the firemen who would then light the miners' candles.

The approximate location of the explosion was agreed to be the far end of No.2 level of the Trencherbone Mine, but it was inconclusive as to exactly how and when the large amount of deadly gas had accumulated, and all the theories put forward could only be regarded as speculation. The explosion happened at 9:20 a.m. on Thursday, June 18th when the day shift of around 300 persons was in full work. There was little doubt that due to the shear force of the blast death must have been instantaneous for all those in the Trencherbone Mine, except at the extreme end of No. 3 level East, where ten men were working, and although unaffected by the blast, the presence of afterdamp prevented their escape for over 13 hours.

Substantial damage was suffered throughout the mine and shafts, including the cages which became jammed for several hours and hindered the rescue operation. There was, however, a tunnel, which connected the Dow Mine, Five Quarters Mine and Trencherbone Mine of Clifton Hall Colliery with the Dow Mine of nearby Agecroft Colliery. By means of this passage 122 men and boys who had been at work in the 'Dow' and 'Five Quarters' mines at Clifton Hall effected their escape to the shaft at Agecroft, and so to the surface. The tunnel had been planned and constructed with a view to the possibility of damage or difficulties at either Clifton Hall or Agecroft. This travelling way was not used in ordinary circumstances, or examined regularly, and was now in a much worse condition than when it was first constructed. Originally it was 5 feet in height and 6 feet wide, but as time had gone on the immense pressure from above lessened the height until at certain places it measured only 3 feet. At another point in the passage there had gathered over two feet of water, and this stretched for over 200 yards. After the explosion this now crucial means of escape became polluted with deadly afterdamp, and nine persons were later found dead in the water, it was thought they had died by inhaling the noxious gases, and not by drowning.

FOURTH DAY.

Wednesday, 8th July, 1885.

BEFORE

Mr. FREDERICK PRICE, Coroner,
Mr. JOSEPH DICKINSON, Government Inspector of Mines,
and
Mr. J. S. MARTIN, Assistant Inspector.

Mr. ARNOLD MORLEY, M.P., attended an behalf of the Home Office.

The names of the jury were called over, and all answered to their names.

SAMUEL LAMBERT sworn.

Examined by the CORONER.

Where do you live? — No. 30, Bridge Street, Pendlebury.

What are you? — A coal miner in the Five Quarters Mine in the Lumbs Colliery.

You were working there on the morning of the 18th of June last, were you not, the morning of the explosion? — Yes.

You were working at the time of the explosion? — Yes.

You made your way to the travelling road leading to the Agecroft Colliery, I believe? — Yes.

Where did you meet with after-damp, do you remember? — In the tunnel.

You made your way up with many other workmen? — Yes, to the travelling way.

Did you come to some water in that travelling way? — Yes.

Did you know, personally, Ralph Crook or John Crook? — I knew them, but I did not see them that morning.

But you knew them? — Yes.

Do you remember seeing them in the tunnel in the travelling way? — No.

Had you a lamp? — Yes.

There were a great many others passing through, I suppose, at the time you did? — Yes.

Did you meet with after-damp? — Yes. I met with a little boy that was blown against the waggon, and he was crying for help.

Where was that? — That was in the travelling road.

What part of it? — It would be in the water.

There was a waggon there, was there? — It was in the water-way that I met with the little boy, and I stopped and put him up.

Was that Robert Worrall? — I cannot tell his name.

Which end of the travelling way was he? — He was in the Clifton Hall Colliery.

Was it nearer to Clifton Hall Colliery or Agecroft Colliery? — The Clifton Hall Colliery.

In the water? — Yes, we went into the water; and after I got through the water with the little boy, I was got down by the after-damp.

You overtook the little boy? — Yes.

Did you ever hear his name? — No, only they told me he lived at Pendleton way somewhere.

Did he appear to be about 13 years of age? — I believe he was about 15 or 16 years of age.

(*A Juryman.*) He was not dead, was he? — No.

(*The Coroner.*) You overtook a boy, you say, that was in the water? — Yes.

Did you assist him? — Yes.

Above. An excerpt from the Inquest held at the Institute, Pendlebury, 8th July 1885.

The inquest lasted ten days, with the jury retiring to consider their verdict at 12:30 P.M on the 9th July. Three hours later they returned and gave various verdicts on how most of the deceased had met their fate, and to confirm that the explosion had occurred on the east side of the Trencherbone Mine. They also stated their opinion that no person was either criminally or censurably to blame and that all had met their deaths by accident. Predictably there were also recommendations as to the discontinuance of naked lights and more frequent and thorough inspections of the mines in the district.

It is worth noting that during the inquest Joseph Dickinson, Her Majesty's Chief Inspector of Mines, made it known that he had received the following foreboding letter from an anonymous source in November 1884. He made the decision not to bring it to the attention of the Managing Director, or owners of the colliery.

"Sir, If there is any necessity for your help at present it is at the Clifton Hall Colliery, Andrew Knowles. It is a disgrace to go in the Trencherbone Mine at present for firedamp, through the smallness of the airways. The manager has been down all week and it is not right as yet, men all complaining about it. Things have gone nearly as far as they can; men's lives are at stake. I think it is time you knew something about it; things are too much neglected, you will find all I have said correct. The manager will be down on Monday morning again. Yours resp, one who knows it to be correct."

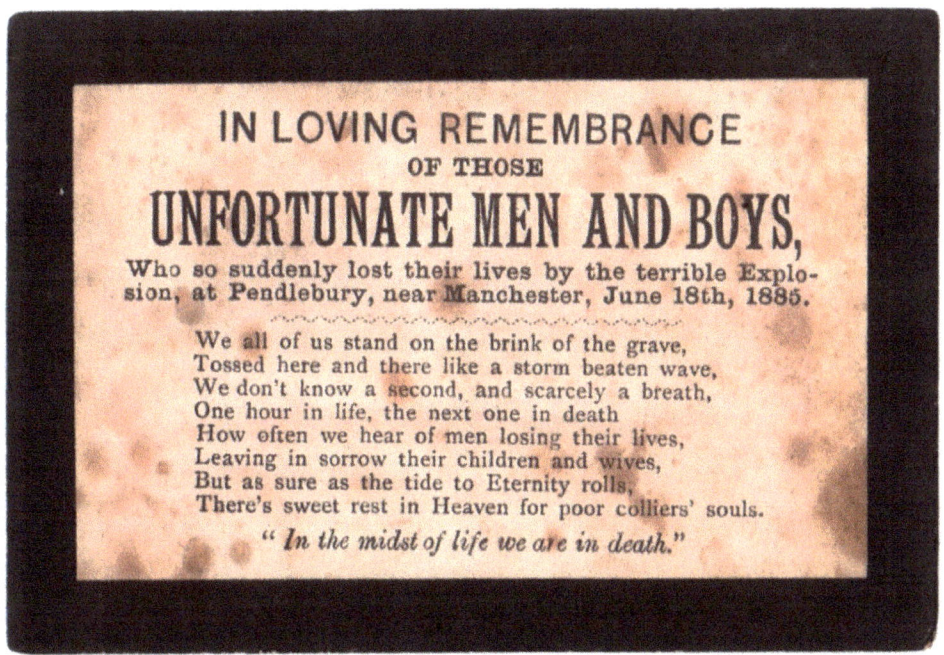

Above. A memorial card for the Clifton Hall Colliery Disaster.

The colliery eventually closed in November 1929, and a memorial stone in memory of those who lost their lives still stands in St. Augustine's Churchyard, Pendlebury.

Clifton Hall Colliery sidings, circa 1910.

Ringley Fold Colliery Explosion

Above & next page. Details from the London Morning Chronicle of the Ringley Fold Colliery Explosion, which occurred on Monday 26th January 1852. Candles were again used in favour of safety lamps in this pit, even though the men often had to beat out the gas with their jackets before commencing work.

MORNING CHRONICLE,

FATAL COAL-PIT EXPLOSION NEAR BURY.

On Monday morning an explosion of fire-damp occurred at the Ringley Fold Colliery, Ringley, near Bury, belonging to Messrs. Knowles and Stott, by which three persons were instantaneously killed, and 13 or 14 others injured more or less severely, including two of whose recovery no hopes are entertained. The *Manchester Guardian* gives the following account of the calamity. The Ringley Fold Colliery comprises four pits, at least two of which are connected by workings, as well for the purpose of ventilation as for that of getting coal. The pit in which the explosion occurred is known among the miners as the "cannel mine;" the seam worked from it is not of cannel coal, but it is surrounded by a coating of this description, a few inches thick, which, according to the plan adopted, is never "got," but allowed to remain, forming the floor, roof, and sides of the workings; and it is supposed to be carefully picked from the other coal, when any of it gets intermixed either by a fall of the roof or an accidental blow of the pick. The shaft is about 130 or 140 yards deep; it having been sunk some distance to the "cannel" seam, some years since, when the seams above, known as the "trencher-bone" were exhausted. The present workings are generally about 5ft. 6in. high. From this pit there is a communication with another called the "Kearsley Hall Mine," which is used as the up-cast shaft; and to aid in the ventilation, there seems to be a furnace fixed at the bottom of an old shaft, which is also joined to the others, but at a distance of 600 or 700 yards from the former. Between 20 and 30 men and boys usually work in the "cannel" mine, and these assembled at the pit's mouth at six o'clock on Monday morning, for the purpose of commencing work. Most of these had got down by half-past six o'clock; but before any of them had been able to get to work, a violent explosion occurred, followed instantly by at least one other. As yet, there is not the slightest approach to a knowledge of where or how the gas was ignited; but one or two points in connection with what appears to have been the custom of the men working in the mine are deserving of notice; although the statement of them must be received with some degree of reservation. Up to the time when, a few months since, the connection with the Kearsley Hall shaft was completed, gas seems to have been very prevalent; an improvement has arisen since then, but it has not been of any very marked or constant character. A state of foulness requiring the men to beat the gas from the different workings, by means of their jackets or other articles of clothing, seems to have been of not unfrequent occurrence; and, as far as we could understand, this has been the case very recently. Sudden changes in the atmosphere, or a prevalence of high winds, will of course interfere with the ventilation of the most carefully-managed mines, at least on the present perilous system; but from the statement of one of the men who was in the pit at the time of the explosion, "after the blusterous nights we've had recently," the gas has been found accumulated in the "cannel" mine to a more than usual extent. We could not ascertain the precise nature or probable power of the ventilating appliances used in connection with this shaft; so that it may prove that they have been all that was possible, and that the accumulations alluded to have been wholly unpreventible. But there is a point which we presume will be specially investigated by the coroner's jury—whether or not there has been a "fireman" or "fire-trier" employed, and if so, what were his duties, and how were they attended to. There appears no doubt that on Monday morning the men went down the shaft before any authorised person had examined the workings, notwithstanding the known probability of gas having accumulated, more especially after the cessation of work during Sunday. If such was not the invariable practice, it is still evident, not only from what occurred on Monday, but also from what was stated at the inquest, that there was no recognised rule forbidding the men to descend until after the mine had been properly inspected. A safety-lamp was always supplied to each couple of men who worked together, and to these seems generally to have been left the decision of the question whether their particular workings were in a state which rendered it safe to enter them. But, notwithstanding this, the general practice seems to have been for the men either to take the tops from their lamps, or to carry naked candles along the air-ways, until they got into or near their workings; although the mine has been known to be so full of gas, that it extended some distance up the shaft, and was there so abundant as to render it unsafe to descend, even with lamps, and to require men to give the signal to be drawn up again ere they reached the bottom. A man named Robert Pilkington seems to have been appointed to some office—either that of firemen or assistant to the underlooker—a few months since; but it is said that he did not usually go down, either before the men or early in the morning; he was at the mouth of the pit when the explosion occurred. The underlooker himself appears not to have been in the habit of going to the pit early in the morning, as he left the superintendence at that time to Pilkington.

The only account yet given of what occurred after the explosion, is that of a young man named Jeremiah Leach. Two of the men who were killed had descended before him; the third (Page) had not. Many of the men in the pit seem not to have left the vicinity of the shaft at the time; and they were all got out very speedily after the explosion. Page was found dead within five or six yards of the shaft. Lindley and Grundy were afterwards found some distance up one of the brows. One of the men who is injured says he believes that Page fired the gas, while looking for some clay in an old that rage fired the gas, while looking for some clay in an old working; but whether this is the case, or whether the explosion was caused by one of the other deceased, can only be known through the inquest. We subjoin a list of the killed and injured :—

DEAD.
Henry Page, 28, wife and four children.
George Grundy, 29, wife and three children.
Thomas Lindley, 20, single man.

BURNED OR OTHERWISE INJURED.
Isaac Barratt, single man, not expected to recover.
James Morris, married, not expected to recover.
Thomas Lindley, severely burned.
Frederick Barratt, severely burned.
Squire Lindley, slightly burned.
Joseph Warburton, slightly burned.
William Sedden, slightly burned, wife and three or four children.
James Lord, slightly burned, and ancle broken.
Samuel Seddon, slightly burned.
Jeremiah Leach, slightly burned.
Joseph Platt, slightly burned.
Two boys, related to the Seddons, slightly burned.

Most of the injured men are much shaken and bruised; and the deaths seem to have resulted as much from other injuries as from burning. Joseph Platt escaped through the Kearsley Hall Pit.

The inquest on the bodies of the three deceased was commenced on Tuesday afternoon by Mr. W. S. Rutter, county coroner, at the Three Crowns public-house, Ringley-bridge.

Jeremiah Leach, who lives in Kearsley, was the first witness called. He said: I work in the coal-pit of Messrs. Knowles and Stott, where this explosion occurred. It is called the Ringley Fold Colliery. I went to the pit's mouth on Monday morning, about six o'clock, at which time none of the men had gone down. I saw John Hunt and Thomas Atherton among the first men who went down, the others I did not notice; neither Hunt nor Atherton were burned, but both of them were knocked and bruised. I went down about a quarter after six. Grundy and Lindley, two of the deceased, had gone down before, but Page had not. Grundy and Lindley had gone to their work places when I got down, as had all the men who were down before me. I took my picks and went on towards my place, in company with James Heathcote, William Molyneux, William Morris, William Bury, and a boy who waggoned for me. We had to go to the top of a jig-brow, and when we got there we sat down, as we usually did there, to strip. I had got my coat off, and was about to fold it up, when I heard a noise which I knew to result from an explosion. I said, " Lord bless me, somebody's fired it," and I wrapped my coat round my face and laid down. All of us who could lay down did so, and the explosion passed over us. I rose and said, " I'm for going to th' pit end," but I heard the explosion coming again, so that I was obliged to lay down. Afterwards we began crawling on our hands and knees to the shaft, and when I got there I found several men who had come down the pit after me, and had not been able to get away to their work. The men were " skriking" to go up, and as the usual means of giving a signal had been blown away, I found a piece of iron and struck the guide rods, to warn them above. Several of the men, including Page, Seddon, and Isaac Barratt, who had not got away from the shaft, were burned. When the tub was let down, I said I would not go up until after all who were burned had got out. Samuel Seddon and me remained to the last, and when we came up we brought out Page, whom we found among some " slutch" just under the edge of the shaft. When I got out of the cage I could scarcely stand from being among the sulphur so long. I did not see anything of the other two deceased. I have no idea how the explosion was caused, but I heard Samuel Seddon say while we were in the pit that he thought " Page had fired it." We thought, when the blast came, that it was from the workings into which we were going; but nobody worked there except us, and we were all together, and none of us were burned.

By the Foreman: Hunt and Atherton are colliers, like myself. Each tubful of men waits at the bottom of the shaft, in order to give lights to those who come next. As I understood, none of the men who came down after me had left the " plates" (some iron at the bottom of the shaft) before the explosion occurred.

By the Coroner: The underlooker is named David Davies. I did not see him that morning before the explosion; he rarely came in the morning, because he had a man named Pilkington to assist him; Pilkington was at the top of the pit when the explosion occurred. It is not a rule for the pit to be examined by the underlooker or his assistant before the men go down. Every man is provided with a safety lamp. The mine makes very little water, and what there is was pumped out by the engine, which winds. I have had no gas in my place for a fortnight, but the mine does make " middling" of gas. I know of men having had to beat out the gas with their jackets before commencing work. Nearly all of us had naked candles on Monday morning; we could carry them in the current of air, which was generally strong enough to blow the flame a little aside, and we thought there was no danger until we came nearer our " facings." There are always two men working together, and there was a lamp for each couple.

Evidence was given identifying the bodies; and the inquest was adjourned to Tuesday next; at which time it was thought that the Government inspector (if one should be sent down) would present a report, and some of the injured men be in attendance to give evidence.

AUSTRALIAN EMIGRATION.—The Salacia, a fine fast-sailing vessel, belonging to Messrs. Gibbs, Bright, and Co., of Liverpool, cleared yesterday from the Liverpool docks for Sydney, N.S.W. She had on board upwards of 130 emigrants, most of them stout and strong young men, all bound for the " diggins."

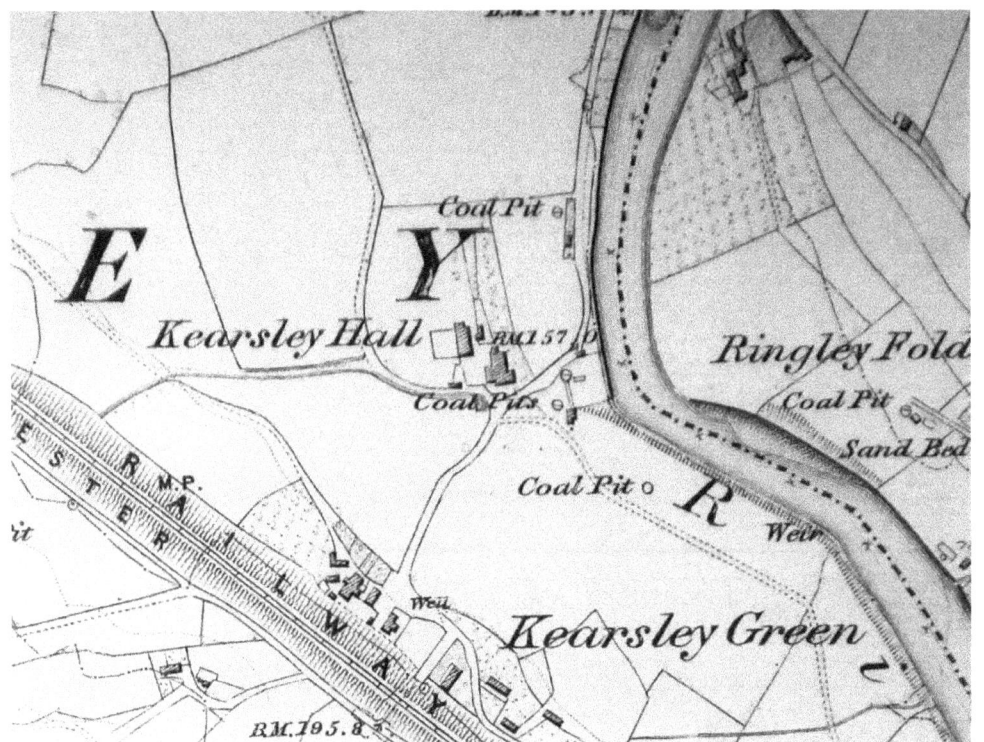

Above. 1848. The Coal Pits that made up Ringley Fold Colliery and Kearsley Hall Colliery are shown close to Kearsley Hall Farm at Ringley. The old Kearsley Hall road winds its way through the site to the tunnel at Slackey Brow. Kearsley Hall was originally built by William Hulme (1631 – 1691) in 1670 as one of his residencies. He was both a wealthy and generous man and amongst his gifts and endowments were grammar schools at Bury, Oldham and the well-known William Hulme Grammar School in Manchester, as well as the Bolton Lectureship Charity.

He and his wife Elizabeth Robinson of Kearsley are buried in Manchester Cathedral and Hulme Road takes its name from the family. The Hall was a strongly built stone edifice of an austere style, which later became a farmhouse owned by the Nuttall Family at the end of the 19th century.

Kearsley Hall and the rest of the farm buildings were located close to where the roundabout on Hulme Road now is. It was demolished in 1927 when the land was sold to the Lancashire Electric Power Company who purchased the site to build Kearsley Power Station, which itself was demolished in the late 1980's to make way for the Ringley Meadows housing estate.

Above. Kearsley Hall Road, which now only extends from the La Roma Italian Restaurant (former Lord Nelson public house) to where it meets Hulme Road.

> SHOCKING CASUALTY: A MAN FALLING DOWN A COALPIT.—A terrible and fatal accident happened on Wednesday evening to a man named James Morris, at the Singing Clough Coalpit, belonging to Messrs. Knowles and Stott, situate near the top of Stoneclough Brow, on the Manchester Road, at Kersley. The pit is being sunk deeper in order to work some cannel; and the deceased, who was ordinarily employed as an engine-tenter, was engaged in assisting to repair or fit up some air pipes in the shaft. About eight o'clock on Wednesday evening, he had got into a bucket or tub to descend the pit, and was taking with him an air-pipe, which he attempted to suspend to a hook. The tub in which he stood was raised a little above the level of the shaft mouth and was out of the "catches" which run down the sides to hold the cage. The movement of his body caused the bucket to swerve a little; and discovering the danger he was in, he endeavoured to reach a chain near him and so save himself. He, however, unhappily missed his hold; the momentum overbalanced the bucket, and he fell out, being precipitated headlong down the pit, which is 169 yards deep. He was killed instantaneously. His wife, who had brought his supper, was standing near at the time, and fainted as soon as she saw her husband's fate. The deceased, who was 44 years of age, was brother to Mr. Thomas Morris, underlooker for Messrs. Knowles and Stott; he leaves a widow and five children.

Above. Another tragedy in the perilous mines, this time at the Singing Clough Coalpit. From the Farnworth Journal of November 25th 1865.

Stonehill Colliery Disaster

On Tuesday 23rd January 1877 a terrible disaster occurred at the Stonehill Colliery in which 18 men and boys were suffocated. It is thought that a lighted rag was placed carelessly by a worker, causing it to ignite wooden pit-props and then the surrounding coal. The fire is believed to have stretched for 100 yards along a wall of coal in the Cannel mine, with around 30 men on the wrong side of the dense fumes that were filling the workings. Those nearest to the inferno managed to make their escape, but 18 of those further away were not so lucky and were overcome by the smoke. A man named James Shorrocks who had escaped, courageously turned back into the smoke to look for his son, Richard. Both were later found dead, lying on the ground, with their arms wrapped around each other.

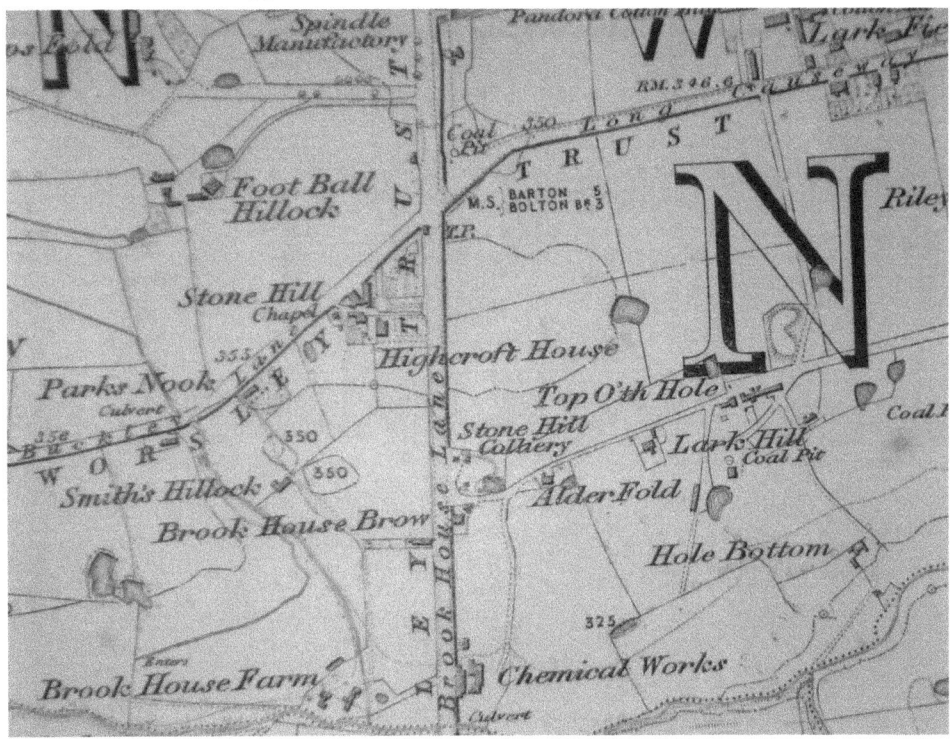

Above. Stone Hill Colliery just off what is now Worsley Road and Stone Hill Road. In January 1964 one of the colliery shafts that had been capped off and covered over suddenly collapsed, and a bungalow that had been built on the site disappeared down the hole. The home had started to subside and fortunately the owners decided to immediately evacuate, escaping seconds before most of it vanished. The bungalow sat on the corner of Bloomfield

Road across from the former Half Way House public house that is currently Sottovento Italian restaurant.

Foggs Pit Disaster

Only two weeks after the disaster at Stone Hill the district was again shaken by a further catastrophe on the 7th February 1877 at Foggs Pit, which stood alongside the MBB Canal at Little Lever. A lighted candle was again the culprit, causing a huge explosion of gas that took ten lives. At this time the pit employed around 50 men and boys, and all those who had survived the disaster volunteered to go back into the mine to search for their comrades. But, unfortunately, the force of the blast had resulted in such enormous damage to the mine that the stricken miners bodies were not recovered for some weeks afterwards. The pit reopened shortly afterwards, and by the mid 1890's employed around 230 miners and surface workers. On 4th October 1907 tragedy once again struck at Foggs, as a cage carrying nine miners became disconnected and plunged down the shaft killing all inside. The pit closed for good on 24th November 1913.

Above. Circa 1910. Foggs Pit on the MBB Canal.

Below. A memorial card dedicated to the memory of those who lost their lives when the cage crashed to the pit bottom in 1907.

Sacred to the Memory of

How hard it is to part with those
We hold on earth so dear ;
The heart no greater trial knows,
No sorrow more severe.

James Mullineaux, collier, 43, Goodwin Street, Bolton
Peter Bleakley, collier, 141, Bridgewater Street, Farnworth.
John William Lambert, collier, 77, Darley Street, Bolton.
Alfred Tomlinson, collier, 38, Bentley Street, Farnworth.
Thomas Yates, taker-off, 3, Osborne Street, Farnworth.
William Bond, day wageman, 24, Lee Street, Moses Gate.
James Berry, collier, 174, Hall Lane, Moses Gate.
William Taylor, collier, 46, Wootton Street, Bolton.
John Bithell, sen., collier, Hall Lane, Moses Gate
John Bithell, jun., son of the above, also of Hall Lane, Moses Gate

Who Lost their Lives at Fogg's Pit, Darcy Lever, Bolton, by the fa'ling of the "Cage," on Friday, October 4th, 1907.

Newtown Colliery

Owned by the Clifton And Kearsley Coal Company the first sod of earth was cut at Newtown on 6th August 1875 by Alfred Pilkington. It remained under their control until it was sold to Bridgewater Collieries in 1925, who themselves were amalgamated with their other subsidiaries into the Manchester Collieries Company in 1929. In 1943 Manchester Collieries wanted to close the pit as it had begun to make substantial losses, but the Ministry of Fuel and Power stepped in to keep it running and to underwrite any financial deficits. Newtown Colliery closed for good in March 1961 with nearly 500 men losing their jobs.

Above. Circa 1930's. Aerial view of Newtown Colliery on the Clifton and Pendlebury border. The newly built houses of Broadhurst Avenue can be seen top left, and what is now Billy Lane is to the left of the colliery chimneys. The inclined tubway for coal transportation can be seen making its way from the pit towards Robin Hood sidings close to the Manchester to Bolton railway. Robin Hood Colliery, which was also owned by the Clifton and Kersley Coal Company, had stood opposite the Robin Hood Public House, just to the side of the slip road that now comes up from the M62 motorway.

Swinton Miner Killed.

GOVERNMENT INSPECTOR ON UNHEEDED WARNINGS.

A verdict of "Accidental death" was returned at the inquest on Monday on Samuel Siddall, a Swinton miner who was killed on Friday at the Newtown Pit, Clifton. The evidence showed that the deceased lost his life while endeavouring, along with another miner, to withdraw a prop which was supporting the roof. Siddall was killed outright, and his workmate was seriously injured by a heavy fall of rock. Mr. Gerrard, Government Inspector of Mines, pointed out that the number of accidents at the Clifton and Kearsley Co's. mines had been reduced considerably by their providing ample timber for roof support. In this case the workmen should either have set two fresh props while they pulled out the one already set, or used the apparatus which enables miners to take out props in safety. In spite of the warnings which they had from time to time, he regretted to say miners too often allowed them to pass unheeded.

Although it did not suffer any major disasters with multiple losses of life, Newtown was, alike many other pits, in that there were fatal accidents and numerous injuries suffered by its workforce. This article from the Farnworth Journal of February 18th 1910 is one such example.

During the early part of 1912 mineworkers all over Britain became increasingly disgruntled at the way in which their wages were paid and how this was calculated. Often the rate of pay was linked to local coal prices, and this varied from district to district, also as coal prices had stagnated, so had the miners wages. Instigated by the Miners Federation of Great Britain, the national coal strike of 1912 officially began on the 1st of March, and its main purpose was the introduction of a minimum wage. Here in Kearsley and the surrounding district every colliery joined in the strike. It is estimated that nationally around one million miners participated, and that the strike was so well supported that very little disorder was reported. At the time of writing (2018) we are all aware of our reliance on oil in daily life, and most of us can remember that in less than two weeks during September 2000 how protesters managed to cause so much disruption to the UK fuel delivery system that very quickly petrol stations and schools began to close, deliveries of food and other essential supplies were severely disrupted as were public transport systems. In 1912 a similar situation existed, but the reliance was on the British coal industry rather than imported oil that is refined in Britain. As the possibility of coal shortages manifested itself in the populace it became common to see whole families digging for scraps of 'black diamonds' in the slack heaps of collieries past and present. The strike was eventually ended after only 37 days when the Government passed the Coal Mines Act that gave minimum wage protection to the miners.

Below. Farnworth Journal, March 15th 1912. Report of Coal Pickers on the site of a former pit known as 'Klondike' which was located between Stoneclough Brow, Hazlemere and the Manchester to Bolton railway line.

The Coal Strike.

Coal Picking at Stoneclough.
Scenes at "Klondike."

Although there is not yet an actual scarcity of coal in the Farnworth and Kearsley district, the rapidly-diminishing stocks, the high prices, and the probability that there will be a serious shortage ere many days has led to remarkable scenes at the site of an old colliery thrown into disuse some years ago. We refer to Messrs. Stott's pit, better known as "Klondike," situated within a stone's-throw of Stoneclough Station and adjoining Messrs. Entwistle's brickworks. When the colliery was working a banking was formed of a mixture of coal, slag, and dirt, and one or two local colliers, aware of this fact, betook themselves to the spot armed with picks, shovels, and other implements, and have made a "good thing" of it. The few pioneers, however, have not held a monopoly by any means. So quickly had the news spread that there was coal to be had for the getting that colliers, and even women, on Monday literally swarmed to the spot in hundreds, coming not only from Farnworth, Kearsley, and Prestolee, but from as far away as Pendlebury, Swinton, Walkden, and Little Lever, bringing with them all sorts and sizes of conveyances, from the humble hand wagon to the horse and cart. At one stage of the day it was estimated there were quite 500 present—men, women and boys, who each played their part in the digging of trenches, filling the sacks and carting away. Throughout Monday and again on Tuesday there was an almost unbroken procession of heavily-laden handcarts and wagons in Stoneclough-rd., but it ceased at noon, the police having intervened on instructions from the agent of Col. Starkie, who owns the land. It has been a case of killing the goose that lays the golden eggs, for there has been the ruthless damaging of fences, and in the disposing of dirt a boundary wall has actually been buried. In many cases the miners have conveyed the coal to their own homes, but the fuel has been turned to profit in not a few instances, bags holding approximately a couple of hundredweights having brought prices ranging from 1s. to 2s. One particular set of men from Farnworth have done good business, one of the orders they fulfilled on Monday being for four bags at 1s. 9d. each—and it was only a few minutes' work filling a bag. The transporting of the fuel—it is not the best coal, but it is said to burn brightly and give off great heat before leaving a residue of dirt—has been the chief difficulty, and some of them have not been very fortunate in this respect. On Tuesday a party of the Farnworth colliers had hauled two handcart loads as far as the Black Horse when one of the wheels of the foremost cart collapsed under its heavy burden. It must have been close on half a ton, and they had not been four hours in the getting of it. The man who stood guard over the broken-down conveyance was subjected to much good-humoured chaff by fellow-miners, who were evidently amused at the spectacle, but a sympathising dame who passed thought it no occasion for laughter, and, taking compassion on the man, handed him sixpence.

Above. The 'Klondike' coal pickers of Stoneclough.

SEARCHING FOR "BLACK DIAMONDS": FAMILY PARTIES GATHERING WASTE COAL FROM A COLLIERY-TIP AT PENDLEBURY.

Owing to the Coal Strike poor people have had to resort to all kinds of shifts to obtain fuel. In the mining districts there has been a run on the waste coal lying about on the coal-tips of the collieries, resulting in scenes such as that shown in our photograph, taken at Pendlebury, in Lancashire. In the poorer districts of Manchester, coal has been sold by the pennyworth. At Sheffield a subsidence of the ground was caused by hundreds of poor folk digging at a coal seam in a brickfield, and two people were injured.

Circa 1890's, sinking of a pit shaft at the bottom of Stoneclough Brow. This picture was taken approximately where the entrance to the Europa Trading Estate currently is. It came to be known as 'Stanley Pit' and was no longer being worked by 1909. In the background to the left are the houses that stand immediately across from the Hare & Hounds public house. They show on maps of 1848 as one residence named Kearsley House. The houses on the right are named Lynton Terrace just off Sulby Street.

Circa 1901. A horse-drawn cart makes its way up Manchester Road. The chimney and pit head of Spindle Point Colliery are visible in the background.

Kearsley Moss Colliery (Tasker's Lane), and Spindle Point Colliery

Owned by Samuel Scowcroft, Kearsley Moss Colliery was located on Tasker's Lane (now Springfield Road), it stood on the site of the former play area across from the top of Waverley Avenue. The colliery was sunk during the early 1860's but closed in 1883 after being put up for sale and remaining unsold. Shortly afterwards though the Clifton & Kersley Coal Company secured the lease and used the site as a pumping station to help drain water from some of their other pits nearby. In 1904 they reinvested in new plant, and once again began coal production at Taskers Lane. The company decided that the coal was to be washed and screened at Spindle Point Colliery some distance away at the top of Slackey Brow. This was achieved by means of a most remarkable arrangement that is difficult to imagine ever existed.

At Spindle Point a quite incredible tub haulage system had been constructed over the main road via what was termed 'The Spindle Point suspension bridge." This system allowed coal tubs access to the colliery washery, because the lines that crossed the road at ground level were mostly in use from the colliery screening plant. The suspension bridge was at a height 20 feet above the traffic on Manchester Road with the electric trams passing underneath. In fact the insulators for their cables were actually attached to its underside. The bridge was of wooden construction and spanned the whole width of the road with no central pillars for support.

Just as extraordinary is the fact that a tram-road for the tub haulage system was constructed from the Kearsley Moss Colliery at the end of Taskers Lane, all the way to connect to the Spindle Point system somewhere close to the rear of Ryder's Farm. It is not known exactly how long this interconnection was in use for, and sadly the route taken does not show on any maps or documents I have examined. As it does not show on the OS maps of 1927 it must therefore be presumed that it was dismantled when Kearsley Moss Colliery closed in 1921. Unfortunately there are also no photographs of the suspension bridge over Manchester Road that linked Spindle Point Colliery to the Manor Pit, Taskers Lane and the Unity Brook sidings on the Manchester to Bolton mainline. These sidings were accessed via a line that ran under the road at a point between the Unity Brook public house and Ryders Farm. There is still today a stone wall at either side of the main road and these served as the parapets for the tunnel that ran beneath.

Spindle Point Colliery closed in 1928, but a constant reminder of this well-worked former coal mining location is the road we call Slackey Brow. The colliery had opened in 1860, but there had been other coal pits on and around the site for decades before this, and so to the rear stood vast slack heaps all along the valley hillside. The steep climb from the railway tunnel up to Manchester Road was at first termed 'slack heap brow' by the locals, whose dialect would have abbreviated this over time to sound more like 'Slackey Brow.' The name stuck, and in October 1866 the Streets Committee of the newly formed Kearsley Local Board made it official. The slack heaps were only cleared in 1961 so that an electricity sub-station could be built at the bottom of the hillside next to the railway line. This has since been demolished and a new one built on the other side nearer to the River Irwell. From the mid nineteenth century to the mid twentieth century there were several houses and a public house called the Miners Arms at the bottom of Slackey Brow, but no trace of them now exist.

Radcliffe and Kearsley Miners' Accident Society. The half-yearly meeting of this society was held on Monday at the Woolpack Hotel, Radcliffe, and on Tuesday at the Miners' Tavern, Lower Kearsley. The president, Mr. Jacob Davenport, was in the chair at both the meetings. It was decided to alter the first part of No. 11 rule, so that instead of £12 for fatal accident for a single man and £8 for a married man, in future it will be £10 in either case. A few members of the society who have been called to South Africa have been presented with £3 3s. each, and should they get shot their widows will receive £10 each. The balance-sheet showed a gain for the half-year of £62 1s. 3d. The lodge, which was formed in July, 1898, is worth £238 13s. 4d. There were 90 accidents during the half-year, the doctors for the same period being paid £49 11s. 6d.

Above. From the Farnworth Journal, February 10th 1900. Details of the Radcliffe and Kearsley Miners Accident Society that was formed to provide financial aid to those injured or killed in the mines. A £10 payment in 1900 would equate to around £1,200 in 2018.

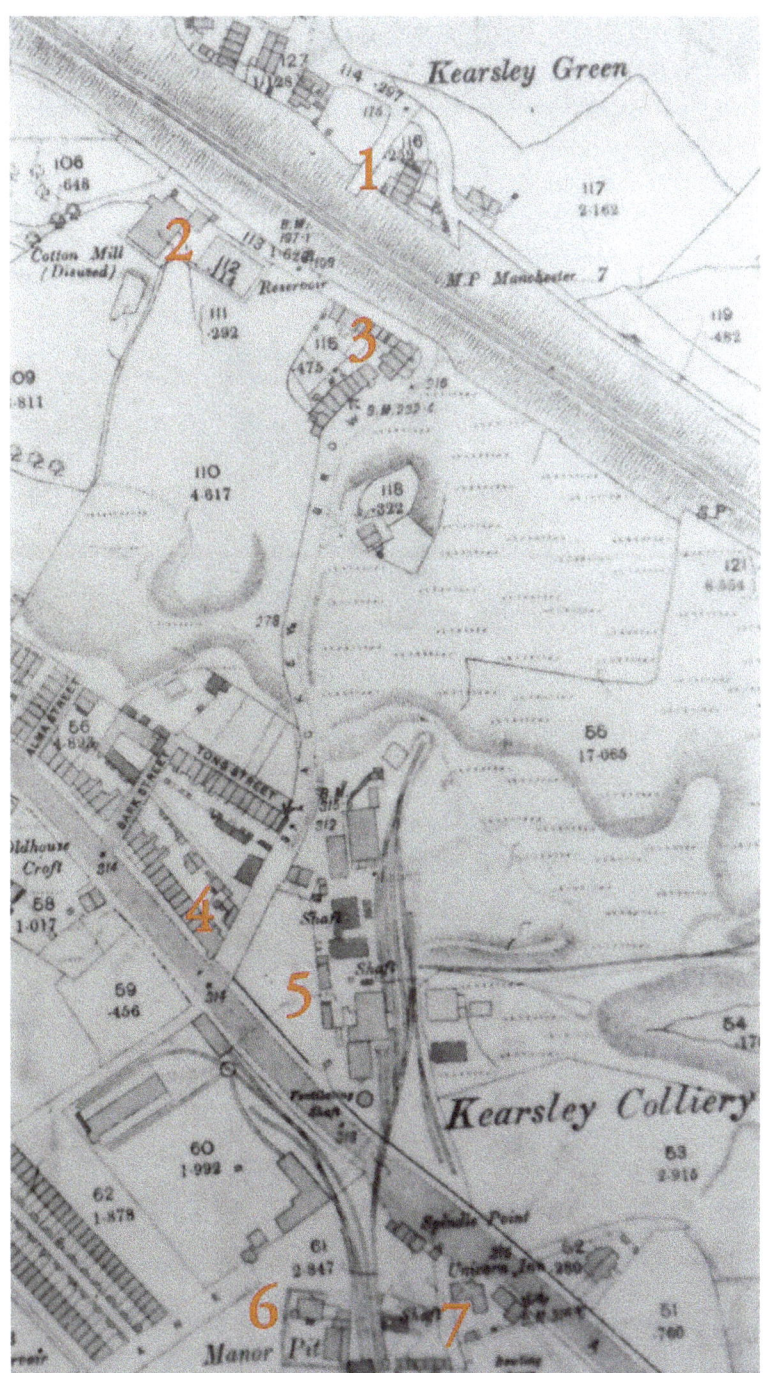

Above. Map of 1890 showing the area around Slackey Brow.
1. The entrance to the tunnel under the Manchester to Bolton railway line at Kearsley Green. **2.** Cotton mill and reservoir formerly ran by the Baker

family. **3.** Houses and a pub named the Miners Arms located here. These were all demolished during the 1950's. **4.** The Spread Eagle public house. **5.** Spindle Point Colliery, also known as Kearsley Colliery. Now the site of the Sunset Business Park. **6.** The Manor Pit on Moss Lane. This was also owned by the Clifton & Kersley Coal Company. **7.** The Unicorn Inn.

> BY MR. EDWIN HASLAM.
> TO BREWERY COMPANIES AND OTHERS.
> VALUABLE FREE BEERHOUSE IN KEARSLEY.
> RE MRS. HANNAH NELSON, DECEASED.
>
> EDWIN HASLAM has received instructions to SELL BY AUCTION at the PACK HORSE HOTEL, BRADSHAWGATE, BOLTON, on THURSDAY, the 3rd day of APRIL, 1919, at 7 o'clock in the evening, subject to conditions:
>
> The OLD ESTABLISHED and well known BEERHOUSE known as the "MINERS ARMS,"
> situate and Nod. 77 and 79, SLACKEY BROW, KEARSLEY, in the occupation of Mr. T. Rushton.
>
> The SITE is leasehold for the residue of a term of 999 years from May 12th, 1846, subject to a yearly ground rent of £1 14s. 6d.; area 414 square yards.
>
> The PREMISES contain: Entrance, Tap-room, Bar Parlour (17ft. 9ins. x 10ft. 3ins.), Side passage, Kitchen, Scullery, 4 Bedrooms, Club-room (28ft. 6ins. x 13ft. 8ins.), 2 Cellars and Storerooms. Good yard and back garden.
>
> The LICENSE (Ante 1869) is for the sale of beer and the house is entirely FREE FROM BREWER.
>
> Further particulars on application to the AUCTIONEER, 24, Acresfield, or Messrs. COOPE & KENYON, Solicitors, 2, Bowkers Row, Bolton.

Above. The Miners Arms at the bottom of Slackey Brow goes up for sale in March 1919. The pub was located on the left hand side close to where you turn right to go into the tunnel toward Hulme Road. It is interesting to note the dimensions and that it was still a private public house not under the control of a brewery, and that the license (Ante 1869) is a good indication of when this pub first opened.

Wet Earth Colliery, Fletchers canal & Pilkington's Tile and Pottery works.

Wet Earth Colliery was located at Clifton, just across the Irwell from Giants Seat, Ringley. This and other surrounding land was owned by a Mr. John Heathcote, and during the early 1740's he first began to sink shafts to the shallow coal seams. One such mine was sank to the Doe seam and then later a much deeper mine to connect to the much lower Doe seam workings. To this end he engaged Matthew Fletcher, a young mining engineer from Bolton. Fletcher sank this new shaft known as the 'Gal' or 'Engine' pit eventually up to a depth of 330 feet in the late 1740's. But unfortunately, the deeper the working, the greater the problems of flooding caused by the irregularity of the rock in the Irwell valley fault beneath the River Irwell. The unremitting problem of flooding at this colliery is the most likely reason it acquired the name 'Wet Earth.'

The 'Gal' Pit, incidentally, derives its name from Galloway ponies, and was a term widely used to describe pit ponies or pit horses in general. The ponies, or horses were tied to a 'Gin', which was a winding drum with ropes attached, and they would trudge one way to wind an empty tub down, and turn around to walk the other way to wind a loaded tub of coal back up. This 'Gin' system would have also been used to try and drain the mine, with empty buckets going down and buckets of water coming back up. The original digging out of the pit shaft may well have used the Gin system as well.

As drainage by bucket and chains was unsuccessful the colliery temporarily closed in 1750. Shortly afterwards it is believed that John Heathcote managed to secure the help of a brilliant engineer from Staffordshire called James Brindley. It also about this time that Matthew Fletcher seems to have become lessee of much of the Heathcote lands and mineral rights at Clifton, indeed it was he who built Clifton House and took up residence there around 1763.

After an inspection of the site in 1752 Brindley came up with an ingenious and original solution. The idea was to reroute water from the River Irwell into the mine, which would then drive a waterwheel and pumps to remove the flood water out of the workings. At Ringley Fold, around 1500 yards upriver from the colliery, Brindley constructed a weir, this gained a considerable head of water which was actually at a higher level than that of the pit-head. The flow of water from the top of the weir was then taken in a tunnel across to the other side of the river around 800 yards away at Giant's Seat, the water then went down under the River Irwell's rocky bed in a syphon tunnel before coming up again on the colliery side into an open leat, or feeder channel, then on to the water wheel which drove the pumps in the Gal Pit. These pumps sucked water from the pit and discharged it into the turbine chamber, from where, together with the water driving from the wheel, it passed back into the River Irwell through a narrow tailrace tunnel. The drop in water from the top of the weir to the wheel in the underground chamber was 35 feet, and this lifted water from a depth of 158 feet, and Brindley became known as the 'man who made water run uphill'. For his labours he received 2s 0d per day; the income from the revived pit is believed to have reached £6,200 per year, giving employment to around 150 persons.

This remarkable scheme took four years to complete and was very effective in its purpose of solving the flooding problem and therefore allowing access to further rich seams of coal. The original waterwheel worked until the 1860's when it was replaced by a more modern turbine which remained in operation until 1924, when it to, presumably was worn out and finally replaced by steam.

In 1790 Matthew Fletcher began work on extending the feeder channel around three quarters of a mile downriver to Botany Bay Colliery, which was located near to where the Pilkington's Tile works currently stands, and this new waterway became known as Fletchers Canal. In total it was around a mile and a quarter long and of crude construction, but in 1801, after some opposition, it was also connected via an aqueduct to the newly opened Manchester Bolton & Bury canal at Clifton, of which Matthew Fletcher was also one of the chief protagonists.

By 1805 the estate interests had passed to Ellis Fletcher, Matthew's nephew, and he sank a downcast shaft to the Doe seem that also used a new steam winding engine which made redundant the horse powered gin winding system. The old Gin itself was actually retained and used for pump and shaft repairs and indeed remained on the site until its final closure.

Circa 1896. Coal Screening sheds under construction at Wet Earth Colliery.

Circa 1930. To the right is Fletcher's Canal where it linked up with the Manchester Bolton & Bury Canal at the Roving Bridge close Pilkingtons Tile and Pottery Works. The MBBC crosses the River Irwell via the aqueduct that can be seen to the left. Further back is the railway viaduct known as the thirteen arches, which made the connection from Clifton Junction station over to Molyneux Brow station. Molyneux Brow station closed in 1966, the same year the elegantly designed Roving Bridge was also demolished.

Matthew Fletcher passed away on 24th August 1808 aged 77 years and his body lies in the family vault in Ringley churchyard, there is also a memorial to him inside the church. A stone tablet was placed above the door of one of the cottages on the colliery site with an inscription which read as follows: *'This stone was placed here at the request of Sir John Edensor Heathcote, of Longton Hall, Staffordshire. To the memory of Matthew Fletcher, Esq., of Clifton, who departed this life the 24th day of August, 1808 aged 77 years. In addition to honour and integrity he possessed a sound understanding, which he employed for the benefit of his neighborhood with the highest credit to himself. Cs. Lever, engineer.'*

The chimney still situated on the site is known as 'Fletcher's Folly' and was connected via lengthy underground flues to the steam boilers that drove the steam winding engine. It is believed that Ellis Fletcher had it built at that location so that it did not spoil the view from Clifton House, and that when a replacement chimney was built in 1905 this one was simply left as a redundant 'folly.'

Ellis Fletcher had two sons, Ellis Fletcher jnr (born 23rd July 1833) and Jacob Fletcher Fletcher (born unknown date 1821/22), and when he passed away in 1834 the estate passed to his youngest son, Ellis Fletcher Jnr. This seems an odd sequence of events as Ellis Fletcher jnr was not even two years old, but it was not uncommon at this period for the youngest son to take priority over an elder sibling regarding inheritance matters. This meant that Ellis Fletcher jnr could not take control of the estate until he came of age, which was on his 21st birthday. Tragedy struck Ellis Fletcher jnr just 3 months after inheriting the estate, as he died from injuries suffered in an accident whilst returning from a hunting trip. The estate now passed to his brother Jacob Fletcher Fletcher who passed away less than three years later on April 1st 1857 after contracting gastritis. The estate was then moved on to his 12 year old daughter, Charlotte Anne Fletcher, but it was placed in the trust of her cousin, John Fletcher until she came of age. Charlotte Anne married Sir Robert Wellington Stapleton-Cotton, 3rd Viscount Combermere of Bhurtpore in June 1866, they had two children, Cecil and Madeline, but the couple were divorced in 1879. In 1872 Charlotte Anne became patron of the newly founded Church of St. Anne, Clifton, and in 1886 she married Major Alfred Wynne Corrie of London. Charlotte Anne did much charity work during her life before she passed away on June 20th 1913. Corrie Drive and Corrie Crescent are named in her honour.

> Mrs. Corrie's Will.
>
> Mrs. Charlotte Anne Corrie, Park Hall, Oswestry, Salop, owner of large colliery estates in Clifton and in the neighbourhood of Wigan, who died on June 20th, left £6,000 for charitable purposes. Testatrix was the wife of Mr. Alfred Wynne Corrie, and only daughter of Mr. Jacob Fletcher Ellis Fletcher, of Peel Hall, and Clifton, Lancashire, and formerly the wife of the Hon. Robert Wellington Stapleton Cotton, and left unsettled property of the gross value of £123,384.

Left. Details of the passing of Charlotte Anne Corrie in the Farnworth Journal of July 25th 1913.

John Fletcher was responsible for sinking mines at the Manor and Spindle Point Collieries in Kearsley during this period, but it is also thought that around this time the good coal seams at Clifton started to run out which put a severe strain on the finances of the business. This may well have been the reason that the coal rights were then leased out to Joseph and Josiah Evans who worked Haydock Collieries near St.Helens, and their nephews Edward and Alfred Pilkington, the sons of Richard Pilkington who was a partner with his brother William at the St. Helens glassworks. Together they formed The Clifton & Kersley Coal Company in 1867, and, as its name suggests, they went on to work a number of collieries in the area, as well as take over the leasehold of about half the land in Clifton village.

By 1885 Edward and Alfred Pilkington had become sole owners and a limited company was formed under the title of Clifton & Kersley Coal Company Limited to take over the business previously run by the partnership. It was while sinking two new shafts around 1889 that were to be called Pepper Hill Colliery, a great deal of good quality Marl was found. As it turned out the two new shafts were constantly flooding and had to be abandoned, but by chance the Pilkington brothers' secretary at the coal company knew a Mr. William Burton who was a chemist with the famous Wedgwood Pottery Company. After some tests Mr. Burton suggested that a good use for the Marl would be in the production of items such as decorative tiles, which at this time were becoming increasingly popular in Britain. The Pilkington's Tile & Pottery Company was formed in 1891 with William Burton as its General Manager, he also helped design the building of the factory located at the end of Fletchers Canal. The pottery manufactured at Clifton was of extremely high quality, but due to falling demand the pottery department was closed in 1937, the company then changed its name to Pilkington's Tiles Ltd. The tile making side of the business continued in production until the 2000's, but by

2010 the company were selling only imported tiles in their factory outlet shop. In June 2010 Pilkington's Tiles finally it went into administration with debts of 23 million pounds and closed its doors for good.

Up until the 1880's at Wet Earth all the coal was still being loaded onto canal boats and without being cleaned, but the Pilkington's started to invest in more surface plant including railway lines, a locomotive, coal screening sheds, washery and a compressed air rope haulage system that now did the work previously carried out by pit ponies. Canal boats did continue in use and around 200 were still carrying coal loaded by crane, the colliery even built a small dry dock next to the loading basin for the purpose of repairs.

The investment paid off and output is believed to have doubled leading up to 1905 with a daily winding of 2,800 pit tubs per day, each of 7cwt capacity giving a total of 980 tons of coal daily from a workforce of between 600 to 700. The Trencherbone, Hell Hole, Doe, Five Quarters, Crambouke and the newly opened Plodder mine were all being worked, as well as a 'Day eye' or Drift mine that was well known for its sizable rat population which displayed considerable inventiveness in stealing the miners 'snap'.

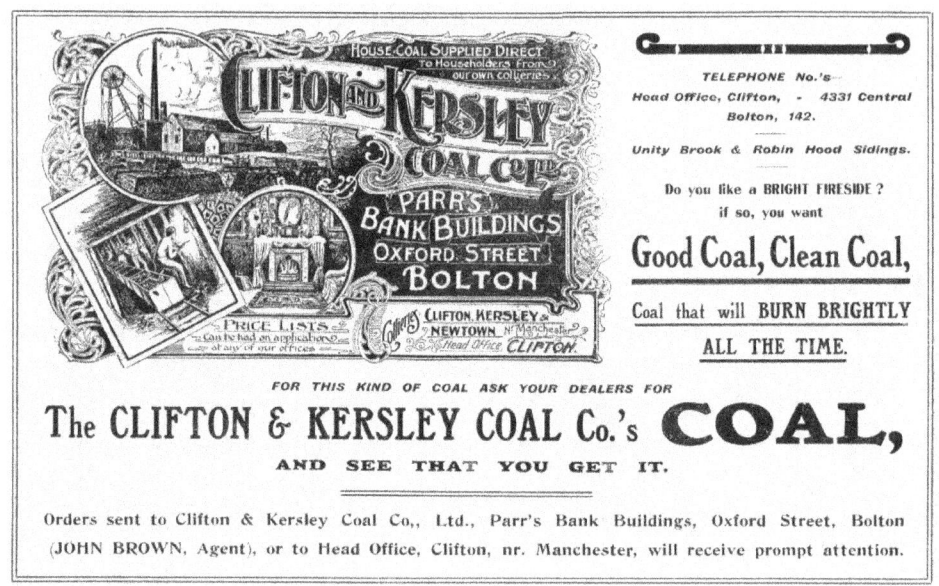

Above. 1914. Advertisement for the Clifton & Kersley Coal Company.

It was not long after this that the colliery entered a period of decline, mainly due to most of the coal seams being worked out, and after the national coal strike in 1921 only the Plodder Mine re-opened. The pit gradually became uneconomic and finally ceased production on 10th February 1928.

The colliery buildings and machinery were removed shortly afterwards and the site lay redundant and derelict for many years, until the 1960's when many tons of soil and gravel were removed for use on the construction of the nearby M62 motorway. The huge hole that remained was filled with water and is known as Clifton Marina, which forms part of the 48 hectare Clifton Country Park that is open to the public. The remains of Wet Earth Colliery are maintained by the Park and continue to fascinate visitors of all ages. Interestingly most of the colliery site was planted with trees during the development of the marina in an attempt to beautify it, unfortunately at that time there seemed to be little regard to the historical importance of the location.

Parish Church of St. Anne, Manchester Road, Clifton shortly after construction. The foundation stone was laid by Charlotte Anne Fletcher in 1872, and the Church was consecrated on August 19th 1874.

Above. St Anne's Church 1914, and below in 1932.

Above. Circa 1930. Stunning aerial view of Pilkington's Tile & Pottery Works and Exide Battery Works at Clifton. The MBB Canal can be seen crossing the aqueduct over River Irwell to where it meets Fletcher's Canal at the Roving Bridge. The Manchester to Bolton railway can be seen at the bottom of the picture, as can the connection over to Molyneux Brow Station across the majestic looking thirteen arches viaduct. A cricket match is also taking place on ground currently covered by industrial units on what is now known as Junction Eco Park.

Above. 1920's Exide Batteries advertisement, the company later became Chloride Electrical.

Left. June 2010. Pilkington's Tiles factory outlet shop shortly before closure. This was the last part of the business to remain open.

Above. The Pilkington's works around 1900.

> On Friday the workings of the Botany Bay Colliery, one of the oldest of the Clifton and Kersley Coal Company, were permanently closed. It is believed the shaft was sunk during the latter part of the last century. The lowest workings were about 400 yards below ground. Originally the pit machinery was worked by a water wheel, and afterwards an atmospheric engine. The Fletchers were owners before the present proprietors, who 20 or 30 years ago had modern plant put down. Fifteen years ago between 300 and 400 miners were employed, but latterly the number had been reduced to about 70, most of whom will be found employment at the firm's other pits. Mr. James Holt has been manager since the completion of the Robin Hood pit. There have been comparatively few fatalities at Botany Bay during the past half century.

Closing of Botany Bay Colliery, Clifton.

Above. Report of the closure of Botany Bay Colliery, from the Farnworth Journal, January 5th 1895. At Botany Bay, there were underground canal arms to allow direct loading onto narrowboats, comparable to the Worsley mines.

Clifton & Kearsley Moss Cultivation Stone

In the wooded area to the rear of Teak Drive sits a large rectangular stone that was placed there to mark the draining and cultivating of both Clifton Moss and Kearsley Moss by the Fletcher family during the 1860's. It became known locally as the 'enclosure' or 'land grab' stone as this land had formally been open and used by anyone for grazing or for digging peat. But the Fletcher's recognized its possibilities and claimed it under the enclosure act.

Above. The stone reads: *CLIFTON MOSS CULTIV NOV 1862. KERSLEY CULTIV NOV 1863. JOHN FLETCHER. RECEIVER.*

Local Governance. Kearsley Local Board and Urban District Council.

The history of local governance is not confined to the last couple of centuries as many people would think, indeed there has been a varied, but continuous, form of local administration stretching back as far as written records exist and beyond. The first of what we would consider local councils were created under the Government Public Health Act of 1848, which allowed the creation of a Government backed Local Board, formed by members who were elected by the property owners and ratepayers of that area, to provide a cohesive approach to matters such as public health, street cleaning, crime, sewerage and the water supply, as well as many others necessary duties.

In the centuries prior to this act there would be public meetings, attended by the ratepayers of the town, and usually chaired by the incumbent of the local Church. As these gatherings were often held in the vestry of the Church they became known as vestry meetings. Here local influential men would decide on any significant matters. These included such things as appointing persons as 'special constables' (there was no Police force at this time), road repairs, how much support would be given to the poor, or even what to do with any unruly townsfolk.

Ancient records of Kearsley survive that show some interesting details of the time. It is estimated the number of townsfolk was no more than 500 in the year 1700, and that the poor rate was around £5 per quarter. The 'poor rate' was a rate of tax levied, usually on property and landowners, by each Parish, and the money collected was used for relief and support of the poor. An 'overseer of the poor' was appointed who would be responsible for setting the poor rate, collecting the money and then distributing it as they saw fit. This important position was usually a landowner or churchwarden, and would have typically been chosen on a yearly basis. The overseer of the poor would assess each case for parish relief on an individual basis, and this could include performing an audit of a persons' possessions. A memorandum made in 1717 states the following items were in the hands of a Kearsley resident named simply as 'ffrances wife,' *these being "a fire irne, fald bord, bed stocks, a table, 3 chears, 2 wheels, a salt box, 8 stools, a mug, an ould smoothing Irn, one pair of Tongs."*

It is believed the position of overseer of the poor in Kearsley was an unpaid endeavor up until the year 1790, with the incumbent generally unhappy at being given the responsibility. There were other occupations also which were allocated to townsfolk, such as 'overseers of the highway,' who would inspect the roads and bridges and organize any repair work. A 'constable' would also be designated to work in tandem with the overseers to help collect taxes and 'church leys' (sometimes referred to as a church rates), which paid towards the running expenses and repairs to the parish churches.

The overseer of the poor for Kearsley in the year 1705/06 was John Doodson, who passed his duties on to the next overseer, Jonathan Greenhalgh, on the 27th May 1706.

Amongst the items appearing in the 1705/06 overseers accounts are *" for making 2 shifts* for Rich Crompton and his wife- 6d.. 'spent at laying ye generall taxes for yr paſt- 5/9, "several payments of 1/6 to ffarnworth" and items amounting to £1 17s. 7d. in connection with Thomas Seddon's wife's illness and funeral, including Dr Low's three attendances, 9/-, for dressing the body, 2/, chapel dues, 2/4, "spent" (evidently on ale) 1/3, and 1 ½ yards of "gladon" for a wrapper, 1/-, A payment of 8/- was made to Tom Post for "Atending Ould Dish," and another of 4/6 "for signing an order on the overseer," and a memorandum in a strange clerkly hand is a reminder of an old impost stating: "You are required to pay your quarterly land for windows duty."* This last statement referring to the property tax of the time which was based on the number of windows in a house.

*The shift was the undermost garment worn by children and women. It served the same purpose as the man's shirt. Made from various qualities of white linen, it had either a drawstring or plain neck, as well as drawstrings or cuffs at the elbows. It could be plain or lace trimmed.

In addition to the poor rate Kearsley's tax paying inhabitants were also expected to contribute towards the upkeep of not just the local area, but the county highways, bridges and institutions as well. The following entry comes from the old Kearsley township record books at a time when a man named Abraham Heywood was overseer of the highways:

Octobr 13 day 1708

A tax upon the inhabitance of Kerſsley for repaire of Conway Bridge and seven other Bridges and houſe of correction and attending several feſsions................... 1-06-05

And for one half of a church ley which is £20 in the parish, our part............ 0-14-03

> *This day Abraham Heywood accounted and he will have in his hands when he hath a tax of 2 ½d, the sum*... 0-07-00¼

> *There is 5-7 due to Abraham Heywood upon highways acct which muſt be deducted out of ye above 07s, 4d.*

(Signed)
Robert Bolton
Samuel Barritt

The next tax was for repairs to Church Bank, Bolton, and Hilstford, Middlebrook, and on June 9th 1709, a tax was laid of 3d, for *"Lancashire Bridge, Stone Clough Bridge, Burnden Bridge, Ratcliffe Bridge, for prisoners at Lancaster, for houſe of correction, for vagarans, the peal day 3, one privl sefsions 6, paid to high constable 6."*

The following year Kearsley contributed to the highways in Rumworth and Westhoughton, in 1711 to Ellenbrook bridge and Cornebrooke bridge, and in 1712 for *'a day of apeall and Stone Clough Bridge and Bury Bridge and such like things"* the amount of this years tax being *"five farthings pounds."*

It was not uncommon during this period for the most compassionate local inhabitants to donate, or leave money in a will, for the poor and needy. The money was not always given directly and not in one lump sum, and often it had conditions attached, such as it was to be used for purchasing cloth or other items to be distributed amongst the poor on an annual basis. An example of this goodwill is the 'gift' to the town by a Mr George Seddon of Farnworth which reads;- *An act of the distribution of a piece of linene cloth given to the poore of Kearfley by George Seddon of ffarnworth in ye year 1707*

George Rediſh......................*7yrd ¾*
Aun fiſh..........................*2yr ½*
Bett fiſher........................*2 yr ½*
Withington......................*3 yr*
Ralph Cromptn..................*2 yr ½*
Sam Holliday....................*2 yr ½*
James Lomax....................*5 yr*
Rich Crompton..................*5 yr*

Ann Balfron……………………2 yr ½
Jon Jackson……………………..2 yr ½
Tho Seddon………….....…………5 yr
Peter Aspinall…………………3 yr
George's wife lad……………..3 yr
Ralph Boardman………….…..1 yr ¾
James Doodfon……………….4 yr
Rich Allen……………………2 yr ½
Tom Poft………………………2 yr ½
Dan Cave……………………3 yr
Edmond Jackfon……………..2 yr ½
………
63 yr

Distributed by Robt Seddon.

On April 30th, 1783, at a public town's meeting held at Joshua Lomax's, it was agreed *"that ye paupers belonging to ye township of Kersley was to have the allowances as follows, that be to pay their allowance monthly on every first Wednesday in the month – Edmund Jackson 4/- per month, Judea Jackson 3/-, Ann Lord 8/-, Thomas Bury 10/-, James Heywood 6/-, James Lord son of Betty Ann Lord 9/-, John Eckersal 4/-, Mary Sixsmith 2/-, Alice Lord daughter of Betty Lord 10/-,"* it was also further agreed *"That all paupers that has children which are at age shall be put forth to an apprentice agreeable to the statute."* This entry signifies that the children of those receiving relief could be compelled into working for a master who would teach them a trade, and in many cases this would mean the child leaving the family home. A further resolution states; *"All paupers that gives the officers any unnecessary trouble shall wear the badge."* The term 'wear the badge' refers to the statute of 1697 in which the poor, or those considered to be deserving support, were required to wear a badge to signify which parish they belonged to and that they were in receipt of relief.

This seemingly draconian measure was brought in for a number of reasons, but in the main it would help to identify those who had been adjudged by the overseer to be worthy of parish relief, but it was also hoped that those wearing the badge would feel ashamed enough to make every effort to depart from parish handouts and seek every means available to support themselves and their families. A change in the badge requirement was introduced in 1782 which permitted 'paupers of good character' to avoid wearing the badge, and although there is no record of whether the inhabitants of Kearsley were ever required to wear the parish welfare badges, this statement made it clear, if they became obstinate, or refused the terms set out by the overseers and constables, then they would have to wear the badge, or otherwise lose their handouts. This highlights a curious problem of the time for both the authorities and the paupers of Kearsley.

The parents who would wish to keep the family together would be unwilling to agree to the terms of the parish welfare system if it meant their children being taken away to work for a master under an apprenticeship, but if they opposed this then their relief payments would cease. The authorities on the other hand were well aware that the system was open to abuse, with some, not all, deciding to simply live off the relief system rather than to find work to support their families, so it was important to dissuade as many as possible from taking this option. A report ordered by the House Of Commons at the time declared *"the poor*

Right. List of Overseers of the Poor for Kearsley from 1700 to 1839.

List of Overseers of the Poor.

1700 John Hardman for Mr. Parr, 1701 Richd Hardman, 1702 Edmund Grundy & Richd Mather, 1703 Robt Seddon for Top of Bank, 1704 Thos Heaps, 1705 Abraham Heywood, 1706 John Doodson, 1707 Jonathan Greenhalgh, 1708 Richd Grundy, 1709 Edmund Grundy, 1710 Jas Smith, 1711 Robt Seddon, 1712 Robt Bolton, 1713 Jas Fletcher, 1714 Mr Antribus, 1715 Robt Halworth, 1716 Mr Raguley, 1717 Saml Barrat, 1718 Jas Walworth, 1719 Jno Ellton, 1720 Richd Hardman, 1721 Jno Hardman for Mr Parr, 1722 Thos Kirkham, 1723 Richd Hardman for Top of Bank, 1724 Thos Kirkham for Caves, 1725 Jonathan Greenhalgh, 1726 Abraham Heywood, 1727 Henry Hardman for Richd Grundy, 1728 James Bullow, 1729 Jas Smith, 1730 Ellis Crompton for Alice Greenhalgh. 1731 Mr Peter Dorning, 1732 Mr Kirkham for Antribus, 1733 Mr Seddon for Walworth, 1734 Thos Kirkham for Works, 1735 Robt Howarth for Jno Farnworth, 1736 Mr Thos Crosse, 1737 Thos Bury for Barrats, 1738-1739 Jas Hollows for Top of Bank, 1740 Joshua Hilton for Mr Parr's, 1741 Mr Kirkham for Barsus, 1742 Robt Aspinall for Tastery, 1743 Mr Kirkham for Cheethams and Caves, 1744 Oswald Mosley Esq for Bothams Yate, 1745 Humphrey Smith for Prestoe, 1746 Henry Hardman, 1747 Jno Hobson for his own house, 1748 Robert Howarth for James Smith, 1749 Nathaniel Topp for Mr Dorning, 1750 Mr William Seddon for Dyehouse, 1751 Thomas Alcock for Antribus, 1752 Robt Aspinal for Fletchers and works, 1753 Mr Wm Seddon for works, 1754 John Blomeley for Mr Henry Mather, hired by the town, 1755 John Blomeley for Kearsley Hall, 1756 Jno Lord for Barrats, 1757 Jno Hobson and Robt Howarth for Top of Bank, 1758 Miles Mather for Mr Parr's, 1759 Lawrence Fogg for Barsus, 1760 Jonathan Dorning for Jas Youngs, 1761 Jas Fogg for High Stile, 1762 Jas Fogg for Adam Chadwick, 1763 Robt Aspinall for Tuskers, 1764 Robt Aspinall hired, 1765, Nathaniel Topp for Prestoes, 1766 Henry Hardman, 1767-8 Henry Hardman hired by the town, 1769 Jonathan Dorning, 1770 to 1778 Nathaniel Topp, allowed £4.4.0 yearly by the town, 1779 John Holker, 1780, James Jackson, 1781 Dan Cave, 1782-3-4 Dan Cave allowed by the town £5, £4.4.0, and £5, 1785 Robert Scholes, 1786 Thos Hamer, 1787, John Laver, 1788 John Laver allowed £5.5.0, 1789 James Lord for Barritts, 1790 to 1794 John Lever hired by the town at £6.6.0 yearly. From this date the overseers were paid, the amounts increasing from £6.6.0 to £8.8.0 in 1806, to £12.12.0 in 1811, and £14.14.0 in 1815, after which there is no record. 1795 Richard Gaskell, 1796 Richard Gaskell for Egerton Crosse Esq, 1797 Samuel Ogden, 1798 Dennis Grundy for Thomas Smethurst, 1799 Thomas Ratcliffe, 1800 Thomas Ratcliffe for Mr Peter Seddon, 1801 Thomas Ratcliffe for Joshua Cross, 1802 Edmd Turner, 1803 Jas Linley for Kersley Green,

1804 E. Johnson for Top of Bank, 1805 Robt Lever for Thos Jackson, 1806 Robt Lever for town, 1807 Robt Lever for Ralph Crompton for Caves, 1808 John Lever for Thos Seddon, 1809 John Lever for Joseph Topp, 1810 Saml Jackson for Botoms Yate, 1811 & 12 John Lever for the town, 1813 James Ridyard for himself, 1814 James Ridyard for Thos Tongo, 1815 James Ridyard for the town, 1816 to 1821 John Lever for the town, 1822 to 1825 Edmund Turner for the town, 1826 to 1828 Joshua Partington for the town, 1829 to 1833 Edmund Turner for the town, 1834 Joshua Partington, 1835-39 John Tickle.

ought to know and feel that the eye of the public is upon them, ready to check fraud and restrain importunity." Charles Jerram, a prominent evangelical priest of the Church of England, who was involved in the administration of the poor laws also called for *"some means to distinguish the profligate pauper from the unfortunate and virtuous sufferer."*

For those unfortunate souls completely unable to sustain themselves and their family, there was another forbidding circumstance, of which the township records show this option was taken on many occasions. At a vestry meeting on July 14th 1797 it was unanimously agreed *"that Samuel Ogden, the overseer of the poor, should take Catherine Jackson to the Workhouse and her two children, Jimmy and Molly, to be provided with sufficient necessaries of life."* At this time the township paid 7s 4d per year to Brindle Workhouse, which was evidently a sort of retaining fee. In 1798 the overseers accounts show a lot of bills paid to Brindle Workhouse amounting to £12 13s 7½d, and from April 1800 are other payments of £9 8s 7 ½d and £10 7s 10d. The Workhouse at Brindle was situated in the hills above Preston in a most desolate and grim landscape, it had been open since around 1734 and by all accounts had a harrowing reputation for cruelty towards its occupants. From around 1812 onwards the Workhouse for Kearsley was at Goose Cote Farm in Turton, Bolton.

The following are examples from the Kersley town meeting minute books in the early 19th century.
"At a public meeting, held at the house of John Hewart, the Black Horse Inn, Kersley, March 26th*, 1824, it was resolved, "that a number of special constables be now appointed, and that the following persons be nominated for the office, namely, Joseph Lord, Clammerclough; Benjamin Cooke, Halshaw Moor; Peter Ditchfield, Kersley Mill; James Crompton, near Kersley Mill; Robert Grundy, Kersley Mount; John Lever, Ralphs; Joseph Hubert, Kersley Hall; and Henry Cross, Clough Side; and they be requested to take the usual oath at the Sessions Room, Worsley, on Wednesday, 7*[th] *April next, for the purpose of being sworn in."*
A further note in one of the books from 1827, signed by Joshua Partington, Constable, states " *Thomas Grundy, Henry Cross, Richard Cross, Robert Dawson, Samuel Topp, Robt Lord, James Lowe, Benjamin Cooke and Thomas*

Tonge have each a truncheon in their possession, Joshua Partington having two truncheons and four pairs of handcuffs." And another note from 1818 shows that *"Robert Linley, John Parr, Jas Greenwood, John Pilkington, Matthew Eckersley, John Green, Thomas Green, John Bowker, Richard Place and Adam Greenhalgh each paid 1s 4d to be exempt from the militia for Kersley."* The militia was a sort of reserve army, which was called upon when the local constables could not cope but full military action was unnecessary. The constables would try to enlist local men, but these men it seems could pay to avoid joining up.

"At a public meeting held on the 4th day of May, 1827, by adjournment from Thomas Tonge's (The Lord Nelson Inn), at Ringley it was resolved, "That the township of Kersley do pay for the cleaning of the linen and the purchasing of bread and wine for the sacrament at St. John's Church, in Kersley, along with the township of Farnworth, in the following proportions, namely, Kersley two-fifths, and Farnworth three-fifths; and that the money collected shall be understood to go and be given to the poor of the said townships in the same proportions."

"Kersley, June 26th; 1808. Belonging to this township there are today six truncheons, two staffs, and one pair of handcuffs for the use of the constables."

The Poor Law Amendment Act of 1834 ended the parish relief system administered by the overseers of the poor. The new organization saw the establishment of a Board of Guardians that oversaw several parishes rather than just one, but a lot of the duties and responsibilities were similar to the previous system. On the 1st February 1837 the Bolton Poor Law Union was officially formed with an elected board of representatives from each of the 26 integral parishes. The Bolton poor law Board of Guardians continued to use the workhouses at Goose Cote Farm, Turton and Fletcher Street, Bolton to give refuge to the paupers, orphans and homeless of the town, but these were becoming increasingly unfit for purpose. In 1856 land was purchased from the Fishpool farm estate in Farnworth for the sum of £2880, and the cornerstones for a new union workhouse were laid in September the same year. Building work was completed in September 1861 and the inmates from Fletcher Street and Turton were all transferred there. These new workhouse buildings became known as Fishpool Institution, and originally housed 900 beds, but this was added to over the following decades, sadly giving an indication of the increasing number of persons falling into extreme hardship. Next to the main workhouse building four large houses were built for orphans and the young children of the inmates, these were called Hollins Cottage homes.

A further 76 acres of land at was purchased next to the Fishpool workhouse in 1894 at a cost of £10,000, and a hospital originally known as Fishpool Infirmary was built on the site in 1896. By 1929 this had become known as Townleys Hospital, the name being taken from nearby Townleys Farm, of which the hospital buildings now occupied part of its land. The workhouse system came to an end in 1929 after Government legislation was passed to abolish Poor Law Guardians and allow local authorities to take over poor relief. Some workhouses remained open and were renamed Public Assistance Institutions, but with the establishment of the National Health Service in 1948 these last vestiges of the workhouse and Poor Law system were no more.

The original workhouse building at Townley's (now the Royal Bolton Hospital) was located on the left hand side after you pass through the gates going up Minerva Road, it was demolished in 2011.

Above. Boxing Day 1922 at Fishpool Workhouse, Farnworth.

The Poor Law Amendment Act of 1834 was superseded in 1848 by the Public Health Act, which granted further powers and encouraged townships to form an elected Local Board to continue with previous duties, but also become more involved in matters relating to public health, in particular the cholera epidemics of the time. Environmental health risks such as slaughterhouses, sewers, and water supply became high priority issues. This was again superseded in 1858 by the Government Local Board Act, which granted additional powers and responsibilities.

A meeting of the principal ratepayers in Kearsley was held on the 24th August 1865 to discuss satisfying the requirements to form a local board for the township. Interestingly, apart from the inhabitants of Kearsley desiring to regulate their own affairs, it seems there were also concerns that plans may be put forward by the Farnworth Local Board, which could impact on, or even absorb, portions of Kearsley. The Farnworth Local Board had been formed in November 1863 with Mr. Alfred Barnes appointed as the first chairman.

A further meeting of Kearsley property owners and ratepayers was held at the house of Mrs. Turner, The Grapes Inn, Stoneclough on 30th August 1865, and amongst those present were the Rev. E. Mather, B.A., St. Saviour's Ringley; Mr. W. Stott (Messrs. Knowles and Stott), Dr. Eames, Captain Topp, and Messrs. John Partington and Thos. Cooke, overseers of the poor; Johnson Martin, churchwarden; Richard Eckersley, collector of assessed taxes; Isaac Gee, Donald McDonald, Samuel Partington, Robert Prestwich, Wm. Holden, John Gerrard, James Fletcher, Samuel Scowcroft, Samuel Gee (Poor-law Guardian), Hugh Topp, Edmund Isherwood, Peter Bradburn, Joseph Grimshaw, J. W. Watkinson, Jesse Baker, John Taylor (innkeeper), Samuel Horrocks, John Taylor (shopkeeper), John Entwistle, John Allanson, James Brearley (poor rate collector), and Mr. James Stott was elected to preside.

The Chairman proposed *"That this meeting doth resolve and order that the Local Government Act, 1858, be and the same is hereby adopted in the township of Kersley."* Mr James Fletcher seconded the motion, after which it was proposed by Mr. Isaac Gee *'That the number of elected members upon the Local Board for the township of Kersley be twelve."* This was seconded by Mr. McDonald, and carried unanimously.

The next meeting was held at the Black Horse Inn on the 30th October 1865, for the purpose of agreeing upon a list of 12 persons to constitute the Kersley Local Board. There was a numerous attendance, which included most of the ratepayers in the township, but after brief discussions the following persons were selected as the first members of the Board.

John Fletcher, Clifton, Harrison Blair, Peel Hall, Samuel Gee, Cotton

Spinner, Samuel Pilkington, Farmer, Johnson Martin, Surgeon, Benjamin Bowker, Innkeeper, Richard Eckersley, Grocer, John Taylor, Grocer, John Partington, Grocer, Thomas Cooke, Spindle Manufacturer, Donald McDonald, Shopkeeper, Robert Prestwich, Grocer.

> **ADOPTION OF THE LOCAL GOVERNMENT ACT AT KERSLEY.**
>
> At three o'clock on Thursday afternoon, a meeting of owners and ratepayers of the township of Kersley was held at the house of Mrs. Turner, Grapes Inn, for the purpose of adopting the Local Government Act, 1858. The meeting was convened by Mr. Johnson Martin, churchwarden, in compliance with a numerously and respectably signed requisition. Amongst those present were the Rev. Edward Mather, B.A., of St. Saviour's Church, Ringley; Wm. Stott, Esq., of the firm of Messrs. Knowles and Stott; Dr. Eames, Captain Topp, and Messrs. John Partington, Thomas Cooke, overseers of the poor; Johnson Martin, churchwarden; Richard Eckersley, collector of assessed taxes, Isaac Gee, Donald Macdonald, Samuel Pilkington, Robert Prestwich, Wm. Holden, John Gerrard, James Fletcher, Samuel Scowcroft, Samuel Gee, poor-law guardian, Hugh Topp, Edmund Isherwood, Peter Bradburn, Joseph Grimshaw, Jesse Baker, John Taylor (innkeeper), Samuel Horrocks, J. W. Watkinson, John Taylor (shopkeeper), John Entwisle, John Allanson, James Brearley, poor rate collector, &c. On the motion of Mr. MARTIN, seconded by Mr. PARTINGTON, Mr. James Stott was appointed chairman. Mr. Charles Holden, of the firm of Messrs. Holden, Andrews, and Holden, solicitors, of Bolton, attended as legal adviser, and read the notice convening the meeting.—In answer to the Chairman, Mr. HOLDEN said the Act required that the requisition should be signed by thirty ratepayers or more; it contained the names of thirty-three owners and ratepayers.
>
> The CHAIRMAN said they all knew the object of the meeting; and he would read to them the resolution he had to propose. It was as follows:—
>
> "That this meeting doth resolve and order that the Local Government Act, 1858, be, and the same is hereby adopted within the township of Kersley."
>
> Mr. JAMES FLETCHER seconded the motion.
>
> The CHAIRMAN asked if any gentleman had any remark to make or any amendment to propose. He wished to allow every one fair play, and would now listen with patience to anything that might be said.
>
> No one attempting to speak, Mr. SAMUEL PILKINGTON said that, so far as the Highway Board was concerned, they had made up their minds to adopt the Act; and he fancied that the silence on the part of the meeting gave consent for its adoption.
>
> The CHAIRMAN: But we must do something more than just give a silent approval.
>
> As no other person offered to speak, the resolution was put and carried unanimously—every one in the room appearing to vote, no hands being held up to the contrary.
>
> Mr. ISAAC GEE said that the resolution having passed so unanimously, there could not be any objection to the one he had now the honour to propose:—
>
> "That the number of elective members of the Local Board for the township of Kersley be twelve."
>
> Mr. MACDONALD seconded the resolution. He was glad to see such a large and influential meeting of ratepayers. It showed that the subject had been thought over, and also proved that the township was anxious to do its own work. Some little sanitary improvement wanted doing in Kersley, and the result of that meeting would show that they were willing and wishful to do it. He believed the adoption of the Local Government Act would be a good thing for Kersley. The township was rapidly progressing, and would, in a few years, be a large town; it was increasing very considerably in the direction of Manchester, which he was glad to see.
>
> The CHAIRMAN: I think twelve a wise adoption: it is better than having a great number.
>
> The resolution was then put and was also carried unanimously.
>
> Mr. SAMUEL GEE said he thought that the largest meeting of ratepayers held in Kersley, and the business transacted the most important for some years past. It was a remarkable circumstance in connection with the management of the public and parochial affairs of Kersley, that they were able to do everything so unanimously. There was no hitch and no dissensions, but everything was done in a comfortable and agreeable manner; and that meeting showed that when the interests of the township required the adoption of an important measure, that they could be unanimous in that also. Although the act had been adopted as it were pro forma, its provisions had been duly discussed amongst themselves, and they were all satisfied with the benefits that were likely to accrue from its adoption. He had now very great pleasure in moving a vote of thanks to Mr. Stott for coming so far (from Southport) and giving them the weight of his influence as well as so ably presiding; all of which showed the interest he felt in the subject of the meeting.
>
> The motion was seconded by Mr. PILKINGTON, and carried unanimously.—Mr. STOTT having briefly acknowledged the compliment, the meeting terminated, the business not having occupied more than thirteen minutes.

Above. From The Bolton Chronicle, 2nd September 1865. A defining moment in the history of Kearsley as the decision is made to form its own Local Board, which would eventually evolve into the Kearsley Urban District Council. This meeting, with local colliery owner James Stott acting as chairman, confirmed that Kearsley would take charge of its own affairs and not be controlled by neighbouring towns such as Farnworth, and remarkably it took less than thirteen minutes.

The first meeting of the Kersley Local Board was held in High Stile Schoolroom on the 15th November, 1865, with all of the members present as well as Mr. Thomas Holden, solicitor, of Bolton. Mr Harrison Blair was appointed as the first Chairman, and a committee was selected to ascertain what officers would be needed, and to define their duties.

Above & next page. In the handwriting of Harrison Blair, newly elected chairman of the Kearsley Local Board, this is the minute book of the very first meeting at the High Stile schoolroom on 15th November 1865.

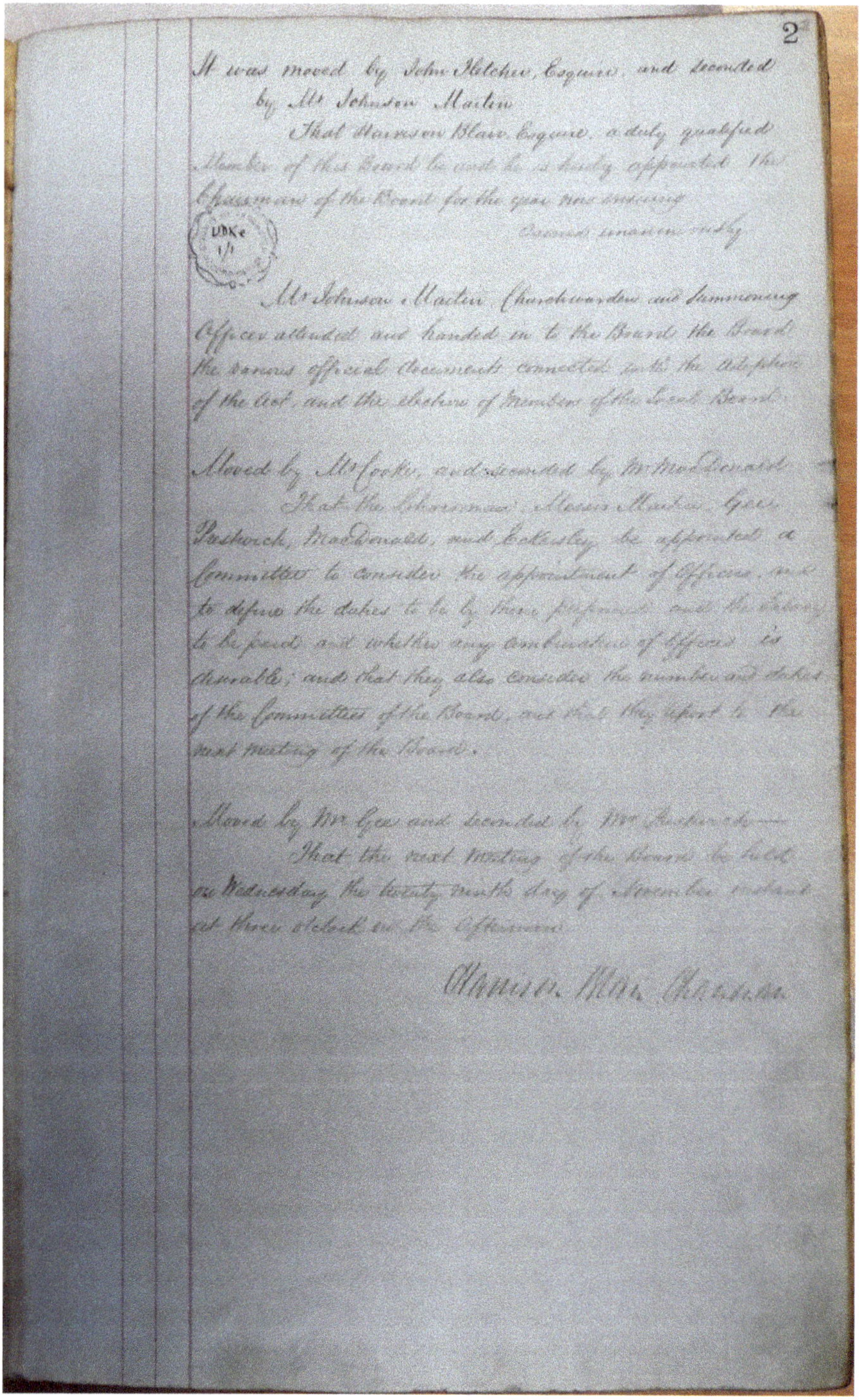

It was moved by John Fletcher, Esquire, and seconded by Mr Johnson Martin

That Harrison Blair, Esquire, a duly qualified Member of this Board be and he is hereby appointed the Chairman of the Board for the year now ensuing

Carried unanimously

Mr Johnson Martin Churchwarden and Summoning Officer attended and handed in to the Board the various official documents connected with the Adoption of the Act, and the election of members of the Local Board.

Moved by Mr Cooke, and seconded by Mr MacDonald

That the Chairman, Messrs Martin, Gee, Pashwick, MacDonald, and Cottesley, be appointed a Committee to consider the appointment of Officers, and to define the duties to be by them performed, and the salary to be paid, and whether any combination of offices is desirable; and that they also consider the number and duties of the Committees of the Board, and that they report to the next meeting of the Board.

Moved by Mr Gee and seconded by Mr Pashwick—

That the next meeting of the Board be held on Wednesday the twenty ninth day of November instant at three o'clock in the afternoon

Harrison Blair Chairman

Left. The Kearsley 'Seal' designed by Harrison Blair and first shown at the Local Board meeting on 10th January 1866. It has a mixture of the Comberbere and Fletcher "arms" because at this time Miss Charlotte Anne Fletcher was Lady of the Manor and was soon to marry the Hon Wellington Cotton, who was heir to the Comberbere title. There is a chevron, palewise, through which is passed an arrow, also palewise, and a sheaf of three arrows on an encircling ribbon.

The Local Board system continued until 1894 when the Local Government Act was again amended to establish Parish Councils with additional responsibilities. Kearsley Urban District Council came into being in 1895.

The Township expanded by 700 acres in 1933, taking in a small portion of Clifton from the Barton Rural District, and also the Ringley and Prestolee portions of the parish of Outwood from the Bury Rural District.

In June 1969 a report by the Royal Commission on Local Government in England put forward recommendations that would mean the disappearance of smaller local authorities all over the country. Kearsley Urban District Council and several other local councils would be absorbed into new a "Metropolitan District" under the control of a larger centralized authority. The report also stated that local councils may continue to exist, however they will have no real power and will be expected to act more as "sounding boards" for local people which can be passed on to the metropolitan district authorities, and in turn to the metropolitan area authority. The die was cast, and, with the Local Government Act of 1972, the system of local governance was reformed completely, and Kearsley Urban District Council was to be no more. Along with other districts of Bolton, Kearsley became a part of Bolton Metropolitan Borough in 1974, and was no longer in charge of its own affairs.

Above. A 1950's Kearsley UDC waste/refuse wagon. In the days before wheelie bins the bin men would carry the metal waste bin from your house to the wagon and tip it in, then return it to your door.

Kearsley Town Hall and Cenotaph

Originally called Highfield House, the Kearsley Town Hall building was purchased by the council in July 1910 for £650, after which a further £500 was spent on alterations and decorating, plus another £150 on furnishings. The council had for many years previously rented just two rooms on the ground floor of this building, but as the town expanded, more staff were also required, and the decision was taken to purchase Highfield House rather than build new premises.

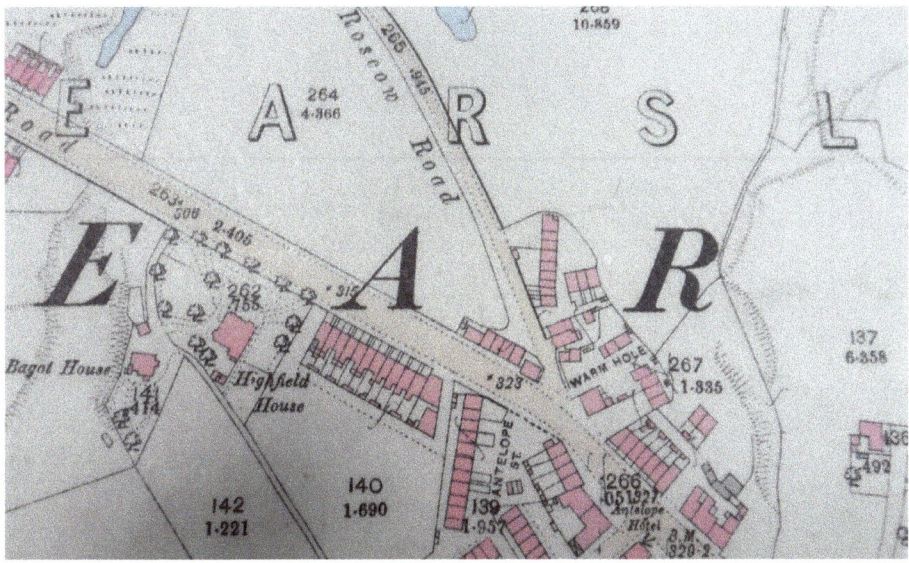

Above. Circa 1890. Highfield House on Bolton Road, which at this time the Kearsley Local Board were renting two downstairs rooms. The area around The Moss Rose public house is called 'Warm Hole,' of which I have been unable to trace how it came by this curious name.

Kearsley Town's Offices.

IMPROVED ACCOMMODATION.

The alterations at Highfield House, Kearsley, which a short time ago was purchased by the Kearsley District Council at a cost of £650, are nearing completion, and yesterday the commodious chamber where the affairs of the township will in future be discussed, was opened in the presence of a representative assembly of townspeople. The necessary alterations and decoration of the premises have been carried out at an estimated cost of £500, with an additional £150 for furnishing, and the much-needed increase of accommodation which the scheme provides will greatly facilitate the work of the Council and its officials. The new Council room is situated on the second floor immediately above the old chamber, and by the removal of the partition wall of a small room above the vestibule the chamber has been given quite a spacious appearance, and with a new horse-shoe shaped table in the centre it will fulfil requirements admirably. A committee room adjoins the new chamber, and two other commodious rooms on the same floor are to be utilized, one by the Surveyor. The Sanitary Inspector will find comfortable quarters in a room in the rear of the ground floor, and whilst the Clerk is to be accommodated in what is at present his assistants' office, the latter will be transferred to the old Council chamber, which will be known as the Rate Office. There is, of course, nothing elaborate about the scheme of decoration, but it is effective. The walls throughout the rooms, corridors, and staircase have been treated in a pleasing shade of pale green parripan wash, the ceiling and frieze in cream duresco; and the dado of leather brown with black bands, is adorned at frequent intervals—too frequent if anything—with the Kearsley Coat of Arms in colours. All the wood work has been oak-grained, the floors have been laid with substantial looking cork carpet, and the premises will be heated with low pressure hot water apparatus, which has been installed in each room. The exterior of the premises has also received attention, and outside the most notable feature is the new entrance opposite the front door of the offices, the approach being made by stone steps. This has been the work of Messrs. E. and S. Street, and the decorations of Mr. John Crossley.

Left. From the Farnworth Journal of 8th July 1910. Details of the purchase of Highfield House, which would now be used solely for Kearsley Urban District Council purposes.

Kearsley Town Hall circa 1950. The original Highfield House building is to the right, and to the left the extension, which was formally opened on Thursday Aug 27th 1936, by Council Chairman Albert Plant.

Above. Late 1940's. Kearsley Town Hall Chamber, and below, the view across from Victoria Road.

Counc. J. Hollinshead, Chairman of Kearsley Council, joined the players in the open roof of the coach outside Kearsley Town Hall and got Nat Lofthouse to say a few words into the microphone.

Above. On Monday 5th of May 1958 the victorious FA cup winning Bolton Wanderers team passed through Kearsley and stopped outside the Town Hall, an estimated 5000 people had lined the streets to celebrate the triumph over Manchester United. They had travelled back from London by train to Manchester, and somewhat unwisely decided to make their way back to Bolton in an open top bus. On the journey through Salford, close to Irlams o'th' height, they were bombarded with stones, sods of earth and fruit amongst many other things. Bolton coach George Taylor described it as 'being ambushed in cheyenne country.'

The Town Hall was sadly demolished at the end of January 2013. The building had been disgracefully left to rack and ruin over a period of several years by Bolton Council, before it was sold, along with the surrounding land, for a pitiful amount.

This wanton act of abandonment was a tragic end for a building that had served the town so well. It had been a focal point in the development of the town and should have been preserved.

Above. 23rd January 2013. The bulldozers stand ominously in front of the Town Hall building.

The stone War Memorial, unveiled in October 1921, still stands in its original location, but, now somewhat bizarrely, against a backdrop of residential houses. At the time of writing the Remembrance Day parade is still fairly well attended even though the number of veterans from the two great wars has diminished.

There are two plaques on the cenotaph, one for WW1, and the other for WW2. The WW1 memorial reads "Lest we forget, in honoured memory of the men of Kearsley who gave their lives in the cause of freedom in the Great War" below this are the names of 151 men who fell in that conflict. For details of all those from Kearsley and Farnworth who died in the Great War the book 'Fallen In The Fight' by Neil and Sue Richardson is highly recommended.

The WW2 plaque reads "To Honour the fallen in the Second World War" below this are the names of a further 61 men, underneath these it reads "May They Rest In Peace."

For the years 1919/20 a temporary cenotaph was placed on the land opposite the top of Stoneclough Brow. The monument, which was an imitation one in the design of a broken column, had the inscription:- Greater love hath no man than this, that a man lay down his life for his friends."-John, ch.15,v.13." Another inscription read, "In loving memory to our fallen comrades;" and a third inscription read "Fervently and sincerely we beg of all classes not to drift into forgetfulness or indifference to the gallant lads who shared in bringing about this victory."

Above. Kearsley folk gather at the temporary memorial opposite Stoneclough Brow in September 1919. The slack heaps from a former colliery at Singing Clough are visible in the background.

Above and right. Some of the local men who lost their lives in the First World War, and the first report that an armistice had been agreed as reported in the Farnworth Journal of November 15th 1918.

THE DAY.

The welcome news so anxiously awaited that an armistice had been signed was received at the "Journal" office, and as it was posted in the windows and the big Union Jack was hung out every passer halted to grasp the truth and immediately hurried off to let their friends know and share in their rejoicings. There were a few doubting Thomases who, not content with the clear statement, tried to get it confirmed in the office. The children who were on holiday owing to the influenza outbreak rushed home with the news and were soon out in the streets again, marching in little processions with their flags and cheering and singing. In half an hour flags were flying from all points of vantage and from the windows of cottage houses in the humblest street, whilst strings of bannerettes soon followed, and in Northumberland-st. was hung suspended an effigy of the Kaiser. The bells of the Parish Church were soon merrily ringing and sending the tidings near and far, buzzers were not slow in opening their throats, and the news was the signal for

A General Cessation of Operations

in works and mills. It was not necessary to pile up the munitions after the fighting had stopped. "Cease firing" on the western front meant "Cease working" on the home front! The army in the trenches having finished their job, the army at home was at least justified in suspending its job. In some

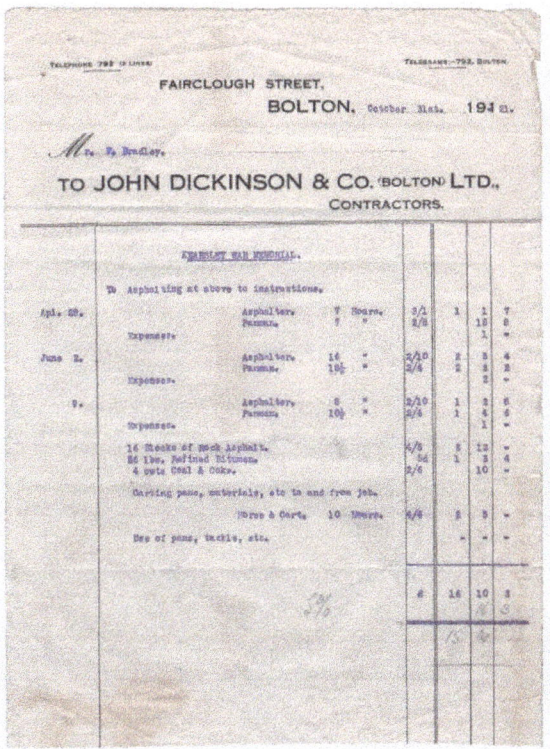

Above September 2013. The Kearsley Cenotaph stands isolated after the demolition of the Town Hall building.

Left. An invoice dated October 31st 1921 for asphalting at the War Memorial. It is interesting to note the transportation method of the materials was still done by horse and cart.

KEARSLEY HEROES HONOURED.

Sgt. J. PARTINGTON.   **Sgt. A. CROOK.**   **Cpl. J. HARDMAN.**   **Pte. R. GOODRAM.**

Four more Kearsley heroes were honoured last week, when, at a meeting in the Council offices, Mr. J. Howard, J.P., the chairman of the District Council, handed to them gold watches and illuminated addresses subscribed for by their own townspeople. He expressed the grateful admiration which the residents had for all the men who had gone from amongst them to fight for liberty and justice and their pleasure that so many of them had been selected for special honours. The following were the recipients:—

Sergeant John Partington, of the Grenadier Guards, living at 135, Primrose-st., whose name is on the Roll of Honour of St. Peter's Church. He worked at the Earl of Bradford's Colliery, Great Lever, and was a member of the Farnworth Anglers Association. He was awarded the Military Medal for gallantry during the heavy fighting of March 1918. The Guards were in a rearguard action and on the morning of March 28th dug in and held the Germans, who made three attacks during the day. Sergeant Partington was in the piquet line, 150 yards in front of which was an outpost of an officer and five men. The officer and three of the men were wounded and Sergeant Partington crawled out and dragged the officer back. He then went out again for the wounded men, when the Germans made another attack. He and two men held the post for 14 hours, up to the waist in water, until the night, when they were relieved. He has been in much heavy fighting and has been fortunate enough to escape being wounded. He has recently returned from Cologne, where his regiment forms part of the army of occupation.

Corporal Alfred Crook, of the Lancashire Fusiliers, lives at 39, Lord-st. He served his time as a plumber with Messrs. Brooks Bros., and his name is on the Roll of Honour of the Kearsley Mount Wesleyan Church. He was awarded the Military Medal for gallantry in warm fighting during an attack by the Germans on April 25th, 1918. Two months later he was taken prisoner by the Germans when wounded in the arm and leg, and has just been repatriated.

Corporal Joseph Hardman, of the Highland Light Infantry, who lives at 18, Manchester-rd., had some difficulty in persuading recruiting officers to accept him for the army, and after some time got into the Royal Scots, from which he was later transferred. He was in charge of the stretcher bearers during a bombing raid by his company on the German trenches on September 22nd, 1917, and was awarded the Military Medal for his fearlessness and skill in collecting and evacuating the wounded under heavy shell fire. Later he was taken prisoner by the Germans and has just been repatriated. His name is on the Kearsley Mount Wesleyan Roll of Honour and he worked at the Drake Mill as a piecer.

Private R. Goodram gained the Military Medal by his gallantry in rescuing wounded soldiers during the Vimy Ridge encounter in May 1916, being under heavy shell fire at the time. Later he was gassed and when he was able to get home in November of the same year he received the Medal at the Council Offices at the hands of Captain Duncan Heyes. Later still he was taken prisoner by the Germans and has recently returned to his home at 13, Grove-st., off Mather-st. He is in the L.N.L. Regt.

Above. Incredible stories of bravery from the Farnworth Journal of January 31st 1919.

Kearsley Mount Convalescent Home on a postcard dated April 1920. I have found no other mention of this facility, but it must have been in the Kearsley Mount area.

STONECLOUGH SOLDIER'S BRAVERY

DECORATED BY FIELD-MARSHAL MONTGOMERY

The bravery of a Stoneclough soldier during the hard fighting immediately after D-Day has earned for him the award of the Military Medal. He is Sergt. Norris Clegg, of 38, Edward-st., Stoneclough. He was serving with the Royal Scots when they crossed into France on D-4 Day, and the following is the official citation of his action, received at his home this week.

"On December 3rd, 1944, in the assault on Blerick, Corpl. Clegg was the leading section commander of 8 Platoon, "A" Co., 6th Batt. the Royal Scots Fusiliers. "A" company was the assault company and Corpl. Clegg's company was in the leading kangaroo. The leading section ran into a minefield and the men in the kangaroos were halted. Corpl. Clegg, without any hesitation, ordered his section to de-tank, and formed them up preparatory to crossing the very open and exposed ground between the obstacle and the company objective. This he organized despite being under enemy small arms fire and heavy mortar and shell fire. He himself then lead a section across the open ground. The going was very difficult, being covered with obstacles and pitted with bomb holes, but Corpl. Clegg continued to advance with his section.

Corpl. Clegg himself was wounded in the leg before reaching the objective. He completely disregarded his wounds, however, and showing great bravery continued to control his section and urged them on. He himself was responsible for the capture of two prisoners on the objective. It was not until the section had reached the objective and he had reported to his platoon commander that he allowed himself to rest and have his wound attended.

Throughout Corpl. Clegg was conspicuous for his leadership, and was an inspiration to the rest of his company. Had it not been for his action and initiative there is no doubt that the company would not have reached its objective until some time later."

Sergt. Clegg, who is married and has two children, attended the Ringley St. Saviour's schools. He was a schoolboy swimmer, and was also keenly interested in football, playing for the school. He is 29 years of age, and before joining the Army in March, 1940, worked at Messrs. Fletcher's Paper Mills, Stoneclough.

Our picture shows Sergt. Clegg being decorated at Lubeck by Field Marshal B. Montgomery.

Seaman's Award

Ringley Honours D.S.M.

O.S .C. WARDLE

"For courage and resolution in pressing home a successful attack on the enemy's forces in enemy coastal waters" is the official citation which accompanies the award of the D.S.M. to O./S. Cyril Wardle (19), son of Mr. and Mrs. H. T. Wardle, 10, Vale-ave., Stoneclough. He is now lying badly wounded in a naval hospital in the south. In the words of his mother, who has been to see him, "It is only his pluck that has brought him through." At a public meeting called by the Vicar of Ringley on Friday at St. Saviour's school, and attended by people of several organizations in the district it was decided to inaugurate a fund with the twofold purpose of turning the tribute of local people into a tangible form and in order to help to reinstate him on his return. A committee, including Messrs. Kirkman and Morgan, treasurer and secretary, and the Rev. Matthews, chairman, was appointed and collectors for various parts of Ringley and Prestolee were appointed. Boxes are to be placed in shops and public houses. Several donations have already been promised and a house-to-house collection will be held. The chairman stressed that although the meeting had been called by the church the effort was strictly undenominational, and it was to be a tribute from everybody in the district and not confined to any one particular body.

Present at the meeting were representatives from Fletcher's Paper Mill where O./S. Wardle worked before his call-up in June, 1942, having volunteered in February of that year. He went to sea three months after joining and had seen action several times. He was a choirboy at St. Saviour's, and was also a member of the St. Saviour's day school football team.

Above Left. Corporal Norris Clegg of Stoneclough receives a medal from Field Marshall Montgomery in January 1946. **Above Right.** Cyril Wardle of Ringley receives the Distinguished Service Medal in October 1943.

Right. From the Farnworth Journal. Bomb damage from the local area which could only be reported after the end of the Second World War.

A bomb had landed on what is now Melville Road, at the side of the Co-Op on Springfield Road. Local ladies Lily Holker and Betty Bostock both lived within 100 yards of the explosion, and still do to this day. They explained *'On the evening of August 28th 1940 the Luftwaffe had carried out a bombing raid on Manchester and the air raid warning siren had sounded in Kearsley, prompting them to take refuge in their Anderson Shelters and to make sure no lighting whatsoever was visible. Around midnight the all clear was sounded and everyone could go back to bed. A short

BOMB DAMAGE DURING THE WAR

By the courtesy of Mr. H. Cunliffe (Farnworth), Mr. F. Roberts (Kearsley), Mr. H. Lomax (Worsley) and Mr. W. Kelly (Little Lever) we are now able to report for the first time the damage done in the district by enemy aircraft during the war.

Farnworth
1940

October 8.—One H.E. bomb at Plodder-lane, no casualties.
October 19th.—Three H.E. bombs in Hall-lane, no casualties.
December 12.—Two H.E. bombs in Hall-lane. No casualties.

1941

January 9.—Fifty incendiary bombs in Harper Green and Plodder-lane, no casualties.

Kearsley
1940

August 28.—One H.E. bomb Springfield-rd., near F. and K. Co-op. branch, one person injured.
December 12.—Two parachute flares at Town Hall and Bolton-rd., no casualties.

1941

April 26.—Four H.E. bombs near Unity Brook, no casualties.
July 9th.—Two H.E. bombs on River Irwell, no casualties.

Little Lever
1940

December 22.—About 100 incendiary bombs in Stopes-rd. area, no casualties.

Worsley
1940

August 8.—Three H.E. bombs near Vicars Hall farm and near Manchester-rd., Walkden, no casualties.
August 28.—Four H.E. bombs near Sandhole Pit, Vulcan Hotel and Bridgewater Hotel, 24 injured.
September 7.—Six H.E. bombs near Mable and Glen-avenues, Mulgrave-rd., East Lancashire-road, near Burton's factory, two injured.
September 26—Ten H.E. bombs near Hill Farm, Linnyshaw Farm, Sandhole Pit, and Moss-lane. No casualties.
October 7.—One H.E. west side Worsley-rd. housing estate. No casualties.
October 9.—Numerous incendiary and six H.E. bombs on Parr Fold Park, Town's Yard, Back Walkden-rd., Brindley-street Memorial-rd. High Level railway bridge, Technical School, Hilton-lane, railway embankment, field opposite Burton's mill, Welbeck-rd., Sandwich-st., between Birch-rd. and Roe Green, Ryecroft, Worsley-rd., telephone exchange and Park-rd. No casualties.
October 10.—One H.E. at coal wharf, Alfred-st. No casualties.
October 26.—Two H.E. bombs near Drywood Hall and field. No casualties.
October 27.—20 Incendiary bombs near Granary-lane. No casualties.
October 28.—One H.E. bomb at Clegg's-lane. No casualties.
December 22.—Two incendiary 5 H.E. bombs at Newearth-rd., Longview-drive., The Cottage, Barton-rd., Clegg's-lane. Four killed, six injured.
December 23.—Several incendiary, five H.E. bombs and two parachute mines at Bridge-water Hotel, Worsley Green, Worsley Station embankment, Wardley Cemetery, and near Wardley Grange Farm. No casualties.

1941

January 9.—Many incendiary bombs at Malkins Wood Farm, between Old Farm and Old Warke Dam, the fields south of Bridgewater Canal. No casualties.
April 6.—One H.E. bomb at Grange Farm. No casualties.

1944

December 23.—One flying bomb (V.1) at Woodstock-drive. One killed, four injured.

time later a terrific bang was heard causing hundreds of windows to blow in on dozens of surrounding houses, and even internal doors to slam shut. The bomb had landed near to the side of the shops that still stand there today, at the time the Co-Op was the closest to the impact. Lilly says her father carried her back outside into their shelter, which was a brick structure with a tin roof, built specially to accommodate all seven of the family. "In the morning we went to look at the large crater which had not been fenced off. Incredibly the shop had suffered little damage, but the house across the road, at number 190 Springfield Road, had the whole side blown off which exposed the stairs and the bathroom. A girl who lived there was injured and had to go to hospital.' As to why the Germans decided to drop a bomb on Springfield Road we will never fully know, but both ladies also gave an account of the story that went around the neighbourhood at the time, it is purely conjecture, but worth noting.

The tale is that around this time the land that now makes up Alderbank Close was used as a pig farm, it was formerly the site of a larger dairy farm named Taskers Lane Farm that had been run by the Co-Op. The man who ran this pig farm had a van and had been out in it that evening, and after the all clear had sounded then decided to drive it home, but with the headlights on, now confident that it was safe to do so. A German bomber still lingering around the area, looking for signs of life on which to drop any remaining bombs,' may have spotted the unwitting farmer and targeted his route, suspecting it may be a built up area. At the time this story remained only as gossip, but nearly eighty years later it is still an interesting anecdote to the event.

Kearsley Library and Kearsley Royal British Legion

The first Kearsley branch library was situated at a large house which stood on Springfield Road next to what is now number 129. This house was known as Moss Dene and had previously been the residence of the Holden family who ran the nearby Moss Rose mill. During the late 1940's the house was used jointly as a library, and as the headquarters of the Kearsley branch of the Royal British Legion.

The Kearsley British Legion had formed in 1941, although before that time there was a committee operating the United Services fund. The branch had no premises but engaged at St. Stephen's school for any meetings they had. Right through the war years and afterwards they were busy recruiting members, and in 1949 had raised enough money to purchase the premises outright as well as to furnish them. Membership was at first confined to ex-servicemen and women but eventually this was relaxed to allow anyone to apply to join.

In 1966 the house was taken down and new purpose built premises erected, but sadly due to decreasing membership these closed in 2002, and were eventually demolished during 2003. The site is now occupied by flats built by St Vincent's Housing Association.

Above. Regulars of the Kearsley Royal British Legion in high spirits as they wait to depart on a day trip in the mid 1960's. In the background are the old terraced houses that dated from the late 19th century, these were demolished at the end of 1968 with the Springfield Gardens complex of flats built over the site.

The second Kearsley Library building on Oakes Street opened on Tuesday 31st October 1950. The opening ceremony was performed by Lady Openshaw, J.P, chairman of the County Libraries Committee who said she *"hoped it would bring pleasure and education to the people of Kearsley. No township was complete without a library service, and that was why she was keen to see that every corner of the administrative county should be covered either by a central library, a branch library or a mobile library van. Reading was on of the most important part of education to-day."*

Above. The interior of the former Kearsley Branch Library on Oakes Street.

The first book was issued to County Alderman, Richard Matthews, Chairman of the Kearsley and Little Lever Library Sub-Committee, who had been instrumental in securing the new library building for Kearsley.

Above. Kearsley Library, Oakes Street, in the late 1950's. The library closed in the mid 1980's and residential houses numbered 54 to 58 Oakes Street now cover the site.

Name Derivations

Kearsley

The name derives from two words, but the first part may have come from two possible sources. It is thought to either be made up from 'cærse' and 'leah', with 'cærse' the Anglo-Saxon name for cress or water-cress, and 'leah' which is Anglo Saxon for an open space, clearing or 'untilled' meadowland. Leah (now usually shortened to 'ley') is often used as a termination for place names. Alternatively it may derive from the word 'gærs' or 'gers', which is grass in Anglo-Saxon, again coupled with the word 'leah.'

In this book you will notice in various articles and documents that Kearsley is often spelt without the letter 'a,' hence Kersley. For example the Ordnance Survey map of 1848 uses Kearsley, but twenty years later the newly formed Clifton and Kersley Coal Company decided against using the 'a' within its name. It seems that up until around 1900 it was simply a matter of choice, but during the early twentieth century the 'a' stuck for good.

Prestolee

There are two likely options, firstly is that the name derives from two words- 'Priest' and 'leah.'

In the early 1500's and probably for some time before this, there was an Oratory or Roman Catholic Chapel upon the site of Farnworth Hall (built 1603, demolished circa 1900), which occupied a site between what is now Hall Lane and Fylde Street in the Moses Gate area. The Oratory owned land at Prestolee so it is thought the name derives from two words, 'Priest' and the Anglo-Saxon word 'leah'. Priests leah' would have been the land owned by the priests at the Oratory, and over time local parlance could have modified this to Prestolee.

Another serious consideration is that it derives from 'Prestall' and 'leah.' The area around what is now Presto Street was known as Prestall after the Prestall family, which owned the land around it. It is intriguing that the name Presto Street is taken rather than Prestall Street, there is no record of how this came about. It is also interesting to note that one of the heirs to this land was Robert Bolton who is named as 'of Prestolee' in the *gentleman, upright and law-abiding men of the county aforesaid, jurors*' in the Salford Hundred document relating to the repair of Ringley Bridge on page 390.

If the Prestall family had owned land at Prestolee it is not inconceivable that this could have been Prestall's 'leah.'

Stoneclough
The name derives from two words, firstly the Anglo-Saxon word 'stán' which means stone, and 'clough' or 'clud', which means hill. So Stoneclough, or 'stan clud' literally means stony hill.

Ringley
The name derives from the old English words 'hring' which means a ring or circle, and 'leah' which is Anglo Saxon for an open space, clearing or 'untilled' meadowland.

River Irwell
First mentioned in Roger De Lacy's Charter Of Brandwood around 1200. The name comes from the old English, or Semi-Saxon, 'irre' or 'eorre' meaning angry, straying or wandering, and 'welle' meaning flowing water. Hence, Irrewelle – the wandering or angry river (flowing water).

Farnworth
Originally Anglo-Saxon or old English 'Ffordword' – Ferneworth- Fearnworth – Farnworth. The old English word 'Fern' can take various similar meanings, with the most likely simply being 'flowerless plants,' of which the area was abundant. The word 'worth' was also used by the Anglo-Saxons to mean 'enclosure' or 'an estate.' The most likely meaning of Farnworth would originate from an 'enclosure amongst the ferns.'

Halshaw Moor
The central and south eastern part of Farnworth, and north western part of Kearsley was also commonly referred to as Halshaw Moor for at least a couple of centuries. There are a number of differing but equally plausible explanations as to how it took its name.

The first of which is that an ancient shoemaker and farmer, named Alec Shaw, owned large areas of land in the locality. And it seems over time that Alec Shaw's moor became altered, probably through ease of pronunciation to Al Shaw's moor then eventually Halshaw Moor.

Old Alec Shaw's home was located nearly opposite to what is now the Clock Face public house, in fact this small area of the town was actually known as Clockface, on account of one of his more unusual acts. Legend has it that Alec became so irritated with people knocking on his door to ask the time, he removed his clock from his kitchen wall and fixed it to the front of his cottage for people to see without disturbing him.

Another credible interpretation is that during the late 16th century and early 17th century a man named Robtus de Halsall was one of the principal landowners in the area. This could again have led to Halsalls Moor being altered slightly by familiarity, and the local dialect, to Halshaw Moor. Either way, no definitive attestation exists.

Clifton

The origin of its name is the cause of some debate, but there are two main theories. One is that part of the village was known as Cliveley, and 'Clive-tún' would have been 'enclosure of Clive,' as 'tún' was the Anglo-Saxon name for an enclosure or settlement. The other is that the old English 'Clif' meaning cliff, slope or riverbank and 'tun' meaning 'town,' 'settlement,' 'enclosure' or 'village.'

Bolton

From the old English 'Bothl' or 'Botl' meaning house or dwelling, and 'tun' meaning 'town,' 'settlement,' 'enclosure' or 'village.' Once known as Bolton-Le-Moors, i.e. Bolton on the moors.

Salford Hundred

The term 'Salford Hundred' is merely the administrative area covered by the judicial and military system that was based in Salford. The term 'hundred' is recorded as far back as the 10th century and there is some uncertainty as to how the term originated. It may have been down to a certain area of land, or how many men under arms it would take to control per 100 homes for example.

The Salford Hundred covered an area slightly larger than what is currently the Metropolitan County of Greater Manchester. A 'Hundred' was usually part of a 'shire' and Salford came under the authority of the historic county of Lancashire, and Interestingly it was also known as 'Salfordshire' during the middle ages. By the early 19th century power had dissolved to other authorities in and around Manchester and Lancashire, but the ancient term survived in use until 1971 when, finally, the High Court known as the Court of the Hundred of Salford was abandoned. John Speed's map of Lancashire from 1610 gives an excellent illustration of the area overseen by the Salford Hundred.

Every so often the argument is raised as to whether Kearsley (or indeed Bolton) is part of, or should be part of, Greater Manchester or Lancashire. Different perspectives and current viewpoints will always ensue, but as far as history goes Kearsley was once under the administration of the Salford Hundred in Salfordshire. But Salfordshire was under the administrative rule of Lancashire, so it can be contended that Kearsley was in both. I hope that clears that up!

Above. Circa 1900. The Grapes hotel at Stoneclough is to the right with a couple of horse-drawn cabs waiting outside. The houses are long gone and the pub car park now occupies the area. The building nearest to the pub has an alleyway that is now bricked up and is incorporated into the main building.

Circa 1893. Barnfield House, Ringley. Currently the home of the Kearsley and Ringley Conservative Club. At this time it was the home of Dr Thomas Boles Eames and family. It is worth noting the ladies in their marvellous attire and a man sat at the window above the main door to the building.

Circa 1893. Another view of Barnfield House from the top of Ringley Road. Note the old gas lamp on the corner and how much narrower the main road leading toward Market Street is. This road was widened and straightened out during the 1930's, but the cobbles seen here remain under the tarmac. A truly wonderful picture giving a glimpse of village life before the housing estates and mass popularity of motor vehicles.

Above. Circa 1890's, the rear of Barnfield House, it is unclear what the building to the right was, but it may just have been a residence or part of a stables for the family horses. The doorway and most of the downstairs windows on this side of the building have been bricked up for many years.

Group at the official opening of the Kearsley and Ringley Conservative Club on Monday evening. Left to right: Mr I. A. Johnston, prospective parliamentary candidate; Mr Kenneth Ross, managing director, Robert Fletcher and Son Ltd.; Stoneclough, the opener; Mr A. J. Johnson, club president; Mr Stanley Windle, ACC representative, and Mr Mark Hobson, who was presented with the badge of honour for long service.

Left. The official opening of the Kearsley and Ringley Conservative Club new premises at Barnfield House on Monday 30th September 1968. For seventy years previous the Club had been situated in two old houses a short distance away on Edward Street. These houses were knocked down to make way for a car park for Fletchers Paper Mill.

New club well and truly launched

THE NEW Kearsley and Ringley Conservative Club was well and truly launched on its way on Monday night with a spate of good wishes from the opener and other speakers—and a bumper attendance which augurs well for the club's future success.

The club president, Mr A. J. Johnson, told the audience in his introductory remarks: "It's a do-it-yourself job, but we have a nice homely little club and all we want now is plenty of support."

He appealed to members who might have any ideas for improving the club in any way to come out into the open with them, and not to keep any likely ideas in their minds only. "We might not be the biggest club in the district — but we're the best," he said.

Mr Kenneth Ross, managing director of Robert Fletcher and Son Ltd, Stoneclough, in officially declaring the club open — it has actually been in use for some time — said: "You are good neighbours and near neighbours and we wish you all the very best for the future."

VERY STRICT

Referring to a framed cutting from a Journal feature about old days at the club, which hangs on the wall of the lounge, Mr Ross said the committee away back in the club's early days were obviously very strict. "They banned clogs and orange peel," he notice."

They had been very careful of the members' money in those old days as the present officials were. "Unfortunately those old days were rather thirsty ones for members for there were no drinks available—

Then eventually came the repeal of Prohibition — which Stoneclough edition — which must have been a very popular move."

Mr Ross said he was delighted that the club allowed women members and he paid tribute to the help the women had been over the years the club had existed in the old premises.

Speaking of the day he first visited the village many years ago, Mr Ross said: "It was pouring rain and I was walking along Market Street when a woman spoke to me and said 'Welcome, isn't this lovely gentle rain.' A remark I've always remembered."

As a result of years of dogged persistence, said Mr Ross, a fine new club had now emerged from what was once the home and surgery of the two Dr Eanes — father and son, whom between them had been there for a period of almost a century.

The audience gave a cordial welcome to Mr I. A. Johnston, prospective Conservative parliamentary candidate, and Mrs Johnston.

Mr Johnston said he was delighted to be present at a pleasant opening of such a pleasant new Conservative Club. "The clubs are the bulwarks of our party throughout the country," he said.

"I don't wish to dwell too long on political matters on such a very pleasant social occasion. But I would like to say a few words on the present situation."

Referring to recent speeches by Mr Enoch Powell, Mr Johnston said: "I think these speeches have done good service to the Conservative party and have given us a jolt."

He added that the Conservative party had three objects — to put this country first, encouragement of free enterprise and to see to it that it would be better for people to be working than out of work. If help had to be given to people in difficulties then this should be given only to the right type of person.

Other guests at the opening were Mr Stanley Windle, representing the Association of Conservative Clubs, County Counc L. J. Brady, chairman, Farnworth Conservative Association, Mr W. Hardman, president, Farnworth Amalgamation, and Mrs Butterworth, the former agent.

From the Farnworth Journal, October 3rd, 1968.

Above and Below. 1987. Work begins on the extension to the Conservative Club. The former storage buildings of Fletchers Paper Mill can be seen in the background of the top picture. These were destroyed by fire just a few years afterwards.

Education and Religion in Kearsley

It is difficult to determine what can lay-claim to have been the first school in the Kearsley locality, but in the will of Nathan Wallworth, benefactor of St. Saviours Church, Ringley, dated October 15th 1640, he clearly states that a schoolhouse has been established, and an endowment put in place to fund it along with a schoolmaster (see page 282). I have been unable to find an earlier record regarding a place of education, but that it is not to say there was not any prior to this time.

The Mather School, also known as High Stile School, does seem to have been the first in the area not directly connected to any specific Church, or place of worship, when founded by Henry Mather in 1752. Henry Mather passed away in 1758 at the age of 79, but the school continued to be funded by the Mather charity which he had setup for that purpose, nearby Mather Street was also later named in recognition of this kind benefactor. Located at High Stile Fold, the school closed in 1837 when the children transferred to the new St. John's school and the Mather Charity Fund of £80 per annum also went to the new school.

Known as Cinderhill School and located at the top of Ringley Brow (now Ringley Road) where it meets the main road towards Stand and Whitefield, there stood a small row of three storey cottages, and the old School was held in the garrets (attics or loft spaces) of these cottages. There are no definite dates as to when this 'cottage school' was in operation, but the best guess is from around the late 1700's to the 1820's. In 1835 another Sunday School was built at Cinderhill and endowed by the eccentric character James Seddon, who was known locally as known as Dictum Factum (Latin - said, done), It is thought this school closed around 1875.

Up at Kearsley Mount a school was started around 1857 in the cellar at 184 Manchester Road, then occupied by Mrs. Maria Unsworth. The teachers were Miss Letitia Brooks and Miss Jane Gooden. At this time a Sunday School was also established in the cellar, the first teachers were Mrs. Maria Unsworth, who lived at the premises, Miss Gooden and John Files. They were later joined by Mrs. Timbrel, Mr James Edwards, Mr Dennis Lever, and Mr. Thomas Partington. From 1861, the scholars would march from the cellar School to Kearsley House, at the top of Taskers Lane, to attend the Church service in a room that Harrison Blair had had licensed by the Bishop of Manchester for Divine Service.

The cellar was also used as a Night School for three evenings a week for the men and boys of the district. They paid one penny per night and were expected to pay for their own candles. Most, if not all, would have also had a long hard day at work before attending. The children of the cellar School were transferred to St. Stephen's day school when it opened in 1863.

In 1806 Mr Roger Holland and family came to reside at Birch House, the magnificent residence that stood approximately where the first houses are on Bolton Road if you turn left out of Bentley Street, Farnworth. The family originated from Manchester, but Roger Holland was determined to establish a school in the locality, and so in February 1808 he made use of the old Grammar school building that stood across from what is now the bottom of Harrowby Street. The school immediately became overcrowded with scholars, so Mr Holland rented another building close-by, but this too was insufficient to cope with the number of children eager to attend. During this time he had been in discussions with the group of nonconformists who were planning to build what was to become Halshaw Moor Chapel at Withington Croft, but eventually they went their separate ways, as Roger Holland wanted the Chapel to be put under a strict Methodist discipline and the other gentlemen found this unacceptable. The Halshaw Moor Chapel went on to open their Sunday school on June 23rd 1816.

Roger Holland went on to build what became known as 'Holland's School' in 1810 at the corner of Church Road and Market Street. The school was rebuilt and enlarged in 1868, and records show that in January 1900 it had 468 scholars attending, which was the highest number of the 18 schools in the area.

Above. The original Holland's School building before it was rebuilt in 1868.

Below. Mr and Mrs Roger Holland.

Above. Another view of Holland's School prior to rebuilding in 1868.

Below. The rebuilt and enlarged Holland's School in 1910. Today the buildings are used as The Holland's Nursing Home.

More Recollections.

By an Old Farnworthian.
HOLLANDS' SCHOOL.

Aw never tak a walk up Market-st. but aw turn mi een to Hollands' Skoo, and mi thoughts wander back to tort sixty yer ago, an th' owd faces come to mi mind as were to be seen at that time. Aw remember th' names o some oth' superintendents un teachers, including Mr. Horrocks, as lived in a big heawse at th' eend of Crow Bank, David Lord, painter, Thomas Crompton, shoemaker, Joseph Leach, Peter Greenhalgh, Charles Thornton, un an owd gentlemon cawd Mr. Walker, as lived in a big heawse on Bowton-rd., to'ther side of George Green Lone. It wer a Sunday skoo for no particular sort, but for folk of aw denominations. Aw were but a little lad when aw were tan to it but aw recollect um givin' mi a paddle wi' th' alphabet an some short texts on it. Aw geet likin' to go in time un dursn't miss, for if aw did un eawr folk geet t' know an aw'd for't go t' bed beawt baggin' that neet. One Sunday some of us lads had a wawk reawnd Darley, isted o goin' t' skoo, but we knowed abeawt it, un as soon as aw geet whoam aw geet a good hidin' un were sent t' bed. Ther were a chap cawd Jim Ansdell teiched t' class as aw were in un he lived facin' us un towd um when aw hadn't bin. One Sunday he'd bin tellin' us abeawt Joseph un his brethren, un at last he ses to us "Neaw why did they put Joseph in the pit?" None on um spoke, so aw says, "Aw know." "Well, why?" he says. "Why, for t' keep him beawt baggin," aw said. He towd mi t' go t' bottom o'th' class. He were tellin' us abeawt th' "Prodigal Son" another Sunday, un at th' finish for t' see what notice we'd tan on him he ax'd us who were sorry as t' Prodigal had come back, un one lad says: "Why, th' fat cawve, aw'll bet." Every Sunday forenoon, at ten o'clock, aw t' scholars used to march fro t' skoo deawn Market-st. to th' owd Chapel facin' th' "Journal" Office, for t' yer a sermon preiched, un every Whitsun Friday aw t' scholars ud meet at t' skoo un march i' procession to Mr. Walker's, on Bowton-rd., where wi'd aw get an orange apiece. We'd free rompin' abeawt th' greawnds for an heawr or two, un then marched back to th' skoo un ha' buns un coffee. There were a band used t' lead us for a deol o' years as we used t' caw th' "ladies' band." It were t' Worsley Yeomanry Band, un they could play, too. There were no lessons for us every fust Sunday afternoon i' t' month, but an address fro' different superintendents un teichers. It were gin cawt i' th' forenoon one Sunday as Peter Greenhalgh—un whoa i' Farn'oth didn't know Peter?—would speak i' th' afternoon, un when aw geet whoam aw towd cawr folk as Peter Greenhalgh were givin' a dress. They towd me t' ax for it; un they kidded me abeawt it a greight while after.

[Photo by Greenhalgh & Sons.]
MR. R. H. CUNLIFFE, Superintendent.

Above. From the Farnworth Journal, September 30th 1910. Superintendant at Holland's School at the time of its Centenary celebrations, Mr. R.H. Cunliffe.

Left. Recollections of Holland's School told in 'Lanky Twang,' from the Farnworth Journal of August 5th 1910.

Ringley Weslyan Chapel and school

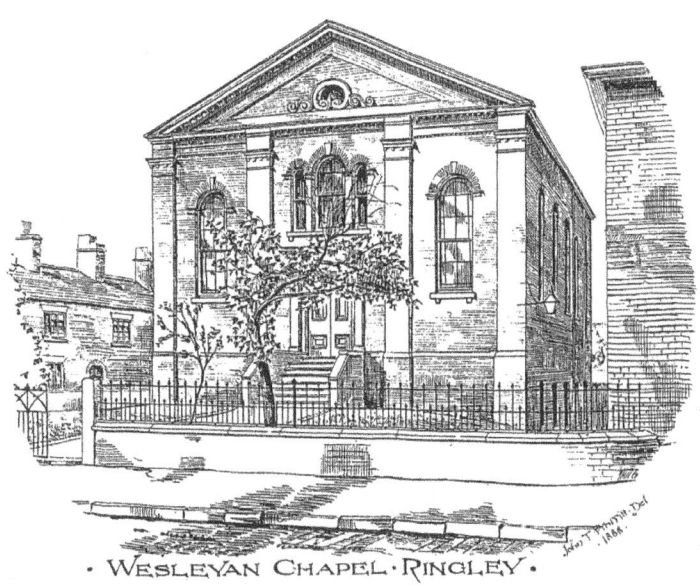

· WESLEYAN CHAPEL · RINGLEY ·

LAYING THE CORNER STONE OF A NEW WESLEYAN CHAPEL AT RINGLEY.

The ceremony of laying the corner stone of a new Wesleyan Chapel was performed at Ringley on Saturday afternoon. A Sunday school and preaching station have been established here by the Wesleyan Methodists for upwards of 15 years, the services as well as the Sabbath school work being hitherto conducted in the upper room of a joiner's shop, not only at great inconvenience but at great discomfort to those engaged. These services have been attended with the most gratifying results, the congregation at the present time averaging from 200 to 250, which is quite as many as the room will accommodate, while the number of scholars upon the books is 280. The project for erecting a chapel was first mooted six or seven years ago, but from a variety of circumstances, amongst which may be mentioned the American war, and the consequent distress in the cotton trade, nothing practical was done in the matter until within the last twelve months, and the energetic exertions then put forth were owing in a great measure to the efforts of Mr. W. S. Lawn, the superintendent of the school, and secretary of the Lancashire and Yorkshire Railway Company. Mr. Lawn made the trustees a gift of a plot of land as a site for the new building, and his liberality being worthily seconded by other gentlemen in the neighbourhood, a sum was soon promised which induced the trustees to proceed at once with the erection. Designs were prepared by Messrs. Simpson and Sons, of Leeds, and with a few slight modifications were accepted; and the building will be erected in a modern style of architecture, 60 feet long by 42 feet wide, and will be capable of accommodating about 400 persons, in addition to which there will be underneath the chapel a spacious room for Sunday school purposes. A gallery for the use of the elder scholars will be constructed at one end of the building, and will be fitted with open benches for seating about 90 children; and a number of free benches will also be provided in the body of the chapel for the accommodation of about 60 persons. The contractor for the erection is Mr. John Lord, of Farnworth, who however has sub-let the joinering to Messrs. Coope Brothers, and the masonary to Mr. Samuel Coucill, of Farnworth. The cost will be about £1500, towards which about £900 has already been promised, and the building is expected to be completed towards the end of the year.

Above. 1888. The Chapel stood to the left hand side of the convenience store currently at 104 Market Street until it was demolished in the early 1960's. Nearby Chapel Street is a reminder of what was sited here previously.

Left. From The Bolton Chronicle, Saturday 10th June 1865, Report of laying the corner stone of the Weslyan Chapel at Ringley on the previous Saturday.

After the stone laying ceremony of the Chapel, Mr J.G. Bradley gave an account entitled 'The rise and progress of Methodism at Ringley,' of which a brief overview is as follows.

"In the year 1797 there was an incumbent at Little Lever chapel of ease, named Dillon, a thoroughly evangelical preacher. Under his ministrations four men residing at Ringley, named John Lord, James Lord, Joshua Lord and Timothy Roscoe were converted, Joshua Lord finding peace with God in the club-room of the public house opposite the Little Lever chapel of ease known by the name of the Hare and Hounds, and occupied at that time by Mr. John Hollows. It appears that after the morning service they went over to the public house to dine, as was the custom in those days, and after dinner used to adjourn to the club-room to hold a prayer meeting, and it was on one of these occasions that Joshua Lord realized the forgiveness of his sins. Soon after this Mr. Dillon removed to London, and was not succeeded by a man of like mind and those men were not able to profit by the ministrations of his successor as they had done under Mr. Dillon. The pulpit of the chapel of ease at Ringley was not filled by a man of Mr. Dillons stamp, and they were consequently forced to look out for a ministry more congenial to their views, which they found in connection with the Weslyan Methodists in the town of Bolton, worshipping in the chapel known by the name of "Ridgwaygates," or the "Old Buildings." They invited the Methodist local preachers to come down and preach at Ringley, these services being held in the Blackhurst Green farmhouse at the bottom of Stoneclough Brow, now occupied by Mr. John Seddon. The preaching was removed to the house Joshua Lord in Halshaw Lane, and a class established; Mr. John Lord being the leader. In this way things went on until the year 1825, with the exception of every now and then preaching being tried at Ringley. In this way a class was established at the house of Mrs. Whittaker, living at Ringley Bridge, which continued to meet there until about the year 1845, when Mrs. Whittaker removed to Runcorn. This class, upon Mrs. Whittakers removal, was transferred to the house of Mary Seddon, in Prestolee, where it continued to meet until the close of the year 1854, when it was merged with a new class which had been commenced in Prestolee in December 1853 by Mr. J.G. Bradley. In the month of March 1847, Mr. W.S. Lawn, secretary of the Lancashire and Yorkshire Railway Company, came to reside at Giants Seat, which is about a mile from Ringley Bridge. Mr. Lawn at once commenced a class at his house and opened the same for preaching on Sunday evenings. The services were conducted for the first 12 months by local preachers from the Salford circuit, invited by Mr. Lawn, the place not being upon the circuit plan. The class commenced at Giants Seat was soon removed to the house of Mr. Berry, at Ringley Bridge, as being more convenient for the

members. Mr. Berry leaving the neighbourhood soon afterwards, it was taken back to Giants Seat, where it has remained up to the present time (1865). In the year 1848 the place was taken upon the Bolton circuit, being much nearer to Bolton than to Salford. The Sunday evening services continued to be held at Giants Seat until the month of November 1850, when Mr. Lawn rented a large building from Mr. John Jackson of Pendlebury at £18 per annum. This building was situated on Market Street, Stoneclough and had formerly been John Entwistles joiners shop. In this large room the floor was dotted with holes where the knots had fallen out, and the children spent a great deal of time dropping things through." When the new Ringley Weslyan Chapel opened in December 1865 a school was added a short time later, and the scholars from the joiner's shop transferred there, and this eventually evolved into what became known as Irwell Bank School.

Irwell Bank Band circa 1910

Harrison Blair and the Blair Family

Harrison Blair stands out as one of the most notable and remarkable individuals that Kearsley has ever known. Being born into the rapidly changing world of the industrial revolution he fully understood the immense social and commercial transformations that were taking place. His devotion, faithfulness and endeavour in the many undertakings he became associated with make it difficult to find local records of the time in which his name does not appear.

Born in 1812 Harrison Blair was the younger of two sons to George Blair, Esq, who came to Bolton from Wigton in Cumberland around 1815. George Blair established a bleachworks plus had other interests in manufacturing and the cotton industry. These enterprises had been extremely profitable and he had amassed a sizable fortune by the time of his death in 1826.

Harrison Blair and his elder brother Stephen had taken up the reins of the family business, but sometime during the early 1830's Harrison along with a Mr Cottingham established their own vitriol works on Linnyshaw Moss (vitriol was used in the chemical bleaching of cloth). The site of this vitriol works was located over pretty much the same area as the current Lyon Industrial Estate at the end of Springfield Road. Upon the death of Mr Cottingham in 1836 Stephen Blair joined his brother in this successful business.

In 1851 Harrison Blair married Frances, the third daughter of Joseph Mann, Esq, of Liverpool, and up until this time he had lived at Kearsley House, which was situated next to the vitriol works. They promptly moved to Outwood Lodge, and Kearsley House then became offices for the vitriol works. They later moved to Clitheroe, but in 1857 he leased Peel Hall at Little Hulton, where he remained until his death on 16th January 1870.

Harrison Blair was appointed chairman of the very first Kearsley Local Board in 1865, a post he held for two years, and during this time he also designed the Kearsley shield. He was greatly involved with obtaining an Act of Parliament to establish The Farnworth and Kersley Gas Company in 1854 to bring supplies of domestic gas to the towns. This was done wholeheartedly in the interests of the consumers, as the only other supplier of the time was the Bolton Gas Company, who could not give any assurances that they would not overcharge or turn off the supply at short notice.

Concerned about the district's water supply he called a public meeting, after which negotiations were opened with Bolton Corporation to supply what was then known as 'Belmont Water.' The mains supply to Farnworth and

Kearsley was extended and operational in 1854. As a man of great intellect, he was not just the proprietor of the Vitriol works, but also it seems being largely involved in the scientific side of the business and applied for various patents regarding improvements to the manufacturing process. He was a trustee of Farnworth Grammar School and prominent in the establishment of St. John the Baptist's Church and School in Little Hulton. It was his passionate determination, coupled with deep religious beliefs and faith in Christian principles that led to the erection of St. Stephen's Schools and Church at Kearsley Moor. Unfortunately Harrison Blair did not live to see the Church which he had endeavoured to be built, but on its south side there is a stained-glass window dedicated to his memory which was paid for by the employees of his chemical works.

> IV
>
> ST. STEPHEN'S NATIONAL SCHOOLS, KEARSLEY.
>
> On New Year's Eve, the annual Christmas tea party was held. Nearly 300 sat down to tea. The school-room was tastefully decorated. The Vicar of Farnworth presided; and on the platform were—Harrison Blair, Esq., of Peel Hall; Rev. E. B. Welburn; Mr. Warburton; and Mr. Jesse Baker. Many pieces were recited, and St. Stephen's choir sang several glees, accompanied by Mrs. Blair on the piano-forte. The evening's entertainment was brought to a close shortly after ten o'clock.
>
> The number of children attending the day schools:—Boys, 60; girls, 50; infants' 50; total, 160. The Sunday School:—Average attendance, about 140.
>
> On the 17th, Mrs. Blair, of Peel Hall, gave her annual Christmas treat to the children belonging to the above schools, of whom 260 were present.
>
> Holy Communion is administered at St. Stephen's Church School on the first Sunday in every month.

Above. An excerpt from the Parish magazine of January 1870, shortly before Harrison Blair passed away on the 16th of the same month.

Also mentioned is a Mr. Jesse Baker who was the proprietor of a cotton mill at the bottom of Baker Street, which takes its name from this family.

Above. Harrison Blair, Esq.

Staff photo at Harrison Blair's chemical works in 1875. The site was at the end of what was called Taskers Lane but is now named Springfield Road. Please take a moment to look closely at this remarkable picture, and note that the workers ages range from men who must be nigh on 70 years old to young boys of around ten years old. It is difficult to imagine the long hours and arduous conditions they endured at the Chemical Works before going home to the most basic dwellings, but the austere expressions may provide some clue. The building in the background is Kearsley House, which was at this time used as offices for the works.

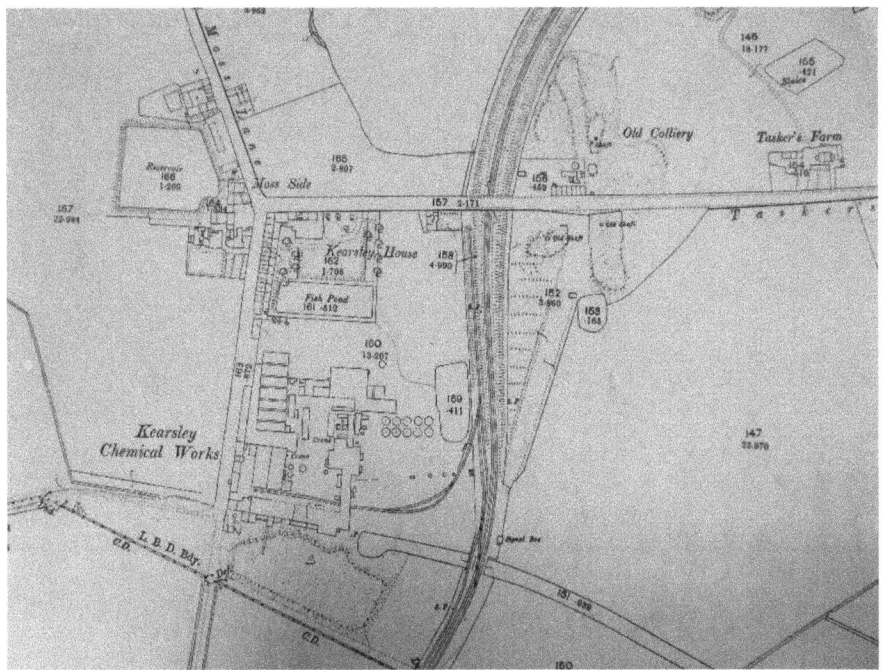

Above. Map of 1890 showing the Kearsley Chemical Works and Kearsley House at the end of Taskers Lane. The vast waste tip from the site is shown at the bottom of the picture, and in the top right Taskers Farm is seen in the location occupied currently by the Spar convenience store at number 200 Springfield Road.

The Cellar School at Kearsley Mount

Prior to the opening of St. Stephen's day school, there was a school setup around 1857 in the cellar at 184 Manchester Road, then occupied by Mrs. Maria Unsworth. The teachers were Miss Letitia Brooks and Miss Jane Gooden. At this time a Sunday School was also established in the cellar, the first teachers were Mrs. Maria Unsworth, who lived at the premises, Miss Gooden and John Files. They were later joined by Mrs. Timbrel, Mr James Edwards, Mr Denis Lever, and Mr. Thomas Partington. From 1861, the scholars would march from the cellar School to Kearsley House, at the top of Taskers Lane, to attend the Church service in a room that Harrison Blair had had licensed by the Bishop of Manchester for Divine Service.

The cellar was also used as a Night School three evenings a week for the men and boys of the district. They paid one penny per night and were expected to pay for their own candles. Most, if not all, would have also had a long hard day at work before attending.

Pictured in 1969 is the colossal chemical waste tip from Kearsley Chemical Works. In the bottom left is the cutting for the M61 which was under construction at the time. During the motorway construction most of the waste was removed, but some remained and was simply covered with clay, and to this day remains as part of the motorway embankment. Locally this was nicknamed 'stink bomb hill' and for good reason, as it odour could apparently be smelled for miles around.

St Stephens Church and School

In the month of July 1860 Mr John Fletcher of Clifton House, and Mr Harrison Blair of Kearsley House, met at Peel Hall in Little Hulton to discuss a scheme for providing a Church and Schools on Kearsley Moor. But no suitable building in the neighbourhood could be found, so it was proposed that a small schoolhouse should be erected as soon as possible. The advantage of building the day School first would also mean it could be used for a Sunday School and Church services until the necessary funds were available to construct a Church.

The cost of building the first School was estimated at around £300, towards which Mr Fletcher promised to contribute £100 and Mr. Harrison Blair £200. Harrison Blair also promised to contribute £30 per annum for the period of five years towards the payment of a Curate.

Both men had extensive business interests in Kearsley, with John Fletcher being the proprietor of the Wet Earth, Manor and Spindle Point pits amongst others, and Harrison Blair the owner of a large vitriol-works at Linnyshaw Moss, of which most of the workforce were also Kearsley folk.

By December 1860 donations from all sponsors and subscriptions had reached £1,005. As this now far exceeded the original sum proposed it was decided that the plans should be extended to also include a master's house. Plans for the new proposed school were submitted to the Council of Education, but it was not until 13th December 1861 that a reply was received, and in this it was made clear they disapproved of what they considered to be the exuberance of the local sponsors. The amended plans were eventually approved in April 1862, and the tender submitted by Mr. Thompson of Manchester was accepted to build the School with master's house for £1,262.

Above. St. Stephen's original school with master's house on the far right hand side.

The first school was built more or less across from where the current school stands on Bent Spur Road. At this time the road was simply known as a Turbary Road (the road to the turf), and the plot of land was generously donated by Mr. Le Gendre Nicholas Starkie, of Huntroyde, who was one of the principal landowners in Kearsley. The total area staked out was 60 yards on the side adjoining the Manchester to Bolton turnpike road (now Manchester Road) and 80 yards 2ft (one statute acre) on the middle Turbary road (now Bent Spur Road). The foundation stone was laid by Mr. William Vickers of the Antelope Hotel.

The new School was completed in April 1863 and opened for the first time on Sunday the 12th, with three services being held that day. The Rev. F.H. Thicknesse, M.A Vicar of Deane and Rural Dean, preaching in the morning ; the Rev J. P. Pitcairn, M.A. of Eccles in the afternoon : and the Rev E.W. Gilbert, M.A, in the evening. Mr. Daniel Taylor and his wife were appointed Master and Mistress on the 20th May at £75 per annum. The first managers of the Day School were Mr. Harrison Blair, Mr. John Fletcher, Mr. John Stott, Mr. Noah Baker, the Rev. E. Gilbert and Dr Eames of Barnfield House, Ringley.

The Day School opened on 13th July 1863 and one hundred children were admitted, this included children of the cellar School which now ceased to operate, and Mr. John Files, who had taught at the Cellar School on Manchester Road, made the following comment in his handbook: "Raw recruits; sound in wind and limb; fresh from pastures green; Kearsley bred, and porridge fed – oh, one can scent war in the camp….."

The number of children attending began to steadily rise, and by the end of 1863 some 212 scholars were on the books of the Day School, with the average attendance being 121. The Night School had 40 scholars with an average attendance of 29. One of the reasons for these fluctuating attendances was that at this time around 50 of the children were 'half-timers' who were also employed at the local mills, and interestingly most of these were girls. Attendance was not compulsory, and if the mill owner wanted them to work instead going to school, it was he who seemed to have the advantage over the headmaster. It is also believed that at times when they were not required to work at the mills the half-timers would simply take the time off in the hope that headmaster would not be aware of them being unoccupied.

By 1876 meetings were taking place to consider enlarging the school to accommodate the increasing numbers. The work involved pulling down the master's house and erecting a further school building on the site as well as extending the classroom in the north-west corner to the boundary wall. Work commenced on 2nd May 1877, and the enlarged school was opened on 11th December that year, by Mr Alfred Pilkington of Clifton House.

St. Stephen's old school on Bent Spur Road shortly after the extension was completed in December 1877.

Above. St. Stephens's old school after the master's house had been replaced with the extension to the right.

Architect of St. Stephen's new school Mr Frank R. Freeman

The number of children attending the St. Stephens Day School continued to rise, and by 1910 an incredible 578 children were on the books, 224 of which were infants. A meeting of parishioners in October that year decided unanimously that a new building was required on a fresh site. The school didn't move very far, as it was quickly decided that the perfect spot lay on the fields across the road. The land was again owned by the Starkie family who generously sold the plot for a nominal 1d per square yard. Architects from Manchester and Bolton were asked to submit plans, and seven responded. Those chosen were from Mr Frank R. Freeman, L.R.I.B.A, of Bolton, with the Board of Education approving them on the 6th June 1912.

Subscriptions were again appealed for, and the four daughters of Harrison Blair immediately donated £500, followed by one from Mrs. A. Wynne Corrie of £100 and the same amount from The Clifton and Kerlsey Coal Company. Further funds were raised from a 'sponsor a brick scheme' at 5 shillings each. Ultimately nine hundred and nineteen bricks with the initial of the donor were placed in the main entrance and corridors.

On the 4th September, 1912, Mrs Jane Pilkington laid the first brick at the north-west corner, Mrs Thomas Wolstencroft laid the first brick at the north-east corner, Mrs. Annie Gregg Scarlin laid the first brick at the south-east corner, and Miss Annie Berry laid the first brick at the south-west corner. Silver plated trowels were presented to each of these bricklayers by Messrs. George Graveson & Sons of Farnworth.

On the 21st September, 1912, in the presence of a large crowd, Miss Florence Blair laid the foundation stone, under-which a bottle was placed containing a list of members of the Building Committee, a financial statement, plans of the new schools, description of the new schools, a view of the new Schools, a copy of the Service Form used on the day, local newspapers – The Farnworth Journal and Chronicle, a Parish magazine, current coins dated 1912 and a chip of stone from the old buildings. As far as it is known this time-capsule is still in position.

Above. Architect Frank R. Freeman's drawing of the proposed new school.

The laying of the foundation stone of St. Stephen's new school by Miss Florence Blair on 21st September 1912. Holden's Moss Rose Mill can be seen in the background.

The new school was opened on the evening of 11th June 1913, by the Right Reverand Lord Bishop of Manchester. After a short service at the Church his Lordship was met at the door of the School by Miss Janet Wolstencroft who, on behalf of the building committee, presented him with a silver key with which he opened the door leading to the girls cloak-room and declared the School open. The total cost of the new School building, with incidental expenses was around £4500.

Although the new school had been opened in June, the children did not transfer from the old school straight away as minor building work continued and the new furniture had not arrived. But on the 28th July 1913 they all gathered in the old school before marching over the road to be the first scholars at St. Stephen's new school.

Above. St. Stephen's Church Army Mission Hall circa 1913, situated at Oldhouse Croft, which was on the opposite side of Manchester Road from Bark Street.

St. Stephen's new school shortly after completion in 1913

The success of the original School encouraged the main protagonists to push forward with the building of the Church, and in what seems to have been a temporary measure the deeply religious Harrison Blair had a room at Kearsley House licensed for the celebration of Divine Service by the Bishop of Manchester in June 1861. Here the Reverand E. W. Gilbert performed the Service of the Church of England for the first time on 7th July 1861. The children from the Cellar School at 184 Manchester Road would march in procession to attend this service.

On the 1st September 1864 a committee was formed to consider the erection of the Church. The committee consisted of Rev W.H. Barnes, Rev E.W. Gilbert, Messrs Harrison Blair, John Fletcher, James Warburton, Noah Baker and Jesse Baker.

Although the plot of land had been donated by Mr. Starkie, the legal process of transferring the property mineral rights of the land caused a delay of several years to the commencement of the Church building work. This must have been a hugely frustrating situation, as it was not until January 1870 that the deeds were obtained and work could begin. The architects of the church were Messrs. Medland and Henry Taylor of Manchester whose design had been chosen in a competition in January 1865. The original design showed the church would accommodate 540 persons and would cost around £4000 to build. The contractors were Messrs. Ellis and Hinchcliffe of Manchester. Sadly though, Harrison Blair did not live to see his beloved Church take shape, as he passed away after a short illness on 16th January 1870 to the great regret of the local inhabitants.

His widow, Frances, and their four daughters, along with his elder brother Stephen Blair, duly announced that work on the Church would proceed as planned, and that no financial loss to the parish would result from the death to its patron and benefactor.

It was now arranged that Stephen Blair would lay the foundation stone, with masonic ceremony, but again tragedy struck, as he was taken ill at his home in Bolton. Stephen Blair was unmarried, and Mrs Blair had him taken to their home at Peel Hall, Little Hulton so she and her four daughters could look after him. Sadly he died on 4th July 1870, but again Mrs Blair continued to fund the project, and even completely paid the costs of building the Vicarage, sited next to the Church on Manchester Road, which was completed in 1873.

Below. Rev. Canon Lowe, Vicar at St. Stephens 1871 – 1881.

The first sod of earth cut on the site was by Mrs Blair on the 28th June 1870, and building operations began on 4th July, the same day that Stephen Blair passed away.

The Church foundation stone was laid at 3'o'clock in the afternoon on 15th October 1870 in the presence of a large crowd. A procession headed by the school band, and consisting of scholars from the school plus workers from the Harrison Blair chemical works, and Stephen Blair's Mill Hill Bleachworks, walked from Farnworth and through Kearsley before taking up a position to the rear of the church.

The laying of the Memorial Stone, which is at the East end (top chancel pillar, now behind the pulpit) was carried out by Miss Constance Blair who spread the mortar, Miss Florence Blair struck the stone on its four corners with a mallet, Miss Ellen Jane Blair applied the square to it and Miss Frances Beatrice Blair manipulated the level. After this they all duly declared the stone to be laid. Building work only took around eight months, with the Church being consecrated on Saturday 1st July 1871 by the Lord Bishop of Manchester, Dr Fraser. On the 1st August 1871, the Rev. Charles Lowe was licensed by the Bishop as the first incumbent.

On Saturday, October 15th, the ceremony of laying the memorial stone of St. Stephen's, Church, Kearsley Moor, took place. The weather was very fine, and there was a large gathering of both clergy and laity. The stone was laid by the four daughters of the late Harrison Blair, Esquire. The assembly was addressed by the Vicar, John Hick, Esquire, M.P., T. L. Rushton, Esquire, and the Rev. E. W. Gilbert, all of whom alluded to the munificence of the founders of the chuch, and the loss the neighbourhood had sustained by their death, and a hope was expressed that their noble example might lead others who had the ability, to "go and do likewise." The school children and workpeople were afterwards, by Mrs. Blair's kindness, entertained at Kearsley Moor; whilst most of those present from a distance returned to Peel Hall. The church is expected to be completed by June next.

On Sunday, 23rd ultimo, the annual sermons were preached at St. Stephen's, Kearsley Moor, in aid of the Day and Sunday Schools. The collections amounted to £23.

Above. From the Farnworth and Kearsley Parish magazine of November 1870

Saturday, July 1st, was a day of great rejoicing at Kearsley Moor, as the Consecration of St. Stephen's was fixed for that day. The circumstances connected with the origin progress, and completion of this Church are well known. It was projected some years ago by the late H. Blair, Esq., and John Fletcher, Esq., of Clifton House. The site was liberally given by L. G. Starkie, Esq. The work which seemed likely to be interrupted by the lamented death first of Mr. Harrison Blair, and soon afterwards of Mr. Stephen Blair—has been zealously carried out by the generous zeal of Mrs. Blair and her family. The Bishop was met at the School by the choir and clergy in surplices, whence they proceeded in procession to the west door of the Church, where the petition for consecration was presented, and its prayer granted. The Bishop then with the choir and clergy walked to the east end of the Church chanting the 24th psalm. The consecration service was completed, and morning prayer followed. The prayers were read by the Incumbent; the first lesson by the Vicar of Worsley; the second by the Vicar of Farnworth-with-Kearsley; the gospel by the Vicar of Bolton; and the epistle by Archdeacon Anson. The Bishop preached both morning and afternoon, alluding in touching terms to the circumstances under which the Church was built, and exhorting the people to use faithfully the sacred building which was now theirs for ever. There were about 180 communicants on Saturday, and 54 on Sunday morning. Numerous costly gifts have been made. The surplices for the choir are presented by various friends and members of the congregation: the pulpit is the liberal gift of John Fletcher, Esq., and the beautiful font is the gift of Miss Ley. The workmen at the Kearsley Works have put in a handsome stained window in memory of their late master and friend, H. Blair, Esq.; and the teachers and scholars have added another. It is proposed to put a bell and clock in the Tower, at a cost of £150, of which £70 are already contributed. The opening services were continued on Sunday, sermons being preached by the Rev. W. H. Taylor, and Canon Beechey. On Wednesday evening, the Rev. E. W. Gilbert, preached, on Friday, the Rev. E. W. Appleyard. The collections amount to upwards of £140.

Above. From the Farnworth and Kearsley Parish magazine of August 1871. A first-hand account of the consecration of St. Stephens Church.

VESTRY MEETING.—On Monday, April 13th, the annual vestry meeting was held; the Vicar in the chair. The accounts were submitted, and the balance due to the treasurer—£6 6s 2d. was generously liquidated by Mr. John Lever and Mr. Thomas Tong. The old officers were re-elected—Mr. Mark Fletcher, Churchwarden, and Mr. John Lever, Sidesman, appointed by the Vicar; Mr. Tong, Churchwarden, and Mr. John Jackson, Sidesman, by the parishioners. Mr. John Lever was also re-appointed Treasurer. A cordial vote of thanks was unanimously accorded to these gentlemen for their past services. Mr. Lever expressed his hope that the offertory would soon advance to £2 a week, which sum was required to provide efficiently for the expenses of the church. The earnest hope was also expressed that the parishioners would voluntarily come forward with their contributions towards the new burial ground, which is now drained, but still has to be levelled, surveyed, consecrated, and planted. It certainly would be a cause of thankfulness if each parishioner according to his means would contribute towards this object of his own free will, and thus obviate the necessity of a house to house solicitation. The necessity of procuring a safe for the church books, and for outside painting this summer, was again urged.

The arrangements for Whitsuntide were not completed in time for publication. Probably they will be much as last year.

Above and below, both from the Farnworth and Kearsley Parish magazine of May 1874.

THE DAY SCHOOLS will be examined by Her Majesty's Inspector, June 25th. Parents are earnestly requested to enforce the punctual attendance of their children previous to and on the day of Inspection.

WHIT-FRIDAY.—The Annual Whit-Friday proceedings passed off with great satisfaction. The Teachers and Scholars having met at the Schools, proceeded to the Church at 12 o'clock, where a considerable number of the congregation was already assembled. After a short Service, the Procession, headed by the Vicar, Churchwardens, and Sidesmen, observed the usual route to Unity Brook, joining the Procession of the Farnworth Church Schools at Longcauseway, returning by Kearsley House and Tasker's Lane to the Schoolroom, where an excellent Tea was provided. The Band obtained through the exertions of Mr. Tong, gave great satisfaction. The weather, which during part of the route, had been most unpromising, now improved, and enabled the Scholars to adjourn to a field kindly lent by E. Pilkington, Esq., of Clifton House, where the usual games and prizes were thoroughly appreciated. We cordially thank Messrs. Warburton and Ansdell for the kind loan of their waggon annd horses. The Procession of Scholars was a great increase upon any previous occasion, and the large number of the congregation and friends who joined us evinced a growing sympathy and interest in our Day and Sunday Schools. Mr. Jonathan Baker and Mr. Joseph Eckersley deserve our best thanks for their exertions in obtaining subscriptions to meet the expenses of the Treat, as do also those who have liberally responded to their appeal.

This picture of St. Stephens Church and Vicarage is undated, but is certainly not long after the buildings were completed. As the ground sloped down from the main road the foundations of the church had to be considerably built up to elevate it to road level.

Left. Mrs Frances Blair, who continued to fund the Church and Vicarage building work after the death of her husband.

Below. From the Farnworth Journal, May 16th 1930. Miss Florence Blair attending a fund-raising bazaar at St. Stephen's School. Also in the picture is Mr A.M. Holden, proprietor of nearby Moss Rose Mill and son of the late John Holden.

The deep interest which the Blair family have always taken in St. Stephen's Church, Kearsley, was again emphasized on Saturday, when Miss F. B. Blair travelled from Sussex to open a bazaar in the school. A group taken at the opening ceremony shows Messrs. A. Clegg, J. Cranshaw, Rev. W. E. Davis-Winstone, Rev. A. Patrick (vicar), Miss Blair, Miss Grundy, Mrs. A. Holden, and Mr. A. M. Holden.

The first baptisms took place on the 2nd August 1871, here is a list of those with the honour of being the first to be baptised at St. Stephens Church:

William, son of John and Ann Harrison.
Joseph, son of Joseph and Sarah Richards.
Joseph, son of Joseph and Mary Entwistle.
Thomas Hardman, son of James and Esther Holt.
Alice Ann, daughter of John and Alice Benyon.
Nelly Gradwell, daughter of Henry and Phoebe Seddon Madelow.
John, son of William and Martha Taylor.
Richard, son of Thomas and Alice Nelson.
Eliza Anne, daughter of Thomas and Alice Nelson

The new Clock and Bell were put up by Messrs, Bailey & Co of Salford at a cost of £240 which was again paid for by public subscription. It was officially rung for the first time by Mr William Wrigley on 25th February 1872. The first marriage solemnized in the Church was that of Mr. Dennis Lever to Miss Martha Eckersley on the 18th March 1872, and the first burial to take place was that of James Whittle, aged 53 years on the 4th of December 1874.

Above. St. Stephens Prize Band, circa 1910. The first band had been formed in 1869 and was originally made up of workers from the local collieries.

Above. Whit Tide procession 1897. The St. Stephens group make their way up Manchester Road.

Whit-tide processions were considered a great event of the year, the following were the marching orders for St. Stephens in 1871:

Meet at School-room at 11:30 am, attend Divine Service at 11:45, march to Unity Brook, then back through Kearsley to Farnworth, where, at Longcauseway, they met the scholars of the St. John's Parish Church. Here one vast Church procession was formed, marching down Albert Road to Moses Gate, then to Darley Hall.

The Kearsley scholars returned home along Old Hall Street, down Mabel's Brow past Kearsley House, and down Tasker's Lane to the School. Here they were treated to coffee, buns and oranges after-which they spent the rest of the day on the fields taking part in sports, racing and dancing.

Note at this time the return route from Old Hall Street would now go down Mabel's Brow, along past the fields that are now at the back of Kearsley West School, then across what is now the A666 Kearsley Spur approximately where the footbridge is, then up Moss Road to the corner of Springfield Road, formerly Taskers Lane, where Kearsley House stood opposite this corner.

St. Stephen's Church Magazine, June 1941.

St. Stephen's Parish Magazine.

VICAR'S LETTER.

My dear Friends,

Our ANNUAL SERMONS this year will be on the 15th JUNE, and as usual I take this opportunity of appealing to your generousity on behalf of our Schoolchildren. I don't wish to spoil them in anyway, but I do want them to be happy, and I want them to have every facility we can give them.

The familiar quotation "we are only young once" still rings in our ears today, therefore, whatever the future may bring forth, never let it be said that we refused to give to every child in our school that opportunity which it is entitled to.

Speaking on behalf of the School Managers and the Day and Sunday School Teachers, they are extremely grateful for all that has been done for them.

In spite of the war, education is playing a more prominent part today, than ever before. To some leaders, they would like to see a national education with religion taking a second place, or even minus religion, but this is a fatal policy. History keeps on repeating itself, and time and time again, we are constantly being warned by experience that no life is complete unless the principles of our blessed Lord are fully taught to every child.

Educate a child without these principles and you produce in all possibilty, a German Nazi, or a Moscow Communist. I have repeatedly stated on many occasion, there are three forces in the world today trying to get supreme power. They are Nazism, Communism, and Christianity. It is left with us to make the choice, the power is in our own hands.

All decent people detest the first two philosophies, but what shall we say about the third?

If Christianity is going to survive, and overthrow the evil influences of so much diabolical teaching, this can only be done through the channels of our Schools and Churches, hence, the importance of giving the right education to all our children. True, education does not mean being prepared with a view to earning L.S.D. only, but it does mean preparing that child to take his or her place in any department of our national life, so that the life may have an influence on the lives of others.

With this in view, I make my appeal for a more greater sacrifice than ever. I don't wish to bore you with figures, but our expenditure on the School never diminishes, but has rather been on the increase this year, owing to the war.

Here is an opportunity for those who have not been able to come to Church owing to war work, to give a direct subscription before the day, to enable us to reach the £100 we are in need of.

If a hundred volunteers would come forward between now and the Sermons day, and promise to give 5/- each, this would be a great step towards reaching our goal.

I cannot force you into this adventure, neither do I wish to argue about it, my business is, to state the facts and the position, and then to leave it to your own free-will and conscience, knowing that "In as much as ye have done it unto these my children, ye have done it unto Me."

Any subscription given, either to the Church Officers or myself will be greatly appreciated and acknowledged without delay.

I would like to had a word of thanks to our numerous friends and supporters outside the parish, who, by their generous support year by year, not only give of their best, but which means a scource of encouragement to us to go forward and keep the flag well hoisted.

May I ask for all Sermon Boxes to be handed in to Mrs. Cranshaw without delay.

Thanking you once again for your help in the past, trusting that our Sermons Day this year will be crowned with every blessing and success.

Your most sincere Friend and Vicar,

ARTHUR PATRICK

Some interesting wartime words from the Reverend Arthur Patrick in the June 1941 Church Magazine.

Above. St Stephens Church December 2006.

Kearsley Mount Methodist Church and school

It is believed that Methodist meetings in Kearsley first began during the early 1800's, and were initially held in the homes of followers. Due to a rapid increase in numbers a more suitable accommodation was required, so a building a little further down the valley at the rear of the present Kearsley Mount Methodist Church was used for gatherings.

This building, opened in 1836, became known originally as the Kersley Sabbath School, and was used for meetings, services and as a Sunday School, it is also believed to have been used as a day school as well during this period.

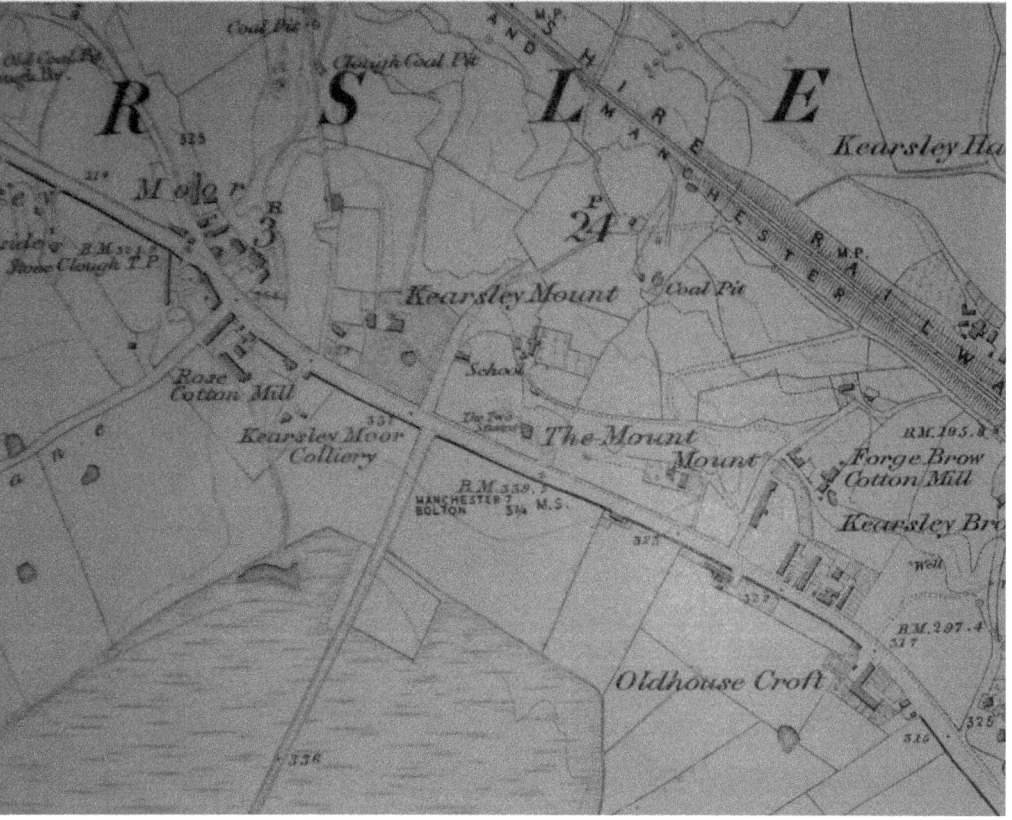

This map of the area from 1848 shows the original Weslyan Sunday School and Chapel further down the valley off what is now Sandhole Road. To the left of this (below the word Kearsley) is the large residence once owned by the Bailey family at a place now covered by Walker Close. The surrounding land had many apple trees and was known as Bailey's orchard.

Further rises in attendances during the following decades meant the school building was becoming unsuitable for meetings and church services, so plans were made for the erection of a chapel. The site, at Kersley Mount, on Manchester Road, was leased from the Earl of Derby, and on the 21st May 1870 the foundation stone was laid by Mr. Henry Blackmore, superintendent of the Lancashire and Yorkshire Railway. The new chapel was opened for Divine service on 8th December the same year, with the first sermon preached by Rev. J. H. James. The total cost of the new chapel was around £1100 and the contractors were Messrs. Coope Brothers of Farnworth.

Above. Kearsley Mount Weslyan School photo from 1898.

Below. From 1925, Headteacher John Flitcroft is seen to the right.

An unforeseen problem had also arisen at this time with the original school buildings, as they had now become unsafe largely due to mining subsidence, which resulted in it having to be bolted and planked to make it secure. Negotiations were held with Messrs . Knowles and Stott, owners of the colliery that was the cause of the trouble, and it is believed they paid the sum of £30 in compensation.

The old school had become increasingly unfit for its purpose, and eventually plans for a new school building, next to the new chapel on Manchester Road, were approved in 1875 by the Kersley Local Board. The new school opened in 1879, with the Cornerstone being laid by Mr. Edward Davies of Knoll Villa, Station Road, Stoneclough, on 24th May of that year. This school was extended in 1890 with further classrooms and accommodation for infants.

The school remained in use until 1976 when the pupils were transferred to the newly built Spindle Point Primary School in September of that year, after this the building was used as a youth club and after that as a private nursery called Rompers. The old school building was demolished in 2009 and replaced by a block of flats built by St Vincent's Housing Association.

Above. Picture dating from shortly after the construction of the new School building on Manchester Road at Kearsley Mount in 1879. On the right is the first Methodist Chapel built in 1870.

The new Chapel, built in 1870, also began to suffer the same difficulties as the original school, triggered again by mining subsidence, and work to secure the building had to be carried out. By 1905 the persisting issues with the underground mine workings had caused ongoing damage, and become a sufficient enough concern that a fund was started toward the construction of a new Chapel, on the same site, but this time on sound foundations.

The present Kearsley Mount Methodist Church was built on the same site as the old chapel, it was opened and dedicated for public worship on 19th January 1916.

In the stone of the centre pillar of the front door there is a cavity, which contains a lead casket. This casket was originally placed in a cavity in the original chapel built in 1870, and it is believed the original documents and papers,

Left. The opening ceremony as reported in the Farnworth Journal 21st January 1916 which include plans of the building, a copy of the New Testament, a letter from the Chairman of the District, a document detailing the rise of Methodism in Kersley and local newspapers from the time are still contained within it.

In 1990 it became apparent that the Church building was once again suffering from structural problems. The decorative triangular façade atop the front of the building was found to be leaning outwards, and the initial estimated cost of repairs was £23000, but, after further inspection, additional issues were found with the steelwork, which would increase the repair bill to around £45000.

Interestingly, this issue with the front of the Church leaning outward was not attributed to mining subsidence as

Kearsley Wesleyan Church.

OPENING CEREMONY.

A handsome new church which replaces one pulled down two years ago, and for which the Wesleyans of Kearsley Mount have for ten years been raising money, was opened on Wednesday afternoon by Miss Doodson, daughter of Mr. J. Doodson, of Southport. Notwithstanding the inclement weather, the ceremony of formally unlocking the door was performed before a large gathering, though the outdoor proceedings were abbreviated considerably. The Rev. F. Taylor officiated, and among those present were the following members of the Kearsley District Council: Messrs. R. Lucas, J.P. (chairman), F. Shippobottom, J.P., J. Howard, T. Ingham, R. Robey, T. Rushton, and H. Martin (clerk). In handing a silver key, suitably inscribed, to Miss Doodson, the Rev. F. Taylor said they were greatly indebted to the members of the Davies and Doodson families for the generosity they had always shown to efforts for the erection of that church. When the Trustees and Building Committee met to consider who they should ask to open it, they were not long in making up their minds. A deputation from the Committee waited on Mr. Doodson to extend to him the invitation, but he had to decline, and as it was apparent that Mrs. Doodson would not be able to accept, Miss Doodson was asked, and she readily consented.—Miss Doodson, in a few remarks, declared the church open, and the company then went into the building, where service was conducted by the Rev. Trevor H. Davies, of Southport, there being also present the previous buildings had been, instead the suspicion was that vibrations from heavy traffic along Manchester Road were to blame.

The members of the Church did not waver at this unwelcome predicament, they became determined to overcome this financial setback, and, over the next couple of years they organized many fund raising events and activities. The Church was also forced to draw on money from trust funds, plus loans from other local Methodist Churches, but the repair cost was met, and all necessary work to make the building safe completed.

Over the next two decades declining numbers in congregation resulted in the possibility of the Church facing closure, possibly during 2007/08, but once again their unswerving members formulated a plan. The idea was to create a community space to generate income, and initially the old school building was considered, but this was currently being utilized by Rompers Nursery and would also require a huge expenditure to bring it up to the required standard. Around this time Church member Stephen Tonge met with the chief executive of St Vincent's Housing Association, and the possibility of selling the old school building and its accompanying land was discussed. A deal was reached whereby the Church would receive a substantial, but not unreasonable, amount of money, with which they could compensate the nursery company and have plenty left over to renovate the Church to also allow it to be used as a community space. St Vincent's also agreed to take down the old school building and to develop some of the land into a car park area for the Church.

The work took less than two years to complete, and the Church reopened in 2009. It is notable that prior to this work taking place, nearby St John Fisher Roman Catholic Church also had renovation and repair work which would see them using Kearsley Mount Methodist Church as a temporary base for around six months. This kindness was reciprocated when St John Fisher opened its doors to their Methodist neighbours during their refurbishments. A wonderful example of mutual support and comradeship, between two congenial and harmonious religious groups. Along with nearby St. Stephen's, these two Churches form a group known as the 'Churches on the Mount' who regularly collaborate on community projects and fundraising schemes.

Kearsley Mount Methodist Church survives today due to the determination and inventiveness of its members, and at present is home to a vast array of beneficial and constructive community activities, including the Kearsley Community Choir, Zumba fitness dance classes, indoor bowling, Kearsley Health Walkers, brass instrument classes, Sunday School and many other recreations, as well as, of course, being an exemplary Church.

Above. The former Kearsley Mount Methodist School pictured in 2008 when in use as Rompers Nursery.

Below. The same building being demolished just a year a later.

Above. Kearsley Mount Methodist Church in 2001.

Below. The impressive interior pictured in 2014.

Above. Kearsley Mount Methodist Church Whitsuntide procession on Bolton Road close to The Moss Rose public house, circa 1951.

Below. The Rose Queen entourage of the Kearsley Mount Methodist Church Whitsuntide procession on Bolton Road circa 1952.

St. John's Church and School

St. John's Church was built on land given by Benjamin Rawson, Esq, of Darley Hall, and funded by a Parliamentary grant from the Government's Church Building Act, the first of which was passed in 1818, which initially allocated £1 million towards the building of new Churches in Britain. It is believed that the original site given by Mr Rawson was at Dial Post Brow, and it would have actually fronted somewhere along what is now Lower Market Street near to where the Town Hall building stands. The reason it was not built there is that two sets of plans, which had been prepared by architect Charles Barry, were being considered at the same time by the Church Building Commissioners, one for St. John's and one for All Saints Church at Stand, and they ultimately decided that the larger of the two designs was to be built at Stand because it would be too extensive for Farnworth at that time. Mr Rawson took exception to this and refused to let the smaller Church be built at the front of his land, but instead agreed to give the site where the Church currently stands.

The first stone of the Church was laid by Benjamin Rawson on 4th March 1824 in front of a substantial crowd. Preceding this there had been a grand procession to mark the occasion consisting of, amongst others, various trade societies, several bands playing music, Gentlemen of the Township, Magistrates, Oddfellows, Freemasons, Overseers of the Poor, the Borough-reeve and constables from Bolton, Clergy and Churchwardens of the Parish, ladies in open carriages and the town crier.

A cavity had been cut in the stone and into this was placed a glass case containing some gold, silver and copper coins. This was then covered with a metal plate, which had been engraved with the following inscription:

> The First Stone
>
> Of
>
> This Church,
>
> Erected at the entire expense of
>
> The Fund under the management of His
>
> Majesty's Commissioners for the
>
> Building of Additional Churches,

And dedicated to
Saint John the Evangelist,
Was laid by
Benjamin Rawson, Esq.,
On Thursday, the 4th March, 1824,
Being the fifth year of the reign of His Majesty King
George the Fourth.
The site was given by Benjamin Rawson, Esq,
The Right Reverend George Henry Law, D,D, Bishop of Chester.
The Rev. Thomas Brocklebank, Vicar of Deane.
Philip Hardwick, of London, Architect.
John Wight, Clerk of the Works.
Thomas Heaton, Contractor.

After this The Rev. Thomas Brocklebank said a prayer and the National Anthem of God Save the King was sung before the proceedings were closed with three cheers from the thousands of spectators. The next morning it was found that the stone had been relieved of the coins that had been placed within it, so replacements of equal value had to again be deposited inside. Suspicion fell on the workmen employed on the site but the culprit, or culprits, were never detected.

There are no official records regarding the building work at St. John's Church, only scant details such as the total cost of construction was around £8000, the Stone for the Church came from a quarry at Green Lane in Bolton and the top stone of the steeple was laid on September 29th 1825.

At a public town meeting held at the house of Betty Walker, the Black Horse Inn, on June 8th 1820, with Rev. Thomas Brocklebank in the chair, the following entry is recorded:

Resolved,-"That the commissioners for building new churches be allowed to get stone in Green Lane for the new church in Farnworth; that Mr. Thomas Heaton, who has contracted to get the stone, do enter into an agreement to be bound in the sum of one hundred pounds to leave the road in Green Lane as wide as good as it is now; and that Mr. Joshua Cross and Mr. Thomas Heaton do request Mr. Adam Howarth, solicitor, of Bolton to draw up such agreement as the nature of the case may require."

As the district was at this time in the Diocese of Chester, the Church was consecrated by Dr. Blomfield, Bishop of Chester on September 9th 1826. Again a large crowd gathered, with much interest and fascination as a visit from a Bishop to a rural district such as Kearsley and Halshaw Moor was not commonplace. The first Incumbent was Rev. Robert Clerk Burton, who remained until 1828.

The first baptisms took place on 15th October 1826, the children were Thomas and Eliza, son and daughter of James Tildsley (collier of Farnworth) and his wife Anne; and also Rebecca, daughter of Thomas Wallwork (collier of Kersley) and his wife Anne. It is noteworthy that the first internment also took place on the same day, that being of a child of only two years named John Arstall of Farnworth.

The first marriage took place on 2nd August 1830, the couple were Thomas Pedley and Mary Robinson, widower and widow. Their names in the marriage register are only confirmed by a mark, it is thought they could not write.

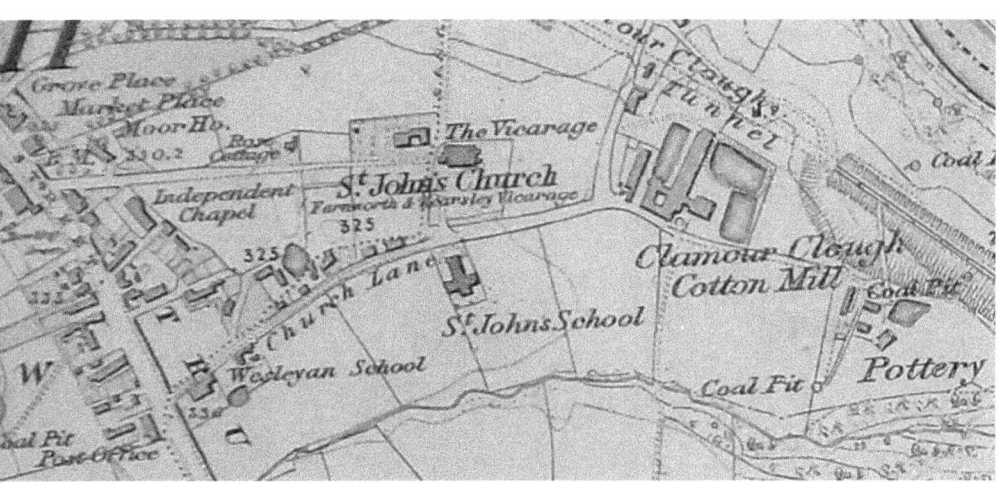

Above. Map of 1848. St John's Church at the end of Church Street and school on Church Lane. Clammerclough Cotton Mill is seen at a place where the A666 St. Peter's Way now cuts through, and in the bottom left the original Farnworth Post Office is shown across from Holland's Weslyan School. The Post Office public house is now on the site.

St. John's Church 1907. The Pinnacles atop the tower were removed in 1912 for safety reasons.

St. John's Sunday School Whitsuntide procession 1927. Leading the way in the bowler hat is Thomas Stanley as Chief Marshall. One cannot fail to be impressed at how smart everyone is turned out for what was a significant event in the Church calendar.

St John's Church circa 1930, picture taken from inside the schoolyard. The iron railings on both the church and school walls were taken off in 1942 to be melted down and used in the war effort.

Above. From the Farnworth Journal, 28th April 1944.

St John's Church, 1905.

This chapel, to the memory of the 27 men of the parish who gave their lives during the second world war, was dedicated at St. John's Church, Farnworth-with-Kearsley on Sunday afternoon. A memorial plaque was unveiled by Mrs. E. G. Botham, whose husband died as a result of the 1914-18 war and who lost a son in the second conflict.

Above. From the Farnworth Journal, 3rd February 1950. The service was attended by over 150 relatives of the 27 men who died, plus 180 members of the Farnworth and Kearsley British Legion. Mr Jack Heighway of Kearsley sounded the Last Post and a collection was taken for the Soldiers', Sailors', and Airmen's Families' Association. The dedication of the chapel was performed by the Lord Bishop of Middleton who said, *"they did well to remember those who died, and to be reminded of their sacrifices and service. In the post-war years it seemed that the country had forgotten God as they drifted into ever increasing divorce, theft and even murder. The question each individual had to ask himself was : Are we proving ourselves worthy of the self-sacrifice of the men who died?"*
Fixed to the wall of the chapel is an oak memorial tablet, with a moulded frame. The 27 names on the tablet, in incised and gilded lettering are: Jack Beech, Wilfred

Benson, James Harold Botham, Fred Bennett, James Cragg, Leslie Dowd, David Denard, Samuel Foulkes, George Gee, Victor Grundy, Herbert Horrobin, Henry Lawton, Harold E. Lees, Robert Longworth, Robert Litterick, Alan McWilllam, Douglas Miner, John Newton, Horace V. Nicholson, Thomas Pennington, Alfred Pearson, Maurice Rose, Ronald Stones, James Smethurst, Harold Taylor, Edmund William Weaver and Harry Whittaker.

When dealing with the local history of this period it is difficult not to come across the name of Benjamin Rawson of Darley Hall, who seems to have been a most influential and formidable character for a variety of reasons. He was born in 1758 as the only son to an Apothecary, also named Benjamin Rawson and his wife Anne.

Substantial land had been in the Rawson family for many years, with Benjamin Senior taking control sometime during the 18th century before this passed to his son. Benjamin Rawson junior was certainly a considerate and generous man, as his copious donations of land and money demonstrate, but there does also seem to have been an ill-tempered and haughty side which could emerge at times.

When Clammerclough cotton mill was built shortly after the Church was finished, Benjamin Rawson remarked "Now when we have just got our beautiful new Church completed they're going to blacken and spoil it with the abominable smoke from a factory chimney." A little contradictory from a man who ran a chemical works that was producing a fair amount of pollution of its own. There is no doubt though he was a shrewd and formidable businessman, as records show he was associated with many businesses as well as being a prominent landowner.

In 1825 he bought and rebuilt Nidd Hall at Harrogate, North Yorkshire, which today is run as a luxury hotel by the Warner Leisure Hotel chain and has a main dining area known as the Rawson Restaurant. He passed away on 31st May 1844 at Nidd Hall, aged 86.

Church Street, circa 1910

Above. Map of 1848 showing Darley Hall and St. John's Church and original School building. The blue line indicates what is now Darley Street, named as such because it led to the Darley area and Darley Hall. It was formerly known simply as 'the Coach Road.' From Darley Hall Benjamin Rawson would have been able to look down the valley onto his chemical works or make the short walk to the old stone bridge over the River Croal to the site.

Darley Hall, the former residence of Benjamin Rawson, pictured in 1905.

St John's School

A Sunday School was started in the early part of the 19th century in one of what were known as Royley's Cottages in King Street, Farnworth. This was soon found to be too small so the school and scholars moved to a hayloft over the stable connected with a house in Church Lane (now Church Road). In 1835 the scholars from the hayloft were transferred to the first St. John's Church Sunday school, which was erected where the present school stands. Originally this was a plain oblong building, but in 1842, due to increasing numbers, two wings were added to give it a cruciform shape. See picture 1848 map on page 225.

On 15th February 1837 permission was granted for the Sunday school to also be used as a day school with the first master being Mr. Rutter who was paid £80 per annum. Shortly after this the children from the Mather Trust School at High Stile were moved to St John's, and the Mather Trust charity fund of approximately £80 per annum also went to the new school.

In 1856 the school was enlarged at a cost of £264 5s 1½d, with Lord and Lady Ellesmere, Lord Brackley, Lord Bradford and Thomas Bonsor Crompton contributing £240 of that sum between them. It is no coincidence that not far from the top of Church Road there are two streets named Ellesmere Street and Brackley Street. The School was again extended and partly rebuilt in 1882 at a cost of around £800, of which £400 was given by Elizabeth Rawson, the daughter of Benjamin Rawson, as well as the land including the playground together with the original ground rent.

Above. St John's School, girls class from 1928. Left to right, back row: Annie Hobson, Ann Bircher, Edith Lord, Mary Schofield, Edith Harrison, Lily Brown and the teacher, Miss Evelyn Howard. Middle row: Dorothy Marsh, Edna Rigby, Nellie Roscoe, Marion Johnson, Madeline Robinson and Annie Seddon. Front row: Alice Mellor, Gladys Brocklehurst, Alice Grimshaw, Annie Berry, Agnes Barnes, Mollie Brown, Rhoda Green, Eva Bromley.

St John's School, November 1934

New Jerusalem Church

The first New Jerusalem Church was completed in 1837 with money raised by groups who followed the teachings of Swedish scientist and theologian Emanuel Swedenborg (1688 – 1772). Swedenborg had many talents and wrote numerous books, most notably 'Heaven And Hell' in which he explains his own ideas on religion and Christianity, but he himself never attempted to form his own Church, or encourage others to do so. Nevertheless groups began meeting and formed societies that followed the doctrine of Swedeborgianism, or 'The New Church' as it was also known. Possibly the first group to form a society was a London congregation who, in 1787, established the Church Of The New Jerusalem – based on the teachings of Swedenborg – as an independent religious body.

Locally there were two Swedeborgian groups regularly meeting, one at Ringley and the other at Stonehill, Farnworth. As early as 1791 the Ringley group held meetings at the house of Thomas Seddon, who was proprietor of the paper mill at Prestolee close to Rawson's chemical works. These meetings were held regularly on Sunday mornings as well as discussions during the evenings, and a main point of reflection was their uncertainty regarding the Trinity. The Rev. John Clowes, of St. John's Church, Manchester, was invited to explain the new doctrines, and after his first visit he met them every six weeks. He could not attend more often as transport was not convenient, but when he did it was on horseback, and a flag was hoisted to let the people in the neighbourhood around Cinder Hill know. On the intervening Sundays Mr. Thomas Seddon and Mr. Thomas Gee led the services and interestingly one of the worshippers was Samuel Crompton, inventor of the spinning-mule.

The Ringley Society was first mentioned in the minutes of the New Church conference in June 1808, and the same year a baptismal register was opened, the first entry on September 28th noting the baptism of Sally, daughter of John and Peggy Gee of Cinder Hill. Because of this the Kearsley New Church celebrated the centenary of its beginnings in September 1908.

There seems to be no definitive date as to when meetings stopped at the House of Thomas Seddon, but it was most likely around 1800 - 1810, but they later started to use larger premises at 'The Meeting House' Top o'th Brow, Ringley (most probably near the top of Ringley Old Brow), when the number of followers increased. Among this group were James and Roger Crompton, proprietors of Stoneclough Mill (later Fletcher's

Paper Mill), who may well have inherited their interest from their uncle who had been part of the original Ringley group.

It is believed that some of the Ringley group joined with the Stonehill group, and they began to raise funds towards the erection of a Church. The plot of land at Bolton Road, Kearsley was acquired and building work was completed in 1837. The total cost of the first New Jerusalem Church was reckoned to be around £400. Interestingly it appears that it was not until 1876 that all of the Stonehill group merged with the Church at Kearsley, and that a large group had continued to meet separately at Stonehill in a little brick building known as 'The Temple' which they had erected in 1843.

The first incumbent at the New Church on Bolton Road was the Rev. Woodville Woodman who lived on Stoneclough Brow, he held the position for 35 years until he passed away at home on the 15th November 1872 after a short illness. He was buried in the churchyard 5 days later.

In May 1838 a piece of land at the rear of the church was rented for the purpose of erecting a Sunday school, and a few weeks later it was declared that a portion of the churchyard should be utilized for the purposes of a burial ground. The church was licensed for marriages in May 1840, and around 1866 a day school was established.

The New Church continued to prosper, and in 1872 proposals for a larger Church building were set in motion. The new Church cost in the region of £7000 to build and it was dedicated on 4th December 1878.

With the opening of Kearsley West County Primary School in 1912 the New Jerusalem day school closed, but its premises remained as a Church Hall and Sunday School into the 1950's. This was replaced in 1958 by a building financed largely by a fund setup by the Church in 1954. This new hall only lasted until 1967 when it was demolished to make way for the Kearsley Spur slip road and roundabout construction.

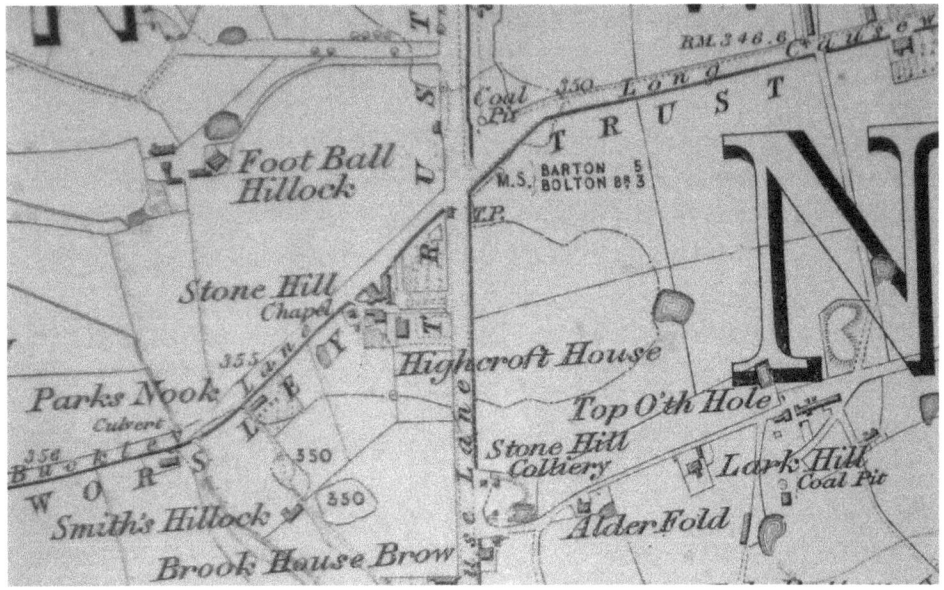

Above. Map of 1848 shows the location of the Stone Hill Chapel known as 'The Temple' on Buckley Lane approximately where the Bridgewater Arms currently stands.

A large section of the graveyard was also removed during this time, and consequently provided a peculiar problem for the road builders. As the burial ground had not been in use for many years it became impossible to trace the descendants of the deceased, so under Home Office license the imposingly named London Necropilis Company were contracted to disinter the bodies then take them away for cremation and re-burial. A six feet high plywood fence was constructed around the site and work began to remove the estimated 30 bodies. The cramped working space was sufficiently unpleasant enough for one of the church ministers who had served on the western front in the First World War to draw comparisons to the conditions, especially when more than twice the expected number of bodies were found.

Above. The Chancel of New Jerusalem Church 1928.

Below. From the Farnworth Journal, August 16th 1946

New Jerusalem Church circa 1910. Opened in 1878 this was the second Church built on the site. During the digging of the foundations the old main road was uncovered which led from Halshaw Lane across to Clock Face then down Old Hall Street.

MEMBERS of the New Jerusalem, Kearsley Church will see their third church hall within 10 years when the new one is built on land at Primrose Street. Meanwhile, the present church hall (above), built about eight years ago, is to be demolished to make way for a mammoth roundabout for the Farnworth and Kearsley by-pass. Church social functions are to be held temporarily in a hut, provided by the County Council.

Removals from the church hall to the temporary accommodation (below) were going ahead yesterday (Wednesday).

Church treasurer, Counc E. Yates, said that the next social function will be a domino drive, and it will be held in the hut.

Access to the building is either through the church yard or via Church Street. There is no direct access from the main road end of Church Street.

The youth club, Sunday School classes and other activities are all to be held in the hut until the new church hall is built.

"If work was started on the new hall next week," said Counc Yates, "it would probably take about nine months to build, so we may be in the hut for about 12 months."

Above. From the Farnworth Journal 12th January 1967.

A new church hall was opened in 1972, but this was abandoned in the mid 2000's due to its run-down state, however a new smaller building opened in 2007. The Gothic style Church built in 1878 was pulled down during 1982 as it too had fallen into disrepair and suffered from dry rot.

The third New Jerusalem Church was rebuilt with a more contemporary compact design with seating for 250 persons, and the remains of the old building were landscaped into a mound close to the cremation plots. At the dedication and opening ceremony in June 1984 visitors from Australia, South Africa and Scotland were among the congregation to hear the dedication service by the President of Conference, the Rev. Christopher Hasler. He was assisted by the area superintendent, the Rev. Leslie Chambers, and the Church's own minister, the Rev. William Grimshaw.

The Rev. Norman Riley, minister of the New Jerusalem Church of the United States in South Africa, and Mr Bernard Cooke, who had been church secretary during the second World War, also attended. After the service, minister's wife Mrs Pauline Grimshaw presented each child with a souvenir booklet and commemorative badge. Representatives of other denominations were at the service and the reception which followed. A collection raised £260.

Above. New Jerusalem Church pictured in 1987.

Kearsley West School

Kearsley West School was formally opened on Saturday June 22nd 1912 by Mr J. J. Cockshutt, Chairman of the Lancashire Elementary Education Sub-Committee. It was originally designed to accommodate 504 children and cost around £6000 to build. As was often the case with schools built at this time, specially fitted out rooms were provided for manual training for boys and laundry work and cooking for the girls. At the opening ceremony Mr. F. Topp, Chairman of the Kearsley area education sub-committee presented Mr Cockshutt with a silver key and testified his appreciation for the good work that the gentleman was doing for education in Lancashire. Mr Cockshutt then declared the school open and dedicated for all time to the service of the children of the district. Both the teachers and children from the New Jerusalem day school transferred to Kearsley West at this time.

Above. Kearsley West County Primary School pupils in 1928.

Kearsley West School football team 1922-23 season. At the rear are members of staff – Mr J. Collier, Mr E.L. Entwistle, Headmaster, and Mr H. Nightingale. Team members are: left to right back row: R. Mayoh, J. Hurst, A. Yates, J. Platt, E. Crompton. Middle row: A. Gerrard, A. Cranshaw, W. Mann, A. Chatton, S. White. Front row: W. Topping, S. Crossley.

Above. Circa 1973. The teaching staff at Kearsley West County Primary School. On the back row in the centre is headmaster Kenneth Roscoe.

St. Gregory Roman Catholic Church and School

The origination of St Gregory's Roman Catholic Church in Farnworth dates from around 1852 when the Canon Boulaye procured land from the Earl of Ellesmere for the purpose of erecting a church. The Bishop of Salford, Father William Turner, sent one of his newly ordained priests, Father William Taylor, to the area to serve the needs of the resident Catholic population and raise funds towards building a place of worship. Within a year, Father William Taylor and the local parishioners had built a stone church, with a school below and a small presbytery at the north end.

Father William Taylor removed to Bolton in 1861, and was followed at Farnworth by Father Micheal Byrne who was well aware that due to the continuing inrush of Catholics from Ireland in search of a livelihood that a larger building would soon be required, and over the next decade he raised around £3500 for that purpose. His successor Father J. G. Boulaye came to Farnworth on Christmas Eve 1871 and commenced the task of building a grandiose Church.

On 16th August 1873 the Right Rev. Dr. Herbert Vaughan, Roman Catholic Bishop of Salford laid the foundation stone, and exactly two years later, on August 16th 1875, the Right Rev. Dr. O'Reilly, Bishop of Liverpool solemnly blessed the newly built Church, which had cost an estimated £4000 to build. The builders were Coupe Bros of Farnworth, and it took almost a year just to lay the foundations, plus two underground passages that ran the full length of the aisles.

The first work of art to grace the church was the baptistery, with its large granite font, the pitch pine receptacle for the things needed, surmounted by the small circular window showing John baptizing Our Lord. It was first used on Whit Sunday 1882. Considered as the crowning glory to the church was the high altar, which was designed and constructed by Mayer & Co of Munich. The prodigious altar, which was carved in oak, weighed five and a half tons, and took five wagon loads to transport from Munich. The altar stone that it sat upon was a flawless seven inch thick piece of granite from Cornwall, it measured four yards by one yard and weighed one and a half tons. An estimated thirty tons of bricks were used in preparing the foundations for this monumental structure. The altar was consecrated by Bishop Bilsborrow in 1894.

The Church building began to suffer from structural difficulties during the 1990's, and this resulted in it being abandoned with worship relocating to the hall at the side of the Presbytery during 1997. Although no longer in use for worship the Church building became grade II listed in 1998. The Presbytery itself finally became vacant in 2003. Many items were saved and put into storage when the church closed, these included the high altar, pulpit, lady altar, war memorial, carving of the last supper and the pews. Sadly the church and presbytery became the target of vandals and thieves during the following years until it was finally demolished in August 2016.

The St. Gregory's primary school foundation stone was laid by the Bishop of Salford, the Rt. Rev. T. Henshaw, on Saturday 5th November 1927 in front of a large crowd despite pouring rain. Designed to accommodate 300 children, the school opened the following year costing an estimated £7,500 to build.

The magnificent high altar of the former St. Gregory's Church, circa 1900. The four saints painted on copper half way up are SS George, Gregory, Patrick and Augustine of Canterbury.

The worshippers at St. Gregory's Roman Catholic Church held their annual procession on Sunday, and although the weather was not of the best, it remained fine until the scholars had just arrived back. One of the most effective features was the Statue of "Our Lady," inside an arch of electric lights.

Picture from the Farnworth Journal of June 15th 1928. St. Gregory's Church procession makes its way along Market Street. In the background can be seen the Market Street Congregational Church (now Trinity Church) and Hollands School building with the clock on the front.

Above. March 2014, view from Church Street of St Gregory's Church. The Presbytery can be seen to the rear and the hall, built in 1929, which was used for worship when the church closed, just behind it. The area behind the church wall was once used for burials.

Below. March 2014 view from Presto Street.

Above. St. Gregory's school 1936.

The Schoenstatt Shrine and gardens at St John Fisher in July 2014

St John Fisher Roman Catholic Church

The Parish of St John Fisher Roman Catholic Church was established from St Gregory's, Farnworth, during 1960. The Church building was purposely designed as a combination of Church and Hall to serve an assortment of purposes and functions. There is a central worship space, which is also used for meetings and other events, plus a kitchen and offices. It was opened in September 1968, but in the years leading up to this, their followers held Sunday morning mass in the tea-room of Kearsley Cricket Club. The Church is built on the site formerly occupied by Kearsley Pool Farm.

Above. Construction work on the St. John Fisher RC Church in March 1968. Building costs were estimated to be around £20,000.
Below. The Auxiliary Bishop of Salford, the Rt Rev Geoffrey Burke, Celebrating the first mass at the opening of the new St John Fisher Church Hall on Friday 13th September 1968.

St John Fisher Church and Hall. August 2014

At the rear of the Church, overlooking the Irwell valley, is the Schoenstatt Shrine, which is a replica of the Marian Shrine built at the town of Schoenstatt, near Koblenz in Germany during the twelfth century. The Schoenstatt Movement, which holds a particular devotion to the Virgin Mary, were offered the opportunity to build the shrine at Kearsley by the Right Rev. Terence John Brain, the Bishop of Salford.

The Schoenstatt Shrine. July 2014

The Shrine of Our Lady of Schoenstatt was dedicated on 1 October 2000 by the Right Rev. Terence John Brain, the Bishop of Salford, and at the time of writing it is the only one in England. The opening was attended by Schoenstatt members from Mexico, Australia, South America, Ireland, Scotland and Germany.

Above. Circa 1920's. Kearsley Pool Farm. The farm and its outbuildings were demolished to make way for the construction of St John Fisher RC Church.
Below. Circa 1920's. A herd of pigs is watched over by a young girl at the rear of Kearsley Pool Farm. The tunnel under the main railway line at Kearsley Junction is seen in the background.

St Peter's Church and School

The origins of St. Peter's school began during the year 1880 when a room was rented in nearby Phoenix Mill, Longcauseway. This day school was originally only for boys and girls under the age of nine, but by January 1881 had gained over 100 scholars and was officially accepted by the Government. On September 17th 1881 the foundation stone of the school in Bradford Street was laid by Mrs W Hulton in a ceremony marred by heavy rain. A bottle was placed inside a recess of the stone by the Rev. J. A. Winstanley which contained an illuminated parchment stating the date on which the stone was laid, and the names of the vicar, curate, churchwardens, sidesmen and Building Committee. The bottle also contained a copy of the order of service, a list of the promoters of the undertaking and those who contributed towards it, a copy of the parish magazine for the month, and copies of the Farnworth Journal and Bolton Chronicle of that day. The school opened in March 1883, and it was stated that the total building cost was £1,604.

Above. St. Peter's School 1903. The Headmaster on the back row is Mr. Ainsworth.

Above. November 1927. A St. Peter's pupil lays a tribute at the Memorial Cross in the Church yard on Armistice Day. The Memorial Cross now stands in the schoolyard.

Above. Circa 1910, St Peter's Church, Bradford Street.

The foundation stone of the Church was laid by the Countess of Bradford on Saturday June 26, 1885, and building work was completed in 1886, at a cost of £3,800. The Earl of Bradford had donated the site and Bradford Street was named in honour of this benefactor. There were many donations to the building costs, including £500 from Miss Elizabeth Rawson, but most of these funds came from a bequest of Mr. George Piggott who lived at Hardman Fold, nearby Piggott Street was later named in his memory. The Church was consecrated on the 20th September 1886 and originally had 635 sittings. Due to decreasing numbers of worshippers the Church was forced to close in July 2007 and never reopened. In July 2012 the Church was demolished and the site used to build an extension on to the original school building at a cost of around £2.4 million.

A sealed glass bottle was also placed into a cavity of the Church foundation stone, which contained similar items to the one at the School. This was retrieved during the Church demolition and opened by a representative from Bolton museum and members of the school staff.

George Tomlinson School and Kearsley Academy

Discussions with regards to a secondary modern comprehensive school for Kearsley had been taking place since the late 1920's, and two sites were considered. These were the Hollands School building and surrounding land at the top of Church Road, and the land on the corner of Springfield Road and Moss Road. The land around Hollands School had actually been purchased during the 1920's for this purpose, and the intention was to incorporate the existing building into the larger school complex. For unknown reasons this plan never commenced, and with the outbreak of the Second World War a further delay transpired.

By the time serious debate on the matter had again commenced, two decades had passed, and there were now serious uncertainties about the suitability of the Hollands School site. It was now desirable to have gymnasiums, cookery rooms, woodwork/metalworking workshops and playing fields all connected directly to the school, as well as enough room for over 1,300 scholars, and there was not enough land to accommodate these requirements. The Springfield Road site was also subject to certain criticisms and complications, one of which was that it was so close to the Harrison Blair Chemical Works, and this would have a detrimental effect on the children's health. The land at Springfield Road had also been earmarked for the building of 250 houses, something which was pointed out to those who had expressed their concerns regarding the chemical works.

Eventually, at a County Council meeting in February 1948, it was finally decided to build at the Springfield Road site, and in October 1949 Councillor Mrs. A.M. Hogg cut the first sod on the windswept fields between Singing Clough and Moss Road. Named after the late George Tomlinson, Farnworth M.P. and Minister for Education, the school opened for the first time on Thursday September 10th 1953. The main contractors were Messrs. J. Cocker Ltd of Walkden and total cost of the build was £175,000.

The first children to attend came from a dozen other schools in the district, and the teaching staff consisted of nine men, twelve women and the headmaster. The school boasted a large assembly hall with a stage, a projector room, dining hall with kitchens, gymnasium, library, craft rooms, art rooms, a dark room, woodwork and metalwork shops, science labs and, in what was a sign of the times, a self-contained demonstration flat for girls to learn practical housecraft and housekeeping.

The opening of the new school meant that four schools ceased to be all-age schools, these were St. Johns, Prestolee, Ringley C.E and Kearsley Mount

Methodist. St. John's provided the largest contingent of new scholars with 162, next on the list was Kearsley West with 114 and 55 transferred from Harper Green Secondary School.

In September 2010 the school dropped the name of George Tomlinson and rebranded as Kearsley Academy, with a new modern building under construction alongside the original 1950's one that was gradually being demolished. The new Kearsley Academy building, costing an estimated £12 million, started taking in pupils in May 2013, but the official opening did not take place until June 2014 when the ceremony was carried out by former Bolton Wanderers footballer Kevin Davies.

September 10th 1953, the very first assembly at George Tomlinson School, Springfield Road. Immediately afterwards the children were allowed to go home, and told come back a week later on the 17th, as the school was not quite ready for them to attend.

Above. The smartly dressed staff at George Tomlinson School, circa 1960.

Below. The staff entrance, circa 1960.

Above. December 2006. The George Tomlinson School sports hall built during the early 1970's, which also served as Kearsley Sports Centre opened in the evenings and at weekends for anyone to use. The top of the school gymnasium can be seen to the right. There were three football pitches to the left and an all weather pitch with floodlights to the rear. **Below.** View from the opposite direction in July 2010. The all weather pitch is seen, and the land between the floodlight and school was where the cookery rooms and science labs once stood.

Above. July 2013, demolition work underway on the old buildings as the new one appears in the background.
Below. July 2014, the entrance to Kearsley Academy.

Ringley St. Saviours clock tower, 1907.

Ringley St. Saviours Church and Schools

Ringley Chapel lays claim to have been the first built and endowed in Lancashire by private benevolence after the English Reformation. Nathan Walworth (sometimes spelt Wallwork) was the benefactor responsible for the building of the first Church in 1625. He was born in 1572 at Ringley Fold farm, which occupied the land at the end of Fold Road, close to where the water treatment works is currently situated. The family had long been settled at Ringley and as early as 1420, in a settlement of the estate of Sir John De Pilkington, William Walwerk is mentioned as the occupier of "one pasture called Ryngleys."

Nathan was employed by the Earl of Pembroke as a steward of Baynards Castle, which was built on the north bank of the River Thames close to St. Pauls Cathedral. This was a momentous time in the history of Britain, as Queen Elizabeth I was on the throne and Nathan would have been about sixteen when the Spanish Armada was defeated. William Shakespeare would have also been presenting his new plays in London at the Globe theatre.

Whilst at Baynards Castle he had employed his friend, Peter Seddon of Ringley, to supervise the building of the Church and they communicated by letter on a frequent basis. Fifty seven letters written by Nathan Wallworth to Peter Seddon survive and, along with other relevant documents, were published in 1880 by the Chetham Society in the book titled "The Correspondence of Nathan Walworth and Peter Seddon of Outwood" edited by John Samuel Fletcher.

The letters provide a most interesting insight into their lives and the times they lived in, it is also clear that Nathan regarded Peter very highly, although at times he would subtly chastise him, for example, a letter dated May 2nd 1631 begins *"Neighbour Peter, Why? What's the matter? Hath the palsye taken your hand? Or is it for want of paper? If I thought so I would send you some, or is it the goute? Or what els? O, no, now I know what it is, you never received my letter, if you had, you would either have acknowledged the receipt, or have reproved what had beene Amisse in it, all the remedye, and Amends ye I now can have is to send no more Ires by ye caryer, and so an end of that songe"*. It is clear from this that Peter has delayed in replying to Nathan for such a length of time as to irritate him.

The Church (or Chapel) was licensed in February 1627 but not consecrated until December 1634 by John Bridgeman, Bishop of Chester, who was also a domestic Chaplain to James I. An interesting side note is that in 1633 Bishop Bridgeman was required by the Kings Council to investigate the infamous case of seventeen witches from Pendle, condemned to death at the Lancaster assizes, thankfully the inquiry resulted in their acquittal. In 1629 Bishop Bridgeman had purchased the manor of Great Lever from Sir Ralph Assheton, whose father had bought the estate from the Radfords some years earlier.

The delay in consecration resulted in Nathan writing a strong letter of complaint to Peter Seddon, dated 7th December 1634, in which he threatens to pull down the building and sell the timber and stones and give the money to the poor. This letter may have taken several days to reach Peter as his reply dated 14th December 1634 describes the consecration of Ringley Chapel by Bishop Bridgeman on Thursday the 10th of December. This fascinating letter also explains how Peter Seddon, Robert Seddon, Thomas Parr and John Walworth rode to the estate of the Bishop at Great Lever on the 7th December to *"persuade him with arguments"* to finally consecrate the Chapel. The Bishop agreed that he would come on the Thursday, and the same four men returned on that morning to accompany him to Ringley, but they found the Bishop unwell. By the afternoon he had recovered sufficiently to accompany them and Peter describes how they stopped at 'the Foxriding gate,' believed to have been at a point up what is now Stonecolugh Brow, where the Bishop looked down on the valley and said of the Chapel "it was a faire and Butifull House."

They then went first to Nathan's house where Martha Walworth, the widow of Ellis Walworth, younger son of Nathan's brother Peter, had laid out a small quantity of wine and food, but the Bishop would not drink as he had been troubled with 'a looseness' the night before.

There then follows an account of the consecration where the Chapel was dedicated to the Holy Saviour, it was Nathan's decision to dedicate Ringley Chapel to no Saint, but to the Holy Saviour. It is believed the first preacher was William Seddon and he remained there until 1629.

Nathan Walworth passed away in 1641 at almost 70 years of age, and a year later the English civil war broke out. The Seddon family along with the other inhabitants of Outwood and Ringley, who were supporters of the Parliament and Oliver Cromwell's puritan cause, were now in an awkward situation as they were tenants on the land of the Royalist supporting James Stanley, the seventh Earl of Derby. Interestingly, Peter Seddon's younger brother, William, decided to join the Royalist ranks and the discord between them was never resolved.

On the 28th of May 1644 the Earl stormed Bolton, then called Bolton-Le-Moors, with around 8000 men. The town was being held by approximately 2000 puritan soldiers and 500 locals. In the fierce fighting the Royalists

Above. James Stanley, 7th Earl of Derby, 31st January 1607 to 15th October 1651. Principal landowner in the Kearsley area at the outbreak of the English Civil War, he was also referred to as Lord Strange.

lost around 300 men but the Puritans suffered a crushing defeat with around 1,600 men lost, the horrific events of that day are known as the "Bolton massacre". James Stanley, the Seventh Earl of Derby was never forgiven for what happened, and when eventually he was captured in battle at Worcester in September 1651 he was later returned to Bolton and beheaded at Churchgate, where he had been forced to await his execution for several hours at Ye Old Man And Scythe public house. The battle at Worcester was the final conflict of the Civil war, as the Royalists were overwhelmed by Cromwell's New Model Army.

The original Ringley Chapel had become run-down, and also inadequate, for the increasing population of the parish by the early nineteenth century, and plans were made for larger premises.

The second church was erected in 1826 more or less on the site of the first one, which was completely demolished. It was consecrated on Monday 6th August 1827 and funded entirely by local landowners and inhabitants of the parish. The architect was Charles Barry, at the time aged 31, who also designed St. Matthews Church, Deansgate, Manchester, and All Saint's Church at Stand, both built out of the £1,000,000 thanks offering by Parliament for church building after the victory at the Battle of Waterloo. Sir Charles Barry, as he later became, received great acclaim for designing the Houses of Parliament, including Big Ben - which was originally known as St.

Stephen's Tower, after much of the original Palace of Westminster buildings were destroyed by fire 1834.

Above. The Jacobean stone with the inscription "NATHAN WALWORTH BUILDED MEE, ANNO DO 1625" was rescued from the very first chapel and placed into the tower of the second church built in 1826. The stone below this was placed to commemorate the building of the second church, and the bottom stone reads " This Tower was Repaired, raised two feet, and a New Clock Erected in Commemoration of the Jubilee of the New Church, Built 1854, Reopened July 1907."

The second church was believed to have been 84 feet in length and 29 feet in breadth without the wall, and though only 27 years old, was deemed to be too small and inconvenient for the growing population of the village and was pulled down in 1854, apart from the Church Clock Tower, which now stands in isolation near the Horseshoe Hotel. The Jacobean stone with the inscription "NATHAN WALWORTH BUILDED MEE, ANNO DO 1625" is from the original church, where it stood on the West front at the apex of the gable, immediately under the bell cote.

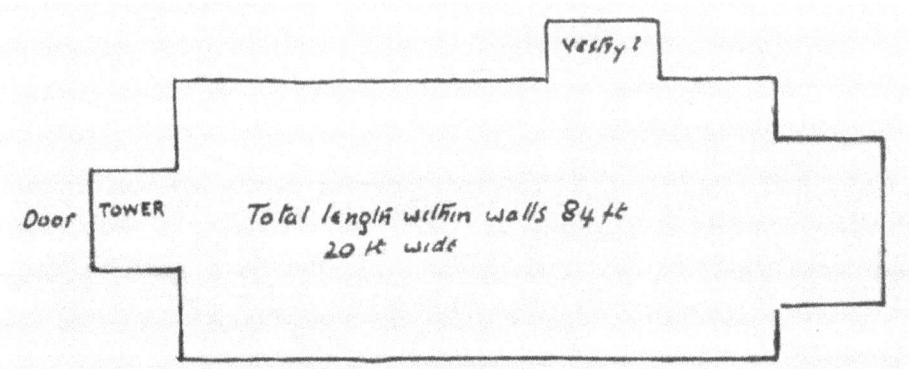

Above. Layout and dimensions of Sir Charles Barry's second Ringley Chapel erected in 1826. Only the Tower remains, as the rest of the building was demolished in 1854, just 27 years after it was built. The tower originally had an outside staircase which led up to a door on the north side.

In 1836 a meeting of subscribers gave the tender for a church clock to "Mr Francis Abbott, of Smithy Door, in Manchester." The surviving accounts show that the clock cost £66 and it's fixing £3 17s. 2d. The original clock had only three faces, looking North, South and West and was situated around two thirds of the way up the tower. In 1907 this clock was removed and the Tower heightened a further two feet to accommodate a new clock, which remains to this day. During 2017 this clock was fitted with an electronic mechanism that is powered by solar energy.

Pre 1907 picture showing the original clock and taller surrounding wall around the churchyard.

Snow covered St. Saviour's front churchyard and tower circa 1892

Ringley Old Bridge circa 1910. The old Tower now heightened by a couple of feet to accommodate the new clock.

Circa 1893 albumen photo of Ringley St. Saviours Church. Built in 1854 it is the third Church on the site and at this time the area at the front was used as burial ground as well as the rear.

Above. Circa 1893 View of the Chancel at St. Saviour's.

The third and current church was built further back than the site of the previous two churches and was consecrated to the solemn worship of God on Saturday, June 10th 1854, by Dr. James Prince Lee, Lord Bishop of the Diocese. The collection was £62. The following day, the Holy Communion was administered to 50 communicants. The offertory, devoted to the Organ Fund, amounted to £22 and the evening service began at six o'clock. The Church is built in a Gothic Revival style and the architects were Sharpe and Paley of Lancaster.

VII
S. SAVIOUR'S, RINGLEY.

1885.	THE OFFERTORY.	£	s.	d.
April 2	—Maunday-Thursday	0	1	6
,, 3	—Good Friday	0	16	11
,, 5	—Easter Day	4	6	6½
,, 12		1	14	5
,, 19	—(For Diocesan Church Building Society)	4	10	4
,, 26		1	4	6½
		£12	14	3

Number of Communions made during the month, 124.

BAPTISMS.
April 4 Annie, daughter of Alfred and Sally Green
   ,, 5 Hannah, daughter of Thomas W. and Mary Elizabeth Bowker
   ,, 26 Wilfred, son of Joseph and Ann Davies
   ,, 26 Mary Jane, daughter of Samuel and Nancy Wolstencroft

MARRIAGE.
William Tonge to Sarah A. Wolstenholme

BURIALS.
April 4 John Chapman, Kearsley Moor, aged 35 years
   ,, 4 Joseph Phythian, Westhoughton, aged 62 years
   ,, 14 Joseph Lord, Gorton, aged 32 years
   ,, 16 John Nuttall, Kearsley Hall, aged 60 years
   ,, 18 Mary Chadwick, Pendlebury, aged 77 years
   ,, 25 William Shermon, Kearsley Moor, aged 2 years

THE EASTER VESTRY MEETING was held in the School on Tuesday evening, April 7th. In the absence of the Vicar, Mr. R. Marsh was voted to the chair. He called upon Mr. Whittaker, People's Warden, to present the accounts. The total receipts amounted to £235 8s. 0½d., and the expenditure was £235 18s. 8½d., leaving a balance due to the Treasurer of 10s. 8d. This did not include the special effort made to improve the Churchyard. For this purpose Mr. Whittaker had received up to that time £86 14s. 1d., and the expenditure had been £82 11s. 9d. The Churchyard had been levelled, a large number of ornamental trees and shrubs planted, kerbstones had been placed to the walks, and the Parishioners might now be congratulated on possessing one of the neatest Churchyards in the neighbourhood. He intimated that about £30 more would be required to complete the improvement, and also explained that a sum of £30 left over from the rebuilding of the Church in 1851 had been obtained from the Bank, and would be devoted to the renovation of the Chancel Arch. The accounts were regarded as very satisfactory, and passed unanimously. The meeting then passed a vote of thanks to the retiring officers, and proceeded to elect officers for the ensuing year. People's Warden, Mr. I. J. Whittaker, Ringley House; Vicar's Warden, Mr. Joseph Seddon; Sidesmen, Messrs. J. A. Baker, T. W. Eckersley, Michael Garside, John Martin. A vote of thanks to the Chairman concluded the proceedings.

ON Sunday, May 3rd, being Wakes Sunday, Special Sermons will be preached and the offertories be devoted to the Churchwardens' Expenses.

An extract from the Parish magazine of May 1885

Two pictures of St.Saviours during the 1930's. It is estimated that at this time it had already hosted around 20,000 burials around the site.

The front portion of the churchyard, on the ground either side of the footpath, was tidied up and landscaped during 1972 leaving the site with a much more orderly appearance. Further maintenance had to be carried out during the mid 1980's as the rest of the churchyard had become unkempt and over-grown.

Children from St Saviour's Parish Church, Ringley, pause for a moment before setting out to take part in the lower Kearsley processions.

Above. From the Farnworth Journal, June 5th 1969. Local children ready to set off on the annual Whitsuntide procession, which became known locally as 'walking day.'

A special service was held on Sunday 14th December 1975 to celebrate the 350th year of the church. Earlier the same year, extensive re-decoration and repairs were undertaken, aided by a grant of £4,500 from the Greater Manchester Council. This included tackling the dry rot in the chancel and vestry, stripping down the walls to the brickwork and re-plastering, plus repairs to the roof over the vicar's vestry.

Circa 1893. Ringley Old Parsonage. This was located at the top of Parsonage Road and was used by the incumbent of St. Saviours. Sometime between 1893 and 1917 a new vicarage was built on Ringley Road overlooking the Church, and the old Parsonage was vacated soon after.

Ringley St Saviours School

After the building of the original Ringley St Saviours Church, Nathan Wallworth also funded the construction of a small building to be used as a school. In his will, dated October 15th, 1640, he states:-

"Whereas I have Lately built a schoolhouse neer to the Chappell, I hereby will the said house to the trustees, their heirs and assigns for ever, upon trust that the said house shall be employed for a school, and for the residence of a schoolmaster. And I hereby divise to the said trustees all my two oxgangs of land within the town of Flamboro', County York, upon trust, that the said trustees employ the yearly rents for the repair of the said house and for the maintenance of an able and honest schoolmaster, to be named by the said Rector of Prestwich, Bury and Middleton, or the greater number of them. And my will is that the children within the Chappellry shall be freely taught without paying anything."

It is believed that these school premises were built between where the Horseshoe Inn stands and the Manchester Bolton Bury Canal which ran alongside it, and they lasted until around 1798 when they fell down. A new building was constructed by subscription on the same site and consisted of a schoolroom only, without the schoolmasters living quarters. This school became known as the Grammar School and had accommodation for 100 scholars who could attend from the age of six years on application to the schoolmaster. They were taught reading free of expense, but to learn writing and arithmetic a small fee would have to be paid, and this was said to have always been the case.

It is worthy of note that at the time of the original school construction around 1640, neither the Horseshoe Inn nor The MBB Canal would have been in existence, but the original Ringley Chapel would have stood where the tower still stands).

Above. Map of 1848 showing the second St. Saviour's Church, of which only the tower remains. Above this are the Horseshoe Hotel and the second school building built on the site. Across the bridge is the Lord Nelson public house, which is currently La Roma Italian restaurant. The bowling green remained in place until the year 2000 after-which it was turned into a car park. A 'Well' can also be seen which would have been used by the locals as a domestic water supply.

A report of the Charity Commissioners from June 1826 states that the schoolmaster was curate of Ringley, the Rev. John Barnsdall and that the number of scholars was 55. The children were transferred to the current St. Saviour Church of England School on Fold Road when it opened in 1872. The centenary of the school was celebrated in 1972 with a Service of Thanksgiving for 100 years of Christian education, which was attended by many past teachers and pupils.

In recent years the school has consistently received outstanding reports from Ofsted (Office for Standards in Education) who attribute much of this success to the school's Christian character and values.

Above. Ringley St. Saviours School 1939.

Cinderhill School

In 1835 a Sunday School was built at Cinderhill and endowed by the eccentric character known as Dictum Factum (said, done), James Seddon. The school was located near the top of Ringley Road as it leads up to the main road to Outwood and Stand. I have been unable to find a map of this time that demonstrates its precise location.

It is unclear exactly how long the school was used for, but it is believed to have been abandoned around 1875, and demolished in 1895 upon which cottages were built on the site. James Seddon (1792 – 1846) was a larger than life character who weighed in at over 22 stones in his later years and the last of his family to live at Seddon Fold Farm, Prestolee.

He bequeathed £1100 towards the school endowment, and the scholars would come and sing under his window at Prestolee during Whit-week to show their gratitude for his generosity, this custom was even continued for a further fifteen years after his death.

It is thought that there was an even earlier school located at the top of Ringley Brow (now Ringley Road) where it meets the main road towards Outwood and Stand. Here stood a small row of three storey cottages, and the old school was held in the garrets (attics or loft spaces) of these cottages.

There are no definite dates as to when this 'cottage school' was in operation, but the best guess is from around the late 1700's to the 1830's.

St. Aidan's Mission, Outwood

St Aidan's Mission Church at Outwood was built on land given by Lord Derby and opened in May 1914. It was burned down in 1987 after being broken into and never rebuilt. A housing estate is now on the site with a road named St Aidans Close contained within it as a reminder.

Above. St. Aidan's mission Church, Outwood 1914.

St Paul's Chapel, next door to St. Aidan's, was first erected in 1920's as a wooden structure but was rebuilt in 1951 as a brick building. This closed in 1991 and was turned into a residential dwelling.

Circa 1910 view of St. Saviours clock tower. The Three Crowns public house can be seen at the bottom of Ringley Old Brow. You will note the section of Fold Road which connects to the main road is not yet built.

Emmanuel Church Mission, Ringley

The beginnings of the Emmanuel Church of England Mission in Ringley are somewhat embroiled in a little controversy. At some time early in the year 1920 a wooden hut was erected for the purpose of worship next to St. Saviours School. This certainly ruffled a few feathers in the locality, not least the resident vicar of St. Saviours Church at the time, the reverend T. Dilworth Harrison, whose indignation at his new neighbours is made palpable in his letter to the Farnworth Journal published 19th March 1920.

CORRESPONDENCE.

CHURCH LIFE AT RINGLEY.

Sir,—A circular which can only be termed misleading, has been distributed in the district during the past week, headed "Emmanuel (Church of England) Mission, Ringley," advertising opening meetings, and giving the names of two clergymen from a distance, neither of whom have ever been to Ringley, as having promised to speak.

As Vicar of Ringley, and in the name of the four wardens and all the 18 sidesmen, who are in complete loyalty to the church, I am bound to point out that the wooden hut which has been erected is neither a "Mission" nor "Church of England." It is not a mission, because the word "mission" means a message or an organization "sent," and this has not been sent nor authorized by anybody. It is not Church of England because the Bishop of the Diocese has definitely and deliberately stated in writing that he has not given, and does not intend to give, any official recognition to it. It would not be possible for his lordship to do so, (he adds), consistently with the duties of his office.

The first time I ever heard a responsible person say that the Bishop had sanctioned the hut was at a secular meeting of responsible officials in a neighbouring town last December. I was obliged to point out that such a thing was incredible; the Bishop had never once mentioned the matter to me, nor had he communicated with any of the wardens or church officers. It was in response to my inquiry as to the origin of these rumours and as to the accompanying story that he had himself suggested the name "Emmanuel" (a rather profane skit upon the dedication of the Parish Church of St. Saviour—"Thou shalt call His name Emmanuel, for He shall save His people from their sins," St. Matthew i. 21)—that the Bishop wrote saying that he could not hold himself responsible for any rumours or reports that might be afloat, and stated, as I have said, his inability to give the hut any episcopal recognition.

The whole story of the origin of the hut is a sad one, and some of us have suffered a good deal from misrepresentation. A pin is a small thing, but an effective instrument if carefully handled. But Churchpeople as a whole have tried to treat matters good humouredly, and many attempts have been made to engender a kindlier feeling. England is, of course, a free country, but even in our own fair land we cannot both have our cake and eat it. And you cannot without your bishop's sanction, and with a view to decoying parishioners from their parish church, erect a hut almost under its shadow, and then in spite of the Bishop's disavowal, and inability even to license a layman to conduct its meetings, call it "Church of England."

I do not write this for the benefit of Ringley and Stoneclough people primarily, for they must by now be more or less acquainted with facts. I have refrained for a long time from writing anything about this little secession, since controversy is a weapon the devil so easily turns to his own uses, but outsiders reading a circular of the kind which has provoked this letter could not but think that the church was erecting a further place of worship. I am told by one of the clergy who has been advertised to speak that he thought he was helping the bishop, and hoped that I should be at the opening meetings!

In conclusion I would point out that it is wise to discriminate between sympathy which people in an official position frequently offer to those with alleged grievances and practical support which is conditioned by the principles involved. In the church a bishop does not overside the authority of a priest whom he has instituted to the cure of souls in the parish, unless that priest is guilty of defection from the church's faith, or failure in morals. The Bishop is bound both by his responsibility to the whole body of the faithful, and to the clergy who hold their commission through him from the Great Shepherd.—Yours, etc.,

T. DILWORTH-HARRISON.
Ringley Vicarage, Stoneclough.

In this month's Ringley St. Saviour's, Parish Magazine the Vicar Ringley. says: "I am loth to make reference to the hut which has been erected between and church and school, as a set off to the church life of the village. It is neither consecrated, dedicated, licensed, nor recognized by the Bishop of the Diocese, and the two gentlemen who came to its opening would have been legally inhibited had the Bishop had time to serve the notice; as it was he wrote to them earnestly requesting them to consider their action from the point of view of the church folk. When one knows the stagnation that exists in many parishes without a murmur of protest, it seems a sad thing that where people have responded so widely to church life and work, that a different spirit should not have animated the seceders. But now the hut is an accomplished fact, we only ask to be allowed to live and let live. "What does it matter," one of the speakers is reported to have said at the opening of the building, "whether we are Church of England or not?" "It is not the surplice and cassock that make union with Christ." With the latter profound statement we are in agreement, but we still value our place in the Church of the ages."

Left. As reported in the Farnworth Journal of April 23rd 1920, the dismay of the reverend T. Dilworth Harrison continues.

The Emmanuel Mission group stayed put though, and continued to grow, below is a picture of the Whitsuntide procession taken during the 1920's.

Emmanuel Church of England Mission group at Giants Seat, Ringley Fold, circa 1920's.

Eventually the wooden hut became unsuitable for the increasing congregation and plans were made for moderately larger premises on the same site, but the money would have to be raised by themselves.

Left. Details of the Emmanuel Church finances from the Farnworth Journal of April 15th 1932.

Below. Notice regarding the opening of the new brick building, from the front page of the Farnworth Journal August 5th 1932.

Emmanuel Mission, Ringley. The annual vestry meeting at the Emmanuel Church of England Mission, Ringley, was held on Wednesday week, when a good gathering assembled in the Mission. The Secretary spoke of the work that had been done during the past year, and thanked all who had helped in the cleaning of the church week by week, the Sunday school teachers, and the members of the choir. All this work was done voluntarily, and they were grateful to those who made it possible. The balance-sheet showed a healthy state of affairs, in spite of the serious industrial depression in the district, which affected many of the members. On the income side the ordinary collections amounted to £86 9s. 10d., and special collections £52 18s. 5d. Other items, together with the balance brought forward, made a total income of £198 17s. 4d. The chief items of expenditure were the Whitsuntide expenses, £12 4s. 4d.; heating, lighting and water, £16 10s.; general expenses, £16 15s.; gifts to various missionary societies, £23 10s. 2d.; and building fund, £23 7s. 5d., leaving a balance in hand of £58 2s. 1d. The Building Fund had grown during the year from £184 to £286 7s. 2d., as a result of the generosity of members and friends. The Minister Fund account stands at £162 17s. 3d., making a total of over £500 standing to the credit of the church.

EMMANUEL (C. OF E.) MISSION, RINGLEY

OPENING OF NEW CHURCH.
SPECIAL SERVICES on
SATURDAY, AUGUST 6th, 1932,
At 3 p.m. and 6-30 p.m.,
When ADDRESSES will be Given by the
Rev. J. P. RICHMOND, M.A.,
of Gee Cross.
On SUNDAY, AUGUST 7th, 1932,
At 10-30 a.m., 2-30 p.m. and 6-30 p.m.
ADDRESSES will be Given by the
Rev. H. E. SMITH,
(of Liverpool).
Holy Communion at the 10-30 a.m. Service.

New Building

Opened at Emmanuel Mission, Ringley

The worshippers at the Emmanuel (C. of E.) Mission, Ringley, were joined by a large number of friends from Bolton, Manchester, Preston, Blackburn, Wigan, Adlington, and Heywood, for the opening on Saturday of their new church which has been built to take the place of the wooden structure which has served the needs of the congregation for several years.

A service was held in the afternoon, conducted by the Rev. J. P. Richmond, of Holy Trinity Church, Gee Cross. In his address he spoke of the good work that had been accomplished by the members of the church, and also reminded them what was expected of them in the future—to see that the church which had that day been dedicated to the glory of God should always be a true witness for Him.

Tea was provided for the visitors by members of the congregation, and the opener gave an interesting account of John Angier, one of the first ministers who came to Ringley about the year 1640, and who ultimately was minister of the Denton Old Church, where he ended his days and was buried in the old church.

Another large congregation assembled at the evening service and listened with pleasure to an address by Mr. Richmond.

The services were continued on Sunday, when the preacher was the Rev. H. E. Smith, of Liverpool. Holy Communion was partaken of at the morning service, when 55 communicants were present at the Lord's Table.

The work of erecting the new church has been carried out without any interference whatsoever to the weekly public devotions of the congregation. The officials overcame the difficult problem of continuing the weekly services by having the new structure built round the existing one. On completion of the new building, the walls of the old church were taken out in sections. Mr. James Davies, builder, Ivy-grove Saw Mills, Kearsley, was the contractor, and the decorations are being carried out by Messrs. Denard and Lowery, of Farnworth.

The new building, which is of brick, measures 62ft. by 23ft. by 25ft. At the been built conveniences, a store house and heating chamber.

It is interesting to note that the new brick building was constructed around the wooden one, and that no disruptions to the weekly services were encountered.

Prestolee Holy Trinity Church and School

Businessman and Prestolee cotton mill owner Thomas Bonsor Crompton had decided to erect a church for the benefit of the local community, but unfortunately did not see his plan commence before he passed away on 5th September 1858.

It is believed that the building of Prestolee Holy Trinity Church began in the early part of 1859 on land from part of an estate owned by Thomas Bonsor Crompton. After the death of Mr Crompton, his nephew, a Mr William Jackson Rideout Esq became the 'legatee' or legal heir to the land and he duly created a freehold by deed of release and preparations were made for work to begin.

The costs of building the church were undertaken by Mrs T.B. Crompton, who agreed an endowment of between £7000 and £8000, and Mr Rideout, who also supplemented this by £150 per year. The architect appointed by Mr Rideout was a Mr George Shaw of Saddleworth, Nr Oldham, who also secured the contract for the erection of the church.

Rev. Edwin William Appleyard.
Incumbent of Ringley, 1853-1862.
First Vicar of Prestolee in 1862.

Building work finished in early 1862 but Mr Rideout and the contractor could not agree on the stability of the tower and spire. This disagreement resulted in the tower and spire both being taken down and rebuilt more securely. Whilst these alterations were taking place the Bishop of Manchester licensed the body of the church for immediate use and the first services of the day were celebrated on Easter Sunday 1862. The church was duly completed and consecrated on the 19th June, 1863.

During the building work Mrs T. B. Crompton had invited the Rev. E. W. Appleyard to the benefice of this new church. At this time Mr Appleyard was the vicar at nearby St Saviours in Ringley but he accepted the offer and took up residence in a house provided by Mr Rideout in Prestolee.

The large stained glass East window shows a representation of the Crucifixion and was the gift of Mrs T. B. Crompton, while the West window depicts the Adoration of the Magi and cost around £200, of which some portion was subscribed by the workers, who had been employed by Mr Crompton, as memorial to their late master. It bears the inscription: - "To The Honour And Glory Of God and in memory of the late Thomas B Crompton, by the people employed at Prestolee, 1862".

Soon after the death of Mrs Crompton in 1864, the large window in the North transept was filled with stained glass as a memorial to her. It was funded by her nephew Mr W J Rideout and the work was carried out by Messrs Ballantyne of Edinburgh, who had also fitted the East and West windows.

The Church has been used for several weddings by ITV soap opera Coronation Street, the first being Deirdre Langton and Ken Barlow in July 1981. After this came dustman Eddie Yates and Marion Willis in October 1983, Mike Baldwin and Susan Barlow in May 1986 and Alec Gilroy and Bet Lynch in September 1987.

Above. Prestolee Holy Trinity Church Circa 1940's. Church Road is to the left and the long gone Church View leads to the right.

HOLY TRINITY CHURCH, PRESTOLEE.

Preparations are being made for holding a Bazaar in the White Row School-room, Prestolee, on Thursday, April 20th, 1871, and the two following days, the profits from which will be expended in providing stalls or benches for the choir, and the fittings required for lighting the Holy Trinity Church with gas. Contributions, either in money or materials, will be gratefully received by Mrs. Appleyard, and Mrs. Rivett, Prestolee; Mrs. T. Bradbury, Mrs. Eckersley, and Mrs. Shaw, Kearsley; Miss Chorlton, Stoneclough; or any of the Sunday School Teachers.

Above. From the Farnworth & Kearsley Parish magazine of January 1871.

THE VICAR'S LETTER.
The Vicarage,
Prestolee,
August 30th, 1943.

My dear People,

We have conquered Sicily, and are preparing to attack Italy. Russia is making great advances, and far-reaching plans have been hammered out at Quebec.

Berlin has been heavily raided, and Nuremberg, that Nazi show-ground, has been virtually wiped out.

Altogether the War news is excellent, and we should fittingly show our thanksgiving and re-dedication on the National Day of Prayer on September 3rd, and again on the Battle of Britain day, Sepetmber 26th.

We wish to build a better Britain. One of the ways is by means of education, and it is with real joy that I record the educational successes of our younger people in another column, for I always stress the importance of education, and always try and urge all to take advantage of the many avenues now open, leading to a richer and fuller life.

The most important way of all to attain that fuller life is, of course, by means of Christian education, and at this stage in our history, we should strive, more than ever, to ensure that our education is indeed a Christian education in the fullest sense.

My Wife and I intend staying in Torquay over Sundays, September 12th and 19th, so the Services on these two Sundays will be, Holy Communion 8-30 a.m. (instead of 8 a.m.) and Mattins and Evensong at the usual times, 10-30 a.m. and 6-30 p.m.

With Best Wishes.

Your Friend and Vicar,
P. WILLMOTT JENKINS.

Above. From the Prestolee Holy Trinity Church magazine of September 1943 are some encouraging wartime words from the vicar P. Willmott Jenkins. To the right is a bookmark from the same period.

Circa 1901. Prestolee Holy Trinity Church is shown with the old wooden Sunday school next to it. The cows are grazing on the fields of the former Prestolee Farm, which was situated on the corner of Crompton Road and Seddon Lane. Within a decade of this picture being taken these fields were replaced by houses making up Alexandra Road, Derby Road and Church Road. At the rear of the Church can be seen Prestolee House, and further back is Irwell Bank Mill which went on to be twice the size seen here by 1904. To the left is thought to be the remains of Thomas Bonsor Crompton's mill built in 1833.

The first official school in Prestolee is thought to have been 'White Row' School which opened around 1845, it was also known as the as 'The Mill School' and was located above one of the old houses known as the 'White Row' close to Thomas Bonsor Crompton's cotton spinning mill.

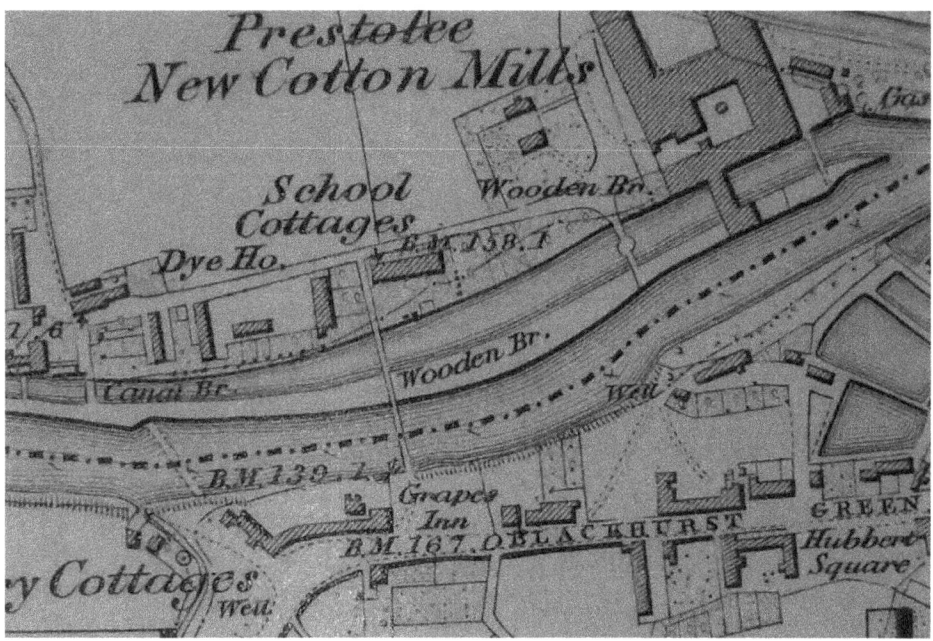

Above. Map of 1848 showing the White Row School Cottages at Prestolee. The School is believed to be above the residence nearest to the mill and was accessed by a series of steps at the end of the building. **Below.** From the Farnworth & Kearsley Parish magazine of January 1870.

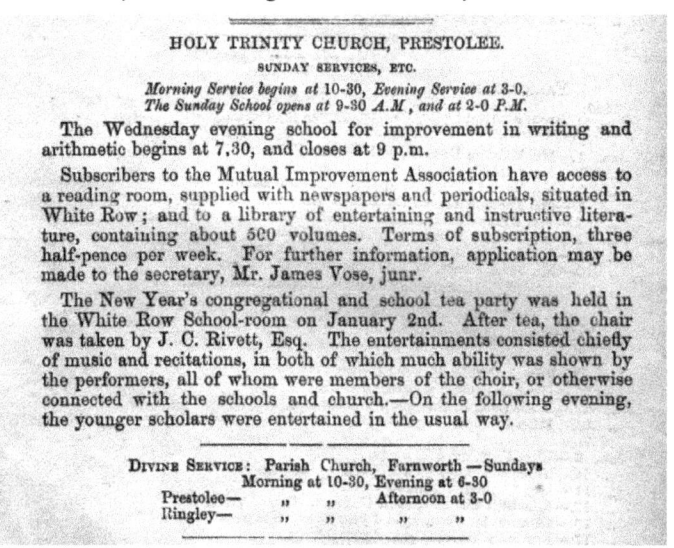

White Row cottages, Prestolee circa 1890. Dating from around the 1830's these dwellings would have been without electricity, inside toilets and possibly running water.

Prestolee Primary School shortly after opening in 1911. The old Sunday school, which was demolished during the 1970's, can be seen further up Church Road, which at this time is still a dirt track with no paving or street lighting.

Prestolee Primary School

The school was formally opened in the afternoon of Saturday 23rd September 1911, in the presence of a large crowd by Mr J. J. Cockshott, Chairman of the Lancashire Elementary Education Sub-Committee. Mr J. C. Woods, on behalf of the builders, Messrs. J.C. and J. Woods, presented Mr. Cockshott with a silver key, with which he unlocked the door.

It was then also known as Outwood and Kearsley Council School and on the first Monday there were 246 children in attendance. Separate entrances and cloakrooms were provided for the boys, girls and infants, and special rooms were furnished for the teaching of laundry work and cookery for the girls, and woodwork for the boys. The cost of building the school, including the paving of the playgrounds, drainage and equipment etc was around £8.000.

At first children were jammed together into rows of long desks with up to sixty pupils in each classroom. During its first ninety years the school had only five headteachers. The first headteacher was Mr J Slack. He was replaced in 1918 by Mr E F (Teddy) O'Neil, who at 28 years old became the youngest headteacher ever appointed in Lancashire, and his methods in running Prestolee School were to be reported on, and debated, around the world.

Teddy O'Neil, M.B.E

Most people are not aware of the quite extraordinary system of education and unorthodox teaching methods that were put into practice at Prestolee School for over thirty years. It was the vision of a man who dreamed of a school where every child would be happy, and education would be by self activity and a minimum of supervision, the children would 'learn by doing'. That man was Teddy O'Neill.

There were many detractors of his methods over the years and at times they came close to finishing his time at the school, but fortunately there were those that wholly believed in what he was undertaking, such as his wife Isabel and his often perplexed colleague Mr Omes.

Edward F O'Neill was born in a back street slum area of Salford where his mother kept a succession of pubs and off-licence shops and his father took work where he could, but whilst in-between jobs would usually be at his wife's place of business or alternative drinking parlour. His fathers excessive drinking would lead to ructions and eventually a separation order from his wife, and when he failed to pay the ten shillings a week for his two children, he was sent to jail. Teddy would help his mother in the Pubs, collecting glasses, watering down the beer and playing the piano, but together they saved enough for him to attend university.

After impressing as a temporary headmaster at a school in Accrington Teddy was advised to apply for the position as headmaster at Prestolee School, he was duly appointed and, at the age of twenty eight, Teddy with his wife and two children made their way to the village during the closing weeks of 1918.

On his second morning in charge the Teachers' schemes of work books were taken away, the framed school time-table was covered with a colour print of the 'Laughing Cavalier' and set lessons were done away with. Playtimes were abolished and teachers could take tea when they wished. The accepted orthodoxies of the education system were swept aside by a man with a vision to not only educate, but to form better people. The children were encouraged to find things out for themselves, as well as reading newspapers and discussing the news of the day, and above all - to ask questions.

Although the children were allowed to do as they pleased in their self-chosen activities for most of the school day, they did have to exercise literacy and numeracy (the three 'R's) and accomplish a minimum amount of work in these subjects, but they could of course continue their work longer if they so wished. The aim of Teddy O'Neil was that by giving the children abundant facilities to use their inborn powers of discovery and interpretation, these faculties would grow and grow through such healthy exercise. The child's knowledge will accumulate as a by-product of this activity and their initiative and resourcefulness will have greatly increased: far more so than can be the case with formal class-teaching and blackboard work. One of his goals was that if a child was asked a question to which they did not at once know the answer, they would be off of their own accord, consulting books and other sources of information, and would return with reasoned answers: whereas the average reaction of the spoon-fed child from elsewhere, if they had not had that particular spoonful of information, would say they had not been taught that, and leave it there.

A sublime example of how the children could be enlightened in this way was the introduction of a school museum. The pupils were made into small groups and everyone was asked to contribute objects to fill the museum, but this is where normal convention ended, as there was one important rule. The rule was that any object put forward to go in the museum must be of no interest whatsoever, and in order for it to be accepted the other groups of children must not be able to find anything of interest about it at all.

This may seem strange or even pointless, but the children set to work fervently, first of all to try and find a completely uninteresting object and also to prove objects brought in by others were of some sort of historical, scientific, artistic or cultural interest. A piece of broken glass was submitted, so a group researched how glass was made, its chemical composition, where the sand may have come from and how the ancient Egyptians had made glass bottles five thousand years ago. A dead cat from the canal was found to be alive with interest and was also rejected. More and more mundane and seemingly bland and banal items were submitted, and none were accepted, the school museum remained completely empty through the hard-work and research by the groups of children as they investigated everything brought in, and always managed to find something of curiosity, relevance and interest in each item.

One of the most interesting techniques employed by Teddy O'Neil was the use of English composition and essay writing to broaden a child's horizons. It is beyond the scope of this book to explain how this was implemented and how it could greatly contribute to a child's character and alertness of their senses, but it is a most fascinating technique that deserves to be acknowledged, and is covered in much greater detail, along with the rest of Teddy's story at Prestolee School in the book 'The Idiot Teacher' by Gerard Holmes, published by Faber and Faber Ltd.

Teddy was named in the New Years Honour's List in January 1951 and awarded the MBE, but just over two years later, in May 1953, he resigned along with his wife Isabella, declaring that the character of the school will be ruined when he loses all the senior scholars to the new George Tomlinson Secondary Modern School opening that September. He went on to say "I suppose it had to come, it is the decapitation of my life's work. With a smaller number of pupils to teach, two teachers would have to resign, so my wife and I decided we would be the two to quit."

Teddy O'Neil passed away in 1977 and a special commemoration service was held at Prestolee Holy Trinity on Sunday 27th March 1977, at which readings were given of Keats and Wordsworth, various hymns were sung, one being Jerusalem, before a procession to the school was undertaken in silence, after which a further hymn was sung by former pupils.

Above. Prestolee School circa 1920.

Below. Prestolee School children at play in 1936.

Below. Prestolee School 1946.

s **and Boys** who go to Prestolee School, Lancashire, are allowed in class out paying much heed to convention. Norma Richardson has been trapeze swinging and hasn't bothered to put her shoes on, while Constance Wr has found some old carpet slippers. Fred Haslam turns round for a

We Learn, By Doing

The Man Who Runs Britain's Most Unusual Council School
E. F. O'Neill, M.B.E., has been its head since 1919. His passion for planting trees has turned the playground into an orchard. Here he shows the children how a carrot-top will grow a fresh root. "But don't imagine that any good will come out of slicing in half your turnip-heads."

Prestolee School 1952

Prestolee School, 1936.

Prestolee School. **Above** 1946 and **below** 1952.

Art and Gymnastics Have Equal Rights in the School Hall
For O'Neill informality is an eternal value in education. His pupils learn to concentrate on their own interests without treading on each other's toes. The picture is an enlargement by the boy on the left of Leonardo da Vinci's 'Warrior.' The 'jungle gym' was built by the children.

Above. Homemade Ice Cream stall at Prestolee School 1952, and below a small selection of the principles expressed by Teddy O'Neill.

"Real poverty is lack of imagination
There Are:
Those who do and those who don't
The educated and the uneducated
The shepherds and the sheep
The riders and the donkeys
The living and the dead"

"Take care of the children and later on- the adults will take care of themselves"

"Self-activity is the habit of starting work without being told to"

"The best way to learn is to live"

"Many teachers die in school but are not buried till later"

Prestolee Primary School with its new extension to the south side of the building, and Holy Trinity Church, 2008.

View from Kearsley Station looking over Prestolee in January 1979. Holy Trinity Church is easily identifiable in the heart of the neighborhood, with the land to the rear having been cleared in preparation for the Riverside housing estate. The former Working Men's Club and bowling green are seen in the centre of the picture. The club closed in the mid 1980's and a small housing development named The Riverbank now occupies the site.

Halshaw Moor Chapel

Just off Market Street in Farnworth Town centre, across the main road from Brackley Street is Chapel Street. By modern standards it is barely a street at all, more an inconspicuous alleyway down the side of the building currently used as the premises of Barclays Bank, but it leads to a small area that has had a colourful and intriguing past.

In the early eighteenth century, and presumably for some time before this, the land around this immediate area was known as 'Withington Croft'. It was owned by a Mr. James Heywood of Little Lever, who, having made his money as a cotton spinner now decided that some spiritual instruction was needed for the locality. He had wanted to simply donate the site for the building of a Chapel, but because the land was not freehold a small charge of halfpenny a yard was charged. Several years later more ground adjoining Withington Croft was secured, and instead of the halfpenny a yard for the land, an original chief rent of £5 5s 0d was paid to Mr. Benjamin Rawson.

The first sod of earth for what was originally called Withington Chapel was cut on 24th June 1808, and on the 7th of July the first stone was laid by Mr. Robert Topp, sen., of Clammerclough. The Topp family were relatively prominent in the district with Robert's father, old Nathaniel Topp, being overseer of the poor for Kearsley around 1750, he was also a tanner and had pits on Holloway Gutter, around 100 yards below the Manchester and Bolton road (the Tannery was to the rear of what is now the Moss Rose public house and Holloway Gutter ran through what is now Holdens Mill and across Manchester Road). Roberts brother, Joseph, lived at Taskers farm at Taskers lane (now Springfield Road, Kearsley) until he was turned out of it by a Mr. Grundy, who was at that time the agent for the Duke of Bridgewater who owned the land, and Robert's wife Peggy ran a school in Farnworth.

It is worth remembering that according to the census of 1801 the population of Farnworth was around 1439, and most of these desperately poor people would have lived in 200 or so small cottages scattered around the fields and commons. The nearest Churches were at Ringley, Little Lever or the Parish Church at Bolton, so the new Chapel could certainly lay claim to have been the first purpose built place of worship in the town.

On Whit Sunday 1809, the Chapel, although unfinished, opened for worship. It seated around 250 and the furniture was very simple; a few forms without backs were placed upon the flagged floor. There was no heating apparatus or lighting, even candles were not required as services were held in the morning and afternoon. The place was originally nothing more than a shell with fifteen windows, six on each side and three at the south end, a roof and two doors. Three months after the opening some high backed pews were fixed down the middle, and on 7th November 1809 a bell was hung. The cupola sheltering the bell stood upon 5 short legs at the South end of the roof. On Sunday 16th July 1809 services began to be held regularly and a subscription was opened for the purpose of providing funds to pay for supplies. The Rev George Kilpatrick was the first to preach at the new Chapel, and in Harold A. Barnes 'The Story Of Halshaw Moor Chapel' the author has it on authority that Mr Kilpatrick's character was described as "austere, gloomy and bordering on moroseness."

Above. The original Independent Chapel at Withington Croft.

Mr Kilpatrick had only been supplied for a year by the Rev. William Roby of Manchester, and for the next couple of years after his tenure a Mr. Paul Partington of Worsley preached, with a Mr. Harrison and the Rev. Noah Blackburn of Delph, in Yorkshire also occasionally preaching. The first permanent minister was the Rev. Joseph Dyson who began his incumbency in 1813. He also originated from Yorkshire, and it seems that his dialect so

Left. Reverand Joseph Dyson

offended his new congregation that they put their heads together and bought him a dictionary, with the modest request that he should use it!, he apparently accepted the gift with good grace. He was also known to have mildly remonstrated with his sometimes weary congregation by bringing his hands down on the pulpit saying "Don't go to sleep my brethren! Don't go to sleep."

The first marriage to be solemnised at the Chapel was between George Redford and Sarah Duckworth, but this was not until February 1838. The reason for this was that previous to 1836 marriages were not legal unless performed in an established Church by a clergyman of the Church of England, and Halshaw Moor Chapel as it was now known, was an independent Church that ran its own affairs. A Sunday school was established in 1816, it was a two storey building erected at the back of the Chapel, that had a ground plan of a mere 21 feet by 15 feet. The lower room was used for the boys and the upper room for the girls. The school opened on June 23rd and in attendance were twenty boys and just seven girls.

Halshaw Moor Chapel continued to flourish with an ever-increasing congregation, then, during 1847 discussions were opened with regard to building a new and larger chapel. A scheme was finally agreed upon and work began shortly afterwards. A plot of land at what was known as Nelson's

Croft was donated by Joseph and James Lord, for the purpose of erecting the new Church. They also donated a significant amount of money to the building fund, and it is believed that nearby Lord Street is named in memory of these generous benefactors, with Nelson Street also taking its name from the ancient location of Nelson's Croft on which it is situated.

Above. Circa 1900. Situated at Nelson's Croft on the corner of Market Street and Church Road, the new gothic style Market Street Congregational Church opened on July 10th 1850. Interesting camera angle seems to be from the top of Hollands School roof.

With the opening of the new Church the old Halshaw Moor Chapel building was converted into a Sunday School. There had been a Sunday School in operation from 1816 and the move to larger premises was a welcome development as the number of scholars had risen rapidly in the preceding years.

The Church and School continued to prosper, so much so that a new large assembly hall building was erected. This was to be used for teaching, meetings, lectures or any purpose that required a large comfortable space. It was given the name Moor Hall, as it was built in the district of Halshaw Moor, and across the road was an old house called Moor House which is now long gone, but the former Police Station stands in what once formed part of its gardens.

Above. The Moor Hall in July 1950.

Above. Circa 1908. The Sunday School building, built in 1850 on the site of the original Halshaw Moor Chapel which had to be demolished. This picture was taken from Church Street approximately from in front of the former Farnworth Police Station. To the right of this building was the Chapel cemetery, and some of the gravestones are still there even today.

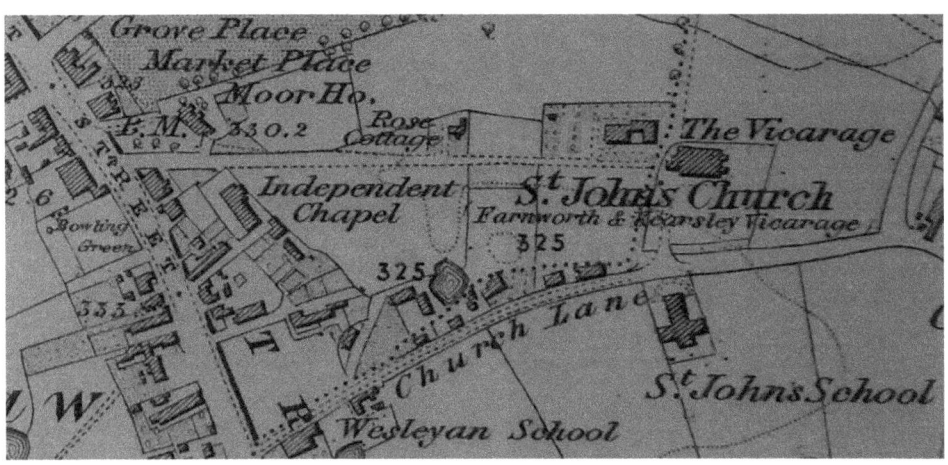

Above. 1848. The Independent Chapel with Sunday School at the bottom of Chapel Street. Moor House & Rose Cottage can be seen across the road on Church Street.

Above. 1908. The Moor Hall which opened on New Years Day 1864.

The Moor Hall became a significant building in the district, and over the next century went on to serve many more functions such as hosting concerts, dances, amateur dramatics society productions, cookery demonstrations and even inquests. During 1950 the hall undertook major restoration work and held a special concert to celebrate the re-opening ceremony.

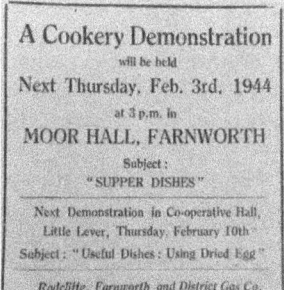
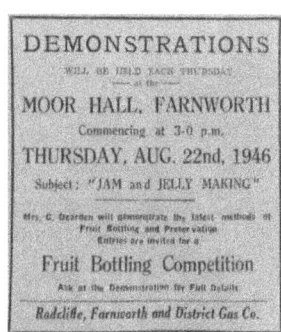

On the left a February 1944 advert for a cookery demonstration at the Moor Hall, and on the right, from August 1946, for a jam making and Fruit Bottling demonstration and competition.

Over the next two decades the Moor Hall and the various Congregational Churches in Farnworth went into a decline. By January 1967 it had become clear that a merger would be a sensible option, and in 1972 the Trinity Church was founded, comprising of the Weslyan Methodist Church, which stood on the corner of Presto Street and Church Street, Queen Street Methodist

Church and the Market Street Congregational Church. Thankfully they were able to remain in the Market Street Church, although much of it had to be demolished and rebuilt during the 1970's leaving only the Chancel of the original building in place.

Above. Circa 1910. The former Weslyan Chapel that stood at the junction of Presto Street and Church Street. St Gregory's Church can just be seen in the background.

Below. The interior of the Church Street Weslyan Chapel.

The Moor Hall at the bottom of Chapel Street however was to have a much more exciting continuation after it was finally abandoned in the early 1960's. It reopened as Club Monaco, operating a late bar with live bands and cabaret acts on every night.

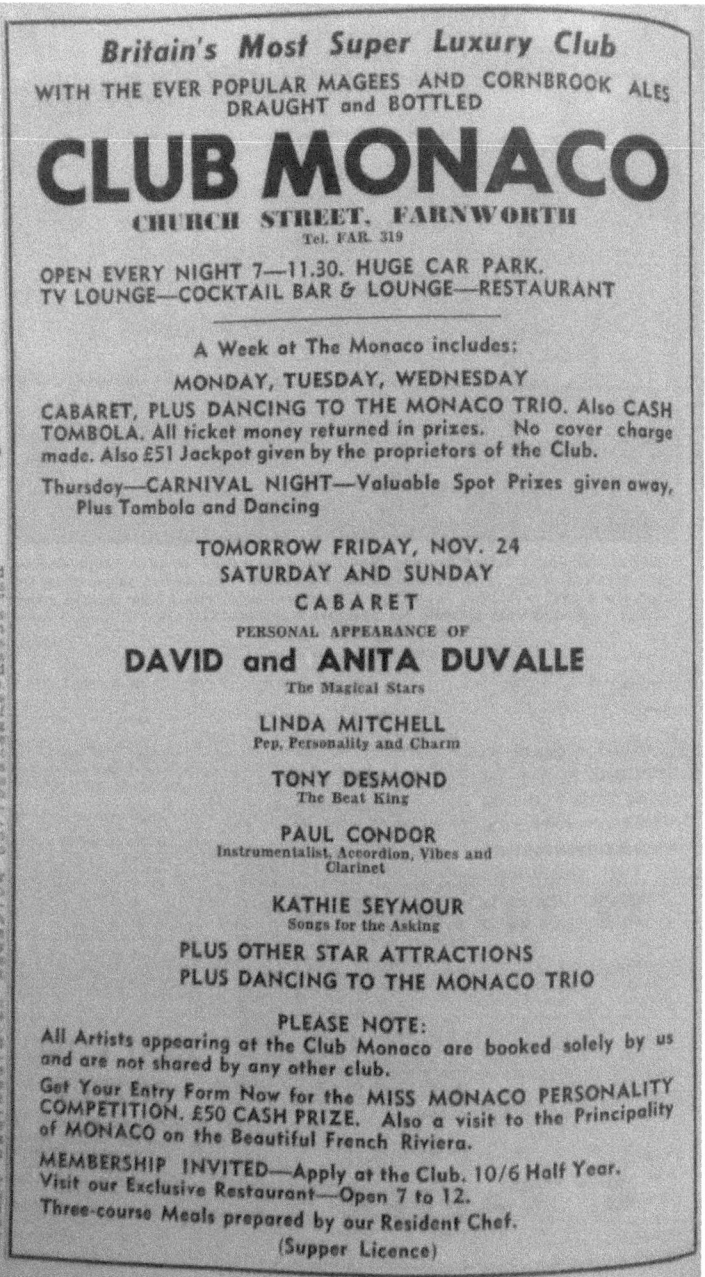

Above. November 1961 Advert for Club Monaco shortly after it first opened.

Club Monaco closed during 1970, but, after major refurbishment, was reborn as Blighty's nightclub, which opened for the first time on November 21st 1971. Blighty's became one of the premier nightspots in the country, with numerous famous stars of music, entertainment and television performing each week. These included, Tommy Cooper, Cannon and Ball, The Three Degrees, Showaddywaddy, Bruce Forsyth, Bob Monkhouse, Martha Reeves and the Vandellas, The Drifters, Slade, Alvin Stardust, and The Four Tops.

Above. Opening night at Blighty's nightclub, Chapel Street. Headline act was the comedian Ken Goodwin, who had starred in the Royal Command Performance that week. The television in his dressing room had not been connected up in time for him to watch the recorded show, so he accepted an offer to watch it across the road in the home of pensioners Mr and Mrs Jim Bradbury. After he had watched himself on television Ken thanked his hosts and went back over to the club to do a 50-minute spot and received a standing ovation from the audience.

The new and impressive layout at Blighty's featured a mahogany lined foyer, which lead into a large cabaret room that was fully carpeted and offered an uninterrupted view of the stage from every one of its 1,000 velvet upholstered seats. A giant chandelier hung over the large dance floor and the bars were designed so that guests could watch the shows in comfort from there if they so wished.

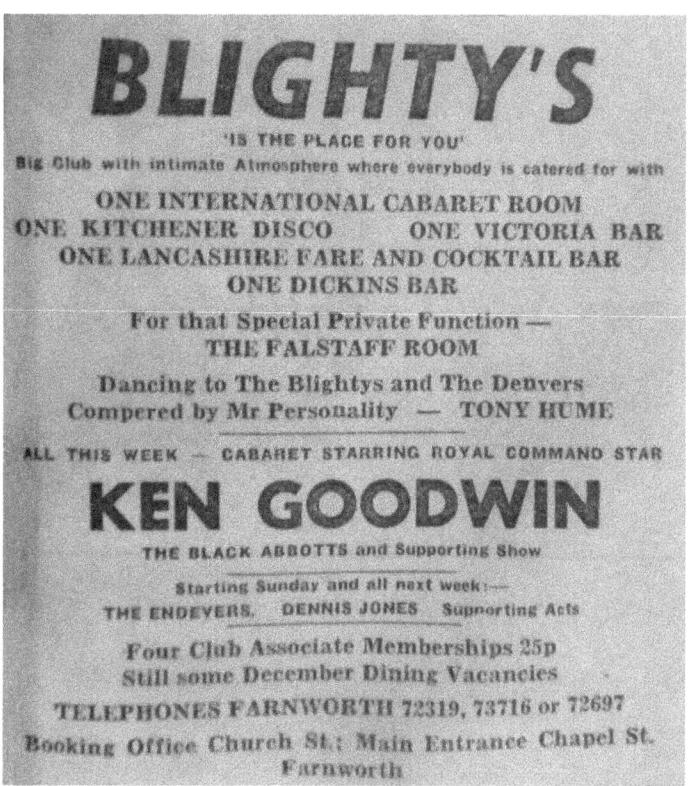

A second floor had been constructed with different rooms and bars, such as the Falstaff Room that could hold 250 people, a Victorian Bar with an elaborate plastered ceiling and marble ornaments and all with its own dance floor, the Dickens Cocktail Bar and the Kitchener Disco Bar. Food on offer included chicken in a basket, hamburger and chips, black pudding and steak and cowheel pie.

There is a story that Frank Sinatra once played at Blighty's, but it is sadly just a myth. But this is not for the want of trying, as in June 1973, Gerry Slinger, manager at Blighty's, offered the star £70,000 plus expenses to appear. Negotiations did take place, but sadly "Ol' Blue Eyes" never made it to Farnworth.

Blighty's remained popular into the 1980's, and under new ownership in 1985 changed its name to City Lites. The interior was brought up to date, and the main dance floor was cleared for a short time during Friday and Saturday nights as we were treated to a bizarre light show to music. The club was often packed to capacity of around 2,500, of which many had travelled by coaches from as far afield as Carlisle, Birmingham, Liverpool and Hull. I can remember the coaches lined up along one side of Market Street and the Police vans lined up along the other, it was mostly good-natured, but occasionally it ended up in unarmed drunken combat between coach parties from different towns, and often the locals.

Due to the popularity of Blighty's, plus the other smaller venues such as the infamous Chuffers and Scarlets (later the RAC club), the surrounding pubs were also packed out. Another club worth mentioning was Brando's, which was situated in the old fire station at the top of Frederick Street. It had a dance floor with different coloured squares that flashed on and off Saturday Night Fever style, but its location meant it was also very popular with the good citizens of Walkden and Little Hulton, again this often meant an interesting few hours for the local constabulary. There is currently a Lidl superstore on the site.

City Lites closed in early 1990, but the doors soon reopened at the bottom of Chapel Street to a whole new clubbing experience. For just over a year between 1991 and 1992 we had The Pleasuredrome. Acid House and Rave music had become immensely popular in Britain, and now Farnworth was once again home to one of the most vibrant club scenes in the country. The Pleasuredrome was often accused of being packed out to over the official capacity and this was doubtless the case, and it was no secret that most, were sky high on illegal drugs. There was very little alcohol sold inside, and the cold-water taps in the toilets did not produce any water, so everyone had to buy it from over the bar. The toilets resembled saunas at times, as only hot water was available for the perspiring and hyperactive clientele that popped in for some relief.

Two centuries previously, at the tranquil site of Withington Croft on Halshaw Moor, plans were made for a humble chapel to give those in the neighbourhood some spiritual instruction. This scheme had proved so successful that a Sunday school was introduced, and later the Moor Hall was erected for the betterment of the locality, but it was now the weekly setting for hundreds of wide-eyed ravers, sweating profusely, popped up on pills plus goodness knows what else, and, somewhat strangely, all directly over the road from the Police station. Only a few decades earlier the Moor Hall held tea parties, amateur dramatic shows and jam making demonstrations. Changing times meant that it had to be put to different uses if it were to survive, and its various reincarnations as nightclubs achieved that goal, but the Pleasuredrome just went too far.

Above. 1992. View down Chapel Street to the entrance of The Pleasuredrome shortly after it had been forced to close.

At the time it was often stated that there was actually very little trouble at the venue, the happy pills were, on the one hand destroying people's minds, but on the other made them somewhat contented enough not to want to start thumping each other. The old Moor Hall was now witness to a most strange state of affairs, and it wasn't going to last. Gradually the authorities took action, public pressure, plus evidence that it had become a drug-dealers paradise meant the Police were compelled to clamp down. In October 1992 the club was forced to close, and its licence also revoked at a hearing at Bolton Crown Court. The owners took their appeal against this decision to London's High Court, but they agreed with the Bolton Crown Court verdict, and The Pleasuredrome was no more.

The building remained unused, until a fire in January 1996 finally destroyed any hopes of it returning to former glories. It was demolished shortly afterwards, and in November 2002 plans for an 80 bed nursing home were approved. Farnworth Care Home now sits peacefully on the historic and noteworthy patch of land once known as Withington Croft.

Circa 1910. Ringley Lord Mayor at the Three Crowns Inn that stood at the bottom of Ringley Old Brow. This pub closed for good during the mid 1920's.

Ringley Lord Mayor

It is unknown exactly as to when the ceremony of instating a mock Lord Mayor to Ringley first began, but the best guess is the late 1800's. It became part of the annual Ringley Wakes celebrations, but in the early twentieth century it appears to have been done sporadically, and often left out altogether for many years before reappearing. It then seems to have been abandoned completely during the late 1930's.

This comic 'Lord Mayor' was elected on the first Monday in May after the Anniversary Sermons in Ringley Church. After he had been elected, the Lord Mayor was carried across the Old Ringley Bridge on a form from the Horseshoe Hotel. He would be dressed in an old-fashioned coat with knee-breeches, buckled shoes and wearing an old shako (an army hat with a peak and feathers) on his head, whilst also carrying a long toasting fork containing a kipper and a piece of toast.

A number of local men would then carry him to all the pubs in Ringley and Stoneclough, as well as often being taken up Slackey Brow to visit further alehouses along Manchester Road and Bolton Road, before returning down Stoneclough Brow. He would be entitled to a free pint in each one, and during his 'Year in Office' he could claim a free drink in all the local pubs every Sunday, providing he was dressed in his Sunday clothes and was wearing a clean shirt with a collar and tie. The only draw-back on the day of his election was the ritual of either having canal water poured over his head from a beer mug or actually being thrown into the canal, usually at the side of the Horseshoe hotel, after he had had his free drinks!

The week of his election was known as Ringley Wakes Week with various rides and stalls near the Lord Nelson Inn. There would be various contests that anyone could enter, such as porridge eating, foot races, a smoking match, a grinning match or climbing a greasy pole. Prizes for each event were given and these included silk shawls, one fat duck, a handsome pair of trousers, money or packs of tobacco.

Ringley Wakes.

The wakes was held last week end. There was foot racing and a bowling sweep at the Lord Nelson, and on Monday afternoon the "Lord Mayor" was elected, the position falling to the lot of a navvy named Charlie Fry. Hoisted on a form, he was carried round Kearsley, the road taken being via Slackey Brow, Bolton-rd., and Stoneclough Brow. Whilst on the higher length he was either knocked or slipped off his perch, and judging by the bandaging upon his cranium he must have been considerably bruised.

Above. The Lord Mayor has to have his head bandaged in May 1900.

Ringley's "Lord Mayor."

An Old Custom Revived.

After a lapse of about 25 years the old custom of "electing" or "selecting" the "Lord Mayor" of Ringley was revived on Monday, when William Pilkington, of the Parsonage Court, took the position. He donned the old peaked cap and braided coat which have been kept at one of the hostelries, picked up the old bell, and mounted a form on which his friends and followers carried him from the Horseshoe Hotel to the Lord Nelson. The Three Crowns used to be on the itinerary, but that inn has meanwhile been closed, and he was instead carried along Kearsley Hall-rd. to and from the Miners' Arms at the bottom of Slackey Brow. Then he was taken to the canal, where he was thoroughly and conscientiously ducked before a large crowd, in which the children predominated, his re- [miners holding] his feet whilst he was "soused." The company then adjourned to the Horseshoe Inn, where the evening was spent right merrily. Seen by our representative on the morning following the "Lord Mayor" looked none the worse for his immersion, but he said his arm was sore from bruises sustained when the carriers of his "civic chair" let him drop in front of the Lord Nelson. In the old days the "Lord Mayor," whose appointment was made on the Monday following the first Sunday in May, was allowed to collect "tolls and taxes" from holders of stalls at Ringley Wakes, which on Monday took up their position on the spare ground near the ancient stone bridge, and were freely patronised. On that day he was carried through Stoneclough on to Manchester-rd. and along that thoroughfare to Slackey Brow and back again to Ringley, he and his following calling at every public house en route for free drinks. For 12 months afterwards on every Saturday night, he was entitled to receive at the three licensed houses in Ringley "a pint of sixpenny beer," as long as he presented himself shaved, wearing a clean shirt, and in an otherwise "respectable" condition.

Above. The Lord Mayor ceremony is reinstated in May 1927.

In the earlier days of the wakes there were also more barbaric and repugnant events on display, such as dog-fighting, cock-fighting and bull-baiting which all took place in a gravel pit near to the Lord Nelson, or on the nearby island on the River Irwell. A form of no-holds barred brawling, by men whom had stripped to the waste, and would then strut across Ringley Old Bridge challenging anyone to a fight (often a fist fight), also occurred. This was known locally as 'up-and-down fighting.' Alternatively, the men would fight by kicking at each other in their wooden clogs until one contestant conceded, this peculiar form of conflict was simply called 'clog fighting.'

Ringley Lord Mayor circa 1910.

Circa 1912. What was known as 'the island' close to Ringley Old Bridge. It is barely visible these days, but in the early years of the Ringley Wakes it was the setting for some of the more vile and barbaric events on display.

The Manchester, Bolton and Bury Canal, (MBBC)

As the industrial revolution began to gather pace during the latter part of the eighteenth century the demand for coal and other minerals increased accordingly. The towns and cities were expanding as a growing number of new large scale manufacturing works and cotton mills sprang up. The latest steam engines were being deployed which meant the demand for coal to power them escalated rapidly, and the expanding population also required more supplies of goods, materials and food.

Up until this time the main form of transport for coal and other goods was by a horse and cart, or by packhorses, which were horses loaded with sidepacks, and this significantly limited the amount that could be carried.

Few roads in Britain during this period were turnpiked, so they were no more than tracks that were either unattended or possibly maintained by the locals or the landowner, and this meant they could be somewhat uneven and often prone to flooding. The eighteenth century solution to these transportation difficulties came in the form of man-made canals.

The Bridgewater canal between Worsley and Manchester opened in 1761 and was the first English completely man made inland waterway. The Duke of Bridgewater employed the famous engineer James Brindley, along with his agent John Gilbert to plan the canal system. Underground canals were dug to the Dukes pits in Worsley where coal was loaded into small boats 47 feet long and 4 and half feet wide. These were towed in 'trains' along the various fingers of the underground system totalling 46 miles. The boats returned full of coal to Worsley and then on to Manchester along the Bridgewater canal. The cost of coal in Manchester was halved because of the new and easier mode of transport.

In 1790, Matthew Fletcher, a wealthy colliery owner who had sunk several new pits in the Irwell valley at Kearsley, Pendlebury and Clifton, realized that a canal from Manchester to Bolton and to Bury would also provide a cheap form of transport for coal (especially his own coal) and other goods, so a preliminary survey was made.

In 1791 an official survey was made by Hugh Henshall, brother in law to James Brindley, and following this Parliament was petitioned to bring in a bill to allow the canal to be built. There were then many meetings by the people who were sponsoring the project, and the mill owners of the area, who were concerned that water supplies to the mills would be affected by the new waterway. After further surveys and reports these fears were allayed and on 13th May 1791 Parliament passed the Bill and work could begin.

The water supply came from Elton Reservoir at Summerseat, which was fed from aqueducts from a weir on the River Irwell and augmented by drainage water from the local land and collieries. The canal was to be cut from Church Wharf, Bolton, to Bury Wharf, with a flight of locks at the Nob End basin joining a further canal through Prestolee, Ringley, and Clifton to Oldfield Road, Salford. The canal was to be a total of 15 miles 1 furlong in length with 17 locks and 3 aqueducts. Between Manchester and the top of the locks at Nob End there is a total rise of 187 feet, the Bolton-Bury level is lock-free.

Cutting the canal finished during 1797, with the work being done by hundreds of navvies. It is worth remembering that this was before the days of any mechanical tools or bulldozers so they had to rely on spades, picks, wooden wheelbarrows and horses and carts. The word navvy came from the word 'navigators' who built the first 'navigation canals' in the eighteenth century. To prevent water from escaping out of the cutting the navvies lined the flat bottom of the canal with puddled clay – that is clay and plenty of water to make a watertight seal.

AN ACT

FOR

Making and Maintaining a Navigable Canal from *Manchester* to or near *Presto-lee Bridge*, in the Township of *Little Lever*; and from thence by One Branch to or near the Town of *Bolton*, and by another Branch to or near the Town of *Bury*, and to *Weddell Brook*, in the Parish of *Bury*, all in the County Palatine of *Lancaster*.

WHEREAS the making and maintaining a Canal for the Navigation of Boats, Barges, and other Vessels, from and to join and communicate with the River *Irwell*, at a certain Place in the said River, at or near the Sugar House or Old Quay, in the Town of *Manchester*, unto, into, or near a certain Meadow belonging to Messieurs *Edward* and *Christoper Whitehead*, in the Township of *Little Lever*, in the Parish of *Bolton*, and near *Presto-lee Bridge*, and from thence to be carried and continued by One Branch to or near a certain Bridge at the Town of *Bolton*, called *Church Bridge*, and by another Branch to or near a certain other Bridge at the Town of *Bury*, called *Bury Bridge*, and from thence to a Place called *Weddell Brook*, in the Parish of *Bury* aforesaid, all in the said County Palatine of *Lancaster*, with proper Conveniencies for conveying and carrying Goods and other Articles to and from the said intended Canal, will afford a useful, short, and easy Communication between the said Towns of *Manchester*, *Bolton*, and *Bury*, and the adjacent Country, open an Introduction to many valuable and extensive Mines of Coal and other Minerals, and will in other Respects be of great Advantage to the Public;

Preamble.

A   And

Above. The 1791 Act of Parliament for constructing the Manchester, Bolton and Bury Canal.

Above. Circa 1905. A horse-drawn boat on the MB&B Canal at Kilcoby Bridge close to Giant's Seat at Ringley.

Below. Circa 1920. Boats queueing at Nob End, Prestolee.

Giant's Seat lower locks at Ringley Circa 1905. The canal has long since been infilled but the coping stones are still mostly visible today. The building on the left was Giant's Seat House and was at one time owned by The Clifton And Kearsley Coal Company. It had a small dry dock next to it and also stable facilities. Agecroft Rowing Club was known to have rented the building in 1899, and around the time this picture was taken the manager of the nearby Outwood Brickworks used it as a residence. It is unclear who resided at the cottage to the right, but both of these buildings were demolished in the early 1970's.

Above. 1960's view of the MBBC aquaduct over the River Irwell at Prestolee. Seddon Fold Farm and Kearsley Mill are seen in the background. According to the book, *The Story Of Halshaw Moor Chapel, 1808-1908,* work on the aquaduct finished in 1793. On the left bank of the Irwell, where some rocks are piled, is the former site of Prestolee Print Works which closed in the mid to late nineteenth century.

On Monday 6th July 1936, about 200 yards from the top of the locks at Nob End toward Ladyshore colliery, the canal breached, and millions of gallons of water plus hundreds of tons of rock and earth cascaded down into the River Irwell below. Boats were torn from their moorings and at least one boat went crashing down with another left perched precariously over the edge of the 40 yard gap. The top cut of the canal emptied almost completely all the way to Bury, and due to the cost of repair and the declining traffic it was decided that repairing the damage would not be worthwhile. The only sections that remained in use after this were from the Bury terminus to Ladyshore colliery which closed in 1951, and another portion from Salford to Clifton. The canal was officially declared as abandoned in 1961 after an act of Parliament.

Above. View of the breach looking down to the River Irwell. The iron rails that had been built into the embankment to protect it from rupturing are clearly seen, and these are still visible even today.

Above. View from the Irwell looking back up toward the canal after it had breached.

A canal boat is seen perched over the edge of where the MBBC breach occurred and millions of gallons of water crashed down the embankment along with its coping stones and tons of earth. This created an unwanted 'dam' in the River Irwell which had to be removed to restore its correct flow.

Above. Circa 1920's. A barge fully laden with cotton bales makes its way down the locks at Nob End. **Below.** The locks a little further down with the lock keepers cottage to the left. The cottage was demolished in 1951 with the debris tipped into the middle pound of the locks.

Above. 1960's view of the Bolton arm of the canal at Nob End. The buildings on the left are the former workshops of the canal company and were built during the mid 1800's. These were demolished in 2012 as they had become increasingly dilapidated and unsafe.

Below. 1912. The MBB Canal winds its way under the road close to the Horseshoe Hotel Public House, which at this time was a three-story building. The long gone Three Crowns Inn can be seen on the far left. On the embankment between the River Irwell and the canal are a wooden hut and several women. It is thought that hen cotes were kept here.

Above. 1970. The remains of sunken barges close to the former Ladyshore Colliery on the Bury branch of the canal.

Left. 1970. MBB Canal Bury branch close to the buildings of the former Ladyshore Colliery. The colliery opened in 1837 and continued to use pit ponies underground until its closure in 1949. After the canal had breached in 1936 a brick dam was built to allow it to remain in use from Ladyshore to Bury. As late as 1941 the colliery was still transporting up to 50,000 tons of coal per year to Radcliffe and Bury.

Above. 1914. Ladyshore Colliery

Below. Scene at Ladyshore Colliery colliery after a fire in the 1920's.

Above. 1970. The basin at Prestolee looking up the filled in locks at Nob End. Out of shot to the left there was a small branch to the canal which led under the bridge to a dry dock.

Below. 1970. Close up view of Nob End locks.

Above. Circa 1960's. The former Nob Inn public house above Nob End locks, which was a popular stop off location for travellers on the canal. **Below.** The same spot pictured in 2013 from the Meccano Bridge that was built during 2012.

Above. Circa 1920's. The lock keepers cottage on the upper section of Ringley Locks between Prestolee and the iron road bridge at Ringley Road. The cottage was demolished and much of the stonework removed during the 1950's. The housing development known as the Ringley Lock estate, which was built around 2005, is directly across the River Irwell from where these locks once stood and is how it takes its name.

The MBBC Society was formed in July 1987 by Steven Parker from Little Lever along with Margaret and John Fletcher OBE from Bolton. Within a couple of months they had over 40 members and 150 by the end of that year. The Society's initial aim was to preserve what was left of this once magnificent waterway, and today, over 30 years later, they are still thriving and pushing forward with efforts to preserve and restore as much as possible, and new members are always welcome.

MBBC Newsletter & fundraising Sponsored walk form from 1989

Above. June 2014. Bridge at Prestolee known as Silver Hill or Seddon's Fold Bridge, and is thought to date from the original construction of the canal. This stretch of the canal was used in the 1970 James Mason film 'Spring and Port Wine' that focused on family life in Bolton.

Seddon Fold Farm, Prestolee

The complex of buildings at Seddon's Fold, Prestolee, lies in an area of particular historical and archaeological interest. The Farm was built on land belonging to the Earl of Derby, with his descendant James Stanley, the 7th Earl of Derby, who was later beheaded at Churchgate, Bolton, reputedly visiting the farm on many occasions, particularly in his younger years.

The stone farmhouse dates from around the 16th to 17th centuries and features period characteristics such as inglenooks* and spice cupboards built into the walls. The Cruck barn is a fine example of a timber framed structure, having four pairs of massive pegged crucks (trees split in two) which rise from the floor to the ridge of the roof. Each of these crucks has been set on a large sandstone block, which would not only be crucial in stabilizing the structure but also alleviate damp and decay.

The Seddon family are known to have held land in the area during the 15th Century, and the majority of this type of cruck framed construction was built between the early 15th and the 17th centuries, so it would be reasonable to assume it was built during this period. Rivington Hall Barn is another fine example of this type of building and is thought to also date from the same era. The brick and stone Gothic style stables are thought to date from about 1800 and probably housed horses for drawing barges along the nearby Manchester-Bolton and Bury canal.

* Note - Inglenook is an enclosed space around a large fireplace.

Above. Circa 1930's. The Aquaduct, drainage pipes and Old Prestolee Pack Horse Bridge at Nob End, Prestolee.

Roads & Highways

Up until the industrial revolution most roads in Britain were nothing more than dirt tracks that would become a deep muddy quagmire after rainfall, or bake into a solid rugged and bumpy surface in the sun. So as the population expanded and larger quantities of goods needed to be transported, some way of improving the road system had to be found. By law, each Parish was supposed to be responsible for the roads that ran through its particular area, with men of the town or village each expected to spend 6 days per year on road maintenance and repair. Needless to say this was not always adhered to, and one can only assume that Kearsley and its surrounding area would have been no different.

In 1663 Parliament introduced the first turnpike act to help raise funds to repair the Great North Road from London to York and on to Scotland, after this only several roads a year were turnpiked, and most of these were around London. The first Turnpike Trusts were run by the Government and non-profit, but they were incredibly unpopular, with travellers often taking longer alternative routes to avoid paying the new tolls.

The term 'Turnpike' comes from the style of the barrier that blocked the roadway. It was originally designed as a military defensive barrier to repel attack by men on horse-back, the construction used 'pikes' which were a long spear type weapon fitted to horizontal beams in an 'X' type arrangement, that would have stretched the full length across the road. This would have to be 'turned' to the side like a gate to let anything pass. The very first turnpike barriers may well have been identical to the original military style ones, but later on much simpler and less hostile looking barriers and gates would have been the norm. Some turnpike gates may well have retained their spikes, but this would probably have been more for ornamental purposes than to prevent horses from jumping over.

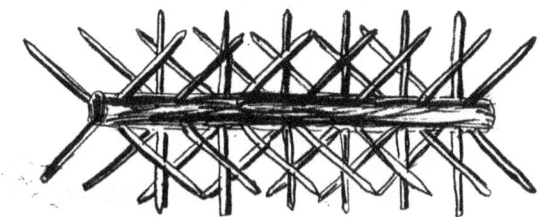

Left. An example of a military style turnpike barrier.

What we now consider the main road from Clifton through Kearsley to Farnworth was turnpiked in 1763, and it took a slightly different course than its current path up until around 1820. The road, which would have been little more than a dirt track, would have come from Clifton passing Unity Brook and Riders Farm, up to Kearsley Mount, then to where the Moss Rose public house stands, at which point it went down what is now Roscow Road, then at the junction with what is now often just called 'the fishbrook', where down to the right is Green Lane or you can stay left through the current industrial units, it took the latter path across to Stoneclough Brow. Here it climbed for a short distance then turned up approximately what is now Oakes Street to Halshaw Lane. The road then continued down Halshaw Lane in a straight line over to the front of where the Clock Face public house now stands, it then turned at 90 degrees down Old Hall Street, then down Higher Market Street past the Black Horse public house.

This winding and circuitous route may seem odd, but up until 1820 the roadway from the former Antelope public house to the junction at the bottom of Longcauseway did not exist. This is now Bolton Road, and previous to this date there existed only a deep hollow, which was filled in by the poor and unemployed of Farnworth and Kearsley. For their work they were paid out of a charity left by the late Ann Cross of Kearsley. If you stand outside the Moss Rose and look toward Farnworth you will see it is a straight line to the traffic lights at the end of Bolton Road at the other side of Kearsley roundabout.

The work of filling up the hollow was let by contract with the poor being employed to do the work. Tenders for the contract were invited and an advertisement was posted in the Manchester Mercury newspaper edition of 8th February 1820 as shown on the following page.

To Stone Masons and Road Makers.

To be LET by TICKET,

At the house of Mr. Thos. Topp, the sign of the Antelope, on Kearsley Moor, in the county of Lancaster, on Thursday the 24th day of February, 1820, at three o'clock in the afternoon;

THE Forming, paving, fencing, and completeing, the new deviation LINE OF ROAD, at Stone Clough, on the Manchester and Bolton Turnpike-road, of the breadth of twenty yards, beginning at the northerly said of the said Antelope Public House, and ending in a straight line towards Bolton, in length about 118 rods, after 8 yards to the rod, in which Line of Road there are to be built two Stone Culverts, the one six feet in diameter, in length about 70 yards, and the other three feet in diameter, in length about 40 yards, also the filling up of the two valleys over the said Culverts, one of which will be about 20 yards in depth.

The Trustees of said road will require the undertaker to enter into a bond, with two sureties, in a penal sum, for duly completeing and finishing the said work.

Sections of the Line of Road will be lodged with said Mr Topp, from the 7th February until 21st, further particulars had of Mr. Hartley, in Pendleton, near Manchester; the Bridge Master for Salford Hundred; and at the Office of John Albinson, in Bolton, Clerk to the said Road

Left. From the Manchester Mercury newspaper of 8th February 1820.

At this time Stoneclough Brow was also improved with the embankment and dry stone wall on the North Eastern side. The old original road from Moss Rose down Roscow Road to Oakes Street remained in use for some years afterwards and this may be the reason the stone walling is of a different construction from this point upwards as it was added at a later time.

The Manchester to Bolton Turnpike road was also known as the 'high road' or the 'coach road', and a toll would have to be paid by anyone passing through on horseback, or with any number of horses, cattle, beasts, wagons, carriages, carts and so on. Remember that people would have to take animals to and from markets in Bolton and Manchester or to slaughterhouses and Butchers shops, so a large number of cows for example could impact quite heavily on the road surface.

The hand drawn map on the next page dates from around the 1790's and shows the original road from Stoneclough Brow to Farnworth. The points of interest are as follows: **(A)** This is Stoneclough Brow approximately 100 yards down from the White Horse, and where you can turn into the industrial units at the bottom of Roscow Road. Note also the spelling of 'Stone Cluff.' **(B)** An ancient row of cottages known as Jackson's Row existed here until the early twentieth century. It is how Jackson Street took its name as they once stood at the top of the road. **(C)** A large farmhouse owned by Joshua Cross that once stood along where Halshaw Lane is situated. **(D)** Approximate present location of Kearsley roundabout. **(E)** The farmhouse reputedly owned by farmer Alec Shaw that became known as the 'Clock House.' The story goes that old Alec owned a particularly reliable timepiece, and many passers-by would knock on his door desiring to know the time. This caused him so much annoyance that to avoid being constantly disturbed he mounted the clock on the front of his house for all to see. The area around this corner became known as 'Clockface' and is of course how the public house that currently stands across from the long gone farmhouse takes its name. **(F)** This is The Black Horse public house, but here it is named only as 'Walton's.' It was not uncommon for public houses to be identified by the name of the owner at this time. They utilized a patch of land close-by where a cock-pit was built and people were charged to enter to watch cock-fighting. This is still known as Walton Place. Former owners of the pub, Magee Marshall's Ltd, were known to have held Deeds that described it in the year 1789 as "a public-house on the road from Manchester to Bolton."

A Plan of the Manchester Road with the various proposed lines from Mr of side of the Cross Lane to New Cliff viz.

The Plan the old Manchester Road distance 1205
Red th. one proposed new line ———— 1140
Blue the Villages proposed etc ———— 1230

Scale of Chains 72.5 to a Chain

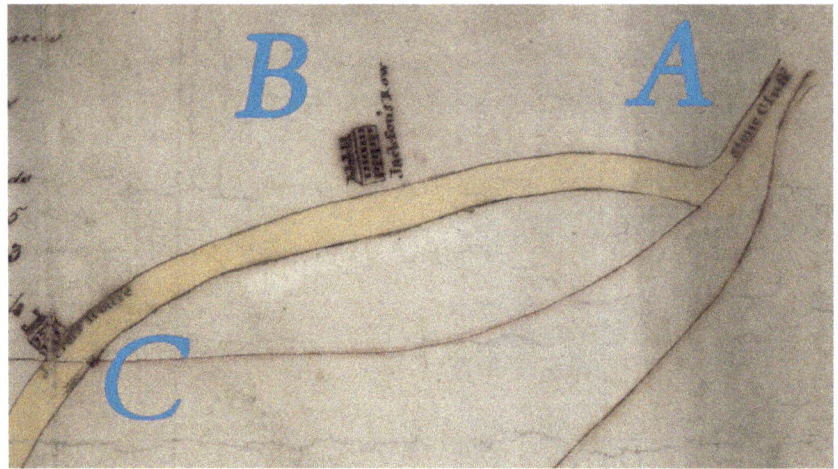

Above and **below** are close-ups of points of interest from the map on the previous page. Stoneclough Brow did not go as far up as it does today because before Bolton Road was constructed during 1820 there was a large hollow at Singing Clough, including the land around the bottom of Pilkington Road. This map must have been drawn up by an official representing the highways, as it is a proposal for building a new road from Stoneclough, through Farnworth and on to Bolton. One of these roads shows up on the 1797 map acompanying the Farnworth and Kearsley Enclosure document, so this map must be a little earlier. It is unclear exactly when the Black Horse public house actually came into existence, as an earlier tavern named The Sun Inn is believed to existed just to the rear of where the current pub stands.

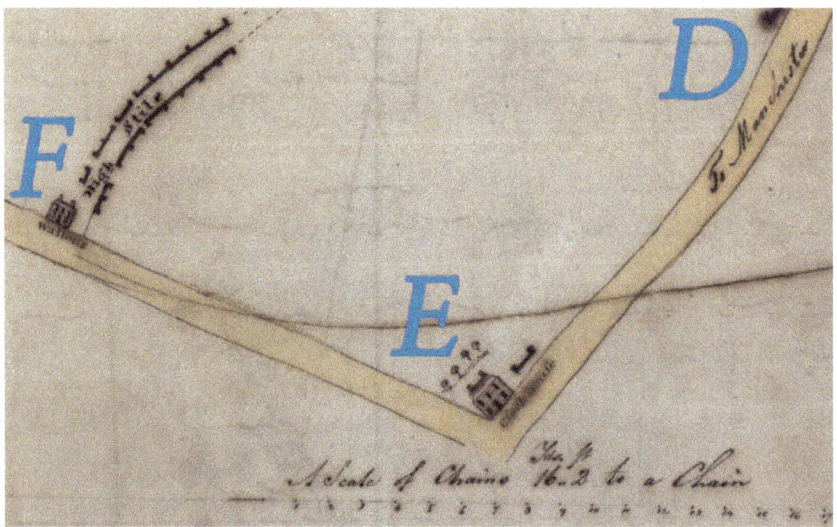

The next seven pages show the 1833 amendment to the original 1821 Moses Gate Turnpike Act.

ANNO TERTIO

GULIELMI IV. REGIS.

****

Cap. xxii.

An Act for more effectually repairing and improving the Road from *Bolton* to *Kearsley* called the *Moses Gate* District of Road, and a Branch thereout from *Stone Clough* to *Pilkington*, all in the County of *Lancaster*. [20th *April* 1833.]

WHEREAS an Act was passed in the First and Second Years of the Reign of His late Majesty King *George* the Fourth, intituled *An Act for repealing an Act of His late Majesty's Reign, for improving the Road from* Manchester *to* Bolton, *and other Places therein mentioned, in the County of* Lancaster, *so far as relates to the* Moses Gate *District of Road therein mentioned, and for granting further and more effectual Powers instead thereof, and for repairing and improving the said District of Roads, and making a new Branch of Road to communicate with the said District of Road*: And whereas the Trustees acting under and by virtue of the said recited Act have proceeded in the Execution of the same, and have borrowed several considerable Sums of Money on the Credit of the Tolls thereby granted and authorized to be taken, which still remain due and owing, and cannot be paid off, or the Interest thereof discharged, nor can the said District of Road and Branch of Road be effectually amended, improved, and kept in repair unless the Term granted by the said recited Act be further continued; and it would be more convenient to the said Trustees and beneficial to the said Roads if the said recited Act was repealed, and if further and more effectual Powers and Provisions were

1 & 2 G. 4. c. 80.

[*Local*.]   4 H   granted

3° GULIELMI IV. Cap. xxii.

Recited Act repealed;

granted in lieu thereof; but the Purposes aforesaid cannot be effected without the Aid and Authority of Parliament: May it therefore please Your Majesty that it may be enacted; and be it enacted by the King's most Excellent Majesty, by and with the Advice and Consent of the Lords Spiritual and Temporal, and Commons, in this present Parliament assembled, and by the Authority of the same, That upon the First Day of *July* next after the passing of this Act the said recited Act of the First and Second Years of the Reign of His said late Majesty King *George* the Fourth shall be and the same is hereby declared to be repealed.

and this Act be put in force for the Purposes herein mentioned.

II. And be it further enacted, That this Act shall thereupon commence and take effect and be put into execution, for and during the Term hereinafter mentioned, for the Purpose of more effectually amending, widening, altering, improving, maintaining, and keeping in repair the Road from the South End of *Burnden Bridge* in *Great Lever* to a Place called the *Four Stumps* in the Township of *Kearsley*, called the *Moses Gate* District of Road, and also the Road from or near a Place called *Stone Clough* in the said Township of *Kearsley* to the Turnpike Road between *Radcliffe Bridge* and *Manchester* at *Stand* in the Township of *Pilkington*, called the *Stone Clough* Branch Road, all in the said County of *Lancaster*.

Streets in Towns not to be repaired.

III. And be it further enacted, That no Part of the Money to be received by virtue of this Act shall be laid out in paving, cleansing, or repairing any Street within any Town through which the said Roads may pass, any thing herein contained to contrary notwithstanding.

Trustees.

IV. And be it further enacted, That all His Majesty's Justices of the Peace for the Time being acting for the County of *Lancaster*, together with *John Ashworth, Richard Ainsworth, Peter Ainsworth, Fletcher Barton Allen, William Atkin, William Rigby Bradshaw, James Bradshaw, Egerton Arden Bagot* Clerk, *Thomas Blackburn* Clerk, *John Baron, Edward Bolling, William Bolling, Robert Barlow, Ralph Beardman, William Balshaw, James Rothwell Barnes, William Barton, John Barrow, George Barnes, Richard Badger, Joseph Badger, John Bolling, Thomas Baron* the younger, *Stephen Blair, John Crompton, Thomas Bonsor Crompton, James Cross, William Crompton, James Cocker, James Crompton, James Crompton* of *Ringley, Roger Crompton, George Cottingham, Thomas Cross* of *Mortfield, John Cross, Elias Chadwick, Thomas Cross* of *Farnworth, Richard Cross, Peter Dorning, Benjamin Dobson, Peter Ditchfield, Ellis Fletcher, James Fletcher, John Fletcher, William Gray, John Gardner, Thomas Grundy, Samuel Grundy, Samuel Gaskell, John Hargreaves, Thomas Howell, Thomas Hardcastle, Thomas Hardcastle* the younger, *Pitt Hewitt, Benjamin Hick, Thomas Gardner Horridge, James Hardcastle, Jonathan Hitchen, Robert Heywood, John Heelis, Stephen Heelis, John Johnson* of *Bolton, Edward Jackson, Andrew Kellie, Andrew Knowles, James Kaye, Robert Lansdale, John Livesey, Robert Lord, Joseph Lord, George Lomas, John Mawdsley, John Moore, Peter Ormrod, James Ormrod, Robert Philips, Nathaniel Philips, George Piggot, Benjamin Rawson, Benjamin Rawson* the younger, *Peter Rothwell, Thomas Rushton, Thomas Lever Rushton, James Ramsbottom, John Rainforth, Robert Smith, Igdaliah Seddon, James Scowcroft, James Slade* Clerk, *John Smith* of *Lever Hall, James Sothern, Samuel Seddon, Ralph Seddon, John Smith* the younger, of *Lever Hall, John Scowcroft, Thomas Scowcroft, Samuel Scowcroft, James Taylor, James Sudell*

3° GULIELMI IV. Cap. xxii.

Sudell Troutbeck, Samuel Taylor, William Garnett Taylor, John Walton, James Watkins, William Weston, Joseph Winter, John Woods, John Ashworth the younger, *Edmund Ashworth, Henry Ashworth, Thomas Ashworth, John Johnson* the younger, *Robert Johnson, Richard Daly, Arthur Sharples, Thomas Brodbelt, Richard Johnson, Thomas Ridgway, Joseph Pope, Giles Ashworth, John Horrocks Ainsworth, Joseph Thwaites, John Hargreaves* the younger, *Thomas Taylor* the elder, *William Taylor, Samuel Taylor, Robert Vicars,* and their Successors, being duly qualified to act as Trustees of Turnpike Roads in *England*, shall be and they are hereby appointed Trustees for putting this Act into execution.

V. And be it further enacted, That it shall be lawful for the said Trustees, and they are hereby authorized and empowered, from Time to Time, at any of their Meetings to be held for that Purpose, to elect and appoint any Number of Persons, being duly qualified to act as Trustees of Turnpike Roads in *England*, not exceeding Three in the whole, to be Trustees for the Purposes of this Act, in addition to the Trustees hereby nominated and appointed; and such Trustees so elected and appointed shall be and they are hereby invested with the same Powers and Authorities for executing this Act as if they had been hereby nominated and appointed. *Power to appoint additional Trustees.*

VI. And be it further enacted, That the said Trustees shall hold their First Meeting at the House known by the Sign of the *Bridgewater Arms* in *Great Lever* in the County of *Lancaster*, or at some other convenient House or Place, on the First Day of *July* next after the passing of this Act, or as soon after as conveniently may be; and the said Trustees shall then and there proceed to carry this Act into execution, and shall and may then and from Time to Time afterwards adjourn to and meet at such Time and Times, and at such Place and Places in the Neighbourhood of the said Roads, as they shall think proper. *First Meeting of Trustees.*

VII. And be it further enacted, That it shall be lawful for the said Trustees, or any Person being a Lessee or Farmer, or appointed or continued to be appointed Collector of the Tolls to be taken by virtue of this Act, to demand and take the several Tolls following; (that is to say,) *Power to take Tolls.*

For every Horse or other Beast drawing any Coach, Berlin, Landau, Chariot, Chaise, Sociable, Curricle, Gig, Hearse, or other such like Carriage, (except Stage Coaches, Vans, Caravans, and other Carriages for conveying Passengers or Goods for Pay, Hire, or Reward, next herein-after mentioned,) the Sum of Three-pence: *Tolls.*

For One or Two Horses or other Beasts drawing any Stage Coach, Van, Caravan, or other Carriage conveying Passengers or Goods for Pay, Hire, or Reward, the Sum of Four-pence for each such Horse or Beast; and for every such Horse or Beast above Two, the Sum of Two-pence:

For every Horse or other Beast drawing any Waggon, Wain, Tumbril, Cart, or other such Carriage, having the Fellies of the Wheels of the Breadth of Six Inches or upwards on the Soles thereof, and having the Tires of the Wheels so constructed as not to deviate more than One Quarter of an Inch from a flat or level Surface, the Sum of Three-

Three-pence; and if such Tires shall deviate more than One Quarter of an Inch from a Flat or level Surface, the Sum of Four-pence:

For every Horse or other Beast drawing any Waggon, Wain, Tumbril, Cart, or other such Carriage, having the Fellies of the Wheels of a less Breadth than Six Inches and not of a less Breadth than Four and a Half Inches on the Soles thereof, and having the Tires of the Wheels so constructed as not to deviate more than One Quarter of an Inch from a flat or level Surface, the Sum of Three-pence Halfpenny; and if such Tires shall deviate more than One Quarter of an Inch from a flat or level Surface, the Sum of Four-pence Halfpenny:

For every Horse or other Beast drawing any Waggon, Wain, Tumbril, Cart, or other such Carriage, having the Fellies of the Wheels of a less Breadth than Four Inches and a Half on the Soles thereof, the Sum of Four-pence Halfpenny:

For every Horse, Mule, Ass, or other Beast, laden or unladen, and not drawing, the Sum of One Penny:

For every Score of Oxen or Neat Cattle, the Sum of Ten-pence, and so in proportion for any greater or less Number:

For every Score of Calves, Swine, Sheep, or Lambs, the Sum of Four-pence, and so in proportion for any greater or less Number:

For every Four-wheeled Carriage not drawn by any Horse or other Beast, but propelled or moved by Machinery, the Sum of One Shilling and Sixpence:

For every Two or Three-wheeled Carriage not drawn by any Horse or other Beast, but propelled or moved by Machinery, the Sum of Nine-pence.

Fractional Part of a Halfpenny in Tolls.

VIII. And be it further enacted, That in all Cases where there shall be a fractional Part of a Halfpenny in the Calculation of the Amount of the Tolls by this Act granted or authorized to be collected, or any of them, the Sum of One Halfpenny shall be demanded and taken instead of such fractional Part.

Limiting the Number of Tolls to be taken on the same Day.

IX. And be it further enacted, That no more than Two full Tolls (except as herein-after mentioned and provided to the contrary) shall be demanded or taken in any One Day for or in respect of the same Horses, Beasts, Cattle, or Carriages for passing through all or any of the Toll Gates continued or to be erected by virtue of this Act upon, across, or on the Sides of the said Road called the *Moses Gate* District of Road; that is to say, not more than One full Toll on that Part of the said Road which lies between the Town of *Bolton* and a Place called *Dial-post Brook* in the Township of *Farnworth*, nor more than One full Toll on that other Part of the said Road which lies between *Dial-post Brook* aforesaid and the *Four Stumps* in the Township of *Kearsley* aforesaid; and no more than Two full Tolls (except as herein-after mentioned and provided to the contrary) shall be demanded or taken in any One Day for or in respect of the same Horses, Beasts, Cattle, or Carriages for passing through all or any of the Toll Gates continued or to be erected upon, across, or on the Sides of the said Road called the *Stone Clough* Branch Road; that is to say, not more than One full Toll on that Part of the said Road which lies between *Stone Clough* aforesaid and *Ringley Bridge* in the Township of *Pilkington* aforesaid, nor more than One full Toll on that other Part of the said Road which lies between *Ringley Bridge* aforesaid and *Stand* in the Township of *Pilkington* aforesaid.

X. And

3° GULIELMI IV. Cap. xxii.

X. And be it further enacted, That in case the Toll hereby authorized to be taken shall have been paid for the passing of any Horse, Cattle, Beast, or Carriage through any of the Toll Gates continued or to be erected by virtue of this Act, the same Horse, Cattle, Beast, or Carriage shall at any Time or Times, and from Time to Time during the Remainder of the same Day (upon a Ticket denoting such Payment on that Day being produced) be permitted to pass and repass Toll-free through every other Toll Gate which shall be continued and erected by virtue of this Act within the Distance of One Mile from the Toll Gate at which such Toll shall have been so first paid as aforesaid.

Toll being paid at One Gate to free others within the Distance of One Mile thereof.

XI. Provided always, and be it further enacted, That in case the Toll hereby authorized to be taken shall have been paid for the passing of any Horse, Cattle, Beast, or Carriage through any of the Toll Gates continued or to be erected by virtue of this Act, the same Horse, Cattle, Beast, or Carriage shall, at any Time or Times and from Time to Time during the Remainder of the same Day (upon a Ticket denoting such Payment on that Day being produced), be permitted to pass and repass Toll-free through the same Toll Gate, and also through such other Gate or Gates (if any) as the said Ticket shall free, except in the Cases of Horses or Beasts drawing any Waggon, Wain, Tumbril, Cart, Van, Caravan, or other such Carriage, or of Carriages propelled or moved by Machinery, laden, both on passing and repassing, with any Loading of the Weight of Five hundred Pounds Weight or upwards, of One hundred and twelve Pounds to the Hundred Weight, in all which excepted Cases the Toll for the Horse or Horses, Beast or Beasts, drawing any Waggon, Wain, Tumbril, Cart, Van, Caravan, or other such Carriage, and for the Carriage propelled or moved by Machinery, so laden as last aforesaid, shall be payable and paid each and every Time any such Waggon, Wain, Tumbril, Cart, Van, Caravan, or other such Carriage, or any such Carriage propelled or moved by Machinery, so laden as aforesaid, shall pass or repass through any of the said Toll Gates, and also except as herein-after is mentioned and provided.

Tolls to be paid but once a Day at the same Gate, except for Carriages laden with 500 Pounds Weight.

XII. And be it further enacted, That the Tolls hereby made payable for or in respect of any Horses or Beasts drawing any Stage Coach, Van, Caravan, or other Carriage conveying Passengers for Pay, Hire, or Reward, or for or in respect of any Stage Coach, Van, Caravan, or other Carriage propelled or moved by Machinery, used for the same Purpose, shall be payable and paid every Time of passing or repassing through all or any of the Toll Gates continued or to be erected by virtue of this Act: Provided nevertheless, that no further or additional Toll shall be payable in respect of any Horse or Beast drawing any Stage Coach, Van, Caravan, or other such Carriage, on account only of the Horses or Beasts drawing the same having been changed.

Tolls in respect of Horses drawing Stage Coaches, &c. to be paid for each Time of passing.

XIII. And be it further enacted, That the Tolls hereby made payable for or in respect of any Horses or Beasts let out to Hire, or any Horses or Beasts drawing any Post Chaise or other Carriage let out to Hire, or any Carriage propelled or moved by Machinery let out to Hire, shall be payable and paid every Time of passing or repassing through all or any of

Tolls to be paid for Horses, &c. drawing Post Chaises, on every new Hiring.

[Local.] 4 I

310   3° GULIELMI IV. *Cap.* xxii.

of the Toll Gates continued or to be erected by virtue of this Act, whenever a fresh Hiring thereof shall take place.

One-horse Carts may be weighed.

XIV. And whereas it frequently happens that Carts drawn by One Horse passing along the said Roads carry a greater Weight than is by Law allowed for Carts drawn by Two or more Horses; be it therefore enacted, That all Carts passing along the said Roads drawn by One Horse only shall and may be weighed at any weighing Machine now erected or to be erected on the said Roads, and the like additional Tolls demanded, received, and recovered for the Overweight thereof as are by Law payable in respect of the Overweight of Carts drawn by Two or more Horses; and all the Powers, Regulations, Penalties, Matters, and Things now in force relating to the weighing of Carts drawn by more than One Horse shall be applicable to Carts passing on the said Roads drawn by One Horse only, and to the Drivers, Masters, and Owners thereof.

Application of Monies on the Moses Gate District.

XV. And be it further enacted, That all the Monies which shall have been raised and produced by virtue of the said recited Act hereby repealed, and which shall remain undisposed of at the Commencement of this Act, and also all the Tolls and other Monies to be collected, borrowed, or received by virtue of this Act, shall be applied and disposed of in manner following; that is to say, in the first place, in Payment of all the Expences of procuring and passing this Act, and all incidental Expences relating thereto; afterwards in paying the Principal Money and Interest already borrowed on the Bonds of any of the said Trustees, and remaining due and owing on the Credit of the Tolls granted by the said recited Act hereby repealed, and in defraying the Costs of continuing, erecting, and providing Turnpikes, Toll Houses, and other Buildings, and making, repairing, and altering the said Roads called the *Moses Gate* District of Road and the *Stone Clough* Branch Road; and in the next place in paying all other Principal Money and Interest due and owing on the Credit of the Tolls granted by the said recited Act, or to be borrowed for the Purposes of this Act, and in defraying all other necessary Costs, Charges, and Expences attending the same, and carrying the Purposes of this Act into execution.

No more Money to be expended in Repair of Roads than is collected thereon.

XVI. And be it further enacted, That none of the Tolls authorized to be taken by virtue of this Act, or any of the Money to be borrowed on the Credit thereof, shall be laid out or expended in the Amendment, Repair, or Improvement of either of the said Roads directed to be amended, repaired, or improved by virtue of this Act, if there be no Toll Gate continued or erected thereupon respectively, and Tolls taken thereat; nor shall any greater Sum of Money be expended in the Repair of either of such Roads than shall be collected at the Tolls Gates continued or to be erected thereupon, or borrowed on the Credit of the Tolls thereof, or received as a Composition for Statute Duty thereon respectively.

Public Act.

XVII. And be it further enacted, That this Act shall be deemed and taken to be a Public Act, and shall be judicially taken notice of as such by all Judges, Justices, and others.

XVIII. And

3° GULIELMI IV. *Cap.* xxii. 311

XVIII. And be it further enacted, That this Act shall commence and take effect upon the said First Day of *July* next after the passing hereof, and shall thenceforth continue and be in force for and during the Term of Thirty-one Years, and from thence to the End of the then next Session of Parliament. Term of Act.

LONDON: Printed by GEORGE EYRE and ANDREW SPOTTISWOODE, Printers to the King's most Excellent Majesty. 1833.

Anything that would possibly cause wear and tear of the road would probably incur a toll, and large boards with the cost of passing through would be at each turnpike gate. Travelling on foot or walking through with a dog for example would not be liable for any charge, plus once a toll had been paid then it may have been possible to travel along all of the roads covered by that particular Turnpike act without further charges for the remainder of the day as long as certain weight restrictions were adhered to, but not all Turnpike acts were the same.

The Moses Gate Turnpike Act of 1821 covered the main roads from Burnden through Farnworth to a place known as 'the Four Stumps' at Kearsley Mount. It also included the roads down through Stoneclough to Stand, which at the time was considered as in the Township of Pilkington.

A Turnpike gate was erected at Moses Gate on Manchester Road near to the bottom of what is now Gladstone Road, but an earlier map also shows this to be nearer to the junction with Egerton Street and the railway station, so either the cartographers were not very accurate or the toll-gate relocated at some stage.

The Kearsley Toll bar was close to the Moss Rose at the top of Roscow Road (see page 361) and there was another one at the bottom of Stoneclough Brow just as you turn the corner towards the Hare And Hounds public house, this was known as the 'Bottoms Toll Bar.'

Left. Notice from the Manchester Mercury, January 5th 1819, stating the Moses Gate Turnpike Trustees intentions to erect a toll-gate at the bottom of Stoneclough Brow. This became known as 'The Bottoms Toll Bar.'

> Moses Gate Turnpike Road,
> NOTICE is hereby given, that an adjourned Meeting of the Trustees of the said Road will be held at the house of Mr. Philip Hughes, the sign of the Bridge Inn, in Little Bolton, on Thursday the 14th day of January next, at two o'clock in the afternoon, at which meeting it will be proposed to revoke an order made at a meeting of the said Trustees held on the 8th day of October last, whereby it was ordered that an offer or tender be made to the Rev. Egerton Bagot, the sum of 340 pounds for the purchase of his land and timber, that will be taken for making the road through his land at Stone Clough Brow. And also at the said meeting an order will be made for the erecting a toll gate on the side of the said turnpike road, at or near a place called the Stone Clough Brow, across a certain highway, there leading to Ringley bridge.
> JOHN ALBINSON, Clerk to the Trustees.
> Great Bolton, 15th Dec. 1818.

Left. Map of 1848 showing the location of 'The Bottoms Toll Bar.' The toll bar may have been administered from the residence at the end of the row of houses shown. This was officially named 'Bar Street' until the houses were demolished around 1900, and is now where the turning into Brook Street takes you to the football pitch.

Many turnpike gate-houses were positioned or constructed so as to allow the occupant to view the roads leading to the gate, and this may explain the angle at which the Kearsley Bar building, shown on the next page, is positioned at, because it allows anyone inside to see up Manchester Road from the front window, a side window would allow viewing down Bolton Road and the rear of the building could still view down Roscow Road, which was the original route before 1820.

Kearsley Bar Circa 1900. This shows the old toll bar building situated at the junction of Bolton Road, Manchester Road and Roscow Road. The Moss Rose public house can be seen in the background behind the horse drawn carriages, but the houses to the left are long gone.

The powers of the Moses Gate Turnpike Act ceased on the 1st November 1876, and a few days later the toll-gates were dismantled by those who had purchased the timber and ironwork by public auction. After this time the responsibility for the upkeep and maintenance of the roads passed onto the local Council or authority, and the next quarter of a century was going to see the steady demise of the horse as the principal means of road transport, as monumental advances in electrical and automotive modes of power began to gather pace.

Circa 1900. Navvies hard at work taking up the cobbles in preparation for laying new tramlines along Bolton Road, Kearsley. The house just visible to the right is number 375 Bolton Road. In the far distance can be seen the ancient row of cottages known as Jackson Buildings. Jackson Street takes its name from these long gone buildings which stood at the top end, on the right as you enter what is now Roosevelt Road.

Trams and Trolleybuses

The first tramways appeared in Bolton around 1880, and were not electrified. Horses pulled the carriages along the metal rails for almost the next twenty years until electrification of the system was made possible. The first tramway in Farnworth ran from Moses Gate along Bolton Road and Market Street to the bottom of Longcauseway, just beyond the Black Horse Public House at Kearsley. This line opened on Friday 3rd June 1881 and formed part of the standard-gauge horse tramway system connected with Bolton; trams had already started to run the two miles from Bolton to Moses Gate on Wednesday, 1st September 1880. The horse drawn tramcars in use at this time were of Eade's patent reversible type, in which the body could swivel right round on the chassis, thus dispensing with the necessity of unharnessing the horse at a dead-end terminus, and also permitting a single-ended body with only one staircase.

The first electric tram routes in Bolton were opened on Saturday, 9th December 1899, and the last horse trams ran on Monday, 1st January 1900. At this time a company named Holden's had held the lease to run the horse tramway service from Bolton to the Kearsley terminus, but this was now taken over by the Bolton Tramways Committee. Moses Gate was among the routes worked electrically from 2nd January, but electrification work in Farnworth had only begun in December and was as yet nothing like complete. As a result Farnworth was left without any service at all. The Urban District Council protested to Bolton Corporation and asked for a horse tram service between Moses Gate and Black Horse, but the Corporation replied that it did not possess any horse trams, and that if it were to buy one or two from Messrs. Holden, it would have nowhere to keep the horses. However Farnworth U.D.C did manage to persuade Holden's to provide a temporary horse bus service.

By the end of March the electrification of the Farnworth section was complete, though not the short length to Kearsley. As in Bolton the track was not re-laid, but merely had the joints bonded. As there was then no electricity supply in Farnworth, the overhead wires were fed from the Bolton distribution system. A trial trip was made as far as Church Lane, Farnworth, on the afternoon of Tuesday, 27th March 1900; the Farnworth Journal commented that this trip occasioned great interest; "the car made a great noise in its passage….The news soon got about, and the return journey was made through the midst of a great throng." The official inspection took place a few days later, by which time the Kearsley section was also ready, but no service began, as Bolton was short of trams. Farnworth U.D.C asked for the line to be opened in time for the Easter holidays, but Bolton Corporation replied that it hoped to open the Horwich extension then, and there were insufficient cars to open Farnworth as well. However, some last-minute difficulties arose in connection with the Horwich line, and so electric tram services to "Black Horse" began on Good Friday, 13th April 1900, without any previous notice. Workmen had spent most of the previous night cleaning dirt and stones out of the rail grooves.

Farnworth U.D.C had actually put forward a Parliamentary Bill for various purposes on the 13th December 1899, and part II of this bill was concerned with tramways. This duly became the Farnworth Urban District Council Act on 6th August 1900 and authorized the construction of 5 miles 56 chains of tramway, and to run this independently of Bolton Corporation. At the same time Kearsley U.D.C applied for powers to construct a tramway along the main Bolton-Manchester Road right through its territory, from the terminus of the 'horse' line near the Black Horse, to the Clifton boundary at Unity Brook; and also a short length into Longcauseway which would connect the Farnworth line with the ex-horse line. These tramways were authorized by a Provisional Order confirmed on 6th August 1900 by the Tramways Orders Confirmation Act (63 & 64 Vict., cap. Cxcviii).

Work on the new Farnworth lines began on Monday 13th May 1901 and the contractor for the work was a Mr. Edmund Taylor of Blackpool. The rails were laid on a six-inch bed of concrete and weighed 98lb per yard, in 60ft lengths, and were supplied by Walter Scott Ltd., of Leeds. The curve from Albert Road into Longcauseway was the sharpest on the system with a radius of 36 feet, except for the curve into the depot yard, which was of 30ft radius. The tramways depot, 120 feet long by 62ft 6in wide was constructed in Albert Road alongside the electricity generating station. Access to the shed roads was by traverser just inside the doors of the depot.

Above. Farnworth bound Horse Drawn tram outside Bolton Town Hall, circa late 1890's.

Below. A procession of horse drawn trams through Market Street, Farnworth, decked out to celebrate the Diamond Jubilee of Queen Victoria in June 1897.

The generating station was opened on Wednesday 28th August 1901. There were two engines and dynamos, one for lighting and one for traction. The station closed down at night, the small quantity of current used overnight being supplied from accumulators. A house by the Depot, No.143 Albert Road, was acquired to serve as offices.

On Thursday, 9th January 1902, the system was inspected for the board of trade by Major Druitt, and, after a meeting at the depot by the Tramways Committee at 11:30a.m, it was decided that services should begin immediately. Services operated every 10 to 15 minutes from 5:30a.m to 11p.m. On Sundays they began at 2:00p.m and on the first day of operation 1792 passengers were carried.

Meanwhile, work was proceeding on the Kearsley U.D.C line from Black Horse along the main road as far as the Clifton boundary at Unity Brook, including a triangular double-track junction connecting the Farnworth U.D.C line on Longcauseway with the higher Market Street line and Kearsley to Clifton line. Farnworth U.D.C had already agreed to work the Kearsley lines, and had leased them for 21 years from 3rd October 1900, at an annual rental of 10% of the cost of construction. Apart from the first few yards, and the junction, mentioned above, the whole line was single track with loops, though originally planned as double track. With a view to doubling later, the track was laid to one side of the road centre, and the overhead was supported by short bracket arms on poles placed in the centre of the road. Side poles and span wires were used only at Black Horse junction, and for a short distance near the Antelope Hotel where the road was narrow.

By the middle of February 1902 most of the line was completed, the final stages having been delayed more than a month by heavy snowfalls. On Thursday, 20th February, Major Druitt inspected and passed the line from Black Horse as far as Spindle Point, including the connections to Longcauseway. The public service began later that same day, certain journeys on the Moses Gate-Albert Road-Longcauseway service being extended to Spindle Point, providing a half-hourly service in the mornings and twenty minute service during the rest of the day.

Rare picture of an electric Farnworth UDC tram in its original livery before they sold out to South Lancashire Tramways in 1906.

The line was divided into three 1/2d stages; Black Horse to Stoneclough Brow, Stoneclough Brow to St. Stephen's and St. Stephen's to "Clifton terminus", i.e., Spindle Point. The route was not very busy, for most of Kearsley's 9,000 inhabitants were concentrated at the Farnworth end of the line. The remaining quarter-mile from Spindle Point to Unity Brook was inspected by Major Druitt on Thursday, 13th March 1902, and the "Clifton" service was extended over it the same day. This section was closed down for almost a month during the spring of 1905 due to the settling of foundations and mining subsidence. A further extension of 1 mile 32 chains from Unity Brook through Clifton to the Pendlebury boundary at the"Oddfellows Arms", Newtown, was opened on Thursday 28th February 1907. This line had been authorized by a Light Railway Order confirmed on 21st December 1901, granted to the Barton-upon-Irwell Rural District Council, of which Clifton parish was a detached part of this Rural District. The destination was still shown as 'Clifton' on the cars, though more usually referred to as "Newtown" on the timetables. Interestingly at this time there was a gap of some 200 yards between the terminus of the Clifton Light Railway at the Oddfellows Arms and the nearest point reached by the Salford trams at the Windmill Hotel.

For some years the financial position of the Farnworth Tramways was a cause of concern and the Council was now anxious to dispose of the undertaking, providing that favourable terms could be obtained. It was, however, determined not to sell to Bolton, for the treatment it had received from that quarter a few years previously in which it seems that Bolton Corporation had hoped to force Farnworth Tramways into bankruptcy, and then take it over. Early in 1906 Farnworth U.D.C opened negotiations with the South Lancashire Tramways Company, and an agreement was reached that the S.L.T Company would take over responsibility for the operation and maintenance of the Farnworth and Kearsley tramways on 1st April 1906, and the lease was for 21 years.

The S.L.T appeared to have made peace with Bolton in 1909 and on 25th May of that year an agreement was reached allowing each company to run trams on some of each others lines, thus allowing trams to run from Bolton, Through the Moses Gate terminus and on through Kearsley to the Clifton (Newtown) terminus.

In 1925 trams operated on Monday to Friday through Kearsley and Farnworth every 11 minutes from the start of service at 4:44a.m until about 7:30a.m, then every eighteen minutes until 2.00p.m after which a 12-minute frequency operated until the end of service at 10:30p.m. On Saturdays, the service started 20 minutes earlier and ended forty minutes later but was less frequent than the Monday to Friday service. A journey from Clifton (Newtown) to Moses Gate would have taken around half an hour.

Circa 1900. Tram lines being laid along Bolton Road. The houses in the background are numbers 421, 423, 425 & 427. The date stone above number 423 reads 'Stanley Terrace 1894.'

Above. Circa 1900. Laying of tramlines at the Longcauseway and Albert Road Junction. Longcauseway is to the left and Worsley Road straight ahead.

Below. The same junction in 1929 but this time looking down Albert Road with Longcauseway on the right.

Above. 1930's tram at the Black Horse terminus often called 'Kearsley Cross.' Bolton Road is in the distance to the right.

Below. Moses Gate circa 1930.

Late 1930's postcard picture of Higher market Street.

Circa 1902. Open topped electric tram makes its way up Bolton Road at Moses Gate. To the right, at the corner of Hall Lane, is the Moses Gate public house; this was demolished in September 2018.

Above. Circa 1930's. A South Lancashire Tram passes the top of Longcauseway at the junction with Albert Road. In the background is the new Oak Mills building, the former Oak Mills building was a cotton spinning mill owned by Thomas Nuttall & Sons and stood to the rear of this one. After it was demolished this became the site for visiting funfairs until the early 2000's. Many will fondly remember the giant puddles in-between the rides and stalls after inclement weather, and the lower section of the mill wall, which remained in place around the site until it was all removed for the Tesco supermarket and car park which currently occupy the area.

Left. Circa 1930s, Bolton Corporation Tram at the Black Horse Terminus.

On the previous page a tram makes its way along Manchester Road Kearsley, circa 1926. The houses on the right were known as 'Plant Pot Row' as they would all have one in the front window, usually containing an aspidistra. On the left hand side can be seen the original location of the Post Box outside of what was then the Kearsley Post Office at number 84. The wall further down is where the Kearsley Social club (originally known as the Reform Club) still stands, and the shop on the far right is where the Post Office relocated to until moving to Kearsley Precinct in July 2016.

The early part of the 1930's saw the winding down of the electric tram system, and the last tram from the Black Horse through Kearsley to Clifton ran on Sunday June 7th 1931, with motor bus services beginning the next day. The tram system of Farnworth and Walkden had also begun to be gradually wound down, with the Longcauseway and Buckley Lane lengths being superseded by motor buses and Trolley Buses in 1932. The last trams ran in Farnworth on Sunday 19th November 1944 with Trolley Bus services replacing these the following day.

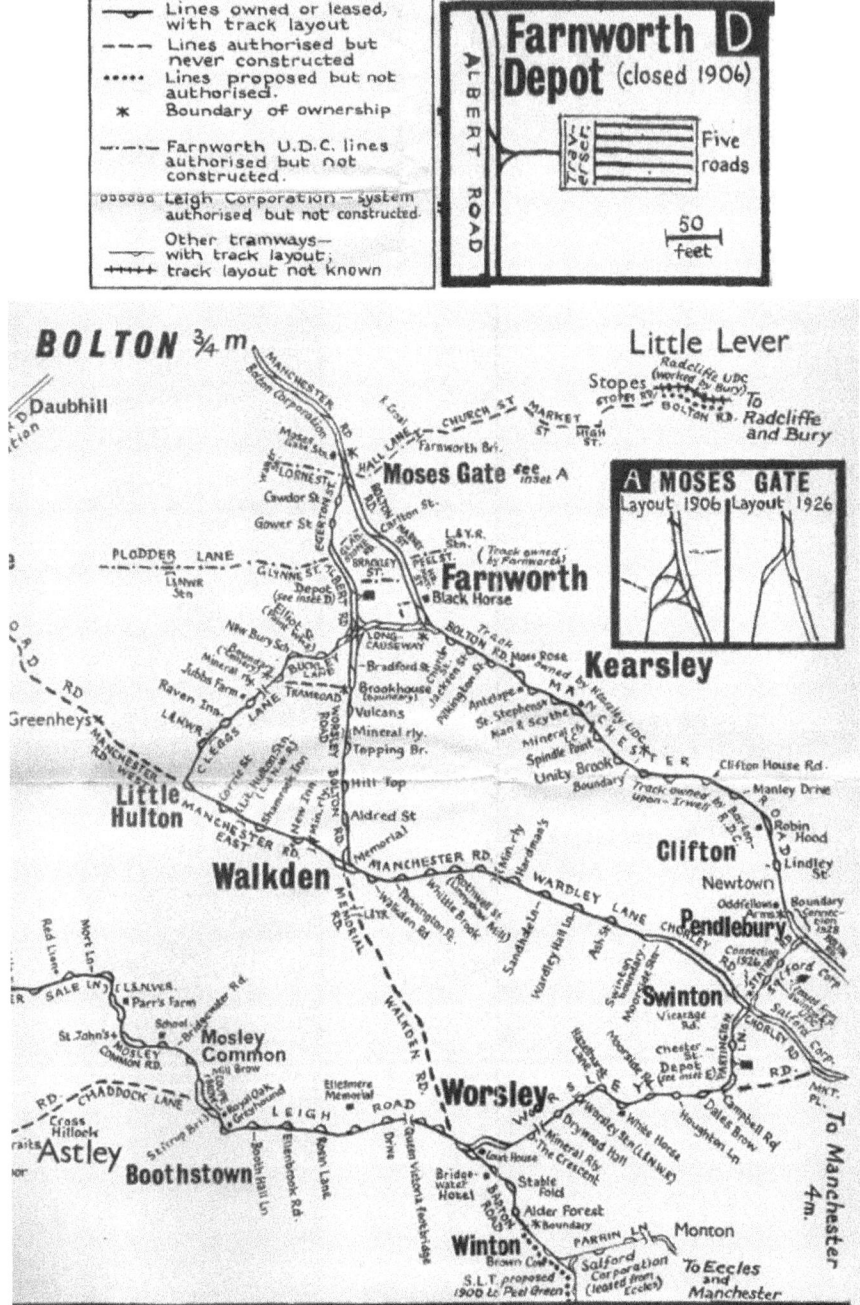

Above. 1920's South Lancashire Tramways route map showing various stopping points, many of which remain in use today for the Bus services.

The picture above shows Bolton Road, Kearsley in mid-June 1931. The entrance to Jackson Street is on the left and the houses on Pilkington Road can be seen in the distance to the right. Even though the trams had stopped running the tram standards were still in place and causing chaos for the motor vehicles, which, as this picture illustrates, were swerving around them on to the wrong side of the road. This era was a particularly dangerous time for drivers and pedestrians. In 1930 there were 7,305 recorded deaths on the roads of Britain, compared to 1,793 in 2017 despite there being much more traffic. It was not until 1934 that driving tests were introduced; previous to this anyone over the age of seventeen could get behind the wheel.

Picture from 1943 of a tram opposite the Black Horse public house. On the pavement is a line of ladies and children quite possibly queueing with their wartime ration books. On the far right can just be seen the sign for 'Lords Café' on the corner of Black Horse Street. This later became a bakery up until the late 1990's.

August 1931. One of the first trolleybuses in Farnworth pictured outside the Bird I'th Hand Hotel at the junction of Old Hall Street and Bolton Road.

Above. Trolley Bus at Brackley Street in April 1958. The old Farnworth & Kearsley Co-Op building can be seen in the background.

Left. Farnworth Journal of August 22nd 1958.

Just as the tram system had been gradually replaced, the Trolleybus system was also succeeded by diesel motor buses. The last Farnworth Trolleybus ran from Brackley Street at 11:15 pm on Sunday August 31st 1958.

Picture dated August 31st 1958 making the trolley bus shown one of, if not the last one to run in Farnworth. The Bird-Ith-Hand pub is in the background as is Farnworth and Kearsley Labour Club. Note that traffic lights had still not been installed at this time.

The Farnworth and Kearsley Bypass (St Peter's Way) and the Kearsley Spur

Plans for a road to ease congestion through Kearsley and Farnworth were first considered around 1960 when Lancashire County Council organized a small team of engineers to explore alternative routes to bypass Farnworth town centre, mostly due to the ever increasing traffic between Manchester and Bolton. Up until the 1950's most people would travel by bus, coach or train, but the rapidly increasing uptake of motorcars and vans meant local roads were becoming clogged and more hazardous.

Official proposals were put forward in 1961, and at first Kearsley Urban District Council opposed the scheme on the grounds that most of the work would be through its territory and would have a significant negative effect on housing projects, playing fields, recreational areas and many homes would have to be demolished along the route.

There was also discontent at the road being designated 'The Farnworth And Kearsley Bypass,' as the road would only by pass Farnworth and merely rejoin the usual route through Kearsley at Bolton Road, and therefore Kearsley had little to gain from its construction. Farnworth Council on the other hand were eager to press forward with the scheme, as it had little impact on the town but provided the huge benefit of reducing much of its unwanted traffic. After over 12 months of negotiations Kearsley UDC finally agreed to the amended proposals, and property purchases and ground surveys could now begin.

Six contractors were invited to tender for the task of building the road as well as the bridges. Sir Alfred McAlpine and Son Ltd and Leonard Fairclough Ltd, working as a consortium, submitted the lowest tender for the work and this was accepted in May 1966. In practice McAlpine did the roadwork and Fairclough the bridgeworks. Work began on the bypass in July 1966 and was estimated to last 24 months.

To make way for the new road one hundred and four houses were taken down in Kearsley, of which 22 had already been allocated for slum clearance. The road was opened without ceremony on Thursday 21st December 1967, six months earlier than was originally calculated. The total cost of construction was estimated around £2,600,000. It became known as St. Peter's Way as it passes close by to the imposing Church of St Peter, which serves as Bolton Parish Church, at the end of Churchgate in Bolton town centre.

Pictured in August 1967, the newly constructed bridge at the lower end of Church Road, Kearsley, built to carry Church Road over the Farnworth and Kearsley by-pass.

Above. Kearsley Roundabout under construction in January 1967. This is a section of the steelwork which supports the road on its northern rim. Houses on Lord Street can be seen to the left. **Below.** The road being laid on this section of the roundabout in April of the same year. Bolton Road is to the right and Halshaw Lane is to the left.

Above. August 1967. The bridge at Grosvenor Street is seen, and on the right is the slip road leading up to Bolton Road at the end of Halshaw Lane. This is the starting point of what became the 'Kearsley Spur' which provides a connection to the end of the M61 Manchester-Preston motorway at the Worsley Braided interchange, this also provides links to the A580 East Lancashire Road, the M62 Motorway and the M60 motorway (formerly M63) which encircles Manchester. **Below.** The view from Grosvenor Street Bridge of the same slip road up to the roundabout in June 2011.

The first members of the public to travel the whole length of the bypass from Kearsley roundabout to Bolton were councillors from Farnworth on Saturday December 9th 1967, they were accompanied on their journey by Mr W.M. Johnson, the County Council's resident engineer on the project.

The south western portion of Kearsley roundabout was built through part of what was New Jerusalem Church graveyard, and special permission from the Home Office had to be granted to exhume the bodies so they could be taken away for cremation and re-burial, even though the graveyard had not been in use for many years.

A six feet high plywood fence was erected and work began to remove the estimated 30 bodies, but it came as a shock when more than twice that number was found. The Church hall also had to be demolished, with a temporary one put up until a permanent new one was built after completion of all the work. A classroom at Kearsley West School also had to be severed to make way for the slip road up to the roundabout.

With the Farnworth and Kearsley by-pass complete, work continued on the southern side of the roundabout to connect the road to the highways and motorway network that was evolving around northern Manchester. This extension from Kearsley roundabout to the Worsley Braided interchange is the Kearsley Spur, and enables a direct connection to the M62 East or West, the M60 Manchester ring road and the A580 East Lancs Road, it also allows traffic from the bottom of the M61 Southbound to get up to the roundabout. The Kearsley Spur was officially opened on December 17th 1970 along with the M61 motorway which linked Manchester to Preston.

The road builders of the 1960's could never have imagined that the number of vehicles on Britain's roads would reach such astronomical figures. For example in 1969 there were 14.8 million vehicles registered in Britain, but by March 2017 this had ballooned to 37.5 million. These early motorway networks were not designed to cope with such numbers, and in certain areas where several motorways and substantial highways converge the system simply becomes overwhelmed. Sadly for us the Worsley Braided Interchange and north west corner of the M60 are two such bottlenecks that during certain times of the working week become so congested that the traffic barely inches along.

Left. Linnyshaw Moss, 1969.

The Worsley Braided Interchange and Kearsley Spur under construction.

Aerial shot of the Worsley Braided interchange shortly after its completion in 1970. The Kearsley Spur winds its way in from the right hand side and finishes approximately at the long footbridge in the centre of the picture. Further up is the yellow railway bridge that was part of the mineral line that carried coal from several Worsley collieries to Kearsley Power Station. Between the bridges there are an incredible seventeen lanes side-by-side, which at the time of writing is considered to be the most anywhere in the UK. The Mossfield Road housing estate is seen on the right, and below it is Bent Spur farm. Blackleach reservoir is also visible in the top left.

Ringley Old Packhorse Bridge

Ringley Old Packhorse Bridge was completed in 1677 at a cost of around £500 to replace a wooden bridge that had been washed away by a flood in 1673. For many centuries this was the only crossing point of the River Irwell for miles around. The bridge was paid for (as well its upkeep) by the taxpayers of the Hundred of Salford.

Below and next page. A letter from 1633 written in Latin which was presented to the Hundred of Salford to inform them that the wooden bridge is in a state of decay.

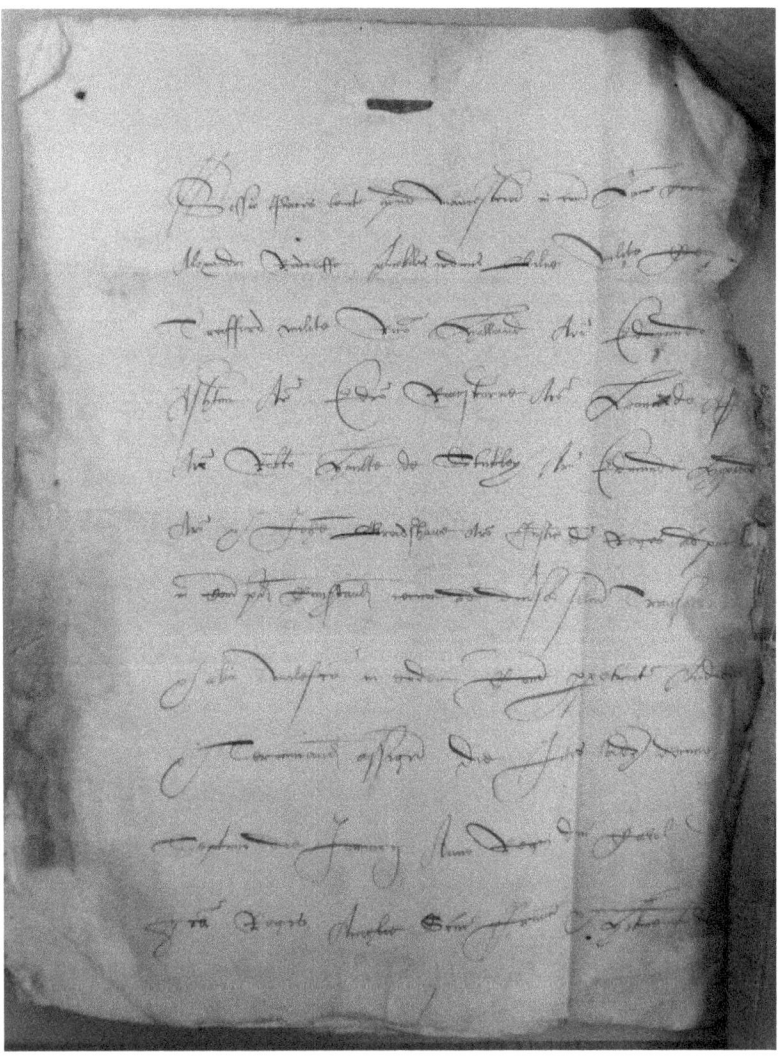

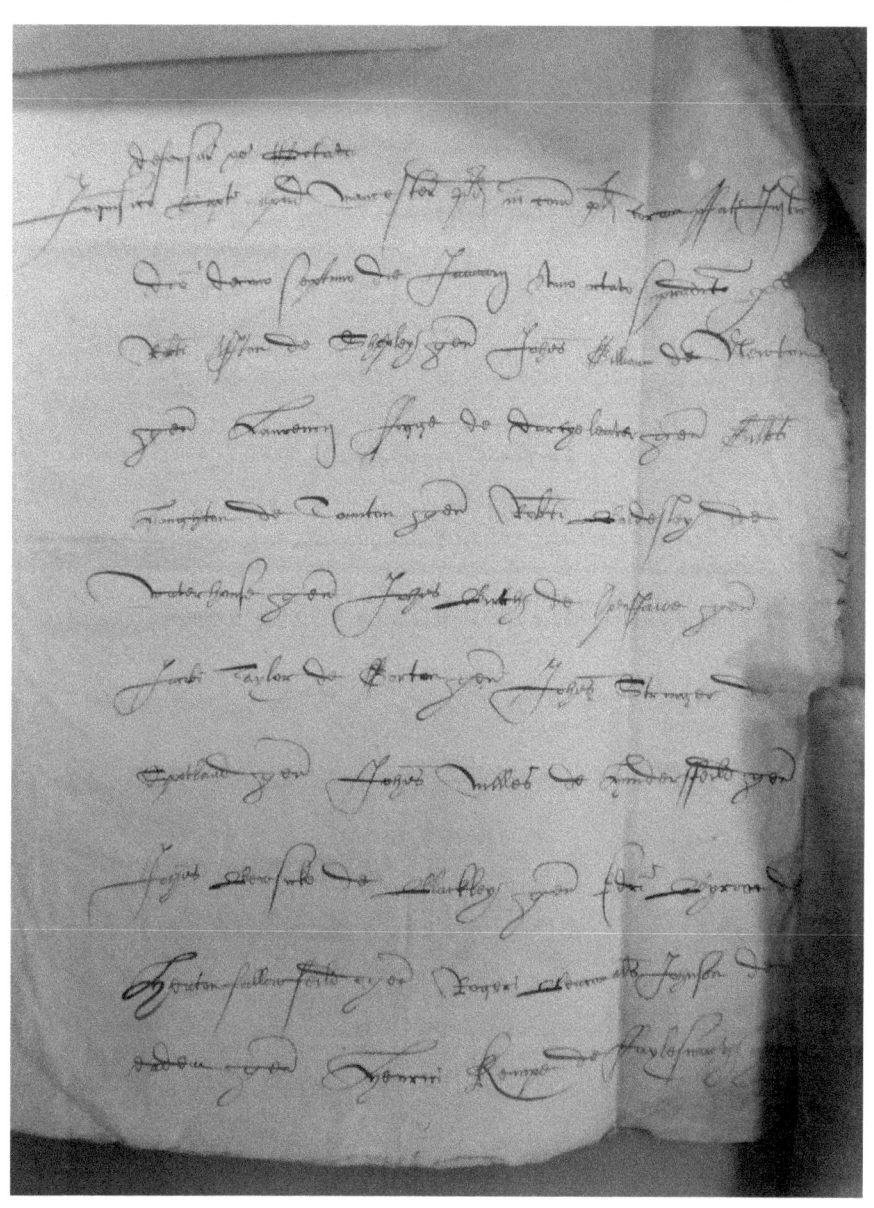

The translation of the letter is shown below.

<u>Session of the Peace, Manchester, 1632/3</u>

Session of the Peace held at Manchester in the county of Lancaster,
 Before Alexander Radcliffe, Knight of the Most Honourable Order of the Bath, Cecil Trafford, Knight, Richard Holland esquire, Edmund Ashton esquire, Edward Rawstorne esquire, Leonard Ash[ton?] esquire, Robert Houlte of Stubley esquire, Edmund Hopwod esquire and John Bradshawe esquire, Justices of our Lord the King assigned to keep the peace in the aforesaid county, and indeed to hear and determine diverse felonies, trespasses and other misdeeds perpetrated in the same county,
 On Thursday, that is to say, the seventeenth day of January in the eighth year of the reign of our Lord Charles, by the grace of God, King of England, Scotland, France and Ireland, defender of the faith etc.

 Inquisition taken at Manchester aforesaid, in the county aforesaid, before the Justices aforenamed, on the said seventeenth day of January in the abovesaid eighth year, by the corporal oath of Robert Ashton of Shepley gentleman, John Gilliam of Newton gentleman, Laurence Fogge of Darcy Lever gentleman, Gilbert Houghton of Tounton gentleman, Robert Bardesley of Waterhouse gentleman, John Birch of Openshaw gentleman, James Taylor of Gorton gentleman, John Stringer of Spotland gentleman, John Milles of Hundersfield gentleman, John Bewsicke of Blackley gentleman, Edward Byron of Heaton Fallowfield gentleman, Roger Beacom alias Johnson of the same gentleman, Henry Kempe of Failsworth gentleman, Roger Whitworth of Castleton gentleman, Robert Boulton of Prestolee gentleman, John Crompton of Farnworth gentleman and William Leightbowne of Halliwell gentleman, upright and law-abiding men of the county aforesaid, jurors,
 Who say and present upon their corporal oath in these English words following, that is to say,
 We do present one long timber bridge over the great River Irwell, lying between the manor of Pilkington and Kearsley, being in the common and usual highway from Leigh to Rochdale, to be in decay,

Which said bridge has from time to time been re-edified, repaired and maintained at the common charge of the whole hundred of Salford, and not by any particular township or person.

> It is examined by George Rigbye
>
> Entered[?]
>
> Mr Holland and Mr Radcliffe to view.

The picture on the next page is from 1913. View from Ringley Old Brow looking down onto Ringley Pack Horse Bridge. The road to link Fold Road to the main road is not yet in place at this time, and the people in the foreground are stood close to the opening that led down to the MBB Canal as it passes beneath. This opening is still accessible today and the 'coping' stones that lined the side of the canal are visible. On the right of the bridge Kearsley Hall Road can be seen winding its way up toward Kearsley Hall farm, which was demolished to make way for Kearsley Power Station just fifteen years after this picture was taken. The silhouette of Spindle Point Colliery, which stood on the left hand side at the top of Slackey Brow, is also noticeable.

Above. Jan 2007. Although it is almost 350 years old at the time of writing Ringley old bridge is still mostly made up of its original stonework, but it is noticeable that much of the parapet has been replaced over the years. The bridge remained open to vehicular traffic until the summer of 1946. It was declared a national monument in 1950, and became grade II listed in August 1986 for its special architectural or historic interest. **Below.** September 2009, looking across toward La Roma Italian restaurant.

Above. September 2015. For several months during 2015 major repair and maintenance work was carried out on the bridge and its foundations. The timing could not have been better, as on Boxing Day later that year the River Irwell rose to record levels through the Irwell valley and the old bridge was put under immense pressure as shown below.

Above. Boxing Day 2015. The old Ringley Pack Horse bridge stands strong against the abnormally high water levels and the vast amounts of debris carried along within it. Confident onlookers stand on the bridge for a better view. **Below.** The stocks on the Tower side of the bridge are thought to date from the seventeenth century, but no records exist of their construction. It is also unknown as to when they were last used.

Ringley Iron Bridge

> SALFORD QUARTER SESSIONS.—At the Salford quarter sessions, on Monday, the Rev. J. S. Birley moved that an application should be made to Parliament in the ensuing session for an act to enable the justices to build a new bridge over the River Irwell, in lieu of Ringley Bridge, and in communication with a proposed new road under the Moses Gate and Ringley Road Act, 1865. The mover of the resolution stated that there were only four bridges across the Irwell between Salford and Bolton. The cost of the new bridge would be £10,000 if of stone, and £8000 if of iron. The trustees of the road would pay £400 towards the preliminary expenses.—The resolution was seconded by Mr. H. Blair, who made a presentment respecting the dangerous state of Ringley-bridge.—A brief discussion took place, the gentlemen taking part being Mr. Dickens, Mr. Ovens, Mr. E. Ashworth, Mr. Walmsley, and others. It was mentioned that, although the expenditure of the hundred had been said to be extravagant, it would be found, when the new valuation was made out, that the inhabitants were not rated higher than any other districts. The resolution having been carried, a committee was appointed to obtain the act of Parliament.—The District Finance Committee recommended the payment of £510 for hundred and £100 for county bridges, according to the bridgemaster's application; and of £432 to the two coroners, for the expenses of the 285 inquests held during the quarter.—The committee appointed to superintend

Above. Bolton Chronicle 28th October 1865. A proposal is put forward at the Salford Hundred for building a bridge over the River Irwell and a new road at Ringley. Mr. Harrison Blair, Chairman of the newly formed Kearsley Local Board, is in attendance to promote the scheme. Building work on the new bridge and road began shortly after this date.

Circa 1930. Ringley Road 'iron' Bridge. During 1931/32 the bridge and road were widened as heavier traffic and larger vehicles became more common.

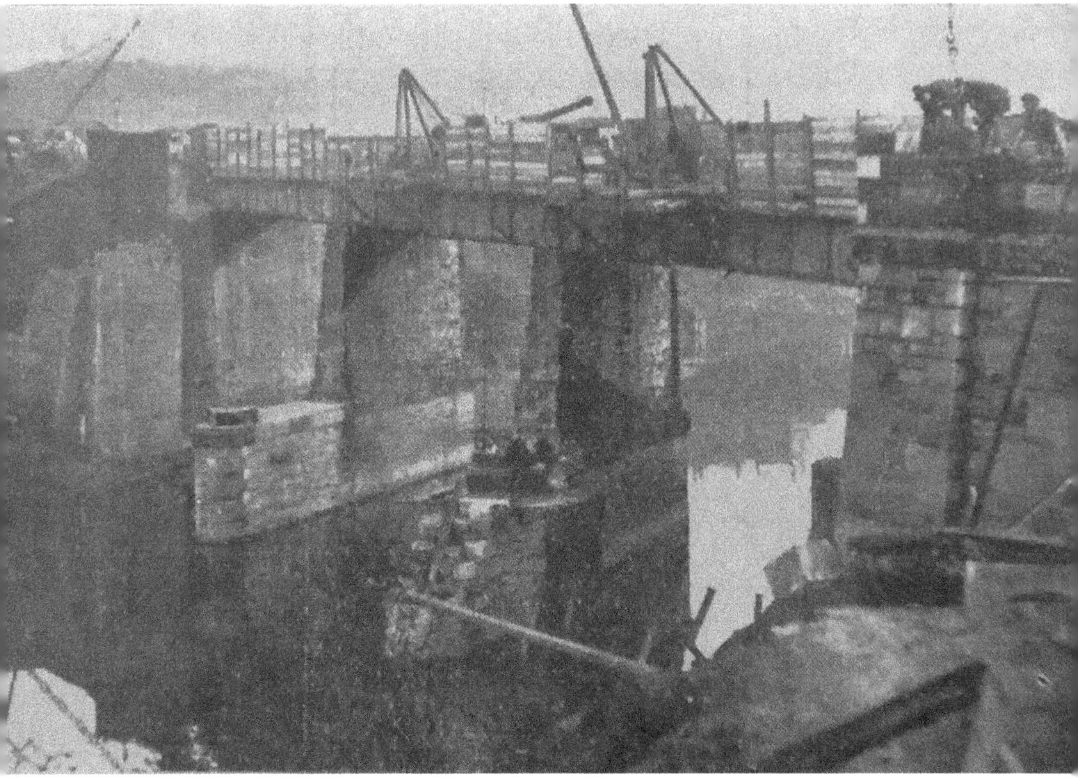

Above. Widening work on the bridge in February 1932.

Below. A ten ton girder is delivered by steam traction lorry in May 1932.

A 64ft. long girder, a 10 ton load, being transported from Bolton L.M.S. station to span the Irwell, in the making of a new Ringley bridge

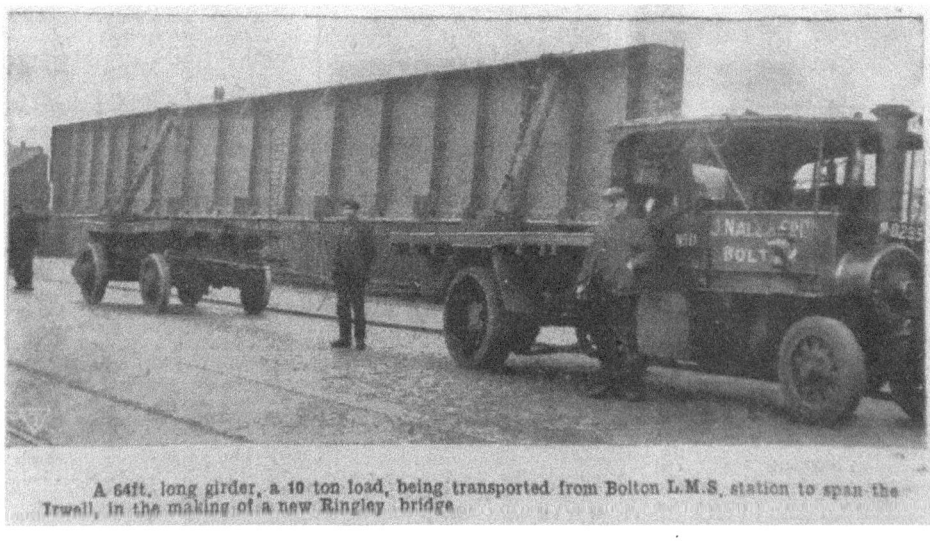

Above. August 1931. Widening of Market Street, Ringley, close to the former Vale House, looking towards the Ringley Road iron bridge that was also undertaking similar work. Note the narrowness of the road, plus the "S" bend in the distance that had become increasingly dangerous for motor transport and so was also removed at this time.

Kearsley Power Station

Kearsley Power Station was built by the Lancashire Electric Power Company, and was the third station built by the company after Radcliffe in 1905 and Padiham in 1927, as Industrial and domestic demand had continued to increase rapidly. The site of the old Kearsley Hall Farm between Stoneclough and Ringley seemed ideal, as on one side was the River Irwell which provided a constant supply of cooling water, while to the south, the nearby LMSR's Manchester-Bolton railway, along with the Kearsley Branch mineral line, would help with the necessary coal supplies required for the boiler furnaces. Kearsley Power Station was not only the biggest of the three LEP Company stations, it was one of the biggest built in Britain in the first half of the twentieth century. Kearsley also broke many records and was regarded as an Industry leader for electricity generation and efficiency.

The station itself was built in three major stages spanning over twenty years, and these became known as A, B and C stations. Work began on the original power station, which came to be known as 'A' station, in June 1927, and eventually began generating its first electricity in September 1929. The main contractor for civil engineering and building work was J. Jarvis & Sons, Ltd with the design of the building being done by Dr. H.F. Parshall who was the consulting engineer to the L.E.P Company.

The original 'A' station had four cast iron chimneys, but these were found to be too low and prone to corrosion, so were replaced in 1935 by two 275 feet high brick stacks. The original 'A' station did not have a cooling tower, instead the water from the turbine condensers was simply discharged back into the River Irwell a little further downstream.

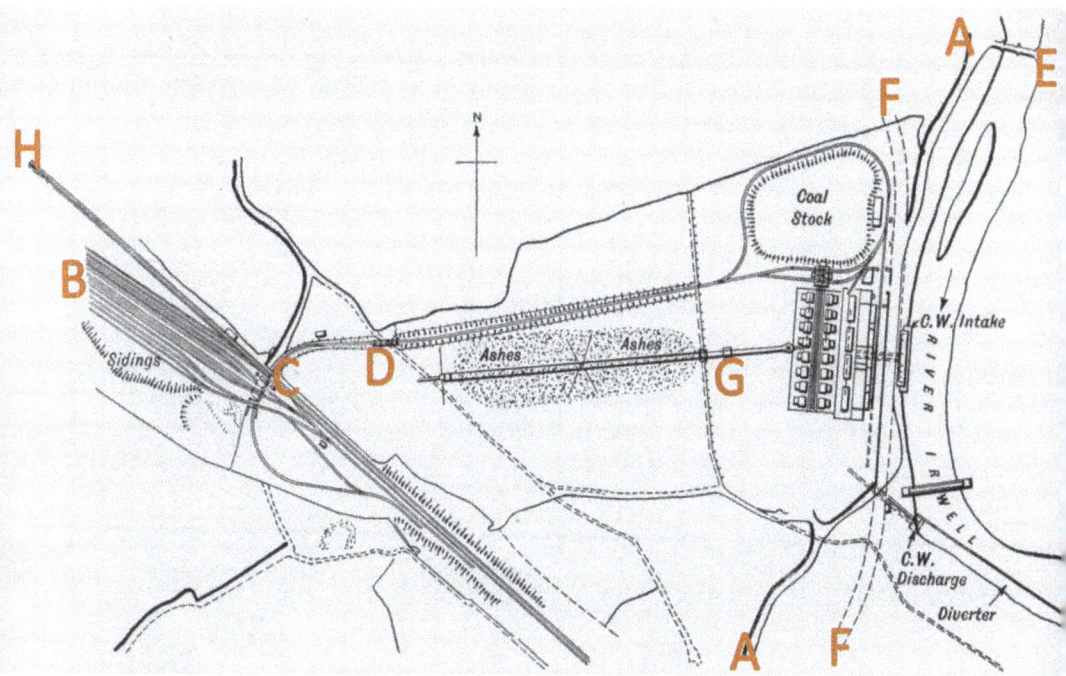

Above. The original site plan showing; **(A)** Kearsley Hall Road. **(B)** Kearsley Branch Railway Sidings. **(C)** Tunnel at Kearsley Junction. **(D)** Location of small bridge over gap in landscape for electric train system. **(E)** Ringley old bridge. **(F)** Hulme Road under construction. **(G)** Aerial ropeway carrying ashes from the furnaces.

On the next page, May 1927, a photograph of the land purchased by the Lancashire Electric Power Co to build Kearsley Power Station. Kearsley Hall Farm and its outbuildings are in the centre approximately where the mini roundabout on Hulme Road is now situated. This whole area across towards Stoneclough Brow was known as Blackbottom. The winding road to the right is Kearsley Hall Road, which lead from Ringley Old Bridge to Slackey Brow tunnel. In the foreground are several old buildings at Kearsley Green.

July 1931. Kearsley Power Station with its original cast iron chimney stacks.

The second expansion of the station was commissioned and officially opened by the Rt. Honourable Earl Of Derby in December 1936, and this became known as 'B' station. This was in fact the first stage of 'B' station, the second part being completed in 1938.

To accommodate for the increased power output, a river intake and screening plant was installed for when the river had sufficient water. But for when it did not, for example, during the summer months when the river flow could be insufficient for the requirements of the new plant as well as 'A' station, the first of what would eventually be 5 cooling towers was constructed on the opposite side of the River Irwell.

Above. Circa 1936. View from a location close to the former weir. This first cooling tower was at the time of erection the largest of its kind in the world at 270 feet high and 175 feet in diameter at its base, with a capacity of 3,370,000 gallons of water per hour. Two further brick chimney stacks, 325 feet high, were also erected at the end of 'A' station's boiler house for the removal of 'B' station's combustion gases.

The second stage of 'B' station was completed in 1938 and four more boilers and a second turbo-alternator were brought into production. The two extra chimneys were encased into the new boiler house and two further cooling towers were constructed identical to the first one, bringing the total at this time to three.

The construction of the final extension to the Power Station began in 1945 and was completed in 1949. The new 'C' station cost £4 million and was intended for peak demand purposes only, rather than continuous running, which 'A' and 'B' stations were performing. Two additional chimneys were built in the middle of the new boiler house, and these were identical in height to the two 'B' station chimneys at 325 feet tall. This brought the total number of chimneys to six, and all using an estimated 9 million Lancashire red bricks.

Above. A section of the Turbine Room, 1931.

Two further cooling towers were also built to deliver the necessary water supply for 'C' station. These were constructed on the land between the Manchester-Bolton railway line and the river, just to the left before you enter the tunnel to go up Slackey Brow. The new towers were bigger than the three previous 'B' station towers, being 290 feet high and 208 feet in diameter at the base.

Above. October 1981. View from above Kearsley Train Station of the two cooling towers that were situated near to the tunnel at the bottom of Slackey Brow. The remains of the old sidings that connected to the Kearsley Branches Railway can be seen to the right, the Hazlemere housing estate is now built over much of this site.

The gradient of 1 in 22 from the Power Station up to the main line meant that the steam trains would not be able to access the site, so sidings for the coal wagons were built at the side of the line, on part of what is now the Hazlemere housing estate. The Power Station had its own standard 4ft 6in gauge 550 volts D.C electric railway system constructed, and electric locomotives would make their way under a tunnel below the main line at Kearsley Junction, then loop up and around to the sidings to fetch the fully loaded coal wagons. The wagons were taken back down and weighed before the contents were deposited into the furnace bunkers, or alternatively to the storage site, roughly where Cloughbank, Dymchurch Avenue and Stanford Close now reside at the bottom of the Ringley Meadows housing estate.

Above. The Power station had four electric trains that transported coal wagons around the site, and also, as shown in this picture from 1969, made the journey up the steep incline to the sidings next to the mainline to collect the coal wagons that had been delivered mostly from collieries in Walkden and Worsley via the Kearsley Branches Railway. Kearsley Junction signal box can be seen but is now long gone, the tunnel though, still remains intact at the time of writing.

Access to these sidings was also made to the Manchester Collieries line via the Kearsley Branches Railway, which ran up Stoneclough Brow beneath the bridge beside the White Horse public house, along the rear of Pilkington Road, under the bridge on Springfield Road, along the top of Mossfield Road to Linnyshaw Moss sidings, then on to collieries at Linnyshaw, Mossley Common and Astley Green.

The first electric locomotive was ordered from Hawthorn Leslie & Co. Ltd of Newcastle in 1927 and actually assisted in the original construction of the site by conveying heavy plant and machinery into the station via a short siding into the turbine hall. This was the only electric loco onsite until the construction of 'B' station in 1936, when a second engine arrived on 18th of June that year, again ordered from Hawthorn Leslie.

The third electric loco was delivered on 24th May 1944, and the fourth a couple of years later on 19th September 1946, both again from the previous supplier who had now changed their name to Robert Stephenson & Hawthorns Ltd.

Above. Hawthorn Leslie Electric Loco Number 1 pictured in 1927. The electric locos were known as Bo-Bo's. The axle arrangements consisted of four wheels on what was called a Bogey, and there were two of these on each loco, so Bo-Bo simply indicated a double Bogey driven loco.

Above. Electric Bo-Bo number 1 at work in the 1960's.

Above. Electric Bo-Bo number 3 makes its way back to the Power Station across a small bridge near to the tunnel at Kearsley Junction.

Left. Electric Bo-Bo number 3 shunts the coal wagons down from the sidings which were next to the main line at Kearsley Junction.

A fully laden coal train makes its way to the sidings at Kearsley Junction via the Kearsley Branch line parallel to Stoneclough Brow, circa mid 1960s. Houses at the end of Station Road and Barnes Terrace can be seen in the background and the bridge that spanned Quarry Road can just be made out in the bottom left hand corner.

At its peak during the late 1940's and 1950's up to 180 coal wagons per day were being delivered to the power station, with 125 tons of coal per hour being consumed when 'A' 'B' and 'C' stations were all generating at full load. Kearsley Power Station was considered at this time as one of Great Britain's premier coal fired power stations, and the number of employees reached a remarkable 550, it even had its own social club on Hulme Road.

Above. Electric Bo-Bo number 2 at the rear of the Power Station in the mid 1960s.

Some of the ash that remained from the burnt coal in the furnace boilers was originally taken offsite or sold to a local company that began to manufacture cement bricks, but most was simply dumped at the rear of the site. This became a serious problem after the second world war, as the power station was now burning its way through up to 125 tons of coal per day, and a large ash pile had now began to form at the western end of the site. It was estimated that the mountain of ash was over 100,000 tons by the early 1960's, and apart from being regarded as an eyesore it also blew around in the wind to cause local residents even more annoyance.

In November 1964 it was removed at a cost of £2000, and the aerial ropeway which carried the skips of ash to the dumping site, was also taken down, with Station-Supt. Mr J. D. Tottman saying "We know the station isn't an architectural gem, but we want to be good neighbours. We knew the ash dump was a nuisance and an eyesore to people living near it, so we devised a more modern method of disposing of the ash."

A conveyor belt system from the boiler furnaces now carried the ash to a hopper, where it could be loaded onto lorries and taken away for brick manufacture or road building, Kearsley Power Station ash was used in the construction of the A666 Farnworth bypass.

After the removal of the ash pile it was considered to grass over the area, but this never happened, a coating of ash remained on the site until the 1980's, and those of us of a certain generation will remember this area as 'the cinders'. Access to the site was fairly easy, and by this time the remaining portions of the electric railway system were fenced off, so 'the cinders' became a popular place to race around on all manner of (mostly illegal) motorcycles.

Kearsley Power Station 1969.

Above. The original aerial ropeway that carried the burnt ash, or 'cinders' out of from the furnaces to be taken away or dumped at the rear of the site.

The run-down of the power station began during the 1960's, but the seeds were sown in 1956 with an Act Of Parliament labelled the 'Clean Air Act,' which sought to reduce pollution, by amongst other things, the burning of coal in urban areas. Around this period Britain also began to import oil from the Middle East plus exploit the reserves of natural gas in the North Sea, and both of these energy sources were cleaner and cheaper than coal. These factors cast a shadow over the economic practicalities of coal fired power stations as a whole.

On the next page is an aerial view of Kearsley Power Station in early 1985. At this time it was being decommissioned internally in preparation for its demolition over the next few years. The Manchester to Bolton railway line is seen running straight through the picture, and the former weir in the River Irwell is visible close to the cooling towers. The whole area comprising the main power station building and the land to the rear all the way to the railway line is now covered by the Ringley Meadows housing estate built during the 1990's.

During 1966 the boilers for 'A' station were converted to oil firing, and two storage tanks that could each hold 153,000 gallons of oil were installed on the west side of the boiler house, and all of this oil would now be brought in by road tankers.

In October 1973 the Arab-Isreali Yom Kippur War erupted, and the price of crude oil quadrupled in a matter of months, this left 'A' station economically impractical to run, and only two years later it was de-commissioned.

Two years later in 1977 'C' station ceased to generate any more electricity, although it was officially put on stand-by it was never used again. This left 'B' station to carry-on until the spring of 1981, when the power station officially ceased generating electricity.

After this the power station was slowly taken apart from within, but it did continue to work in some capacity for the next few years with the remains of the on-site electric railway system being used for various experimental purposes, including remote controlled trams that were tested for driverless operation. The CEGB also used the site as a workshop and several locomotives were sent there for repair or storage, but, by the end of 1985 the power station building was abandoned for good.

Above. Sunset on Clifton Marina, 1984. The prodigious chimney stacks and five cooling towers of Kearsley Power Station reflect serenely on the man made lake.

On Sunday 12th May 1985 the five giant cooling towers that had displayed such an imposing presence over the valley for almost fifty years were brought crashing down. John Turner of Northern Explosives Ltd pressed the button that triggered the explosives attached to the legs in each tower. Thousands turned out to watch the spectacle from the various vantage points overlooking the area, and the next day it was shown on the local television news.

Above and below. Aerial shots taken on the morning of 12th May 1985. The picture below shows the three towers that stood next to the St. Saviour School football pitch on Fold Road.

Onlookers watch the demolition of the cooling towers from the fields next to Slackey Brow on May 12th 1985.

Above. 12th May 1985. The two towers nearest to the Slackey Brow tunnel were the first to be destroyed, the third now comes crashing down.

Left. One of the cooling towers that was situated across the river from the main Power Station building comes crashing down. These towers were normally accessed along a concrete road that had an entrance at Red Rock Lane close to the end of Fold Road. The old Power Station Club can also be seen.

Below. Pictured here in 1986 the Power Station is being slowly dismantled. The left hand side of the building is approximately where the entrance to Fernside from Hulme Road is now situated.

Kearsley Power Station in the midst of demolition, summer 1986. This whole area is now filled with houses on the Ringley Meadows estate. To give perspective, this picture would have been taken from more or less where you would turn into Cloughbank from Ringley Meadows.

Above. Demolition of the turbines during 1986.

The power station building and surrounding site took another 3 years to fully decommission and clear, until the only structures still standing were the six majestic Lancashire red brick chimneys that stood in dignified isolation awaiting their fate. The chimneys were brought down on Sunday 18th September 1988 and again large crowds came out to watch.

Above. Explosives detonate at the foot of the chimneys on 18th September 1988. At the bottom of the picture are the former farm buildings currently used as a cattery and boarding kennels.

Left. View from the fields between Slackey Brow and Baker Street, 18th September 1988.

The clearing of the site was not straightforward however, as various areas were contaminated with dangerous blue asbestos, of which tons had been used for lagging the boilers, combustion chambers and pipework. John Preston was an engineer working on the site during the summer in 1986 & 87, he says "I remember the site was very big! And the main recollection of my time there (It was 2 consecutive summer vacations from University) was that we discovered that the ash from the furnaces, which was stockpiled all around the site, was contaminated with asbestos. Suddenly, we were told we had to wear safety overalls and breathing masks whenever we walked over the site. We had some very strange looks from the commuters in the trains on the railway line that ran along one edge of the site! It also made the local papers with questions being raised about the level of contamination and whether it might become airborne."

Eventually the site was cleared, with some of the debris and brickwork being piled at the rear of the site near the Manchester to Bolton railway line where it has been landscaped and trees planted.

In May 1989 permission was granted to build houses on the site and The Bolton Evening News of December 1st that year announced that a £100,000 community centre would also be built, but this never materialized. The site is now occupied by the Ringley Meadows housing estate built during the 1990's.

Above. February 2013. The former power station office and laboratory buildings being demolished to make way for the Kearsley Green housing development on Hulme Road.

The Manchester To Bolton Railway

The Manchester, Bolton & Bury Canal Company began to promote the establishment of a railway along, or very near to, the line of the canal from Salford to Bolton around the year 1830. This would have meant filling in sections of the canal, which had only been in use for less than 40 years and constructing the line along the general course of the waterway. Indeed in 1831 an Act of Parliament was obtained which authorized the demise of the canal in favour of the railway, but this was amended after protestations from colliery proprietors who still relied on the canal as a supply route. It was agreed that the canal would remain unaltered and the new railway would be built along the course it still takes today.

The shareholders now changed the company name to "The Manchester, Bolton and Bury Canal Navigation and Railway Company" and they employed engineer Jesse Hartley to undertake construction of the line in 1833.

The Manchester and Bolton Railway construction was delayed at Halshaw Moor tunnel owing to troublesome quicksand which had perplexed the engineers, but the line was finally opened for passenger traffic on 29th May 1838, and in an effort to encourage confidence in this modern means of travel all journeys were free for this day. Construction costs of the line ran at around £60,000 per mile, a most prodigious amount for the time.

The new steam trains could run at maximum speeds of between eighteen and twenty miles an hour, but it was decided that such haste was not necessary or workable. The original journey of ten miles from Salford to Bolton, along with all the required stops, took up to an hour. First class carriages were covered and enclosed on all sides and carried only 18 passengers maximum. Second class carriages were calculated to hold 32 passengers and measured 14 feet long by 6 feet 4 inches wide, and the height just 5 feet 6 inches. These had covers supported by iron pillars but were open on each side and at one end. There were seats along each side and at each end, plus a double row of benches down the middle where passengers sat back to back. Meagre lighting was provided by an oil lamp, which would leak its contents when the train jolted, sometimes onto any unfortunate travellers sat below.

Third class carriages were introduced on 11th June 1838, but were not covered and had no seats, leaving travellers standing and open to the elements. These were discontinued on 1st December 1838 in consequence of the number of passengers choosing this cheaper option rather than first or second class

The guard of each train would ride on a raised seat outside the first class carriage, he had a brake to stop the train and he always made his way through the carriages to check and collect tickets. The original fares from Halshaw Moor to Bolton single fare were: first class, 1s 0d, second class, 9d, third class, 6d. There were no double or return tickets for many years afterwards. In these early days of the railway smoking was not allowed in the stations or carriages, but some separate compartments were provided for smokers. It was not uncommon for disputes to develop when ignorant passengers would flout this rule.

The line originally ran between New Bailey Street, Salford to Bridgeman Street in Bolton, and Farnworth Station was at first simply referred to as 'Tunnel' Station, and Kearsley Station as 'Stoneclough.'

The following is an excerpt from *"The Railway Companion, from Manchester to Bolton" (pamphlet) By Arthur Lacey, 1838,* in which the author describes most eloquently the journey and scenery. At this point Mr. Lacey is approaching Slackey Brow tunnel from the direction of Clifton.

"The embankment over which we are now passing is about 37 feet high, and contains 300,00 cubic yards of earth. The village to the left is Kearsley Green; upon the right is Ringley Fold. From this embankment is an interesting prospect. The houses below seem to have a most undesirable approximation to this formidable-looking bank, which appears to threaten to overwhelm them; such is however, the force of habit, that no danger is apprehended; perhaps, indeed, none now exists, as there are heavy retaining walls at its foot, and it is daily acquiring more solidity. The large range of buildings on the right is Mr. Crompton's cotton mills, which employ about 800 hands. Blakhurst Green is just beyond them, and on the summit is Knob End. We now pass over Stoneclough Bridge- the high road to Bolton passes under it. Mr. Knowles collieries are a little further on. We here enter an excavation of some extent, on the side of which are occasional openings, affording interesting views. There is one at the 7 and half mile-post which is worthy of attention: the gentle Irwell wends its way immediately below us, and Nature in her loveliness here triumphs; but at a mile distance, as if to give effect to contrast, is Mr. Rawson's vitriol works, the walls of which appear blackened by the subtle acid; the trees around them are blighted, and all things, for some distance, by their appearance, acknowledge the terrible effect of this power. Beyond the works, a series of locks belonging to the Bolton and Bury canal may be seen; they are six in number, and raise the canal about 80 feet. (7 ½ miles) Just before this post we enter the Halshaw Moor Tunnel: it is 290 yards long, 22 yards wide, and 18 feet 9 inches above the rails. Just through it, we arrive at Tunnel (Now Farnworth HM Station).

The Church of Halshaw Moor is just to the left of the tunnel; it is a neat edifice, with a square tower. (7 ¾ miles) Strong retaining walls have here been erected upon each side of the excavation, which have been more than once destroyed by the pressure upon them, arising from the peculiarity of the ground; and it has been found necessary to support them with strong abutments.

This fascinating first-hand account illustrates how the natural beauty of the landscape coexisted with the numerous industrial premises that filled the Irwell valley, Mr. Rawson's vitriol works rightly being singled out for its unpleasantness and detrimental effect on the area.

During construction of the Manchester and Bolton Railway gangs of rival navvies often caused uproar in the surrounding area with conflicts amongst each other and the locals. There are two such incidents worthy of note from this time. The first commenced on Sunday 3rd April 1837 when a drunken navvy named Daniel Quigley insulted, threatened and jostled the Rev. William Burns, Vicar of St. Johns, and a collier named Peter Boardman. Quigley returned to the Black Horse to continue drinking and cause further nuisance, upon which the landlord, Mr. William Tyldesley, called for special constable Robert Dawson of Kersley, who was also a clogger and shoemaker. Dawson managed to get Quigley out of the Black Horse, but a large crowd had now begun to assemble. Other constables arrived named Nathan Coucill and James Dootson, along with Reverend Burns, but as they made their way to the recently constructed dungeon at Princess Street to incarcerate Quigley a mini riot erupted, with several other navvies, spurred on by the baying crowd, managing to free their workmate. Quigley was apprehended in Manchester several days later and brought back through Kersley to Farnworth on the outside of a horse drawn coach. He was sentenced to nine months imprisonment at Lancaster Castle, with several of the other rioters also being locked up for six months and three months.

Only a few weeks later, on the 24th May 1837, the railway navvies again caused a great drama as between 150 and 200 of them appeared on Stoneclough Brow armed with picks and spades. Constable James Dootson was immediately sent to Bolton to obtain the services of the military (as there was no Police force at this time) to quell the imminent battle. The reason for the disturbance was that an excavator had fallen to his death and the navvies on the Farnworth side wanted the body interred at Bolton, whilst the navvies on the Clifton side wanted the man interred at Manchester, and it was they who held the body. As no resolution could be found they agreed to fight it out, and Stoneclough Brow was the arranged meeting place.

The navvies from the Farnworth side did not show up though, possibly thinking "discretion was the better part of valour" or maybe concerned at the arrival of the military, either way the navies on the Clifton side left the scene after waiting for half an hour, happy that their opponents did not want to contest the matter further.

Above. July 1963, Moses Gate Station.

Left. July 1963, Farnworth And Halshaw Moor Station, which was simply known as 'Tunnel' Station when the line first opened in 1838.

Below. F&HM station in August 1970. The old station buildings were taken down in 1975 due to their run-down state. In the background is the 3 storey Rawson Arms Public House. After a ruinous fire in June 1998 the pub never reopened.

Above. Kearsley bound train emerges from Farnworth tunnel in the mid 1960's.

Above. Train passing Horridge Brook in September 1966. Houses on Church Road and Alfred Street can be seen atop the hill.

Mid 1960's view of Kearsley Train Station.

Stoneclough Brow Bridge circa 1925. Constructed for the Manchester and Bolton railway during 1837 the imposing bridge over Stoneclough Road was designed and built by engineer Jesse Hartley who later went on to design Liverpool's Albert Dock and its warehouses. The bridge became a listed building for its special architectural or historic interest on 19th August 1986. The houses either side of the bridge were demolished in the late 1960's.

Above. February 2011, The Grade II listed tunnel at Slackey Brow is of pure canal architecture. **Below.** Mid 1960's Scene close to the location the former Dixon Fold station at Clifton which closed in 1931. The chimney known as 'Fletchers Folly' is to the right and the cooling towers of Kearsley Power Station are seen in the background.

Late 1960's view of the Manchester to Bolton line at Clifton. The construction of the M62 motorway can be seen in the background with the incomplete section of the bridge that now spans the River Irwell clearly shown. The lake at Clifton Marina was created when earth was taken from the site to help create many of the embankments for the motorway in the surrounding area.

Above. Train passing Pilkingtons Tile Works in the late 1960's with the M62 construction in the background.

Below. A similar view from 1984, showing the completed M62 motorway and bridge over the River Irwell with its now built up grassy embankments.

When the Manchester and Bolton Railway (M&BR) originally opened in 1838 there was no station between Ringley and Agecroft, but in 1844 the Manchester, Bury and Rossendale Railway (MB&RR) gained consent to build a line to connect to the M&BR at Clifton that would pass through Bury and terminate at Rawtenstall. The line crossed the River Irwell over the viaduct known locally as the 'Thirteen Arches' and the station became known as Clifton Junction. The line closed in 1966 and in 1974 the station was renamed simply as Clifton.

Above. 1908, The Thirteen Arches viaduct at Clifton. **Below.** Clifton Junction station circa 1910.

The MB&RR line began at Clifton Junction, with the next stop being Molyneux Brow at a point now obliterated by the M62 motorway. It then passed under Ringley Road West, close to Wood Street, in the Outwood area as shown in the picture below. It continued on to Radcliffe, Withins, Bury, Summerseat, Ramsbottom, Stubbins and finally to Rawtenstall.

Above. A coal train passes beneath the A667 road bridge at Outwood in 1963. The houses on the left are on the main road and Wood Street is to their right. Ringley Road station, which was built when the line first opened, was located at the other side of the bridge. This station closed in January 1953 and only scant remnants of the platforms remain today. The route followed by the old railway line now forms part of the Outwood Nature Trail which is popular for cycling, walking and horse-riding.

1913. Ernest Seddon's shop on Ringley Road West where it adjoins Wood Street. The shop is now converted into a residential dwelling.

Left. A circa 1940's first class ticket from Ringley Road station. This line and the main Manchester to Bolton line were ran by the London, Midland and Scottish Railway from 1921 until nationalization in 1948 when they became part of British Railways.

Below. Circa 1920's view of Ringley Road station

The Kearsley Branches Railway

The Kearsley Branches Railway was a mineral railway which commenced at sidings at Kearsley Junction on the main Manchester to Bolton line, before making its way parallel to Stoneclough Brow to a point just after the bridge spanning Bolton Road close to the White Horse public house, where it originally split off into what was called No.1 and No.2 branches. Number 1 branch continued along the rear of Pilkington Road and terminated at Linnyshaw Moss, where the line then joined the railway system of the Bridgewater Trustees and connected to the Patricroft line, the Worsley line and other branches that joined the whole network of railways in the county. Number 2 branch took a route along Singing Clough, through Lark Hill to Stonehill Colliery on Worsley Road.

The first sod of earth was cut on the 4th of June 1874 by Mr Samuel Scowcroft, owner of several coal pits in the area, including Kearsley Moss Colliery, which was situated at the field where Birch Road, Waverley Avenue and Springfield Road now all convene.

The line officially opened on 28th February 1878 and was always intended to be used for transportation of coal, chemicals and general merchandise, and never for carrying passengers. The total cost of work was approximately £100,000, but for the businesses that would now utilize the line the savings in conveying their goods was regarded as money well spent.

When the line first opened there was accommodation for around 40 or 50 wagons each for both the Harrison Blair Chemical works and Scowcroft's Kersley Moss Colliery at the Linnyshaw Moss sidings. Prior to this line opening any goods that required transportation by rail would have had to be taken by horse and cart to Moses Gate station, so the new Kersley Branches Railway now meant huge financial savings in cartage as well as a significantly more convenient system.

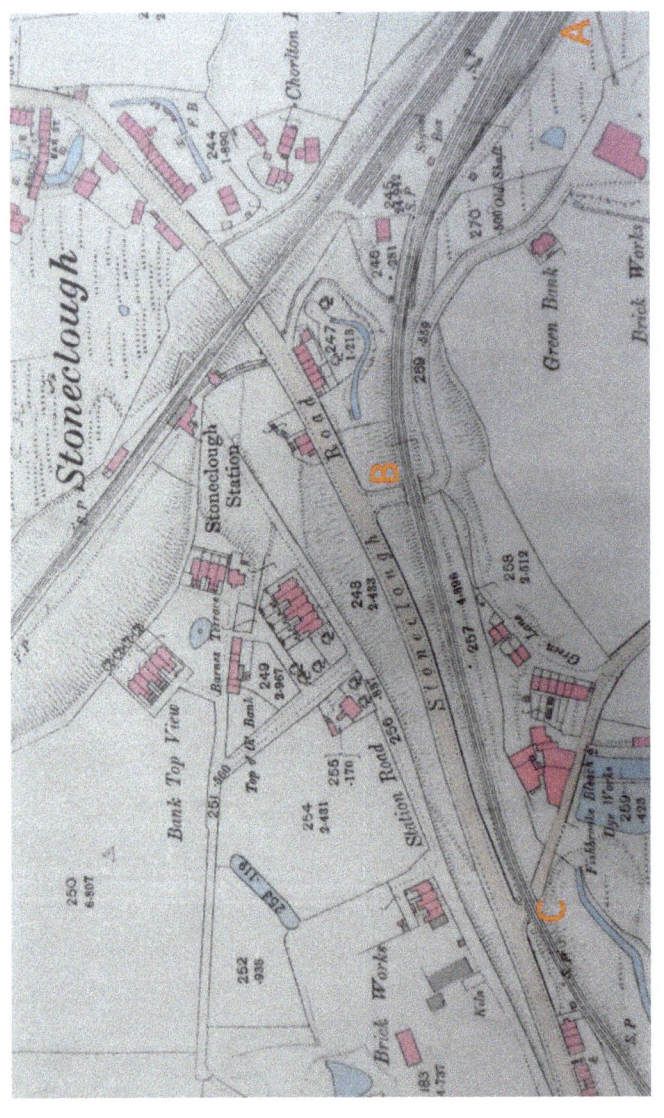

Above. Map of 1890. The line commenced at what were originally called the Little Hey sidings (A) at Kearsley Junction on the Manchester to Bolton line. These sidings could accommodate over 300 wagons and are now covered by the Hazlemere housing estate. The line made its way past a signal box around to a bridge that spanned Quarry Road (B), this bridge was demolished in the 1990's. A little further up the railway there was a level crossing (C) where Roscow Road joined Stoneclough Brow, but this was closed around 1970.

Above. Circa 1970, The Kearsley Branches Railway signal box at Stoneclough. Houses on Station Road and Barnes Terrace can be seen in the distance.

Below, picture taken at the side of the White Horse public house in the mid 1960's, a steam train makes its way back past the Fishbrook Bleach & Dye Works after leaving its delivery of coal wagons for Kearsley Power Station at the Kearsley Junction sidings. The houses to the left were demolished in the late 1960's.

Circa mid 1960's. Coal train emerges from the Bolton Road bridge. Singing Clough is to the left and Pilkington Road is up on the right hand side. The top corner of the White Horse public house can just be seen on the left. It is at this point that Branch Line number 2 would have taken a route across Singing Clough and Lark Hill to Messrs. Roscow and Lord's Stonehill Colliery. It is unclear exactly when Branch Line number 2 became redundant, but maps of the area dated 1909 show that it was no longer in use. This train is on Branch Line Number 1 which connected to the Manchester Collieries lines at Linnyshaw Moss.

Above. Coal train approaching the bridge at Springfield Road in October 1967. At the top of the embankment to the right would be Waverley Avenue, and up to the left would have been George Tomlinson School, which has now been demolished to make way for the Kearsley Academy Secondary School and Sixth Form.

Below, Train and wagons below the bridge at Springfield Road in the mid 1960's. This bridge has now been filled in due to the increasing weight of the heavy goods vehicles visiting the nearby Lyon Industrial Estate.

Linnyshaw Moss sidings, April 1964. Springfield Road bridge is in the background and the Harrison Blair Chemical works would be to the left. The house on the right hand side is number 133 Mossfield Road.

Branch line number 1 remained in use until October 1970 when the last train travelled the route on Friday the 2nd of that month. The route from Linnyshaw Moss to the collieries at Linnyshaw, Walkden, Worsley and Ashton's Field crossed the path of where the new M61 motorway and the Kearsley Spur formed part of the Worsley Braided interchange, and during the construction of these roadways two bridges to carry the railway over them had to be put in place. The first, and smaller, bridge spans the end of the southbound M61, and the longer steel bridge spans the Kearsley Spur and northbound M61. This bridge is easily identifiable as the exterior is painted yellow and the internal design is that it is split down the middle with a walkway on one side and the rail tracks were on the other side.

It is interesting to note that these bridges only fully opened to rail traffic in June or July 1970, so only saw a few months of service taking deliveries of coal to Kearsley Power Station, which had now began taking most of it supplies in by road. The steam driven loco's that had worked the line for almost a century were to make no further journeys and the track was dismantled shortly after.

Above. 1994. The former site of where the Kearsley Branch Line Number 1 terminated at Linnyshaw Moss sidings. At this time the bridge on Springfield Road was being filled in to secure it against the increasing weight of HGV's visiting the Lyon Industrial Estate which can be seen to the right. Houses on Mossfield Road are on the left as is the former play site known as Birch Road park. This whole area is now completely overgrown.

Tasker's Farm and Tasker's Lane Farm

Tasker's Farmhouse stood on the site currently occupied by the Spar convenience store at 198 Springfield Road and the houses to its rear on Melville Road. Although it is shown on a map of 1798 it is unclear exactly when the farm was first established, and it has been a fruitless exercise when trying to trace the name 'Tasker' from all of the ancient documents I have perused. It is surely the case that the original incumbents of the farm would have had the surname 'Tasker,' and, as was often the case, the appellation stuck. The lane that ran through its fields and past the farmhouse also became known as Tasker's Lane until it was renamed Springfield Road in 1930.

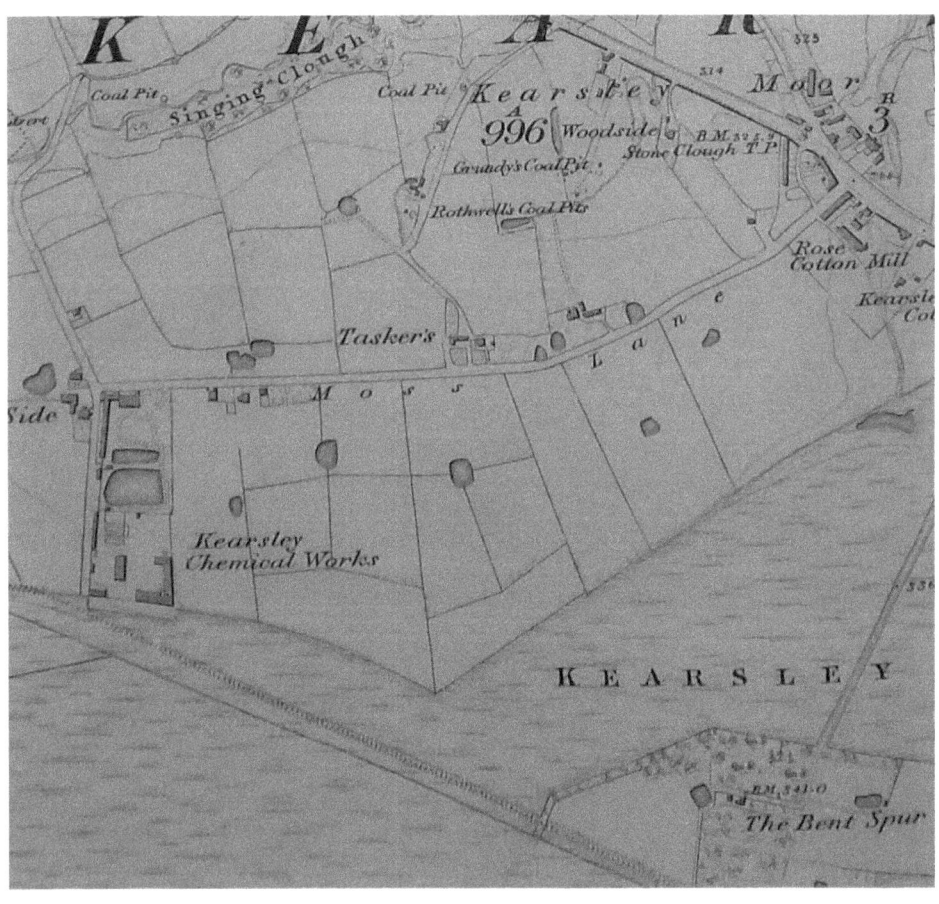

The map on the previous page of 1848 shows Tasker's Farm in the centre surrounded by the fields which were tended to by its proprietors. The lane passing the farmhouse is shown as Moss Lane as it was not officially named Tasker's Lane until October 1866. Further to the right are the buildings of what became known as Tasker's Lane Farm during the late nineteenth century and early 20th century. At that time this farm and its surrounding fields were under the control of the Co-Operative Society.

There are occasional references in books and documents that mention residents of the farm, but it is difficult to build a full picture of its history. In the book 'The History Of Halshaw Moor Chapel' Robert Topp, of the prominent Topp family, is stated as living at Taskers Farm sometime in the early nineteenth century until he was turned out of it by a Mr Grundy, who was at that time a local colliery owner and the agent for the Duke of Bridgewater who owned the land. Around 1928 the farm was taken over by Mr Edward Livingstone and his wife Mary, and they worked Tasker's Farm until its final closure in 1967. During their time in charge they certainly saw the greatest transformation of its surrounding area, as more and more of their fields were sold by the landowners, Bridgewater Estates, for housing developments. Most of the land around Springfield Road, Mossfield Road and Pilkington Road were rich in potatoes, swedes, cabbages, barley, oats, wheat and corn. They would often sell their produce around the district on a horse and cart, this was known as 'hawking.' In January 1931 part of the farmhouse became utilized as the farm shop and also sold other groceries such as milk, bread, cigarettes and sweets.

By 1965 only the farmhouse, stables and yard remained, but the shop remained open until it was forced to close due to the land being sold to a private developer in 1967. The farmhouse was demolished in March 1968 and the Spar store and several houses built in its place immediately after. These are distinguishable as they are constructed of a pale pinkish type brick instead of the red brick of the surrounding houses.

Taskers Farmhouse, Springfield Road, 1953. The shop is to the left and was accessible by the entrance in the middle and also from a door to the rear from what is now Melville Road. The lean-to on the right was the coal shed, and out of shot to the left was a barn and stables. Mary Livingstone can be seen at the top right hand window.

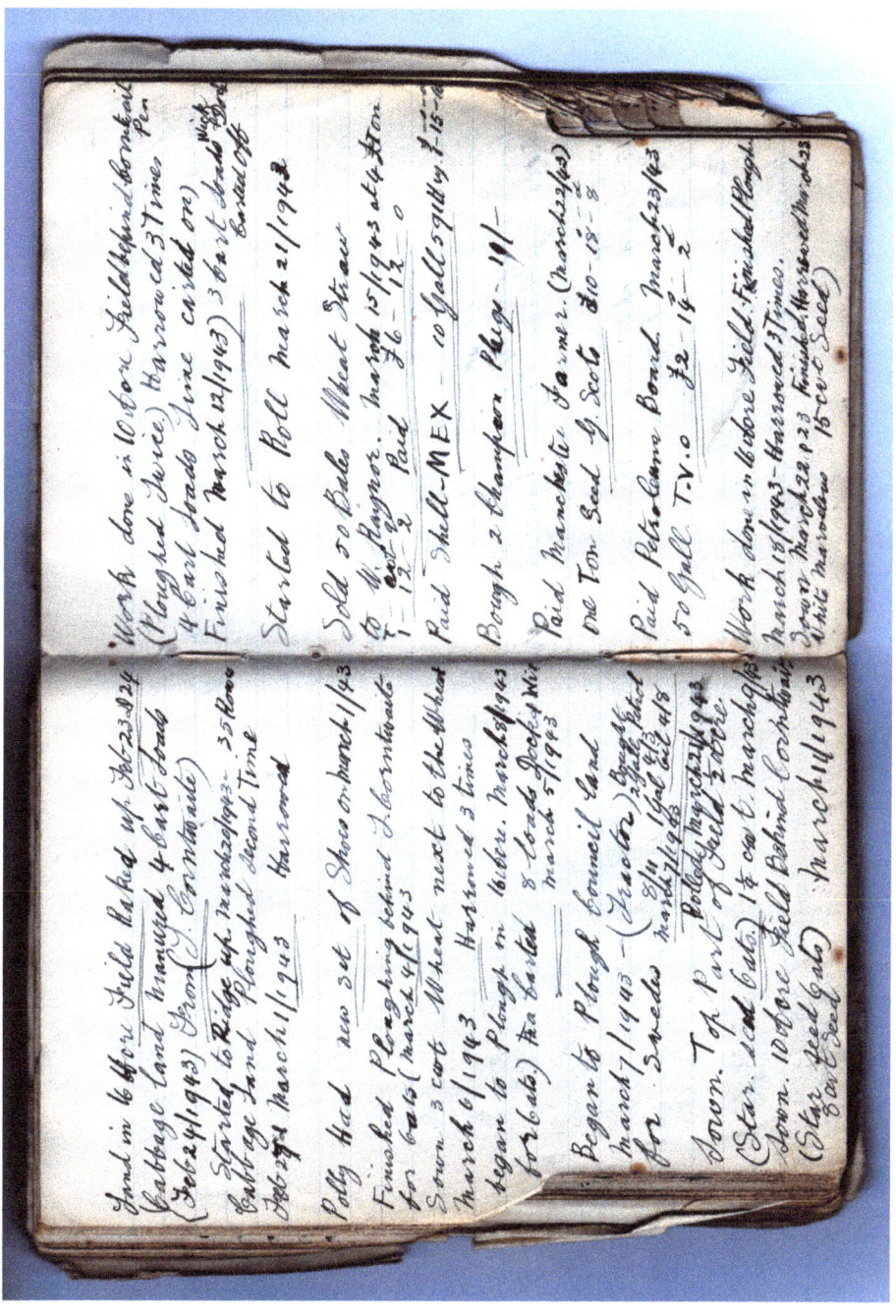

A section from the diary of farmer Edward Livingstone of Tasker's Farm, March 1943.

 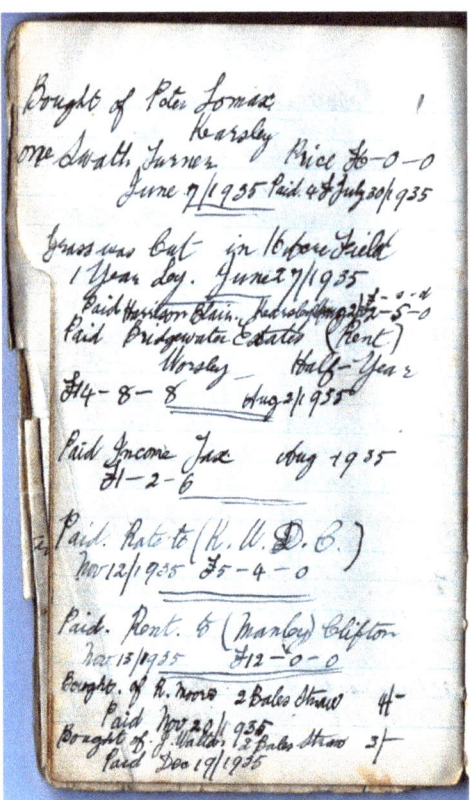

Above. Edward Livingstone pictured in 1967 and diary entries from 1935 showing payments to Peter Lomax of Pool Farm (for a swath turner), Harrison Blair Chemical Works (for rent of a field), Bridgewater Estates (landowners) and Kearsley Urban District Council (Rates) amongst others.

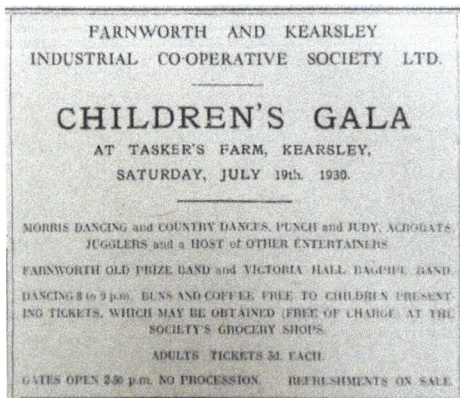

Left. Advertisement from the Farnworth Journal. An annual Gala was held on the land at the Co-Operative society's Tasker's Lane Farm, which was located around the Alderbank Close area, in later years these galas were conducted at Kearsley Cricket Club.

Tasker's Farmhouse and shop, Springfield Road, January 1968. Demolished just a few weeks after this picture was taken, there are newspapers visible at the windows and a Brooke Bond tea sign outside of the former shop window. Out of shot to the right was a gate which allowed access straight through to St Kilda Avenue.

Right. Children at play in 'the hayfield' of Taskers Farm in the 1940's. This later became part of Mossfield Road. The houses in the background are on Princess Avenue, which was built during the 1930's.

Left. Mary Livingstone at Taskers Farm in the 1940's. The house to the right is 192 Springfield Road.

Above. Circa 1949. Jean Livingstone, Arthur Hinks, Marion Livingstone and Mary Livingstone next to a small lodge that was located in the middle of where the Mossfield Road estate was built. The Harrison Blair chemical works can be seen in the background with the huge chemical waste pile known as 'stink bomb hill' to the left.

Left. Circa 1949. Mary Livingstone with pet collie Rex at the rear of Tasker's farmhouse. St Kilda Avenue can be seen in the background.

December 2006. The Spar convenience store at 198 Springfield Road, built on the site of the old Tasker's Farmhouse. The shop was run by John and Brenda Roberts from 1970 to 2007. At the left hand side of the shop is the former launderette which closed during the 1990's.

Circa 1920's. The Co-Operative Society's Tasker's Lane Farm which stood around the area now occupied by Alderbank Close. By the beginning of the second world war this was still in use but as a pig farm only. In the late nineteenth century the farm was tenanted by Mr William Chatton who ran it for many years up until 1902, before turning it over to his son, Charles, who was still at the helm into the 1920's.

Top o'th Bank Farmhouse

The following information has been adapted from the wonderful little book, *Recollections of Farnworth and Kearsley 1900-45, The Family Chatton. By Agnes Fish.*

Around the year 1900 Sam and Agnes Chatton ran a small dairy at the end of Lord Street on Bolton Road, opposite the New Jerusalem Church. They then moved into a farmhouse called Top o'th Bank (sometimes referred to as Bank Top), which stood overlooking Kearsley Railway station.

The front of the farmhouse faced a picturesque lane now known as Clifton Street, which at the time was an avenue of trees with fields on either side, and a duck pond lay in the left hand field roughly where the Bank Top Park is now. The land was made up of good growing agricultural soil, and splendid cabbages and turnips found a ready sale in Manchester's wholesale Smithfield market. Oceans of gold corn rolled over toward the horizon on the Clammerclough side (now the Grovsenor Street area), and mother Chatton would sow seeds along the furrowed fields using an odd violin shaped instrument. The family would often go for tea at their uncle Charlie's farm at Taskers Lane (now Springfield Road) on a Sunday, and as a child young Agnes would remember swinging on the five-barred gate at the bottom of Pilkington Road on the path leading up to the Farm.

During the building of Kearsley Spinning Mill at Prestolee, Sam Chattton entered a prosperous phase through carting contracts he obtained, and he and several associates had a fleet of horse-drawn lorries ploughing their weary way up and down Stoneclough Brow to deliver bricks and other building materials.

Bank Top farm was eventually sold to the local authority in 1938 after running into financial difficulties. The farm buildings and property, plus land adjoining Clifton Street, Oakes Street and Back Station Road, totalling 11,287 acres passed into the hands of Kearsley Council for the princely sum of £1,100. Practically the whole of this amount went to the Building Society to clear off outstanding debt.

During the latter part of the Second World War along Clifton Street and what were once the fields of Bank Top Farm (now the Roosevelt Road and Randolph Road area), a number of German prisoners-of-war were engaged on building works for new streets and housing. Young Agnes Fish describes them as "*working away contentedly; in fact one would have hardly have found them any different from our own workmen, had it not been for the distinguishing* circles of coloured cloth sewn into the back of their tunics – for easy identification if they decided to try and run away".

In the following extracts Agnes Fish describes how births, deaths and common illnesses were often dealt with and her experiences during the Second World War.

"Another method of warding off winter ailments was Thermogene. This thick, orange coloured wadding was impregnated with some kind of heating element which virtually set you on fire when worn next to the skin. It was always considered safer to "lose it in bed", as opposed to straightforward shedding of the impenetrable armour. Some older people placed a "collop" of fat bacon inside a stocking and wound this "cure" around a sore throat. Many gardens were stripped of "nipbone", or comfrey, a weed like substance which was stewed and placed on a sprained ankle or other injured joint. Bad bouts of bronchitis were treated by bowls of heated water laced with balsam; the resulting rising vapours were inhaled by the patient. This felt as if a chimney sweep had vacuumed out the nose and throat passages. Severe earache would find the sufferer with a hot potato, nestling in a scarf, hugging the troublesome ear. A cheap way of warming one's bed was to keep a brick in the oven until it was sufficiently hot to be wrapped in an old piece of blanket and placed at the foot of the bed of some shivering patient.

Spectacles could be bought inexpensively from Woolworths; the style of the frame deciding the wearers choice, rather than the suitability of the lenses. It has been known for several members of one family to share the same pair of glasses.

A brew of nettles, dandelions and other edible hedgerow plants was supposed to help one "keep reg'lar". Rhubarb, too, was thought to be "good for the blood", although one could easily be put off this health-giving aid by seeing it nurtured in the garden with buckets of urine as well piles of ever-abundant horse manure. Boils and carbuncles would eventually pop after home-made bread poultices had been applied to them.

Each street seemed to have its own untrained "district nurse" who dealt willingly – but with suitable financial reward – with births and deaths. A mature woman came in and took over during a confinement, the common request being "Give us plenty of hot water." She delivered the baby, cleaned up mother and child, and then summoned the rest of the family to greet their new sister or brother. Her opposite task was dealing with the dead. Arriving with her bag (contents unknown) she would conduct the "laying out", for which she received a fee. Such women commanded respect from their neighbours, who looked on them as "t'salt of th'earth."

Whenever a death occurred in the family, the body was kept in the house until the day of the funeral. Members of the clan thought it only fitting to sit with it, so as not to leave the deceased alone, and took turns until the day of the funeral. All the neighbours, as well as relatives and friends, were thus given the opportunity to pay their last respects. Gramophones and wirelesses were silenced.

<u>Wartime</u>
A demented German dictator began to feature in the Pathe newsreels shown at the local cinemas. Leslie Mitchell would carry on his excellent newsreading as alarming armies of goose-stepping Nazis strutted across the screens. And to think we laughed at them, seated comfortably and remotely in our cinema seats, because their arrogant stamping appeared to us so ridiculously childish.

As war seemed imminent, the AFS (Auxiliary Fire service) practiced fire fighting on a row of derelict houses fronting the main road opposite the Moss Rose. After the debris had been cleared, a flat bottomed lorry was left on the spare ground and this is where a crowd of people listened to an impassioned speech given by Mr George Tomlinson, MP.

Preparations for war went ahead speedily in Kearsley at the beginning of 1939. Air raid shelters were erected; public ones for the use of the community at large were spacious and built of brick with concrete roofs. Individual families assembled their own from corrugated metal which were installed in gardens, although one or two people I knew had these built inside their houses.

When war was finally declared on 3rd September, 1939 I reported for ARP (Air Raid Precaution) duty in the whitewashed cellar below the Council Offices. Strong wooden stanchions held up the ceiling and camp beds were installed for use if all-night duties were to be put into practice (and they were!).

Kearsley Electric Power Station was deemed to be a prime target for the German air force as it stood by the banks of the River Irwell – easily discernible on a moonlit night. A bunch of protective barrage balloons floated above the area and listeners to the traitorous Lord Haw-Haw (the Irishman, William Joyce) would tremble with fury as he threatened to send "explosive eggs to fit into the gigantic egg cups (water cooling towers) at the Power Station".

Being the nearest resident to the headquarters (Kearsley Town Hall), I spent many nights on duty before being given a respite, but then so did many more of the volunteers. We would sit by the telephones with our forms ready to fill in should any necessary action be required at our end. Initially, unknown to the public, the army would ring us with an air raid warning "purple" which meant, generally, that an air attack was headed in our direction. When the air raid warning "red" was 'phoned we knew, of course, that this meant business! (Sometimes the ground beneath our feet would lurch and shudder as nearby Swinton and Pendlebury got *a pasting but we still had to wait for the official 'phone call' before switching on the siren.) Gradually we took turns in flicking this ordinary looking light switch, which we realized would cause our neighbours to make their nocturnal trek into the shelters. Nevertheless, as the war wore on, some Kearsleyites would remain in their warm beds, ignoring the warnings. Mother was one of these, saying: "if Hitler wants me, he can come and get me!"*

Death of Mr. W. Chatton.

Kearsley Farmer for Many Years.

The death occurred yesterday week of Mr. William Chatton, of 47, Halshaw-lane, Kearsley, one of the oldest and best-known farmers in this district. Always healthy, Mr. Chatton had been singularly free from illness until recently, but was bedfast for practically the last three years. The owner of considerable property in the district and a keen business man he controlled his affairs almost to the last and about six months ago bought a lot of property in Ann-st. and Bent-st., whilst confined to bed. When quite young he became tenant of Taskers-lane farm of which he made a great success, turning it over to his son, Charles, when he retired 20 years ago. He occupied a house in Lord-st., behind which he kept a considerable number of his cattle and distributed his milk from a dairy there. Having led a very active life, even in his retirement he felt he must be doing something and established a wholesale and retail hay and straw business which took him into all parts of the country. A Churchman and a Conservative, he devoted his time and energy to his business and could not be induced to take up public work. His remains were laid to rest in St. John's Churchyard on Monday. He leaves a widow, a daughter and three sons, two of whom are occupiers of farms—Charles at Taskers-lane and Samuel at Bank Top.

Left News of the passing of William Chatton, from the Farnworth Journal of December 1st 1922.

As dawn approached on the morning of 28th August 1940 I had returned home from a lengthy night's ARP watching and prepared to climb into bed. Suddenly, in the distance, a limping aircraft could be heard. Drowsily I thought, "it must be one of ours," as, after all, hadn't the "All Clear" been sounded ages ago? As the plane thundered overhead there was the most deafening volley of screaming whistles, one after the other, as a stick of bombs hurtled past my bedroom window. There they were, rushing earthwards with fancy tails and an ear-splitting din. I could not believe it! I felt an angry personal reaction, thinking, "why don't you come down here and fight like a man?"! Pulling on my slacks, jumper and sandals, I prepared to leap downstairs to find out where the bombs had fallen; I knew it must be quite near. Mother met me on the landing where she fastened her hands into my arms until I thought her fingers would meet in my flesh. It was a terrifying experience. Dust and acrid smells filled the air. Our windows had been blown out and our doors ripped off in the blast.

I soon found out where the bombs had landed – on ground beside the then Co-Op shop on Springfield Road. Thankfully there were no casualties but the brickwork on the front of the council houses was badly pitted by the flying shrapnel which followed the explosion.

Toward the end of the war we were subjected to "buzz" bombs. These were remotely controlled missiles which suddenly cut out their droning as they plummeted to earth. As daylight approached one morning, I stood at our gate with a neighbour and watched this advanced method of warfare. When the noise ceased we were rooted to the spot as the object fell in the direction of Worsley. A Doctor, his wife and two children were the victims of a direct hit.

I was highly surprised during the latter part of the war to pass along Clifton Street, where a number of German prisoners-of-war were engaged on building works across what were once our fields. They seemed to be working away contentedly; in fact one would have hardly have found them any different from our own workmen, had it not been for the distinguishing circles of coloured cloth sewn into the back of their tunics – for easy identification if they decided to try and run away.

Getting to work in Manchester from Kearsley was a problem after the Germans had wrecked the railways and roadways. Standing at the Moss Rose with others hoping for a lift in the city direction, I managed to gain lifts in just about every type of conveyance, once swinging my legs behind a Steptoe-like horse and cart! The journeys were certainly adventurous: from dodging craters in the road to finding gaping holes where familiar buildings had previously stood.

When the War in Europe finished there was great jubilation in Kearsley. Local shopkeeper John Southern scaled the cenotaph outside the Council Offices clutching the inevitable bottle! Others danced around the base and a wonderful air of freedom filled the district. VJ day found Bolton Road ablaze with light, blackout curtains being hurriedly and delightedly snatched from the windows."

The 'Monster' from outer space, as Mrs Fish describes the chara-banc which is seen here about to take a party of people from the White Horse Hotel, Kearsley, on a trip. On the running board are (left to right) Mr Charlie Chatton, Mr Sam Chatton and Mr Thomas Larner. At the wheel of the chara is Mr Billy Chatton.

Above. Circa 1920 picture of day-trippers from the White Horse. It was first printed in the Farnworth Journal during the early 1920's, but was then reprinted in the edition of October 27th 1967. Agnes Fish then contacted the newspaper to explain that the Charabanc used to be kept in the yard of Bank Top Farm, it was nicknamed 'the monster' and when it could be persuaded to start the noise it made would make her quake in her boots.

The picture on the next page is Manchester Road, Bolton Road, from 1928. On the left are the cottages fronting the main road, opposite the Moss Rose, which Agnes Fish is referring to when the AFS (Auxiliary Fire service) practiced fire fighting whilst preparing for the start of the Second World War. This picture shows the cottages being structurally altered to allow the bend of the road to be much smoother as it turns into Bolton Road. The houses further back went along what was then Antelope Street at the side of Wilson's Pie Shop.

Listed Buildings & Monuments of Kearsley

Building or Structure	Grade and List Number	Details
Stoneclough Railway Bridge	Grade II 1067302	First listed on 19th August 1986 for special architectural or historic interest. It is unclear as to when the Iron strainer beams on the North-East side were added, but they do show on pictures from the early 1900's.
Vale House, Stoneclough	Grade II 1067300	First listed on 19th August 1986 for special architectural or historic interest. Vale House closed in October 1987 and was later badly damaged by fire and vandalism. The frontage and other parts of the structure were restored during the 1990's and it now makes up part of the Parklands residential housing estate.
Prestolee Pack Bridge	Grade II 1162287	First listed on 19th August 1986 for special architectural or historic interest.
Manchester, Bolton & Bury Canal Aqueduct over River Irwell.	Grade II 1162420	First listed on 19th August 1986 for special architectural or historic interest. Construction believed to have been completed during 1793.

Manchester, Bolton & Bury Canal milestone approx. 230M North of Prestolee Road.	Grade II 1067303	First listed on 19th August 1986 for special architectural or historic interest. Inscribed 'M8 ¼' showing the distance to Manchester.
Manchester, Bolton & Bury Canal milestone approx. 60M East of Prestolee Road.	Grade II 1162509	First listed on 19th August 1986 for special architectural or historic interest. Inscribed 'M8' showing the distance to Manchester.
Manchester, Bolton & Bury Canal milestone approx. 50M south of Prestolee Aqueduct.	Grade II 1067299	First listed on 19th August 1986 for special architectural or historic interest. Inscribed 'M7 ¾' showing the distance to Manchester.
Manchester, Bolton & Bury Canal milestone approx. 60M East of Prestolee Road.	Grade II 1356799	First listed on 19th August 1986 for special architectural or historic interest. Inscribed 'M7 ½' showing the distance to Manchester.
Manchester, Bolton & Bury Canal milestone approx. 4180M North West of Kearsley Road.	Grade II 1067298	First listed on 19th August 1986 for special architectural or historic interest. Inscribed 'M7 ¼' showing the distance to Manchester.

Manchester, Bolton & Bury Canal milestone approx. 180M North West of Kearsley Road.	Grade II 1067297	First listed on 19th August 1986 for special architectural or historic interest. Inscribed 'M7' showing the distance to Manchester.
Cruck-barn at Seddon's Fold Farm, Prestolee.	Grade II 1309621	First listed on 3rd February 1976 for special architectural or historic interest.
Byre at Seddon's Fold Farm, Prestolee. (a 'Byre' being an old English name for a cowshed)	Grade II 1067301	First listed on 19th August 1986 for its importance as an exceptionally rare example of pre eighteenth century cattle-housing, and the survival of pre nineteenth century cow-house interior features. Also the design and craftsmanship: of its vernacular architectural detailing including the historic timber roof.
Stable at Seddon's Fold Farm, Prestolee.	Grade II 1356801	First listed on 3rd February 1976 for special architectural or historic interest. An important rare example of a substantially complete C18 farm building, probably combining stabling with ancillary accommodation.

Seddon's Fold Farmhouse, Prestolee.	Grade II 1309613	First listed on 3rd February 1976 for special architectural or historic interest. An example of a substantially complete pre-1700 house including the timber roof structure and internal partitions with wattle-and-daub and lath-and-plaster infill.
Ringley Old Pack Bridge.	Grade II 1356800	First listed on 19th August 1986 for special architectural or historic interest.
Old village Stocks to the South of Ringley Old Pack Bridge.	Grade II 1067296	First listed on 31st May 1966 for special architectural or historic interest.
Boundary Stone to the West of Ringley Old Pack Bridge.	Grade II 1162452	First listed on 19th August 1986 for special architectural or historic interest. Inscribed 'Parish Prestwich:Dean/Outwood: Kersley.
Tower to former St. Saviour's Church.	Grade II 1356797	First listed on 31st May 1966 for special architectural or historic interest. The Jacobean stone from the first Church with the inscription "NATHAN WALWORTH BUILDED MEE, ANNO DO 1625" is incorporated into the front of the tower

Church of St. Saviour.	Grade II 1067295	First listed on 31st May 1966 for special architectural or historic interest.
Kearsley Mill, Prestolee	Grade II 1267954	First listed on 4th November 1996 for special architectural or historic interest.
Railway Underbridge, Hulme Road/Slackey Brow.	Grade II 1356798	First listed on 19th August 1986 for special architectural or historic interest. Constructed for the Manchester to Bolton Railway circa 1837.
Clammerclough Railway Tunnel	Grade II 1067330	First listed on 19th August 1986 for special architectural or historic interest. Constructed for the Manchester to Bolton Railway circa 1837. Two 270M long brick tunnels that are often referred to as Farnworth Tunnel.
Church of St. John The Evangelist	Grade II 1356796	First listed on 31st May 1966 for special architectural or historic interest.
Gates and Piers to the West of St. John's Church	Grade II 1067294	First listed on 19th August 1986 for special architectural or historic interest.
St Stephen's Church, Kearsley Mount.	Grade II 1391095	First listed on 9th May 2003 for special architectural or historic interest.

| Holy Trinity Church, Prestolee | Grade II 1350354 | First listed on 9th May 2003 for special architectural or historic interest. |

*Kearsley Town Hall had also been Grade II listed until its demolition at the end of January 2013.

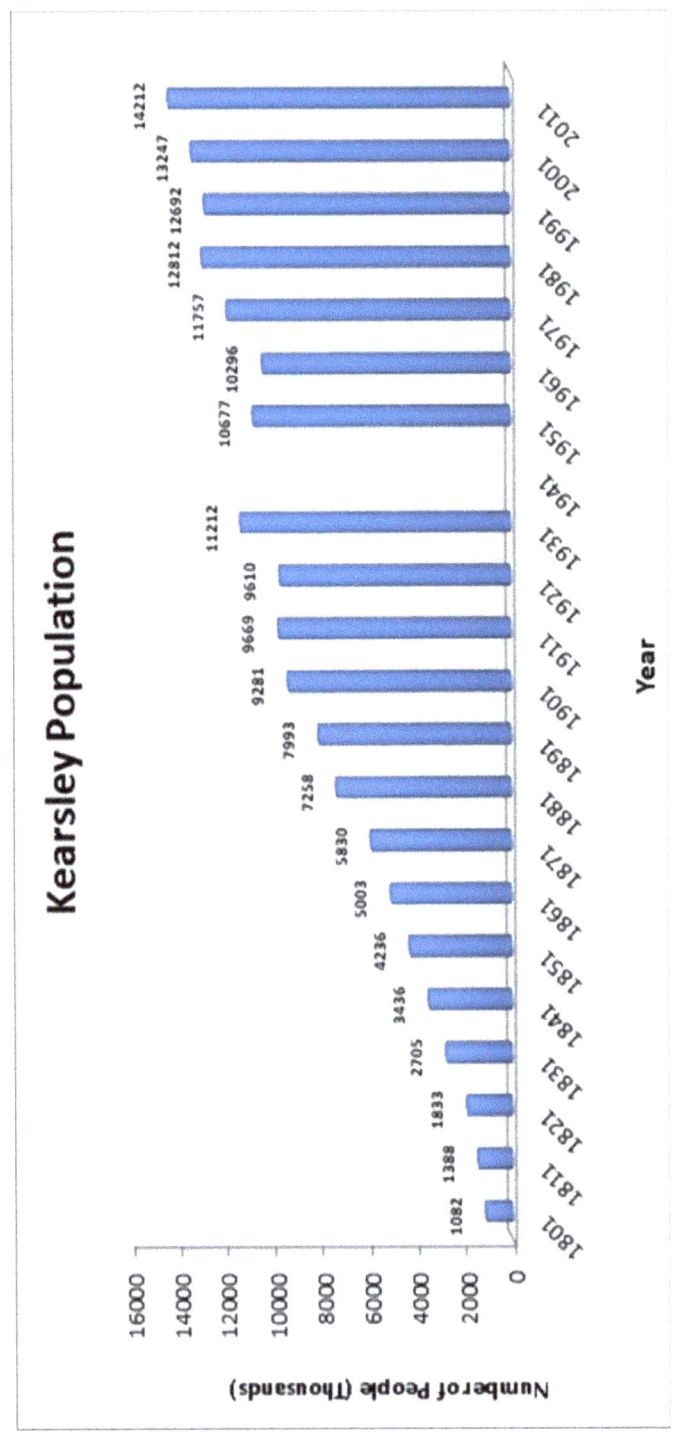

No census undertaken for 1941 due to Second World War

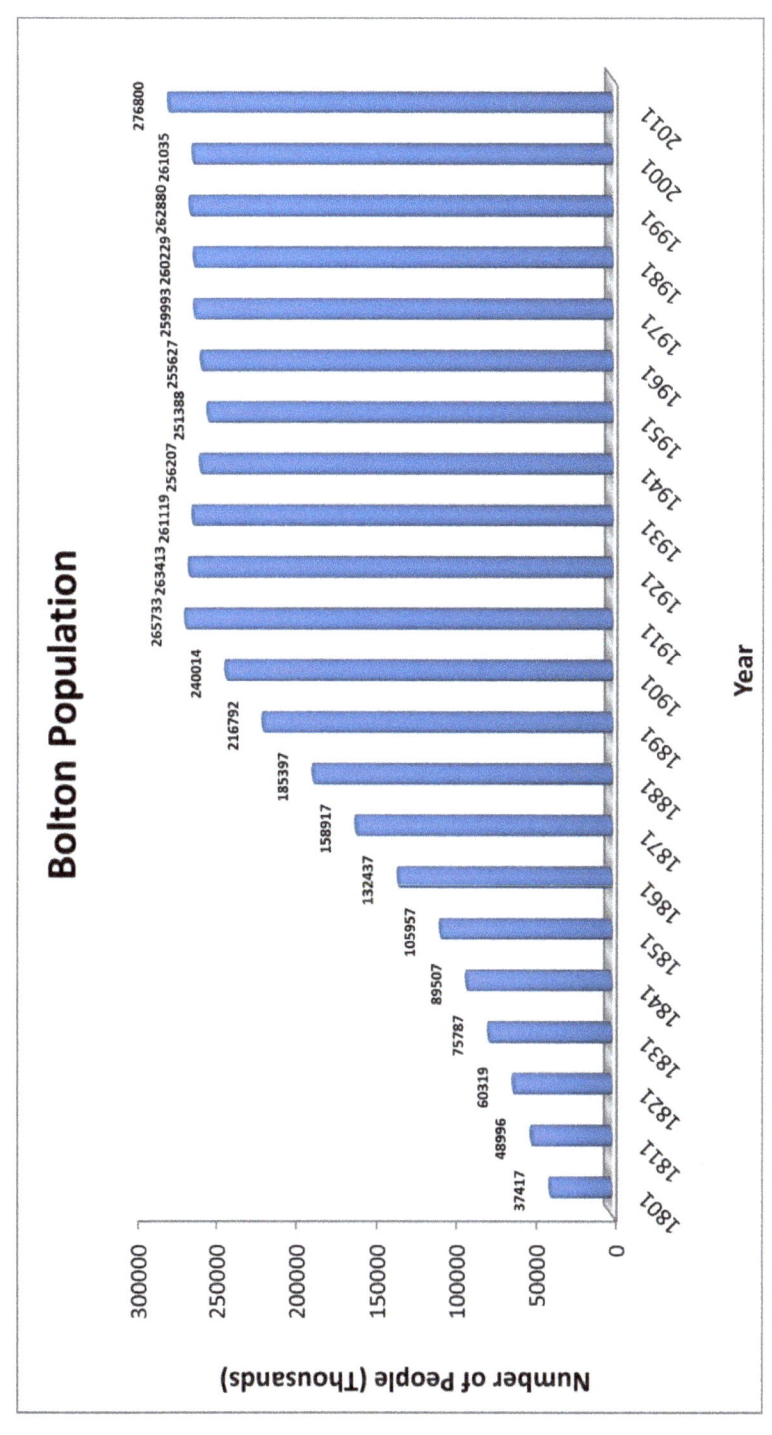

Kearsley Cricket Club

Kearsley Cricket Club was formed in 1875 and originally called the Kearsley Mount Weslyan Sunday School Cricket Club, although this extended appellation did not last long. The notion of establishing a club had been conceived a few years prior to the official formation date when a number of boys would get together to play 'bat and ball' in the old sand hole, at the area that is now Sandhole Road. The Kearsley Mount Weslyan School was also situated down here at this period.

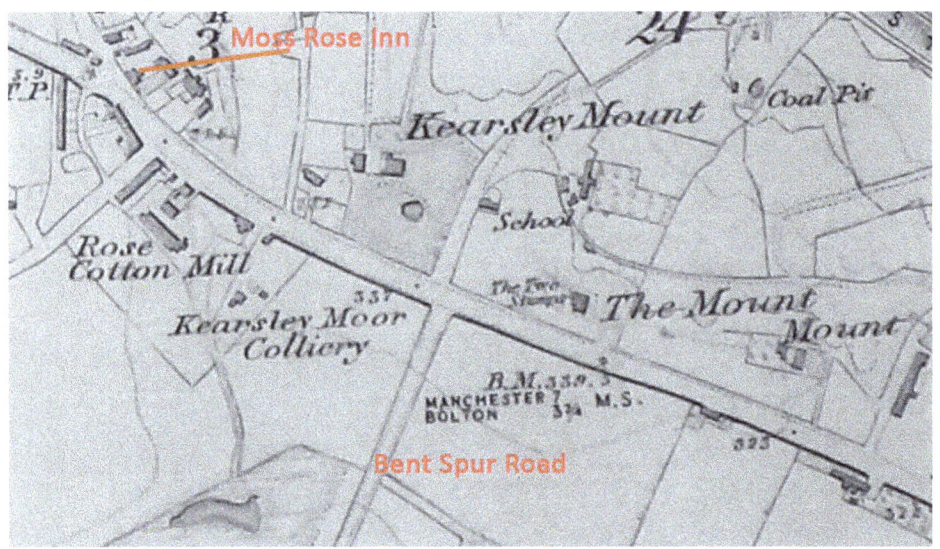

Above. Map showing the area around Sandhole Road around 1848. The original Weslyan School is seen set back from Manchester Road.

They would first meet in front of the Moss Rose Inn where a man named 'Old Copper Jim' lived, and it was here that discussions began with regards to forming a club. Each player paid a shilling, and they commenced playing in a field behind what were known as 'Crompton's Houses' (I am unable to find any mention of these on any maps of the period so cannot give a location). The playing area is described as being like a saucer, as the ball would roll back down toward the centre of the pitch. A short time later the team removed to a field near to St. Stephen's school, where the first pitch was prepared by some of them going down their hands and knees and cutting the grass with pairs of scissors (surely just the central area containing the crease). After this they moved again to another field near the Bolton and Manchester Railway line where they merged with a team from an adjacent field to form the first club.

The club finally found a home at Taskers Lane (now Springfield Road) by renting a field from land owned by the Co-Op. When they first started they did not play matches every week as there was no league, instead they took on teams from Longcauseway, Larkfield (Larkhill), St.John's and Ringley, and once or twice they went to Kirkham and Llandudno.

> **Kearsley Cricket Club.** In the Kearsley Mount Wesleyan Schools, on Monday evening, the Cricket Club were the promoters of an excellent concert. The entertainers were Miss Jessie Martin, who delighted the company with her songs, Mr. Whitehead, of Manchester, a humourist, Mr. Berry, Mr. Palmer, of Manchester, clarionet solos, and Mr. George Gettins, a rising cornettist, the son of the leader of Irwell Bank Band. Thirty living pictures were thrown upon the screen and gave every satisfaction. The lighting was nearly perfect, and there were none of the hitches which often occur in these exhibitions.

Above. Article from the Farnworth Journal of 10th December 1898. The Cricket Club still maintained a connection with the Weslyan School and Church at Kearsley Mount where it was originally formed.

In 1925 a new pavilion costing several hundred pounds had been funded by club president Mr. J. O. Paynter who was one of the founders, and indeed one of the boys who had paid that first shilling over fifty years previously. The new building measuring 36 feet long and 12 feet wide was constructed of asbestos and cement tiles in a wooden frame. The official opening was carried out by seven year old Master W. J. Lawton, the grandson of the president, who unlocked the door with a special gold key handed to him by the architect Mr. T. Fielding. Entertainment was provided in the evening by St. Stephen's band.

Kearsley C.C.'s New Pavilion

OPENED BY DONOR'S GRANDSON.

Above. 14th August 1925, opening ceremony of the new pavilion at Kearsley Cricket Club before a match against local rivals Farnworth. Club president Mr. J. O. Paynter (centre) had been one of the original founders of the club.

Above. 1934 Hamer Cup winning team, with officials and members of the committee. The players are: back row: J Ryder, C Wallis, H Stockton, J Dugdale. Centre Row: G.H. Wigglesworth, Smith (Professional), F Williams (captain), W Tyldesley, A Berry. Front row: W.C. Ashton, T Riding.

Free from Debt

Kearsley Cricket Club

Nine years ago, when pressed by the bank to reduce their overdraft, Kearsley Cricket Club borrowed £135 from friends interested in the club's welfare. At the annual meeting on Saturday it was announced that the last £30 owing on these loans had been repaid.

In his report as secretary, Mr. S. Gittins said that six of their matches last season were spoiled by rain, which had affected their gate money. He expressed the view that the gate money in the finals should be divided as one-third to each of the clubs, and the other third to the League. F. Williams had topped the first team batting, and J. Dugdale the bowling averages; and K. Elliott headed the second team batting. There was no outstanding bowler in the second team.

Mr. J. Hales (treasurer) presented a balance-sheet, which showed that the credit balance of £24 18s. 10d. brought forward had increased to £62 7s. 3d. He went through each item in the accounts, comparing them with the previous year's figures. Both these reports, together with those of the auditors, were adopted.

The following officials were re-elected: President, Mr. A. Gittins; secretary, Mr. S. Gittins; treasurer, Mr. J. Hales; auditors, Messrs. A. E. Williams and G. Pilkington. Acknowledging his re-election the secretary said in spite of calls of national service there was great enthusiasm among the players who turned up for matches. It was the club's intention to keep the game going for the sake of the 27 players who were serving with the Forces. The appointment of League representative was left to the general committee, which was elected as follows: Messrs. Holehouse, Hobson, Dugdale, Booth, Wainwright, Rushton, Lomax, A. and F. Williams, Pilkington, Whalley, Challenor, Wolstenholme, Brooks, Litterick, Stockton, Tatlock, Ridings, Cooke, Grundy, Hampson, Longworth, Irving, Lomax and Wallwork, with power to add.

The Ladies' Committee was thanked for their splendid contribution to the club's finances, and the Press for their interest in the club; and the treasurer mentioned that they had just repaid the last £30 of debt owing by the club. Thanks were expressed to the interested friends who had lent them money totalling £135 in the last nine years, free of interest. Mr. Hales also urged the building up of a reserve fund so that they could meet contingencies after the war without going into debt again. Counc. J. Lomax, J.P., (Bolton) who was present, expressed his good wishes to the club.

Above. Report on the club's now healthy finances in February 1943. Despite have 27 players called up for duty in the Second World War, Kearsley Cricket Club managed to continue fielding teams.

Kearsley were one of the founder members of the Bolton Association in 1889 and played their first match in that league in 1890. They then became one of the founder members of the new Bolton Cricket League in 1930 after breaking away from the Bolton & District Cricket Association along with eleven other clubs in a decidedly acrimonious split.

Chance of the double

Kearsley win Hamer Cup for third time

Kearsley, who won the Hamer Cup for the third time when they beat Heaton by 48 runs in an exciting finish at Green-lane on Friday evening, have an excellent chance of bringing off the double this season. Walkden's failure to beat Heaton at " The Oval " on Saturday allowed the Springfield-rd. team to step up into second position in the Bolton League, three points behind the leaders, Farnworth.

Kearsley, who were dismissed for 249 in the Hamer Cup final last night week (J. H. Davies contributed 68), set Heaton to score 119 to win on Friday with seven wickets still standing (writes "Boundary").

With the Heaton total at 183 for four on a wicket which still seemed to be full of runs, the outlook was none too rosy. Then came Harry Bromley's second devastating spell with the ball. Bob Lilley, Heaton's top scorer (70), lost his middle stump to the fast bowler at 183, and the whole side was back in the pavilion for 201.

Bulcock finished with six for 79 and Bromley had the other four for 61.

Championship too?

Kearsley had five wickets to spare in their league victory at Astley Bridge on Saturday, and are well placed for championship honours.

Above. From the Farnworth Journal, July 15th 1949.

FACTS OF THE FINAL

GATE RECEIPTS: An all-time record of 16,620 people paid £383 3s. 8d. to watch the four nights' Hamer Cup final last week. The previous record receipts were taken at the 1946 final (£204).

COLLECTIONS: The three batsmen who topped the half-century were rewarded with collections bigger than any previously known in local cricket. On Wednesday, Bill Alley (Heaton's Australian deputy professional) received £46 14s. 6d. in recognition of his 67; on Thursday, J. H. Davies (Kearsley) scored 68 and received £50; and on Friday, Bob Lilley (Heaton) topped the scoring with 70 and the cash rewards with £51.

SCORING: Kearsley's total of 249 beat the previous highest score of 243 for 9, also by Kearsley against Little Lever (236) at Farnworth in 1934.

APPEARANCES: Kearsley have made three Cup final appearances (1934-40-49), and have won each time. This was Heaton's fifth cup final. They won in 1932-42-46.

Two members of the Heaton team, J. Fearnhead and C. Lawson, were playing in the final for the third successive season. They helped Horwich to win the trophy in 1947-48.

Kearsley won their third Hamer Cup in 1949, beating Heaton by 249 to 201 in a rain interrupted match that ran over four seperate evenings. With average crowds of four thousand turning up on each occasion the aggregate attendance reached an incredible 16,620, with gate receipts of £383.

In order to bolster its finances the club would hold an annual Gala on the August Bank Holiday Monday. There would be a large fun-fair, morris dancing competitions, vintage motor cycles, coconut shy, Pomagne spin (Pomagne was a sort of cider that came in a champagne type bottle) and Tombola stalls amongst many other attractions.

Above. August 1970. Tombola stand at the Kearsley Cricket Club gala.

In January 1969 the club was given the green light to build a social clubhouse with a bar. A number of local residents had opposed the idea, expressing concerns about noise from music and extra traffic. At the time Kearsley was the only club in the league without a social club.

During the Hamer Cup semi-final against Heaton at Springfield Road in July 1995 Kearsley pro Steve Dublin scored 48 in one over by smashing eight sixes. This was made possible by there being three 'no balls' in the over in addition to the usual six. Dublin, who came from Montserrat in the West Indies, had earlier in the season knocked a century in only 35 balls against Horwich. At the time of writing both of these astonishing feats are Bolton League records.

Above. Kearsley Cricket Club in August 2014. The social clubhouse is to the right and the new players pavilion with clock to its left.

Above. Team of 1923. Back row, left to right: W. Rushton, snr, Peter Collier, Jack Hales, Edward Williams. Second row: Stanley Balshaw, Richard Bleakley, James Berry, Frank Rushton, Arthur Berry, *last two players unknown*. Seated: Richard Rushton, Frank Williams, William Rushton, James Partington (Captain), Stanley Kilner, Robert Hardman, Frank Eckersall.

Above. The 1981 programme for the annual gala held at Kearsley Cricket Club. By the end of the 1980's this gala had ceased altogether.

BOLTON CRICKET LEAGUE

HAMER CUP FINAL

AT HEATON C.C. — SUNDAY, JULY 31st, 1983

Kearsley v Tonge

TEAMS

KEARSLEY (from)	TONGE
T. HOUSLEY	I. TATTERSALL
C. VARLEY (W/k.)	B. KRIKKEN (W/k.)
REIDY (Pro.)	ALI (Pro.)
M. PRICE	A. DALPAT
W. HARPER	N. PARTINGTON
G. HARPER	W. ENTWISTLE
A. MOFFATT	J. MITCHINSON (Capt.)
M. HALL	B. FARNWORTH
N. HARRIS	K. KIRKPATRICK
B. QUIGLEY (Capt.)	D. SUTCLIFFE
P. MORT	R. HAWKE
K. STEPHENS	

Umpires: Messrs. J. Beckett & F. Bradley

Kearsley (Winners 1934/40/49/53/54/75)

beat

Round 1 — Astley Bridge

Round 2 — Farnworth

S/F — Horwich

Tonge (Winners 1968/74)

beat

Round 1 — Bye.

Round 2 — Bradshaw

S/F — Heaton

Above. Programme for the 1983 Hamer Cup Final between Kearsley and Tonge, played at Heaton C.C. Kearsley ran out winners hitting 126 for 3, whilst Tonge could only amass 123 for 8.

Dr. Charles Hassall – Medical Herbalist

One of the most notable characters around Farnworth and Kearsley area during the late nineteenth and early twentieth centuries was Mr. Charles Hassall, a Medical Herbalist who originated from Penkhull, Stoke-On-Trent.

Above. The lid from a jar of Dr. Hassall's Hair Restorer.

He was President of the Medical Herbalists Association of Great Britain, and probably had more honours in his profession than any other man in England. In 1870 he appointed a Mr. Henry Boydell of New Bury to sell his specialities in the district, and he himself would visit patients here from time to time. Around 1871 he came to Farnworth and opened a shop in Brackley Street, but moved to different premises on Market Street a short time later, and then on to Peel Street.

In 1905 he opened further premises on Longcauseway, but also continued to run the Peel Street shop until 1914. People would visit from all parts of the country, with some of his 'cures' being described as remarkable. He passed away at his residence in Bradford Street on Wednesday 28th March 1923 aged 75.

DR. HASSAL'S
WART SOAP.

GOOD TO REMOVE WARTS OR OTHER GROWTHS FROM THE HANDS, FACE, FEET, OR BODY.

2D.   PER TABLET.   2D.

A Lady writes—"DR. HASSALL'S WART SOAP removed every Wart from my hands before the first 2d. Tablet was used."

A Gentleman says—"THANKS TO DR. HASSALL'S WART SOAP, every vestige of WART IS ENTIRELY GONE, and barely used it a week yet."

WE WANT HUSBANDS TO REMEMBER that the Worries and Duties incidental to Home Management are Particularly Trying to the System, causing Irritable Nerves, Loss of Appetite, Lassitude and Depression.

COCA-KOLA WINE
WITH QUININE

A combination of the marvellous stimulating properties of Coca Leaves and Kola Nuts, with the tonic properties of Quinine, should be taken by all who are OVER-WORKED, WORN-OUT, OR RUN DOWN.

IMPARTS TONE AND VIGOUR TO THE WHOLE BODY.

ALL LADIES SHOULD TAKE COCA-KOLA WINE WHEN THE RED GLOBULES OF THE BLOOD ARE DEFICIENT IN QUANTITY AND QUALITY, CAUSING THEM TO GROW ANÆMIC, PALE, THIN AND MELANCHOLY.

PRICE 1/- PER BOTTLE.

PREPARED BY
DR. HASSALL,
(U.S.A.) F.S.Sc., F.C.S.M., F.T.S.,
ECLECTIC AND BOTANIC PRACTITIONER,
76, 78 & 80, PEEL STREET, FARNWORTH.

Established 1864.

CAUTION.—BEWARE OF IMITATIONS.

THOUSANDS OF TESTIMONIALS.

Left. Advert from the Farnworth Journal, December 3rd 1898. The Coca-Kola that Dr Hassall would have been selling here in 1898 is most likely the original recipe that contained around 4.3 milligrams of cocaine for every six ounces of drink. Therefore its claim to 'IMPART TONE AND VIGOUR TO THE WHOLE BODY' may well have had some accuracy, although the unwitting customers would not have been aware of its addictive and destructive ingredients. The recipe was only changed in 1903 to take out all but a negligible amount of the drug, and not until 1925 were all traces of cocaine removed from Coca-Cola's recipe.

Farnworth and Kearsley Labour Club

See Picture on Previous Page. In September 1921 the Farnworth and Kearsley Labour party purchased the Old Royal Oak Hotel public house, which stood at the bottom of Longcauseway facing Market Street, for the purposes of providing a permanent meeting place for its members. At first only the ground floor rooms were used, with one set aside for playing cards, dominoes and other games. There was also a bar that served drink during the usual hours. The picture from the late 1920's shows the Old Royal Oak building on the right with the Labour Club signage above it. The Bird-I'-Th'-Hand public house is behind the tram on the other side of Old Hall Street. Just nine years later the Old Royal Oak Hotel was demolished and brand new purpose built premises were erected on the same spot.

Mr. Guy Rowson, M.P., and Mr. T. Greenall, J.P., surrounded by a number of women workers and members prior to the opening of the new Labour Club at the corner of Longcauseway on Saturday.

Above. Saturday 13th September 1930. In spite of drenching rain several hundred members gathered for the opening ceremony. A gold key was presented to Mr. Guy Rowson, after which he unlocked the door and everyone followed him in.

September 1968, The Bird-I'-Th'-Hand public house which stood at the end of Old Hall Street. Pictured here shortly before it was demolished after being declared structurally unsound.

Left Top. The Bowling Green Hotel, Farnworth. Thought to have been built in the late 1700's or early 1800's, it still retained the name even though the hotel's green was taken over for use as part of the Farnworth market ground in 1870. It was completely rebuilt in the 1840's after the partly thatched roof fell in on the original building.

Left Below. The Travellers Rest Hotel.
Both pictures are from September 1968 when owners Magee Marshall & Co decided to close these two public houses plus the Bird-I'-Th'-Hand. The Bowling Green was demolished but the former Travellers Rest building is still used today as retail premises at 85 to 87 Market Street.

Above. June 2011 view from Higher Market Street.

Below. The Clock Face public house in November 2013.

Black Horse, in Kersley.

TO BE SOLD BY AUCTION,

By JOHN HOLME,

At the House of Mr. JOHN HEWART, the Sign of the *Black Horse*, in KERSLEY, on WEDNESDAY, the 7th Day of JANUARY, 1829, at Four o'Clock in the Evening, subject to such Conditions of Sale as shall be then and there produced;

LOT I.

THE LEASEHOLD INTEREST of and in all that old established PUBLIC HOUSE, known by the Name of the BLACK HORSE, in KERSLEY aforesaid, with the Brewhouse, Stable, Garden, Yard, and Appurtenances thereunto belonging, containing, in the whole, 975 square Yards of LAND or GROUND, including the Site of the Building, be the same more or less, which said Premises are held by Lease for 999 Years, about 40 of which are expired, subject to the Yearly Chief or Ground Rent of £5. 5s.

LOT II.

ALL that COTTAGE, Messuage, or Dwelling-house adjoining the aforesaid Premises, with the Appurtenances thereunto belonging, containing in the whole 75 superficial square Yards of LAND, or thereabouts, now in the Occupation of *Peter Boardman*, as Tenant thereof.

Sale notice for the Black Horse public house from the Bolton Chronicle of December 27th 1828. Of particular interest is that at this time the site is Leasehold for a term of 999 years, about 40 of which are expired. This may well be the best indication as to when the pub was originally built on the site.

Black Horse & High Stile Fold

John Dootson who was better known locally as "Owd Bummy" lived at High Stile Fold for over 80 years up until 1863, and he claimed that it was his Grandfather who built the first public house which stood on the same site, or a little further back from where the Black Horse pub currently resides. It was called the Sun Public House, and the lower end served as a kitchen to the present Black Horse for many years. The Sun was a one-storey building with a clay floor, and was the only public house in the neighbourhood at that time.

Mr Dootson explained that you could stand in the fold and see all over the moor at once, and the whole of the locality was one vast piece of wasteland, mostly covered with rushes, with here and there a hut built of clay and straw and 'radlins.' These were only one storey high, with clay floors, and the roofs covered with thatch. Indeed, before the enclosure act no-one cared very much about the payment of ground rent and that if a man wanted to erect one of these huts, or take a piece of ground for a garden, he was allowed to take the land for free and plant it as he thought fit. Every three or four years Peter Seddon, of Dyehouse Brow, Prestolee, who was in some way connected with the Lord of the Manor, would come and walk through it, as a sort of assertion of his right to the soil. No rent was paid except the oak leaf or peppercorn. Even today nominal or very low ground rent payments are referred to as 'peppercorn rents.'

In old John's younger days there were very few inhabitants and he claimed to know every family, and lad and lass for miles around. There were no factories and only two or three coalpits, from which coal was wound with a gin. Turf was mainly consumed for heating, and people were allowed to get their own from Kearsley Moss. There were only two farmers in the district, yet there was a horse kept at every door and these were allowed to pasture on the wasteland free of charge.

The hand drawn map on page 351 dating from around the 1790's shows the public house named simply as 'Walton's,' which presumably would be the surname name of the proprietor, and how nearby Walton Place took its name. It is difficult to ascertain exactly what date the pub took its name 'The Black Horse' or whether it was always called this, but township records and newspaper articles from around 1800 onwards use the established name.

Perhaps the moral condition of some of the inhabitants can be assumed by the fact that cockfighting was carried on to a great extent. A cock-pit was constructed nearby on a spot known as "Th Back o'th' Hedge" which is roughly where Walton Place is situated, and a charge was made for permission to enter and see the 'sport'. At High Stile Fold Mr. Henry Mather erected a school around 1755, which was the first in the area, and it was considered the best for many miles around. The High Stile schoolrooms were also used for many important meetings, for example the first official gathering of the Kearsley Local Board was held there in 1865. Nearby Mather Street is named after the founder of this school.

Up until around the 1840's the landlords of most public houses in Farnworth and Kearsley would have brewed all of their own beer. The scum or foam that formed on top of the fermented alcohol was in this part of Lancashire commonly called 'Barm,' this was removed and sold locally as it was found to be an ideal raising agent in the making of bread, and this is where the term 'barmcake' originated.

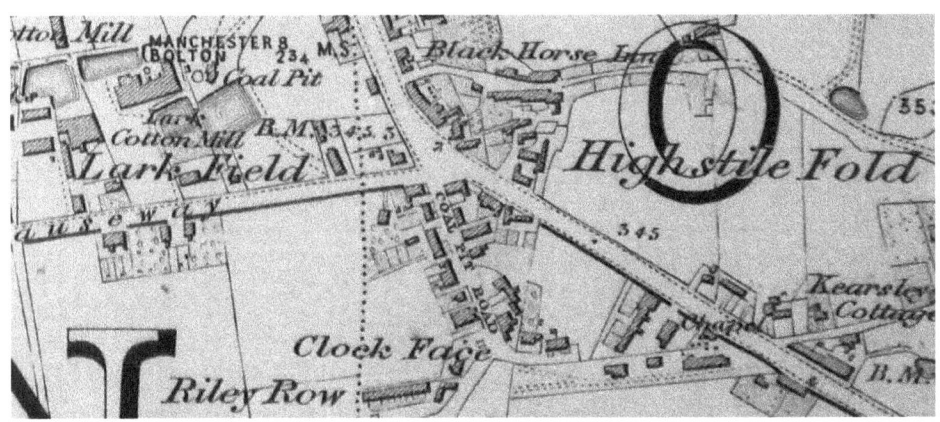

Above. The Black Horse and High Stile Fold area in 1848.

Below. Circa 1908 view of Higher Market Street, note the marvellous ornate lamp above the front door of The Black Horse Hotel.

From September 1949 to March 1950 The Black Horse underwent major renovation work, as the original structure dating from the late 1700's had got into a dangerous condition. A lot of the building had to be rebuilt from the cellar up, including the frontage, roof, gable and the first floor, but throughout this work the pub managed to stay open for business. The black and white façade, which is thought to have been added during the early 1920's was also refitted, but it is interesting to note that Ye Old Three Crowns Inn, which is a little further down, already has this feature in place.

Above. The Black Horse in the late 1940's shortly before the rebuilding work.

Below. The former King's Hall Cinema, which stood to the rear of the Black Horse, is seen here during demolition in April 1970. The cinema closed during the 1950's but the premises were later used for several years by Farnworth Little Theatre. The site is used for car parking at present.

The Black Horse Hotel, 1908.

Circa 1910. A captivating view of the Longcauseway, Albert Road junction. The children seem to have their best clothes on, so it is probably a Sunday, and clogs are certainly the footwear of choice.

Longcauseway

Above. Circa 1907. Looking up Longcauseway with the Pandora Cotton Mills on the right. The Pandora Mills were demolished during 1965.
Below. Top of Longcauseway in August 1958. The traffic lights at the Albert Road, Buckley Lane junction were not installed until the mid 1960's, as were most of the others in Farnworth and Kearsley.

In the early part of the 19th century Longcauseway was fenced on each side by a high copse plus thorn hedges containing hollies and brambles. Extensive meadows and pasture fields stretched out on each side, with scores of hares and rabbits making it a popular place for poachers to lay their snares and traps. The ground nesting Skylark was so numerous in these fields that one locality became known as Lark Hill, a name which remains to this day.

Above. October 2010. The top of Longcauseway at the site now covered by the Tesco super-market.
Below. A late 1930's view from the bottom of Longcauseway looking down Market Street.

The popularity of the annual Whitsuntide processions is apparent by the huge crowds in this 1907 view at the Bolton Road, Longcauseway and Higher Market Street junction. This location was also often referred to as Kearsley Cross.

Postal Services

Above. July 2014. Kearsley Post Office on Manchester Road. These premises closed in July 2016 when the postal services removed to the Costcutter store on Kearsley Precinct, but this only lasted until the 19th of January 2019 when the store terminated its connection with the Royal Mail. The nearest postal services for Kearsley are now at Farnworth and Pendlebury Newtown.

Originally letters for Farnworth and Kearsley were sent to Bolton and then taken to The Bull's Head Inn on Bradshawgate, and they remained there until the receiver called for them, the letter would then be delivered for a small charge as decided by the landlord. If any letters were not called for within a reasonable time the landlord would simply send them on with any persons who happened to call in the Bull's Head and lived near the persons to whom the letters were addressed. When the first Post Office opened in Bolton the sender of a letter would have to take it there for delivery, or if receiving they would be required to attend to collect it. There would be lists in the windows giving details of any letters that required collection, and it was customary for persons to inspect this list and inform anyone in their locality if a letter was awaiting their attention. In his book, 'Local Notes and Reminiscences,' Simeon Dyson states that "Up until the opening of the Manchester to Bolton Railway, the Royal Mail coach would pass through Kearsley at half past seven in the morning, drawn by four horses, with its driver and guard clad in scarlet coats and gold laced hats. The guard, sat at the rear, and would blow his horn awakening any sleepers within hearing distance."

Around this time a man named John Lindley, of Stoneclough, carried goods between Bolton and Farnworth in a carriers cart, and letters were frequently entrusted to him for delivery. He did this for some time, and hoped to become the regular letter-carrier between the two towns, but instead a Mr Robert Myers obtained an official appointment from the Government to carry out this service, and in 1836 a small cottage on Market Street, opposite Holland's School was rented for the purposes of a receiving and delivery house. These premises became redundant when the postal business was transferred to another building further up Market Street sometime during the 1870's, and then to the building next to the bank at the bottom of King Street, a date stone is still visible to this day which indicates the year of construction and its former purpose. Although this date stone indicates 1894 these offices did not officially open for business until 1st May 1895. The Post Office public house was built on, or next to, the site of the original cottage post house and is how it takes its name.

Above. May 2013. The Post Office public house on Market Street, which sits on the site of the cottage first used for postal services in 1836. To the right can be seen the steel frame of new retail premises being built on the former site of The Queen's public house.

Farnworth Post Office. The handsome new premises in Market-st., for the Farnworth Post Office, will be ready for occupation next Wednesday, when it is proposed to remove from the present building. The new property is suitable to the requirements of the town. It will accommodate more than double the number of people, and better facilities are afforded for sorting and despatching letters, accommodation having been provided for more than twenty sorters. The sorting and telegraph rooms are in the back portion of the premises, easy means of access being afforded.

Above. Details of the opening of the Farnworth Post Office premises next to former Bank on the corner of King Street. From the Farnworth Journal of April 27th 1895.

Above. 1940's view of Market Street Farnworth. Note the Post Office on the left. It had moved here in April 1895.

Below. Circa 1960 and Farnworth Post Office is now in the building at 99 Market Street on the corner of Darley Street. The Post Office moved again to the top of Brackley Street in the early 1970's. On the left is the long gone Horse Shoe Hotel, which stood on the corner with King Street.

Above. Circa 1930's. Rush hour at Moses gate.

Below. Circa 1910. St. Stephen's prize band make their way through Farnworth. The building furthest left is the former Travellers Rest public house at 87 Market Street.

A motor bus makes its way along the cobbled Manchester Road at Kearsley Mount in 1932. The electric tram service through Kearsley had only ceased the previous year. Within a few months of the cessation of the tram service the tram standards that ran along the middle of the road were taken down and electric lampposts installed onto the pavements.

Above. Cemetery Road, June 1971. Throughout the 1960's the residents had to endure a constant stream of lorries from Salford Corporation and Fletchers Paper Mill dumping waste at three tipping sites at the end of the road and to the rear of their houses. The lorries caused danger to children playing and the waste sites attracted rats and plagues of flies. By the early 1970's further lorries were using the road to attend a quarry to get stone for local motorway building, and things began to boil over. Protests were organised and mothers began to block the road, they became known locally as the 'militant mums.' Eventually their efforts paid off, when in April 1972 Secretary of State for the Environment, Mr Peter Walker ruled that the lorries must no longer use the road.

Above. Circa 1990. The Lord Nelson Public House which is now La Roma Italian restaurant.

Above. Circa 1930's. Margaret Barlow's Tea Rooms and Gardens. This now forms part of the Giants Seat Garden Centre.

Above Circa 1900. Margaret Tatlock outside her shop on Fold Road, Ringley.

Below. The small red brick building which still stands to the rear of the White Horse public house now forms part of a motor repair garage. This clipping from the Farnworth Journal of May 10th 1912 shows that it was originally built for use as a smithy, and the builders decided not to bother obtaining permission to put it up.

BUILDING WITHOUT PLANS.

Mr. Noah Smethurst wrote explaining how a smithy behind the "White Horse" came to be erected without a plan being submitted, and he was informed that the building was not in accordance with the by-laws. Mr. Shippobottom and the Clerk were deputed to attend the annual conference of the Lancashire District Council's Association at Grange.

Above. Advertisement for the new 'villas' being built along Springfield Road in March 1934.

Above. View of the Albert Road, Longcauseway, Buckley Lane junction circa 1930.

Below. Circa 1920's delivery tricycle for Cunliffe & Son of Farnworth.

Above. This ornate 'marker stone' reads "Green T&A 1777" and was dug up in the grounds of St. John Fisher RC Church by Stephen Bromley, a member of the church's site management team, in June 2018. Ringley St. Saviour Church records show that Thomas and Alice Green are listed as 'farmers of Kersley' at this time, and were known to have had at least four children, Thomas, James, Elizabeth and Hannah. It is most likely that this stone was placed at the entry to their home and the land they worked. Although we cannot be certain exactly where their farm was located, the map drawn up in 1797 for the Farnworth and Kersley Enclosure Act shows a small number of buildings around the area on which St. John Fisher is now situated, which is of course the former site of Pool Farm. The stone measures 17.5 inches tall, 13 inches wide and almost 5 inches thick. This unique artifact is certainly one of the most ancient connected with our town.

Above. December 2012. The Antelope Public House shortly before it closed for good.

Below. April 2013. The Moss Rose Public House at number 1 Manchester Road.

The White Horse public house, November 2018.

Above. Circa 1984 view looking down Hulme Road. The cooling towers of Kearsley Power Station dominated the skyline until their destruction in May 1985.

Below. June 1984. Stoneclough Post Office across from the Grapes public house. The Post Office closed in January 2004 and at present the premises are used as a hairdressing salon.

September 2018. Unity Brook public house. Records show that John Lever sold the lease to Solomon Jackson on 16th February 1861, and that Lever also owned the dozen or so adjoining cottages. It is therefore most probable that this was when the pub and cottages were built. The Unity Brook public house was in the hands of Ann Jackson, daughter-in-law of Solomon, when it was sold, along with the cottage next door, to the Cornbrook Brewery Company for £2350 in 1922. The adjoining cottage was then incorporated into the main building.

Above. The Clock Face public house at the top of Old Hall Street in November 2013. The pub has since closed and been converted into living accommodation.

Below. June 2018. Wilsons Pie Shop, Bolton Road. Winners of the Best Pie in Bolton 2017.

Above. September 2010. Crompton Street close to Lark Hill.
Below. November 2018. The Horseshoe public house, Fold Road, Ringley.

Above. The Market Street Tavern, St. Georges Day 2009.

Below. July 2014. GEP motor garage, Springfield Road.

Numbers 97, 99 & 101 Manchester Road Kearsley preparing for the visit of King George V and Queen Mary as they passed through the town on 12th July 1913. The Kearsley Urban District Council coat of arms can be seen on the Tram Standard in the middle of the road.

Above. Ticket entitling the holder to a small gift to celebrate the Royal Visit in 1913.

Below. Circa1920's. Horse and cart taking part in the Whit Walk along Manchester Road close to the junction with Springfield Road. Irving's Butcher shop at number 19 is seen in the background, which is now a residential property. Two of the houses to the right of this were once believed to have been a public house named The Starkie Arms. To the left is the shop which is still open today.

IRVING'S MEAT PURVEYOR All Orders Receive Prompt Attention — Families Supplied on Reasonable Terms  **19 Manchester Road** KEARSLEY	*The* **Kearsley Grocery, Provisions and Confectionery Stores** "*The People's Providers*" **220 Manchester Road** Weddings and Funerals Catered for
J. CLAYTON High-class English and Foreign **FRUITERER** *Fishmonger, etc.* Wreaths and Crosses to Order Light Portering **209 Manchester Road** KEARSLEY	For all kinds of **WINES and SPIRITS** *Try* **W. STONES** The Antelope Hotel Manchester Rd., Kearsley
FRED COOPE Property Repairer & Decorator MASTIC POINTING A SPECIALITY ALL KINDS OF PROPERTY REPAIRS Estimates Free **5a Manchester Road** KEARSLEY	You will be sure of getting the Best if you get your MILK and EGGS from **LOMAX'S** **Pool Farm** KEARSLEY 

Local advertisements, 1930.

Circa 1901. Manchester Road. To the right is the Spread Eagle public house. The building furthest left in the distance is the Man & Scythe public house, which was demolished during the 1990's to make way for the Melrose Court residential apartments.

The Horseshoe Hotel, Ringley. This picture of the then three-storey building must have been before 1907, as the clock in the tower is the one installed during 1836 and is much lower down than the present one. The current clock was installed in 1907 when the tower was raised around two feet to accommodate it.

Circa 1930. A view of Manchester Road, Clifton. Taken at a spot where junction 16 of the M62 motorway now passes beneath the road. The bell tower of St. Anne's Church is easily recognizable above the houses to the right.

Above. Circa 1910. View down Stand Lane from where the mini roundabout is now situated at the Ringley Road junction. The buildings of Stand House can be seen to the left.

Below. Circa 1910. Looking the opposite way from the same spot we see the entrance to Stand Lodge. The two pillars remain to this day, but the buildings are long gone.

Circa 1905. Ye Olde Three Crowns public house on Higher Market Street. It is built on the former site of a shop known as "Ted o' Neddy's" that sold, amongst other things, castor oil, laudanum, epsom salts and magnesia which were used for common ailments that did not require a doctor. At this time the pub was under the ownership of the Cornbrook Brewery and the landlady's name above the door is Miriam Pilling. It is unknown as to why this pub is commonly known as 'Smokies.'

Above. 1960's view of Market Street with the former Farnworth and Kearsley Co-Op building at the bottom corner of Brackley Street. **Below.** An advertisement from the Farnworth Journal of May 31st 1935.

Above. Circa 1920. Brabin's outfitters shop in the centre of the picture was later turned into an ice cream parlour by a man named Tognarelli. These premises were still known as Tognarelli's café into the 2000's before sadly closing.

Below. An advert for Brabin's from March 21st 1919.

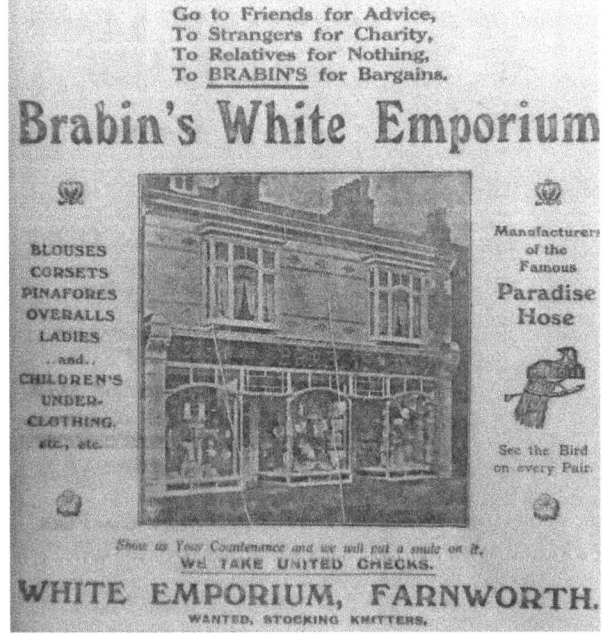

Above. 1907. The former electricity works building on Albert Road, note there is a children's play area to the left.

Below. Circa 1920. The Albert Road Congregational Church with the Sunday School to the rear. The small patch of land to the right of the church was once used as a burial ground. In recent years the church became the Farnworth United Reformed Church.

Above. Circa 1902. The Black Horse Public House. The Bird-I'th'-Hand Public House can also be seen at the Old Hall Street and Bolton Road junction.

Below. Circa 1910. Farnworth, Market Street at the junction with Brackley Street on the left.

Circa 1910. Former cottages next to Farnworth & Halshaw Moor train station. This site is now a short distance over from where the A666, St. Peter's Way bypass, crosses over Farnworth tunnel towards Cemetery Road.

Circa 1905. Market Street, Stoneclough. The clog wearing children are playing in the road as there would be little or no vehicular traffic passing through at this period. The houses nearest the camera, left and right, are still standing, as is the shop to the right and Wells House in the background.

For the Best BACON, BUTTER & GROCERIES

E. A. ROBEY,

DRAPER AND MILLINER

Agency for Patons and Baldwins Wools

119, MARKET STREET,
STONECLOUGH

WILFRED DAVIES,

PLUMBING, SANITARY
AND HEATING ENGINEER,

2, Chapel-St., off Market-St.,
STONECLOUGH

Residence:
53 Market Street   Telephone: 245 Farnworth

All Orders Promptly Attended to.

Did you say Confectionery? TRY

MRS. HULME,

BREAD, PIES, COOKED MEATS

Orders receive prompt attention

17, MARKET STREET,
STONECLOUGH.

J. PARTINGTON,

HIGH-CLASS GROCER and
CONFECTIONER

Funeral Parties Catered for.

—**43, CROMPTON ROAD,**—
PRESTOLEE

S. SIXSMITH,

Newsagent, Stationer & Tobacconist.
Ironmongery and Hardware.

89, Market Street, Stoneclough.

Newspapers and Periodicals delivered promptly

Agent for SLATERS, FLORISTS.

Everything in Flowers, Wreaths, Crosses,
Bouquets, etc.

Mrs. J. GREEN, L.V.C.M., A.V.C.M.

(Former Pupil of the late R. Froude Cowles, F.R.C.O.)

Teacher of Pianoforte, Organ, Harmony,
Counterpoint, Theory, &c.

29, CHURCH ROAD, Prestolee

Lorna Carrington,

LADIES' AND CHILDREN'S
HAIRDRESSER,

15, MARKET STREET,
STONECLOUGH.

EUGENE, NESTLE, KERKA,
PERMANENT WAVING.

Try WILLIAMSON,

—FOR—

Tobacco, Cigarettes and
: Stationery :

THE POST OFFICE, Stoneclough

Go to any of SEDDON'S BRANCHES (See Advt. on last page)

Above. Advertisements for local businesses from the Prestolee Holy Trinity magazine of September 1943.

Above. c1923. Market Street, Stoneclough. To the left is the turning for Bridge Street with the Grapes Hotel public house just out of shot. The building to the right with the people standing outside is the old Co-Op, this stood at the corner with Sulby Street but was demolished during the 1960's.

Below. Walking Day, Stoneclough 1951, with the Co-Op building in the background.

Above. Circa 1910. Ringley Old Bridge, and The Horseshoe Hotel, which was still a three-storey building at this time. The long gone Old Three Crowns public house is the building furthest left at the bottom of Ringley Old Brow.
Below. Circa 1910. These cottages, known as 'Buildings Row,' formerly stood at the end of Fold Road just across from the now filled in MB & B canal. The picture was probably taken from the side of the canal, where, out of shot fifty yards to the right was a loading bay at the bottom of a rail track that brought tubs of coal from Outwood Colliery to be loaded onto barges.

Above. The Lord Nelson public house circa 1920. The bowling green was situated behind the wall to the right.

Below. A local collier decides not to attend his own wedding at St. Stephen's. From the Farnworth Journal of January 5th 1895.

A Kersley Wedding "Off." New Year's day should have seen a pitman united in matrimony with a mill worker at St. Stephen's Church. Guests had been invited and a cab ordered, and, of course, the neighbours were on the qui vive. The bride-elect was ready to the minute, but her intended was non est. He was however, in the locality, but did not see fit to show himself, and though he has "caught it" quite as hotly as he deserved, the well-wishers of the young woman are now congratulating her that the usually "happy event" was opportunely frustrated.

Above. Circa 1910. Prestolee Farm which stood on Crompton Road at the Junction with Seddon Lane.

Below. Seddon Gardens, Prestolee, under construction in October 1981.

Above. Alderbank nursing home on Alderbank Close. Pictured here in September 1969 during the latter stages of building work. The home sadly closed during 2014 after being run down for many years by Bolton Council.
Below. Advert from 1950.

YOU WILL BE **GLAD** IF YOU REGISTER

WITH

H. ROBERTS

4 Lord Street, Kearsley

(Telephone—FARNWORTH 239)

FOR

MEAT - BACON

AND EGGS

A. BRAMMALL

Monumental Sculptor

Manchester Road
GREAT LEVER, BOLTON

HARRISON'S
NOTED
High-class Confectioners

BRIDE and BIRTHDAY CAKES
made to order

ALL CONFECTIONERY
our own make.   Fresh daily

Our own Boiled Ham and Ox Tongue a Speciality

All Orders promptly attended to

217 Manchester Rd., Kearsley

MOORES Farmers

MILK, EGGS
and all kinds of
Farm Produce

We deliver in your
District daily

BENT SPUR FARM
KEARSLEY

If you want Quality

Try

ROTHWELL'S

The Noted Supper Bar

Civility and Cleanliness our Speciality

211   Manchester   Road
KEARSLEY

All Classes of Household Coal supplied in Large or Small Quantities at Moderate Prices
by
C G. SKELTON
324 BOLTON ROAD, KEARSLEY

W. Wolstenholme

Painter and Decorator

Wallpapers in Great
Variety

Prompt Attention

18   BOLTON   ROAD
KEARSLEY

Local adverts from 1930.

Above. Circa 1902. Looking down Bolton Road at the junction with Longcauseway. Local children play in the road in relative safety as there would be very little vehicular traffic apart from the electric trams.

Sources of information and pictures

Introduction
- *Cockersand Chartulary held at the British Library, Euston Road, London. © The British Library Board. Ref – ADD MS37769*
- *http://www.merriam-webster.com/dictionary/frankalmoign*
- *The Victoria History of the County of Lancaster – Edited by William Farrer and J. Brownbill. Originally published by Victoria County History, 1907.*
- *DDHU/14/3. An Act for dividing, allotting and enclosing certain commons and waste lands, within the Manors or Lordship of Farnworth and Kersley. Held at Lancashire Archives, Bow Lane, Preston.*
- *The River Irwell – problems of social and economic geography. Kenneth Colley, 1965.*

The Industrial Revolution
- *The Effects of the Factory System – Allen Clarke, 1899. Publisher G. Richards.*
- *DDHU/14/3. An Act for dividing, allotting and enclosing certain commons and waste lands, within the Manors or Lordship of Farnworth and Kersley. Held at Lancashire Archives, Bow Lane, Preston.*
- *Picture - Kearsley Mill above Kearsley Train Station, postcard, authors' collection.*
- *Pictures - Beautiful Farnworth and Bolton-Work and Rest, both postcards authors collection.*
- *The River Irwell – problems of social and economic geography. Kenneth Colley, 1965.*

Irwell Bank Mills
- *Pigot's Trade Directory, Bolton 1836*
- *Picture – Indenture dated 1798, authors' collection.*
- *Picture – Sketch of 1816, authors' collection.*
- *Picture - The sale of machinery from Prestolee Old Cotton Mill. From The Manchester Mercury, September 14th 1819.*
- *Picture – Opening of Rawsons Bridge. Farnworth Journal 14th April 1927.*
- *History Of Farnworth And Kersley (1887). Benjamin Thomas Barton.*
- *Bolton Chronicle, Saturday June 30th 1838.*
- *Farnworth Journal 15th September 1894*
- *Picture - Irwell Bank Mills postcard, unknown publisher. Authors' collection.*
- *Picture - Irwell Bank Mills 'Black Gang' postcard, unknown publisher. Authors' collection.*
- *Picture - Irwell Bank Mill engine room (Jack Howard and Simeon Howard). Authors collection*
- *Irwell Bank Mill flood article. Farnworth Journal of 27th September 1946.*
- *A.J. Flatley advert. Kearsley Urban District Council Booklet, 1960.*
- *Picture - 'Irwell Bank Mills being demolished' – Kevin Lane, Dunstable.*
- *Picture - View from Prestolee Bridge on Boxing Day 2015 – Simon Colley, authors collection.*
- *Picture – Rawsons Stone Bridge. Farnworth Journal 15th April 1921.*

Kearsley Mill
- *Farnworth Journal June 3rd 1965.*
- *Picture - Kearsley Mill during the latter stages of construction, postcard, authors' collection.*
- *Farnworth Journal May 19th 1966*
- *Picture - Kearsley Mill, January 1979, unknown, authors' collection.*
- *http://www.richardhaworth.co.uk/history*
- *R.A.Arnold - 5th Report of M.O. of P.C. (1862), Appendix V., No. 1, p.111*
- *Kevin Heaton & Joanne Shaw, Belledorm, Kearsley Mill.*
- *Picture - Circa 1905. Farnworth Fire Brigade. Postcard, authors' collection.*
- *The River Irwell – problems of social and economic geography. Kenneth Colley, 1965.*

The Lancashire Cotton Famine
- *Bolton Chronicle, 14th October 1865.*

The Mills of Baker Street
- *Worrall's Trade Directory, Bolton 1871*

Bankfield Mill
- *Kearsley Urban District Council Booklet, 1960*
- *Worrall's Trade Directory, Bolton 1891*

Moss Rose Mill
- *Farnworth Journal 26th August 1904*
- *Picture - The former site of the Kearsley Royal British Legion. Courtesy Peter Harrison, Springfield Road, Kearsley.*
- *Farnworth Journal 13th December 1946*
-

Fletchers Paper Mill
- *Picture – Paper by the mile. Farnworth Journal Jan 26th 1961.*
- *Picture - Circa 1910, Ringley Locks and Lock House, authors' collection.*
- *150th Anniversary History of Robert Fletcher & Son Ltd, C.G Hampson, 1973.*
- *Commercial Directory of Manchester and Salford, 1805.*
- *History Of Farnworth And Kersley (1887). Benjamin Thomas Barton.*
- *Farnworth Journal, November 12, 1877, The death of Mr James Fletcher.*
- *Barratt, S T, Stoneclough Mill Of Yesterday, The Archer, Vol II, No 10, p 379.*
- *Picture - Fletchers Paper Mill Water Treatment Plant, Kearsley Urban District Council Booklet, 1960.*
- *Picture - Fletchers Paper Mill in the early 1970's, authors' collection.*
- *Picture - The gates of Fletchers Paper Mill shortly after it closed for good in 2001. Courtesy Stephen Tonge, Kearsley.*
- *Picture - March 2005. The Ringley Lock estate under construction, Simon Colley, authors' collection.*

- *Picture - March 2005. Fletchers Paper Mill buildings being demolished, Simon Colley, authors' collection.*
- *Farnworth Journal May 17/18/19 1865 death of Robert Fletcher.*
- *Picture – Kearsley children's pageant, Farnworth Journal Aug 25th 1944.*
- *Picture - August 1946. A welcome home party was held at Vale House for employees and staff. Courtesy Maude Haydock, Ringley.*
- *Farnworth Journal Aug 16th 1946*
- *Picture - Some of the regulars enjoying a drink at Vale House in May 1968. Farnworth Journal May 2nd 1968.*

Creams Paper Mill
- *Picture - Creams Paper Mill circa 1904. Authors' collection.*
- *150th Anniversary History of Robert Fletcher & Son Ltd, C.G Hampson, 1973.*
- *Picture - Creams Paper Mill on the bank of the River Irwell, circa 1920. Authors' collection.*

Local Governance. Kearsley Local Board and Urban District Council.
- *Article – "A defining moment in the history of Kearsley." The Bolton Chronicle, 2nd September 1865*
- *http://www.bolton.mlfhs.org.uk/Poor.php*
- *Farnworth Journal Feb 5th 1970*
- *Farnworth Journal June 12th 1969*
- *http://www.workhouses.org.uk/Bolton/*
- *Kearsley Local Board minute book 15th November 1865, held at Bolton Museum Archives.*
- *Kearsley Township and cloth charity account books 1706-1835, held at Bolton Museum Archives.*
- *History Of Farnworth And Kersley (1887). Benjamin Thomas Barton.*
- *http://www.bolton-le-moors-townships.co.uk/424003182. The Poor Law, John Isherwood.*
- *Picture - Boxing Day 1922 at Fishpool Workhouse, Farnworth. Farnworth Journal December 29th 1922.*
- *Picture - A 1950's Kearsley UDC waste/refuse wagon. Authors' collection.*

Kearsley Town Hall, Cenotaph and War information
- *Farnworth Journal 8th July 1910*
- *Pictur – Lilywhite Postcard, FNM16. Author's collection.*
- *Kearsley Urban District Council Booklet, 1959*
- *Farnworth Journal 9th May 1958*
- *Farnworth Journal 19th Sept 1919*
- *Farnworth Journal 15th November 1918*
- *Farnworth Journal January 31st 1919*
- *Farnworth Journal January 18th 1946*
- *Farnworth Journal October 22nd 1943*
- *Fallen In The Fight, Neil and Sue Richardson, ISBN 1 85216 058 6.*

- *Lily Alker, Springfield Road Kearsley*
- *Betty Bostock, Springfield Road, Kearsley*

Name Derivations
- https://en.wiktionary.org/wiki/well
- http://bosworth.ff.cuni.cz/
- http://www.wilcuma.org.uk/wanderings-in-anglo-saxon-britain/anglo-saxon-place-names/
- *The Story Of Halshaw Moor Chapel 1808 – 1908. Harold A Barnes M.A*
- *Local notes and reminiscences. Simeon Dyson, 1895. Held at Farnworth Library*

Barnfield House and Conservative Club
- *Farnworth Journal October 3rd 1968*

The First Schools in Kearsley
- *The Bolton Chronicle, Saturday 10th June 1865*
- *Chapel Picture, Stephen Tonge, Station Road, Kearsley*
- *Hollands School. Farnworth Journal, September 30th 1910*
- *Hollands School. Farnworth Journal of August 5th 1910*

Harrison Blair and St. Stephen's
- Farnworth and Kearsley *Parish Magazine January 1870.*
- *Item Ref - DDX 669/12 - Photograph of employees, taken May 1875. Held at Lancashire Archives, Bow Lane, Preston.*
- *Chemical Waste picture ,Lancashire County Council. Picture is courtesy of the Motorway Archive Trust.*
- *St. Stephen's Grand Bazaar Booklet, April 1914. Joseph Files.*
- *Farnworth and Kearsley Parish magazine, November 1870.*
- *Farnworth and Kearsley Parish magazine, August 1871.*
- *Farnworth and Kearsley Parish magazine, May 1874.*
- *Farnworth Journal, May 16th 1930.*
- *St. Stephen's Church Magazine, June 1941.*
- *The London Journal of Arts and Sciences and Repertory of Patents (page 406). Mr W Newton, 1841*
- *A History of St. Stephen's School, Kearsley. Bernard Blakely, 1968*
- *Local Notes and Reminiscences, Simeon Dyson, 1895*
- *History Of Farnworth And Kersley (1887). Benjamin Thomas Barton.*

Kearsley Mount Methodist Church and School
- *Farnworth Journal 21st January 1916*
- *'...But Excepting The Tower" A Chronicle Of Methodism In Kearsley. – Edited By Carol A. Dyson.*
- *Pictures – Courtesy Stephen Tonge*
- *A Brief History of Kearsley Mount Methodism – 1836 to 1936 Centenary Celebrations.* http://www.kmmc3c.org.uk/latest-news/km-1836-1936
- *Farnworth Journal April 3rd 1969*

St. John's Church and School
- *Farnworth Journal, 28th April 1944.*
- *Farnworth Journal, 3rd February 1950.*
- *The Story Of Halshaw Moor Chapel 1808 – 1908. Harold A Barnes M.A*
- *History Of Farnworth And Kersley (1887). Benjamin Thomas Barton.*
- *Farnworth Journal Nov 7th 1968.*
- *Farnworth Journal, Nov 2nd 1934*

New Jerusalem Church and Kearsley West School
- *Farnworth Journal, December 14th 1928.*
- *History of the A666, Motorway History A666, Lancashire, W M Johnson MBE BEng CEng FICE FIHT*
- *http://www.lan-opc.org.uk/Farnworth-with-Kearsley/jerusalem/index.html*
- *New Church worthies, or, Early but little-known disciples of the Lord, Rev. Dr. Jonathan Bayley, New Jerusalem Church, Kensington, London. James Speirs, 36 Bloomsbury Street West, London, 1884. http://www.newchurchhistory.org/articles/jb1884/00_Early_Worthies.php#index*
- *Farnworth Journal, January 25th 1968.*
- *Farnworth Journal, June 28th 1912.*

St. Gregory's Church and School
- *Farnworth Journal June 15th 1928.*
- *Farnworth Journal, November 11th 1927.*

St John Fisher Roman Catholic Church
- *Farnworth Journal March 21st 1968*
- *Farnworth Journal September 19th 1968*
- *Pictures – St John Fisher Schoenstatt Shrine July/August 2014, courtesy Will Mclellan, Alderbank Close, Kearsley.*
- *Lily Alker, Springfield Road, Kearsley.*
- *Kearsley Pool Farm pictures – Courtesy, Dave Lomax at Bent Spur Farm*

St Peter's Church and School
- *Farnworth Journal February 27th 1969*
- *Farnworth Journal September 20th 1946*
- *Farnworth Journal November 18th 1927*
- *Bolton News July 15th 2012*
-

St. Saviours Church and Schools
- *Farnworth Journal, June 5th 1969.*
- *Picture - Ringley St. Saviours clock tower, 1907. Postcard, unknown publisher. Author's collection.*
- *Picture - The Jacobean stone with the inscription "NATHAN WALWORTH BUILDED MEE, ANNO DO 1625." Simon Colley.*

- Picture - Pre 1907 picture showing the original clock. Postcard, unknown publisher. Author's collection.
- Picture - Snow covered St. Saviour's front churchyard and tower circa 1892. Author's collection.
- Picture - Ringley Bridge circa 1910. Postcard, unknown publisher. Author's collection.
- Picture - Circa 1893 albumen photo of Ringley St. Saviours Church. Author's collection.
- Picture - Circa 1893 View of the Chancel at St. Saviour's. Author's collection.
- Parish magazine of May 1885.
- Pictures - Two pictures of St.Saviours during the 1930's. Postcards, both unknown publisher. Author's collection.
- Picture - Circa 1893. Ringley Old Parsonage. Author's collection.
- Picture - Ringley St. Saviours School 1939. Courtesy Maude Haydock, Market Street, Stoneclough.
- The Story Of Halshaw Moor Chapel 1808 – 1908, page 46. Harold A Barnes M.A
- Picture - St. Aidan's mission Church, Outwood 1914. Postcard, unknown publisher. Author's collection.
- Three Centuries of a Village Sanctuary. The Rev. T. Dilworth-Harrison, 1925
- Bolton Evening News 10th December 1975.
- Picture - Circa 1910 view of St. Saviours clock tower. Postcard, unknown publisher. Author's collection.
- The Correspondence of Nathan Walworth and Peter Seddon Of Outwood, and other documents chiefly relating to the building of Ringley Chapel. Edited with notes by John Samuel Fletcher. Printed for the Chetham Society, 1880.

Emmanuel Church Mission, Ringley
- Farnworth Journal 19th March 1920.
- Farnworth Journal April 23rd 1920
- Pictures - Emmanuel Mission group 1920's. Courtesy Maude Haydock, Market Street, Stoneclough.
- Farnworth Journal of April 15th 1932.
- Farnworth Journal August 5th 1932.

Prestolee Holy Trinity Church and Schools
- Farnworth & Kearsley Parish magazine of January 1871.
- Picture - Rev. Edwin William Appleyard. Three Centuries of a Village Sanctuary. The Rev. T. Dilworth-Harrison, 1925.
- Prestolee Holy Trinity Church magazine of September 1943
- Picture - Prestolee Holy Trinity Church Circa 1940's. Lilywhite Postcard, SCH7. Author's collection.
- Farnworth & Kearsley Parish magazine of January 1870.
- Picture - Circa 1901. Prestolee Holy Trinity Church. Postcard, unknown publisher. Author's collection.
- Picture - White Row cottages Prestolee circa 1890. Postcard, unknown publisher. Author's collection.

- *Picture - Prestolee Primary School shortly after opening in 1911. Postcard, unknown publisher. Author's collection.*
- *Picture - Prestolee School circa 1920. Postcard, unknown publisher. Author's collection.*
- *Pictures – Prestolee School 1936. Courtesy Maude Haydock, Market Street, Stoneclough.*
- *Picture – Aerial view, Prestolee Primary School with its new extension, courtesy Prestolee Primary School.*
- *The Idiot Teacher' A Book About Prestolee School And Its Headmaster Teddy O'Neill, by Gerard Holmes, published by Faber and Faber Ltd.*

Halshaw Moor Chapel
- *The Story Of Halshaw Moor Chapel 1808 – 1908, page 46. Harold A Barnes M.A*
- *Bolton Evening News 13th January 1996*
- *Bolton Evening News 23rd October 1992*
- *Farnworth Journal, August 16th 1946*
- *Farnworth Journal, August 23rd 1946*
- *Farnworth Journal, November 23rd 1961*
- *Bolton Evening News November 22nd 1971*

Manchester Bolton and Bury Canal
- *Item – PDC/1. 1791 Act of Parliament for constructing the Manchester, Bolton and Bury Canal. Held at Lancashire Archives, Bow Lane, Preston.*
- *The Story Of Halshaw Moor Chapel 1808 – 1908, page 46. Harold A Barnes M.A.*
- *The Manchester Bolton And Bury Canal History in pictures. John and Margaret Fletcher, Steven Parker and Richard Chester-Browne, 1995. ISBN 0951905813*
- *A Tow Path Guide. Steven Parker and Richard Chester-Browne. 1989.*
- *The Manchester Bolton & Bury Canal. V.I. Tomlinson. 1991.*
- *Circular Walks On The Manchester Bolton And Bury Canal. John and Margaret Fletcher. 1992. ISBN 0951905708.*
- *On The Manchester Bolton & Bury Canal. Alec Waterson. 1985. Published by Neil Richardson. ISBN 0907511791.*
- *Exploring The Croal Irwell Valley, edition number 1.Nob End Local History Booklet. Date unknown.*
- *https://historicengland.org.uk/listing/the-list/list-entry/1309613*
- *The cruck-framed barn at Seddons Fold, Prtestolee. V Tanner, 1984*

Roads, Kearsley
- *History Of Farnworth And Kersley (1887). Benjamin Thomas Barton.*
- *Picture – Military style Turnpike barrier by Emily Colley*
- *The Manchester Mercury, 8th February 1820*
- *Hand drawn map c1790's, authors' collection.*

- *1833 amendment to the 1821 Moses Gate Turnpike Act.*
- *Manchester Mercury, January 5th 1819.*
- *Picture – Kearsley Bar, Rotary Club of Farnworth Magazine, September 1958*

Trams and Trolleybuses
- *Farnworth Journal, June 12th 1931*
- *Farnworth Journal, August 14th 1931*
- *Farnworth Journal August 22nd 1958.*
- *South Lancashire Tramways. E.K. Stretch. 1972*

A666 The Farnworth and Kearsley Bypass and Kearsley Spur
- History of the A666, Farnworth-Kearsley By Pass - W M Johnson MBE BEng CEng FICE FIHT
- *Picture - Worsley Braided Interchange, Simmons Aerofilms Ltd, Picture is courtesy of the Motorway Archive Trust.*
- *Picture - Linnyshaw Moss, 1969. Courtesy Lily Alker, Springfield Road, Kearsley.*
- *Farnworth Journal, August 31st 1967*
- *Farnworth Journal, January 5th 1967*
- *Farnworth Journal, April 20th 1967*

Ringley Old Packhorse Bridge
- *Item – QSB1/119/83. Pilkington & Kearsley. Presentment of decay of 'one long timber bridge,' 1633. Held at Lancashire Archives, Bow Lane, Preston.*
- *Bolton Chronicle 28th October 1865.*
- *Picture - Circa 1930. Ringley Road 'iron' Bridge. Chas Wilkinson Postcard. Author's collection.*
- *Farnworth Journal, May 13th 1932*
- *Farnworth Journal, February 26th 1932*
- *Farnworth Journal, August 7th 1931*
- Farnworth Journal June 7th 1946

Kearsley Power Station
- Farnworth Journal May 27th 1927
- *Pictures - Mortons Media Group Ltd*
- *Pictures – John Preston*
- *The Record Breakers Of The Lancashire Electric Power Company. Graham Edge, first published 2006 by Gingerfold Publications. ISBN 1902356187.*
- *Railway Bylines, Vol 4, Issue 5, April 1999. Irwell Press Magazines Ltd. Kearsley Power Station by Adrian Booth*
- *Archive Magazine, Issue 6, June 1995, Aticle by Graham Edge, Published by Lightmoor Press.*
- *Souvenir Of The Official Opening Of The Extension At The Kearsley Power Station, December 1936. Produced by The Lancashire Electric Power Company.*
- *http://bancroft.berkeley.edu/ROHO/projects/debt/oilcrisis.html. The 1973-74 Oil Crisis*
- *http://www.bbc.co.uk/history/domesday/dblock/GB-376000-405000/page/12. Cooling Tower destruction.*

- Susan Oliver. Visitors Centre, Clifton Country Park.
- Farnworth Journal 26th November 1964, (Ash pile removal).
- Lancashire Electric Power Company News Bulletin, October December 1936, Vol 2 – Number 4.
- Lancashire Electric Power Company News Bulletin, April June 1936, Vol 2 – Number 2.
- ***Note, at the time of writing the locations of the four Kearsley Power Station electric locomotives is as follows:**
- **No.1** originally went to Manchester museum of science and industry, then to a private collector in Shropshire. Currently at The Electric Railway Museum near Coventry.
- **No.2** went to Padiham Power Station July 1983 but this closed in 1992, then converted to battery operation and sent to Heysham Power Station. Currently at Tanfield Railway Museum, Tyne and Wear.
- **No.3** Initially bought by West Yorkshire County Council for the proposed Spen Valley Electric Railway system, but this never materialized. Currently at Tanfield Railway Museum, Tyne and Wear.
- **No.4** Also sent to Heysham power station, was renamed Doug Tottman. Currently at The Electric Railway Museum near Coventry with its sister loco No.1.

Kearsley Branches Railway
- Farnworth Journal March 2nd 1878
- Picture - Coal train approaching the bridge at Springfield Road. P Eckersley.
- Picture - Coal train emerges from the Bolton Road bridge. P Eckersley.
- Picture - The former site of where the Kearsley Branch Line Number 1 terminated at Linnyshaw Moss sidings. Simon Colley.
- Picture - The Kearsley Branches Railway signal box at Stoneclough. Photographer unknown.
- Picture - Picture taken at the side of the White Horse public house in the mid 1960's. Photographer unknown.
- Picture - Train and wagons below the bridge at Springfield Road in the mid 1960's. Photographer unknown.
- Picture - Linnyshaw Moss sidings, April 1964. Photographer unknown.

The Manchester to Bolton Railway
- History Of Farnworth And Kersley (1887). Benjamin Thomas Barton.
- Pictures - July 1963, Moses Gate Station. Kearsley bound train emerges from Farnworth tunnel in the mid 1960's. Train passing Horridge Brook in September 1966. July 1963, Farnworth And Halshaw Moor Station. Mid 1960's Scene close to the location the former Dixon Fold station. Train passing Pilkingtons Tile Works in the late 1960's. P Eckersley
- Picture - F&HM station in August 1970. Postcard, unknown photographer.
- Picture - Circa mid 1960's view of Kearsley Train Station, unknown photographer.
- Picture - Stoneclough Brow Bridge circa 1925. Shacklady Postcard. Authors collection.
- Picture - February 2011, The Grade II listed tunnel at Slackey Brow. Simon Colley
- Picture - The completed M62 motorway and bridge over the River Irwell. Barrie Watkins.

- Picture - 1908, The Thirteen Arches viaduct at Clifton. Authors Collection.
- Picture - Clifton Junction station circa 1910. Authors Collection.
- Picture - A coal train passes beneath the A667 road bridge at Outwwod in 1963. P Eckersley.
- Picture - 1913. Ernest Seddon's shop on Ringley Road West. Postcard. Authors Collection.
- The Railway Companion, from Manchester to Bolton" (pamphlet) By Arthur Lacey, 1838 (BT Barton Book page 35).
- Slackey Brow Bridge info. https://historicengland.org.uk/listing/the-list/list-entry/1067302
- The Railways of Great Britain and Ireland Practically Described and Illustrated
- By Francis Wishaw. Griffith Farran Browne & Co Ltd (1969).
- Manchester As It Is – Benjamin Love, 1839.

Taskers Farm
- Information and access to diaries etc, all courtesy of Marion Keyte (Livingstone), Ramsbottom.
- Pictures - Taskers Farmhouse, Springfield Road, 1953. Edward Livingstone pictured in 1967. Tasker's Farmhouse and shop, Springfield Road, January 1968. hayfield' of Taskers Farm in the 1940's. Mary Livingstone at Taskers Farm in the 1940's. Circa 1949. Jean Livingstone, Arthur Hinks, Marion Livingstone and Mary Livingstone next to a small lodge that was located in the middle of where the Mossfield Road estate was built. Circa 1949. Mary Livingstone with pet collie Rex at the rear of Taskers farmhouse. All courtesy of Marion Keyte (Livingstone), Ramsbottom.
- Picture - December 2006. The Spar convenience store. Simon Colley.
- Picture - Circa 1920's. The Co-Operative Society's Taskers Lane Farm. Courtesy of Dave Lomax, Bent Spur Farm, Kearsley.
- Bolton Chronicle 13th October 1866

Top O'th Bank Farmhouse
- Recollections of Farnworth and Kearsley 1900-45, The Family Chatton. By Agnes Fish.
- Farnworth Journal October 27th 1967.

Unity Brook Colliery
- Farnworth Journal March 16th 1878
- Bolton Chronicle March 16th 1878
- Farnworth Journal March 23rd 1878
- Farnworth Journal March 30th 1878
- Farnworth Journal April 6th 1878
- Farnworth Journal April 13th 1878
- Farnworth Journal April 20th 1878
- Farnworth Journal April 27th 1878
- Pictorial World March 30th 1878, held at the British Library, Euston Road, London.

- Sketches from Pictorial World by Mr. S.H. Ashley Oakes, of Silverwell Street, Bolton.
- Picture - The Unicorn Inn Public House, courtesy of Stephen Tonge.
- Mining and Mineral Statistics of the United Kingdom of Great Britain and Ireland (1884-1887) Plans of abandoned mines.
- Kearsley Local Board minute book and Relief Fund books all courtesy of the Archive Centre, Bolton Central Library, Le Mans Crescent, Bolton.
- Pictures - June 2018. The Unity Brook disaster memorial on the former site of the Unicorn Inn public house on Manchester Road. Simon Colley. (Memorial site prepared by Stephen Tonge, Stephen Bromley, Chris Ward, Harry Morton, Councillor Mark Cunningham, Simon Colley, Paul Cooper, Bernie Lomax, Lynn Cope, Stuart Horribin (memorial base brickwork), Mark Birtstall (memorial base groundwork, concreting & stone setting).
- Picture – Bowling Green circa 1895. Authors' collection.
- Farnworth Journal Thurs Oct 21st 1965 Council centenary supplement.
- St Stephens bazaar booklet March 1914.
- Collieries and their railways in the Manchester Coalfields, Geoffrey Hayes. ISBN 184306-135X.

The Clifton Hall Colliery Explosion
- Official Inquest Report By Arnold Morley, Esq., M.P. Upon the circumstances attending a fatal explosion which occurred on the 18th of June 1885, in the Trencherbone Mine of the Clifton Hall Colliery
- A memorial card for the Clifton Hall Colliery Disaster. Authors Collection.
- Picture - Clifton Hall Colliery sidings, circa 1910. Postcard. Authors Collection.

Ringley Fold Explosion
- London Morning Chronicle January 31st 1852
- Picture – Kearsley Hall Road. Simon Colley
- Farnworth Journal of November 25th 1865.

Stonehill, Foggs & Newtown Collieries
- Lancashire Mining Disasters 1835-1910 – Jack Nadin. ISBN 10: 1903425956
- Bolton Chronicle January 27th 1877
- Bolton Chronicle February 10th 1877
- Picture - Circa 1910. Foggs Pit on the MBB Canal. Postcard. Authors' collection.
- Picture - memorial card. Authors collection.
- Picture - Circa 1930's. Aerial view of Newtown Colliery on the Clifton and Pendlebury border. Original negative, authors collection.
- Farnworth Journal of February 18th 1910
- Farnworth Journal, March 15th 1912.
- Picture - 1890's, sinking of a pit shaft at the bottom of Stoneclough Brow. Authors' collection.

Kearsley Moss Colliery & Spindle Point Colliery
- Farnworth Journal July 6th 1961
- Farnworth Journal March 21st 1919

- *Tramroads in the Irwell Valley Lectures 1972-73 Part 5 by JB Smethurst & RB Schofield*
- *Collieries and their railways in the Manchester Coalfields, Geoffrey Hayes. ISBN 184306-135X*
- *https://www.nmrs.org.uk/mines-map/coal-mining-in-the-british-isles/lancashire-coalfield/bolton-bury-coalfield/kearsley-moss-colliery-1860-1910/*
- *http://www.nmrs.org.uk/mines-map/coal-mining-in-the-british-isles/lancashire-coalfield/bolton-bury-coalfield/clifton-moss-colliery-1840-1922/*
- *Bolton Chronicle 13th October 1866*
- *Farnworth Journal, February 10th 1900.*
- *Farnworth Journal, March 21st 1919.*

Wet Earth Colliery, Pilkingtons' Tiles & Fletchers Canal
- *Picture - Circa 1896. Coal Screening sheds under construction at Wet Earth Colliery. Postcard, authors' collection.*
- *Picture - Circa 1930. Fletcher's Canal. Postcard, authors' collection.*
- *Farnworth Journal July 25th 1913.*
- *Collieries and their railways in the Manchester Coalfields, Geoffrey Hayes. ISBN 184306-135X*
- *Picture - 1914. Advertisement for the Clifton & Kersley Coal Company. St Stephens bazaar booklet March 1914.*
- *Picture – Greenhalgh, Farnworth. Authors' collection.*
- *Pictures - St Anne's Church 1914, and 1932. Postcards, authors' collection.*
- *Picture - Circa 1930. Aerial view of Pilkington's Tile & Pottery Works and Exide Battery Works at Clifton. Original negative, authors' collection.*
- *Picture - The Pilkington's works around 1900. Authors' collection.*
- *Picture - 1920's Exide Batteries advertisement, the company later became Chloride Electrical. Postcard, authors' collection.*
- *Picture - June 2010. Pilkington's Tiles factory outlet shop. Simon Colley.*
- *Farnworth Journal, January 5th 1895.*
- *http://www.pittdixon.go-plus.net/denton-colliery/denton-colliery.htm*
- *The Industrial Railways of Bolton, Bury and the Manchester Coalfield Part 1 - Bolton & Bury, by C.H.A. Townley, C.A. Appleton, F.D. Smith & J.A. Peden. ISBN 1 870754 30 9*
- *Susan Oliver. Visitors Centre, Clifton Country Park.*

Kearsley Cricket Club
- *Farnworth Journal December 10th 1898.*
- *Farnworth Journal August 21st 1925.*
- *Farnworth Journal September 7th 1934.*
- *Farnworth Journal February 26th 1943.*
- *Farnworth Journal July 15th 1949.*
- *Farnworth Journal September 3rd 1970.*
- *Farnworth Journal September 14th 1923.*
- *Picture - Kearsley Cricket Club in August 2014. Will Mclellan, Alderbank Close.*
- *The 1981 programme for the annual gala. Authors' collection.*

- *Kearsley Cricket Club 1875 – 1975 Centenary Brochure.*
- *Programme for the 1983 Hamer Cup Final. Authors' collection.*

Dr Charles Hassall
- *Farnworth Journal December 3rd 1898.*
- *Farnworth Journal April 6th 1923*
- *http://www.salon.com/2013/05/22/ original_coca_cola_had_a_very_small_amount_of_cocaine_partner/*

Farnworth and Kearsley Labour Club
- *Picture - The picture above from the late 1920's shows the Old Royal Oak building on the right with the Labour Club signage above it. Postcard, authors' collection.*
- *Farnworth Journal September 9th 1930.*
- *Picture – Labour Club June 2011. Simon Colley.*
- *Pictures - The Bird-I'-Th'-Hand public house, The Bowling Green Hotel & The Travellers Rest Hotel. All Farnworth Journal September 5th 1968.*

Black Horse and High Stile Fold
- *Ben Higginbotham's "Annals Of Farnworth" (Farnworth Weekly Journal, August 4th 1911)*
- *Local Notes and Reminiscences, Simeon Dyson, 1895*
- *Bolton Chronicle December 27th 1828.*
- *Farnworth Journal January 27th 1950.*
- *Picture - Circa 1908 view of Higher Market Street. Authors' collection.*
- *Picture - The Black Horse in the late 1940's. Postcard. Authors' collection.*
- *Picture - View of Higher Market Street from the bottom of Longcauseway. Postcard. Authors' collection.*
- *Picture - The Black Horse Hotel, 1908. Postcard. Authors' collection.*
- *Picture – King's Hall, Farnworth Journal 16th April 1970*

Longcauseway
- *Picture - Circa 1910. A captivating view of the Longcauseway. Postcard. Authors' collection.*
- *Picture - Circa 1907. Looking up Longcauseway. Postcard. Authors' collection.*
- *Picture - Top of Longcauseway in August 1958. Postcard. Authors' collection.*
- *Picture - October 2010. The top of Longcauseway. Postcard. Authors' collection.*
- *Picture - A 1940's view from the bottom of Longcauseway. Postcard. Authors' collection.*
- *Picture - The popularity of the annual Whitsuntide processions. Postcard. Authors' collection.*

Postal Services
- *Picture - July 2014. Kearsley Post Office. Will Mclellan, Alderbank Close.*
- *Picture - May 2013. The Post Office public house. Simon Colley.*

- *Farnworth Journal, April 27th 1895.*
- *Picture - 1940's view of Market Street Farnworth. Postcard. Authors' collection.*
- *Picture - Circa 1960 and Farnworth Post Office. Postcard. Authors' collection.*

Various
- *Circa 1930's. Rush hour at Moses gate. Postcard. Authors' collection.*
- *Circa 1910. St. Stephen's prize band. Postcard. Authors' collection.*
- *A motor bus makes its way along the cobbled Manchester Road at Kearsley Mount in 1932. Lilywhite Postcard. Authors' collection.*
- *Cemetery Road militant mums, Farnworth Journal June 10th 1971.*
- *Lord Nelson public house circa 1990, Kenneth Colley. Authors' collection.*
- *Circa 1930's. Margaret Barlow's Tea Rooms and Gardens. Postcard. Authors' collection.*
- *Circa 1900. Margaret Tatlock outside her shop on Fold Road. Picture – authors collection.*
- *Building without plans, Farnworth Journal of May 10th 1912*
- *Springfield Road 'Villas,' Farnworth Journal of March 16th 1934*
- *View of the Albert Road, Longcauseway, Buckley Lane junction circa 1930. Picture – authors collection.*
- *Circa 1920's delivery tricycle for Cunliffe & Son of Farnworth. Postcard. Authors' collection.*
- *1777 Marker Stone, picture and information courtesy of Stephen Bromley, Kearsley.*
- *Picture - December 2012. The Antelope Public House. Simon Colley.*
- *Picture - April 2013. The Moss Rose Public House. Simon Colley.*
- *Picture - The White Horse public house, November 2018. Simon Colley.*
- *Picture - Circa 1984 view looking down Hulme Road. Unknown photographer. donated by Andrea Jones, Prestolee.*
- *Picture - June 1984. Stoneclough Post Office. Unknown photographer.*
- *Picture - 2018. Unity Brook public house. Simon Colley. Other information from The Lancashire Archives, Preston.*
- *Picture - The Clock Face public house at the top of Old Hall Street in November 2013. Simon Colley.*
- *Picture - June 2018. Wilsons Pie Shop, Bolton Road. Simon Colley.*
- *Picture - September 2010. Crompton Street close to Lark Hill. Simon Colley.*
- *Picture - November 2018. The Horseshoe public house, Fold Road, Ringley. Simon Colley.*
- *Picture - The Market Street Tavern, St. Georges Day 2009. Simon Colley.*
- *Picture - July 2014. GEP motor garage, Springfield Road. Will McLellan.*
- *Picture - Numbers 97, 99 & 101 Manchester Road Kearsley. Postcard. Authors' collection.*
- *Ticket entitling the holder to a small gift to celebrate the Royal Visit in 1913. Authors' collection.*
- *Picture - Circa1920's. Horse and cart taking part in the Whit Walk along Manchester Road. Courtesy Jean Haslam, Stephen Tonge.*
- *Local advertisements,1930 – St. Stephen's fund raising magazine. Courtesy Dave Lomax, Bent Spur Farm.*

- *Picture - Circa 1901. Manchester Road. Postcard, authors' collection.*
- *Picture - The Horseshoe Hotel, Ringley. Postcard, authors' collection.*
- *Picture - Circa 1930. A view of Manchester Road, Clifton. Postcard, authors' collection.*
- *Picture - Circa 1910. View down Stand Lane. Postcard authors' collection.*
- *Picture - Circa 1910. Stand Lodge. Postcard authors' collection.*
- *Picture - Circa 1905. Ye Olde Three Crowns public house. Postcard authors' collection.*
- *Picture - 1960's view of Market Street with the former Farnworth and Kearsley Co-Op. Photograph, authors' collection.*
- *Picture - An advertisement from the Farnworth Journal of May 31st 1935.*
- *Picture - Circa 1920. Brabin's outfitters shop. Postcard authors' collection.*
- *Picture - An advert for Brabin's from the Farnworth Journal of March 21st 1919.*
- *Picture - 1907. The former electricity works building on Albert Road. Postcard authors' collection.*
- *Picture - Circa 1920. The Albert Road Congregational Church. Postcard authors' collection.*
- *Picture - Circa 1902. The Black Horse Public House. Postcard authors' collection.*
- *Picture - Circa 1910. Farnworth, Market Street at the junction with Brackley Street. Postcard authors' collection.*
- *Picture - Circa 1910. Former cottages next to Farnworth & Halshaw Moor train station. Postcard authors' collection.*
- *Picture - Circa 1905. Market Street, Stoneclough. Postcard authors' collection.*
- *Picture - Advertisements for local businesses from the Prestolee Holy Trinity magazine of September 1943. Authors' collection.*
- *Picture - c1923. Market Street, Stoneclough. Postcard, authors' collection.*
- *Picture - Walking Day, Stoneclough 1951. Photograph, authors' collection.*
- *Picture - Circa 1910. Ringley Old Bridge, and The Horseshoe Hotel. Postcard, authors' collection.*
- *Picture - Circa 1910. Cottages, known as 'Buildings Row.' Postcard, authors' collection.*
- *Picture - The Lord Nelson public house circa 1920. Photograph, courtesy Stephen Tonge, Kearsley.*
- *Article - A local collier decides not to attend his own wedding. Farnworth Journal of January 5th 1895.*
- *Picture - Circa 1910. Prestolee Farm. Postcard, courtesy Stephen Tonge, Kearsley.*
- *Picture - Seddon Gardens, Prestolee. Barrie Watkins, Worsley. Authors' collection.*
- *Picture - Alderbank nursing home on Alderbank Close, September 1969. Farnworth Journal, September 11th 1969.*
- *Advert from 1950. Kearsley Urban District Council Booklet, 1950.*
- *Local advertisements,1930 – St. Stephen's fund raising magazine. Courtesy Dave Lomax, Bent Spur Farm.*
- *Picture - Circa 1902. Looking down Bolton Road. Postcard, Authors' collection.*

Many thanks to all who have contributed with pictures and information. There are a number of postcards and pictures of which the photographer or publisher is currently unknown, it is never the intention to take credit for any of these, and any information as to who should correctly be acknowledged is most welcome, with further editions amended accordingly. I have endeared to trace and contact all persons concerned, and hope that no upset is caused in my attempt to show Kearsley in as many ways as possible. I can only wish for latter forgiveness if any dismay arises.

Email:- kearsleyhistory@colley123.plus.com

Index

A.J. Flatley Ltd, Irwell Bank Mill 39
Albert Road 44, 210, 365, 367, 371, 375, 498-499, 512, 531
Alderbank Close 164, 454, 459, 540
Antelope public house 90, 194, 348, 367, 514
Antelope Street 466
Baker Street 53, 188, 425
Baker, Jesse 145, 188, 202
Baker, Noah 53, 194
Bankfield Mill, Ringley 48
Barnes Terrace 412, 445
Barnfield House 173-175, 194
Bent Spur Farm 389
Bent Spur Road 75, 194, 196, 389
Birch House, Farnworth 179
Birch Road 443, 449
Bird-I'-Th'-Hand public house 381, 383, 488-490, 532
Black Gang, Irwell Bank Mill 36
Black Horse public house 142, 145, 224, 348, 350, 352, 364-365,
.... 367, 369, 372, 375, 377, 380, 429, 492-497, 532
Blackhurst Green 18, 33, 56, 59, 184
Blair, Constance 203
Blair, Florence 198-199, 203, 207
Blair, Frances 187, 202-203, 207
Blair, Harrison 145-147, 149, 178, 187-191, 193-194, 198,
.... 202-204, 261, 398, 443, 448, 454, 457
Blair, Stephen 187, 202-204
Blighty's 320-322
Bo-Bo (electric loco) 409-411, 413, 415
Bolton Road 49, 93, 151, 179, 222, 239, 311, 325, 348,
.... 352, 360-361, 363-365, 370, 372, 374, 379, 381, 384,
.... 386-387, 443, 446, 460, 465-466, 501, 518, 532, 542
Bomb Damage, Springfield Road 163-164, 464
Botany Bay Colliery 124, 135
Bottoms Toll Bar, Stoneclough 359-360
Bowling Green Hotel, Farnworth 90, 92, 99, 490
Brackley Street 235, 311, 382, 485, 505, 529, 532
Brando's Nightclub 44, 322

Bridge Street, Prestolee	536
Brook Street, Stoneclough	360
Cellar School, Kearsley Mount	178-179, 191, 194-195, 202
Cemetery Road	508, 533
Cenotaph, Kearsley	151, 156-157, 159, 465
Chapel Street, Stoneclough	183
Chapel Street, Farnworth	311, 316, 319-320, 322-323
Chuffers	322
Church Road	179, 235, 261, 314, 385, 433
Church Road, Prestolee	294, 296, 299
Church Street, Farnworth	225, 232, 251, 316-318
Church Street Weslyan Chapel, Farnworth	318
Churches on the Mount	97, 219
Cinderhill School	178, 284
City Lites	321-322
Clifton and Kersley Coal Company	112, 119, 122, 128, 130, 168
Clifton Hall Colliery	91, 96, 100-104
Clifton Junction	126, 439-440
Clifton Marina	130, 418, 437
Clifton Street	460, 465
Clock Face	169, 348, 350, 491, 518
Club Monaco	319-320
Coal, formation of	75
Corrie, Anne Wynne	127-128, 198
Creams Paper Mill	22, 73-74
Crompton Road, Prestolee	19, 42, 296, 539
Crompton Street	519
Crompton, James	55, 58, 142, 238
Crompton, Ralph	55-56
Crompton, Roger	56, 58, 238
Crompton, Thomas Bonsor	30-32, 34, 235, 292, 296-297
Cross Street	80
Cross Street, Farnworth	24
Cultivation Stone	136
Darley Hall	210, 223, 231, 233-234
Darley Street	41, 44, 233, 505
Dixon Fold Station	436
Dublin, Steve	481
Duke of Bridgewater	20, 311, 329, 451

Eames, Dr Thomas Boles 81, 145, 173, 194
Earl of Derby. 20, 55, 215, 269-270, 345, 406
Emmanuel Church Mission, Ringley.. 287-291
Enclosure, Farnworth and Kersley Act 8, 10, 13, 18, 20, 136,
. . . . 352, 493, 513
Farnworth & Kearsley Bypass. 384-387
Farnworth and Halshaw Moor Station 427-428, 431-432, 533
Farnworth and Kearsley Co-Op, Springfield Road 163-164, 451,
. . . . 454, 459, 464, 477
Farnworth and Kearsley Co-Op, Stonelough. 536
Farnworth and Kearsley Co-Op, Farnworth 382, 529
Farnworth and Kearsley Labour Club. 383, 487-488, 491
Farnworth and Kersley Gas Company 187
Farnworth and Kersley Relief Committee. 47
Farnworth Fire Brigade. 41, 44
Farnworth Police Station.. . . . . 314, 316, 322
Farnworth Post Office 225, 502-505
Fish, Agnes. 460-461, 466
Fishbrook 348, 445
Fishpool Infirmary & Institution 143-144
Fletcher, James, Fletchers paper Mill 58-59, 61-62, 64, 94, 145
Fletcher, John, Fletchers paper Mill. 58-60
Fletcher, John, Colliery Owner 127-128, 136, 193-194, 202
Fletcher, Robert, Fletchers paper Mill. 55-56, 58
Fletchers Folly, Wet Earth Colliery.. . . . . 127, 436
Fletchers Paper Mill 16, 22, 55-72
(Robert Fletcher & Sons Ltd)
Foggs Pit.. 110
Fold Road 268, 283, 286, 393, 419, 422, 510, 519, 537
Funfair, top of Longcauseway. 375
Gee, Giles 49
Gee, Isaac 49, 145
George Tomlinson School and Kearsley Academy. 261-266, 302, 447
Giants Seat 123, 184-185, 289, 509
Grapes public house 34, 59, 145, 172, 516, 536
Grosvenor Street.. 387
Halshaw Lane 184, 242, 348, 350, 386-387
Halshaw Moor.. 18, 33, 142, 169-170, 179, 225,
. . . . 311, 427, 428-429, 431

Halshaw Moor Chapel 179, 311-323, 334
Hare & Hounds public house 117, 359
Harrison Blair Chemical Works 188, 190-192, 203, 261,
.... 443, 448, 454, 457
Hartley, Jesse 427, 435
Hassall, Dr Charles 485-486
Hazlemere 114, 408, 444
High Stile Schoolroom 146-147, 178, 235
Higher Market Street 348, 367, 373, 491, 495, 501, 528
Highfield House 151-153
Holland's School 179-182, 225, 250, 261, 314, 503
Holy Trinity Church, Prestolee 30, 42, 57, 292-296, 309
Horridge Brook 433
Horseshoe Hotel, Ringley 271, 282-283, 325, 339, 519, 525, 537
Hulme Road 107-108, 122, 403, 413, 422, 426, 472, 516
Hulme, William 107
Industrial Revolution 8, 15, 17, 75, 187, 329, 347
Irwell Bank Band 186
Irwell Bank Mill 16, 30, 35-41, 57, 296
Irwell Bank School 185
Irwell Valley 8, 14-15, 22, 26, 123, 255, 329, 396, 429
Jackson Street 350, 363, 379
James Brindley 123-124, 329
James Stanley, the Seventh Earl of Derby 269-270, 345
John Gilbert 329
Kearsley and Ringley Conservative Club 173-177
Kearsley Bar, Toll Bar 49, 89, 359-361
Kearsley Branch Railway 402-403, 408-409, 412, 443-449
Kearsley Cenotaph 151, 156-157, 159, 465
Kearsley Cricket Club 254, 454, 476-484
Kearsley Cross 372, 501
Kearsley Green 54, 121, 403-404, 426, 428
Kearsley Hall Farm 107, 393, 402-404
Kearsley Hall Road 107-108, 393, 403-404
Kearsley Junction, on the Manchester to Bolton Railway 257, 403,
.... 408-409, 411-412, 443-445
Kearsley Mill, Prestolee 19, 41-43, 142, 334, 460, 472
Kearsley Moss Colliery 119, 443
Kearsley Mount Convalescent Home 161

Kearsley Mount Methodist Church and School 214-222, 476-477
Kearsley Post Office 377, 502
Kearsley Power Station 107, 389, 393,
. . . . 402-426, 436, 445, 449, 462, 516
Kearsley Roundabout 239, 350, 386-388
Kearsley Social Club 49, 376
Kearsley Spur 210, 239, 384, 387-389, 449
Kearsley Town Hall 151-159, 462, 473
Kearsley Train Station 408, 428, 434
Kearsley Urban District Council 29, 59, 62, 137, 149, 151-153
Kearsley Vale House 58-59, 61-62, 71-72, 401, 468
Kearsley West School 210, 239, 245-246, 262, 388
Kersley Local Board 59, 93-94, 120, 137, 145-147,
. . . . 149, 151, 187, 216, 398, 494
Klondike coal pickers of Stoneclough 114-115
Ladyshore Colliery 22, 334, 340-341
Lancashire Cotton Famine 22, 45-47
Lark Hill 443, 446, 477, 500, 519
Linnyshaw Moss 187, 192-193, 389, 409, 443, 446, 448-449
Livingstone, Edward, Taskers Farm 451, 453-454
Longcauseway 210, 258, 348, 364-365, 367, 371,
. . . . 375, 377, 477, 485, 488, 498-501, 512, 542
Lord Nelson public house 87, 108, 143, 283, 325, 327, 509, 538
Lord Street 314, 386, 460
Lyon Industrial Estate 187, 447, 449
M61 Motorway 192, 387-388, 449
M62 Motorway 112, 132, 387-388, 437-438, 440, 526
Man & Scythe public house 524
Manchester Bolton & Bury Canal (MBBC) 31, 57, 68, 110, 124,
. . . . 126, 133, 282, 325, 329-346, 393,
. . . . 427-428, 468-470, 537
Manchester Road 49, 78, 80, 83, 97-98, 118-120,
. . . . 131, 178, 191, 194-195, 197, 200, 202, 209,
. . . . 215-217, 219, 311, 325, 349, 359-361, 365, 377, 466,
. . . . 476, 502, 507, 514, 521-522, 524, 526
Manchester to Bolton Railway . . . 100, 112, 114, 121, 133, 402, 407, 416,
. . . . 425, 427-439, 442, 444, 472, 502
Margaret Barlow's Tea Rooms 509

Market Street Congregational Church, ... 250, 314, 318 now Trinity Church
Market Street Tavern.. .. .. 65, 70, 520
Market Street, Stonelough/Ringley .... 59, 174, 183, 185, ... 401, 520, 534, 536
Market Street, Farnworth. .. 179, 223, 250, 311, 314, 318, 321, 348, 364, ... 366-367, 373, 485, 488, 490-491, 495-501, ... 503, 504-506, 528-529, 532, 536
Mather School.. .. .. 178, 235, 494
Mather Street. 178, 494
Mather, Henry.. 178
Melville Road 163, 450, 452
Militant mums 508
Miners Arms public house 120, 122, 326
Molyneux Brow 126, 133, 440
Moor Hall 314-315, 317, 319, 322-323
Moses Gate. .. .. 31, 168, 210, 364, 367, 369-370, ... .372, 374, 431, 443, 506
Moses Gate Turnpike Act. 353-362
Mossfield Road. 389, 409, 448-449, 451, 456-457, 552
Moss Lane 78-79, 122
Moss Road.. .. .. 210, 261
Moss Rose Mill. 49-52, 164, 199
Moss Rose public house .. .. 80, 89, 151, 222, 311, 348-349, 359, ... 361, 462, 465-466, 476, 514
Mossfield Road. 389, 409, 448, 451, 456-457
Mount Vale Mill.. 53
Name Derivations 168
Nelson's Croft 313-314
New Jerusalem Church. 59, 238-245, 388, 460
Newtown Colliery 111-113
Nob End 14, 73, 330, 332, 334, 338, 339, 342-343, 346, 428
Oak Mills, Longcauseway 375
Oakes Street 166-167, 348-349, 460
Old Hall Street. .. .. .210, 242, 348, 381, 488-489, 491, 518, 532
Old Royal Oak Hotel. 488
Old Three Crowns, Ringley 286, 324, 326, 339, 537
Oldhouse Croft 86, 89, 200
Outwood.. .. ..149, 187, 268-269, 284-285, 300, 333, 440- 441, 471, 537

564

Overseer of the highways	138
Overseer of the poor	137-138, 140-142, 145, 311
Pandora Cotton Mill	499
Pilkington Road	352, 379, 409, 443, 446, 451, 460
Pilkington, Alfred	111, 128, 195
Pilkingtons Tile and Pottery Works	123-124, 126, 128-129, 133-135, 438
Pleasuredrome	322-323
Pool Farm	254, 257, 454, 513
Population Graphs	474-475
Post Office public house	225, 503-504
Post Office, Kearsley	377, 502
Post Office, Farnworth	225, 503-505
Post Office, Stoneclough	516
Presto Street	12, 168, 251, 317-318
Prestolee Farm	42, 296, 539
Prestolee Holy Trinity Church and School	261, 292-310
Prestolee New Cotton Mill	22, 30-32, 34
Prestolee Old Cotton Mill	22, 24-28
Prestolee Print Works	22, 334
Princess Avenue	456
Quarry Road	412, 444
Randolph Road	460
Rawson Arms public house	432
Rawson, Benjamin	24, 29, 223-224, 231, 233-235, 311
Rawsons Bridge	24, 29
Rev. Canon Charles Lowe	88, 93, 96, 203
Rev. Edwin William Appleyard	292
Reverand Joseph Dyson	312-313
Rideout, William Jackson	31, 292-293
Riders Farm	78, 348
Ringley Fold Colliery	105-107
Ringley Lock	16, 57, 68-70, 344
Ringley Meadows	107, 408, 416, 423, 425
Ringley Old Bridge	14, 168, 184, 275, 283, 325, 327-328, 390-397, 403, 471, 537
Ringley Old Brow	238, 286, 324, 393-394, 537
Ringley Old Parsonage	281
Ringley Road	174, 178, 281, 284, 344, 399, 401

Ringley Road West 440-441
Ringley Road Station 440, 442
Ringley St. Saviours Church and Schools 97, 145, 178, 267-284,
. . . . 286-287, 292, 419, 471-472, 513
River Croal 14, 22, 24, 26-27, 29-30, 233
River Irwell 8-10, 14-16, 22, 24, 26-27, 31, 34-35,
. . . . 38, 40, 55, 57, 64, 67-68, 73, 74, 120, 123-124, 126, 133,
. . . . 169, 327, 330, 334, 335-337, 339, 344, 390, 392, 396, 398,
. . . . 402, 406, 416, 428, 437-439, 462, 468
Riverside Drive 16, 39, 310
Rock Hall 30-31
Roosevelt Road 363, 460
Roscow Road 13, 49, 348-350, 359-361, 444
Rose Cottage 316
Salford Hundred 10, 168, 170-171, 390, 393, 398
Sandhole Road 214, 476
Scarlets 322
Schoenstatt Shrine 253, 255-256
Seddon Fold Farm 284, 334-345, 470-471
Seddon Gardens 539
Seddon Lane 42, 296, 539
Seddon, James (Dictum Factum) 178, 284
Seddons Paper Mill 22, 24-25
Singing Clough 108, 157, 261, 352, 443, 446
Sir Charles Barry 223, 270, 272
Slackey Brow 53-54, 107, 119, 120-122, 325,
. . . . 393, 403, 407-408, 420-421, 425, 428, 436, 472
Spindle Point Colliery 78, 82, 118-122, 128, 393
Spindle Point Primary School 216
Spread Eagle public house 121, 524
Springfield Road 50, 51, 119, 163-165, 187, 190-191, 210,
. . . . 261, 263, 311, 409, 443, 447-452, 455-456,
. . . . 458, 460, 464, 477, 481, 511, 520, 522
St John Fisher Roman Catholic Church 98, 219, 253-257, 513
St Kilda Avenue 455, 457
St Peter's Church and School 258-260
St Peter's Way 384-389
St. Aidan's Mission, Outwood 285
St. Anne's Church, Clifton 131-132

St. Gregory Roman Catholic Church and School . . 97, 247-252, 254, 318
St. John's Church and School. 143, 178, 223-237
Stand Lane 527
Starkie Arms 522
Starkie, Le Gendre 20, 194
Station Road 216, 412, 445, 460
Stink Bomb Hill 457, 192
Stonelough Brow 114, 117, 156-157, 184, 239, 269, 348-350, 352,
.. .. 359-360, 369, 403, 409, 412, 428-429, 435, 443-444, 460
Stonelough Railway Bridge 435
Stonehill Colliery. 109, 443, 446
Sulby Street 117, 536
Taskers Farm 191, 311, 450-458
Taskers Lane, now Springfield Road 50, 119, 178,
.. .. 190-191, 210, 311, 477
Taskers Lane Farm 164, 460, 454
Teddy O'Neil, M.B.E 300-308
The Grapes Inn (Grapes Hotel). .. .. .34, 59, 145, 172, 516, 536
Thirteen Arches 126, 133, 439
Three Crowns Hotel, Ringley 286, 324, 326, 339, 537
Top o'th Bank Farmhouse 460-466
Tottman, Mr J.D 414
Townleys Hospital 144
Trams and Trolleybuses 364-383
Tramways route map 378
Travellers Rest public house 490, 506
Turbary Road. 75, 76, 194
Turnpike, Acts and roads 18, 49, 194, 329, 347-362
Unicorn Inn public house 78, 82-85, 87, 97-98, 122
Unity Brook Colliery. 77-99
Unity Brook public house 78, 119, 517
Vale House 58-59, 61, 64, 71-72, 401, 468
Walker Close 214
Wallworth, Nathan 178, 268, 282
Walton Place .. .. .350, 493
Waterwheel 15, 24, 26-27, 123-124
Waverley Avenue 119, 443, 447
Wells House 16, 534
Weslyan Chapel, Ringley 183-186

Wet Earth Colliery.. 123-130
White Horse public house 350, 409, 443, 445-446, 466, 510, 515
White Row houses & School, Prestolee. 295, 297-298
Whitehead, Sydney Dean. 61-63, 65, 67, 72
Whitsuntide Procession 222, 227, 280, 501, 522, 536
Wilson's Bridge. 24, 26, 29-30
Wilson's Pie shop. 22, 26
Wilsons' Chemical Works 518, 466
Withington Croft 179, 311-312, 322-323
Wood Street, Outwood. 440-441
Workhouse 8, 61, 142-144
Working Men's Club, Prestolee 310
Worsley Braided Interchange.. .. .. 387-389, 449
Ye Olde Three Crowns, Market Street, Farnworth 528

www.ingramcontent.com/pod-product-compliance
Lightning Source LLC
Chambersburg PA
CBHW040326300426
44113CB00020B/2667